COLIN MARTIN AND GEOFFREY PARKER

# THE
# SPANISH
# ARMADA

*revised edition*

MANDOLIN

Copyright © Colin Martin and Geoffrey Parker 1988, 1989, 1999

The right of Colin Martin and Geoffrey Parker to be identified as the
authors of this work has been asserted by them in accordance with the
Copyright, Designs and Patents Act 1988.

Published by Manchester University Press
Oxford Road, Manchester M13 9NR, UK
and Room 400, 175 Fifth Avenue, New York, NY 10010, USA
www.manchesteruniversitypress.co.uk

Distributed exclusively in the USA by
Palgrave, 175 Fifth Avenue, New York NY 10010, USA

Distributed exclusively in Canada by
UBC Press, University of British Columbia, 2029 West Mall,
Vancouver, BC, Canada V6T 1Z2

*British Library Cataloguing-in-Publication Data*
A catalogue record for this book is available from the British Library

*Library of Congress Cataloging-in-Publication Data*
A catalog record for this book is available from the Library of Congress

ISBN 1 901341 14 3  paperback

First published 1988

First digital, on-demand edition produced by Lightning Source 2005 *for Paula & Jane*

# CONTENTS

# FIGURES, MAPS AND TABLES

## Figures

## Maps

## Tables

# PREFACE TO THE 1988 EDITION

This book saw its genesis, gestation and birth in the 13 years from 1973 to 1986, during which we were colleagues at the University of St Andrews. We are deeply grateful to that institution for encouraging our work, and for the generosity of its Research and Travel Fund in sponsoring so many of our rewarding quests. Other grants have helped us to conduct further research in archives and libraries, and to investigate Armada wrecks off the coasts of Scotland and Ireland. We are indebted to the British Academy, the Carnegie Trust, the Leverhulme Trust, the MacRobert Trusts and the Russell Trust, all of which have given generous support over the years.

The archaeological work which has yielded so much new information about the Armada would not have been possible without the far-sighted encouragement of the Ulster Museum, Belfast, and the Shetland County Museum, Lerwick. This has resulted in financial support, conservation services and – most important of all – the safe housing of the recovered items as intact collections which have been, and remain, rich resources for study. We warmly thank these institutions, and the staff with whom we have had the pleasure of working, for their unstinting and enthusiastic help.

Yet another debt is to the phalanx of friends and colleagues who have supported us along the way. We can only name the leading few, but we remember and acknowledge our indebtedness to the remaining many. Mr Sydney Wignall must top the list for demonstrating, in 1968, that the discovery of Armada shipwrecks could contribute through archaeological method to a fuller understanding of the campaign. He also put Colin Martin through the stern apprenticeship of diving in Blasket Sound, the exposed seaway off south-west Ireland where the wreck of the Guipúzcoan vice-flagship *Santa María de la Rosa* was discovered. We salute him, and all the other divers with whom we have been associated – especially the members of the City of Derry Sub-Aqua Club, whose unselfish forethought has safeguarded for posterity the relics of *La Trinidad Valencera*. We have also received valuable assistance from the Streedagh Armada Group and the Moville Sub-Aqua Group. Special acknowledgment is due to the professional diving archaeologists who have helped with the work on the wrecks – Dr Nicholas Dixon; Mr Andrew Fielding; Mr Jeremy Green; Mr Tony Long; the late Mr Keith Muckelroy; and Ms Celie O'Rahilly.

Help in a variety of forms has freely been given by scholarly colleagues, and we gratefully record our debt to them – Dr Simon Adams, University of Strathclyde; Professor José Alcalá-Zamora, University of Madrid; the late Dr Richard Boulind; Professor J. R. Bruijn, University of Leiden; Dr Trevor Dadson, University of Birmingham; Mr Alan Ereira, BBC; Mr Laurence Flanagan, Keeper of Antiquities, Ulster Museum; Mr Tom Glasgow Jr; the late Mr Tom Henderson, Shetland Museum; Dr John de Courcy Ireland, Maritime Institute of Ireland; the late Mr Paul Johnstone, BBC; Dr Piet van der Merwe, National Maritime Museum, Greenwich; Dr Marco Morin;

Dr Jane Ohlmeyer, University of Aberdeen; Professor Peter Pierson, University of Santa Clara; Mr Ray Sutcliffe, BBC; Dr I. A. A. Thompson, University of Keele; Dr Brian Scott, Queen's University; Dr Robert Sténuit; and Mr Andrew Williamson, Shetland Museum. We are also grateful to the following for assistance with research: Nico Broens; Lucy Byatt; Louis Haas; Jill Hawthorne; James Reid; and Bill van de Veen.

Officials and staff of the many libraries and archives in which we have worked have been, as always, unfailingly helpful and friendly. The institutions concerned are listed in the sources, and our gratitude to them all is immeasurable. We also thank Ms Penelope Hoare of Hamish Hamilton for her sympathetic editing of a work which grew in scale and scope far beyond the limits originally set for it.

Our final debt is to Paula Martin, who has been associated with the project almost from its inception. As a diving archaeologist she has worked on two of the wreck sites; as a historian she has generously placed at our disposal the fruits of her own researches, and made many helpful comments on the text; as a secretary she has provided us with a meticulous typescript; and as the book's picture researcher she has imparted upon it her own stamp of originality.

# PREFACE TO THE 1999 EDITION

*The Spanish Armada* was first published in April 1988, just as events to mark the fourth centenary of the momentous conflict between Elizabeth of England and Philip of Spain were getting under way. Over a hundred other books and learned articles on the subject, in several languages, appeared that year or shortly afterwards. Many shed light on issues and problems which had escaped or baffled us during our own researches, and it has been a pleasure to incorporate this new material into our revised account – correcting errors, filling gaps and adding clarification. We would like to express our thanks to all those who have helped us to keep abreast of recent research, or facilitated our use of new sources, especially the following: Simon Adams, Fernando Bouza Álvarez, José Luis Casado Soto, José Ignacio González-Aller Hierro, David and Marsha Karpeles, Paula Martin, Brendan McCarthy, Hugo O'Donnell, Peter Pierson, Nicholas Roger, María José Rodríguez-Salgado, Joost Schokkenbroek and José Ignacio Tellechea Idígoras.

Little fresh archaeological material has emerged during the past 10 years, although the exciting discoveries made off Streedagh Strand in 1985 have been protected by the Irish state for further investigation at some future date. Steve Birch, a member of the Streedagh archaeological team, has generously provided us with unpublished information about artillery and gun carriages from these three important wrecks. We are also indebted to Alan Ereira of the BBC for arranging comparative tests of Spanish and English gun mountings, replicated at full scale for his award-winning documentary *Armada*, and to the Portsmouth field-gun team of the Royal Navy for putting them through their paces with such skill and gusto.

Paula Martin has been a pillar of strength throughout the unexpectedly complex process of revising this book, untangling the electronic muddle as chapters batted between us across the Atlantic, proof-reading the results with a keen and constructively critical eye and compiling a new index. Robert Rush played a correspondingly helpful role at the Ohio end of the operation.

It is also our pleasure to record that the reissue of this book marks a quarter-centenary of friendship and scholarly association between its authors.

Colin Martin, St Andrews, Scotland
Geoffrey Parker, Columbus, Ohio

# NOTE ON THE TEXT

Dates throughout have been adjusted to conform with the new (Gregorian) calendar (NS) which the Spaniards, but not the English, used in 1588. Contemporary English dates, which were still based on the old (Julian) calendar (OS), would otherwise appear to fall 10 days earlier than their Spanish equivalents.

Four Spanish ducats were roughly equivalent to an English pound. The latter, prefixed '£', has been used as a common standard, and conversions to it from currencies other than Spanish have been made where appropriate. The results are necessarily approximate. With regard to weight units, equivalency has been assumed between the Castilian *libra* of 460 grams and the English pound of 454 grams. The Spanish *quintal*, like the English hundredweight, represents units of 100 pounds (the modern 112-pound hundredweight includes an allowance for the weight of the barrel).

In some important respects Spanish names for gun-types do not equate with their apparent English translations, and so the Spanish names have been used as appropriate in the text, set in italics. A discussion of these differences is incorporated in the section on weapons: Appendix 2 (pp. 269–77 below).

Spelling from contemporary English sources has been modernised, while the modern forms of proper names have been preferred.

# ABBREVIATIONS

AGI  Archivo General de Indias (Seville)

AGRB *SEG*  Archives Générales de Royaume (Brussels), *Secrétairerie d'Etat et de Guerre* (with register and folio)

AGS *CMC*  Archivo General de Simancas (Spain), *Contaduría Mayor de Cuentas* (with *época* and *legajo*)

AGS *CS*  Archivo General de Simancas, *Contaduría del Sueldo* (with *época* and *legajo*)

AGS *Estado*  Archivo General de Simancas, *Sección de Estado* (with *legajo* and folio)

AGS *GA*  Archivo General de Simancas, *Guerra Antigua* (with *legajo* and folio)

AGS *MPyD*  Archivo General de Simancas, *Mapas, Planos y Dibujos*

AHN *OM*  Archivo Historico Nacional, Madrid, *Órdenes Militares*

ARA  Algemene Rijksarchief, The Hague

AS  Archivio di Stato

ASV  Archivio Segreto Vaticano

LP  *Lettere principi*

NS  *Nunziatura Spagna*

BAV *UL*  Biblioteca Apostolica Vaticana, *Urbinates Latini*

BL *MS*  British Library (London), Department of Western Manuscripts (with collection, volume and folio)

BMO  J. Calvar Gross, J. I. González-Aller Hierro, M. de Dueñas Fontán and M. del C. Mérida Valverde, *La batalla del Mar Océano* (3 vols, Madrid, 1988–93)

BNM  Biblioteca Nacional, Madrid, manuscript collection

BNP  Bibliothèque Nationale, Paris (with manuscript collection, volume and folio)

BPU  Bibliothèque Publique et Universitaire, Geneva

BRB  Bibliothèque Royale, Brussels, Manuscript Section

Brugmans  H. Brugmans (ed.), *Correspondentie van Robert Dudley, graaf van Leycester en andere documenten . . . 1585-8*, vol. III (Utrecht, 1931)

CCG  E. Poullet and C. Piot, *Correspondance du Cardenal de Granvelle, 1565-86* (12 vols, Brussels, 1877–96)

Co.Do.In.  *Colección de documentos inéditos para la historia de España* (with volume number)

CSPD  *Calendar of State Papers, Domestic Series: Edward VI, Mary, Elizabeth 1581-90* (London, 1865)

CSPF  *Calendar of State Papers, Foreign Series, of the Reign of Elizabeth,* vols XIX: 1584-5 (London, 1916), XXI: 1586-8 (London, 1927–31) and XXII: 1588 (London, 1936)

CSPI   *Calendar of State Papers Relating to Ireland in the Reign of Elizabeth*, vol. IV: 1588–92 (London, 1885)

CSPScot   *Calendar of State Papers Relating to Scotland*, vol. IV: 1571–4 (Edinburgh, 1905)

CSPSp   *Calendar of State Papers Relating to English Affairs Preserved . . . in the Archives of Simancas. Elizabeth*, vols I–IV (London, 1892–9)

CSPV   *Calendar of State Papers and Manuscripts Relating to English Affairs Existing in the Archives and Collections of Venice*, vol. VIII (London, 1894)

Duro   C. Fernández Duro (ed.), *La Armada Invencible* (2 vols, Madrid, 1884–5)

EHR   *English Historical Review* (with volume number)

HMC   Historical Manuscripts Commission: *Reports* (with volume number and description)

HS   Archivo de la Casa de Heredía Spínola, Madrid (also known as the Archivo y Biblioteca de Zabálburu, with *caja* and folio number)

IVdeDJ   Instituto de Valencia de Don Juan, Madrid (with *envío* and folio number)

Japikse   N. Japikse, *Resolutiën der Staten Generaal van 1576 tot 1609*, vols V and VI (The Hague, 1921, 1922)

KML *MSP*:   Karpeles Manuscript Library, Santa Barbara, California, *Medina*
CR   *Sidonia Papers: Cartas Reales*

Laughton   J. K. Laughton, *State Papers Relating to the Defeat of the Spanish Armada, Anno 1588*, Navy Records Society, I–II (London, 1895)

LCP   J. Lefèvre (ed.), *Correspondance de Philippe II sur les affaires des Pays-Bas*, vol. III (Brussels, 1956)

Lyell   J. P. R. Lyell, 'A commentary on certain aspects of the Spanish Armada drawn from contemporary sources' (Oxford University B.Litt. thesis, 1932; and Houghton Library, Harvard, fMs Eng.714. Harvard also owns the sources used)

Maura   G. Maura Gamazo, duke of Maura, *El designio de Felipe II y el episodio de la armada invencible* (Madrid, 1957)

NMM   National Maritime Museum, Greenwich, Manuscript Library

NS   New Style: Gregorian calendar used by the Spaniards

OÖLA *KB*   Oberösterreichisches Landesarchiv, Linz, *Khevenhüller Briefbücher*

Oria   E. Herrera Oria, *La Armada Invencible*, Archivo Documental Español, II (Valladolid, 1929)

OS   Old Style: Julian calendar used by the English

Pepys   Pepys Library, Magdalene College, Cambridge

PRO *AO1*   Public Record Office, London, *Audit Office*

PRO *E*   Public Record Office, London, *Exchequer Papers*

PRO *MPF*   Public Record Office, London, *Maps, Plans and Figures*

PRO *SP*   Public Record Office, London, *State Papers*

PRO *WO*   Public Record Office, London, *War Office*

RAZ   Rijksarchief Zeeland, Middelburg

*Reivindicación*  F. Pérez Minguez, *Reivindicación histórica del siglo XVI* (Madrid, 1928)
Tenison  E. M. Tenison, *Elizabethan England* (14 vols, Leamington Spa, 1933–60)
Vázquez  A. Vázquez, 'Los sucesos de Flandes y Francia del tiempo de Alejandro Farnesio', *Co.Do.In.*, LXXII–LXXIV (Madrid, 1879–80)

**1580**

25 August  Philip II's forces capture Lisbon

**1581**

January  Parma begins reconquest of South Netherlands

**1582**

26 July  Spanish victory of São Miguel

**1583**

July  Conquest of Terceira; Santa Cruz suggests follow-up attack on England

**1584**

23 June  Santa Cruz appointed captain-general of the ocean sea

31 December  Spain signs treaty of Joinville with duke of Guise and French Catholic League

**1585**

March  Henry III signs treaty of Nemours with French Catholic League

May  Philip II embargoes all foreign ships in Iberian ports; Sixtus V elected pope

August  Anglo-Dutch treaty of Nonsuch; fall of Antwerp to Spain

7 October  Francis Drake occupies ports in Galicia (to 17th), and goes on to sack Canaries and Caribbean islands

24 October  Philip declares readines to invade England

December  Philip II invites Parma to prepare invasion plan (reply sent April 1586); earl of Leicester arrives to govern northern Netherlands

**1586**

February  Philip II's accepts Santa Cruz's offer to prepare invasion plan (sent March)

8 June  Recalde appointed to command new Squadron of Biscay

20 June  Parma's invasion plan arrives at court

26 July  G. B. Piatti takes master plan to Parma

17 November  Philip II orders Naples and Sicily to send ships, munitions and troops to Spain

**1587**

February  Execution of Mary queen of Scots; English garrison betrays Deventer to Parma

March  Hulks embargoed in Andalusian ports

12 April  Drake leaves Plymouth to 'singe the king of Spain's beard'

29 April  Cadiz raid (to 1 May)

*2 May* Recalde and Biscayan ships arrive in Lisbon

*26 May* Philip II too ill to work (until early July)

*18 June* Drake captures *São Felipe* off Azores and returns to England

*16 July* Santa Cruz and Recalde lead Armada from Lisbon to the Azores to meet treasure fleets

*29 July* Papal-Spanish accord on future government of Catholic England; one million ducats deposited in a Rome bank by pope

*4 August* Ships gathered in Andalusia arrive at Lisbon under command of Don Alonso de Leiva; Parma captures Sluis

*4 September* New Instructions issued for invasion of England

*25 September* Santa Cruz brings Indies treasure fleet safely to Seville

*29 September* Santa Cruz arrives at Lisbon; Armada begins to refit

*10 October* Recalde's squadron returns to Lisbon

*16 November* Storm damage to ships in Lisbon

*December* Dutch blockade squadron assumes permanent guard off Dunkirk

**1588**

*January* Division of ships in Lisbon into seven squadrons: Andalusia, Biscay, Guipúzcoa, galleasses, Levant, hulks and Portugal

*9 February* Santa Cruz dies

*26 February* Medina Sidonia reluctantly accepts appointment to command Armada

*8 March* Anglo-Spanish peace talks begin in Netherlands

*15 March* Medina Sidonia arrives in Lisbon

*end March* Squadron of Castile arrives in Lisbon

*1 April* Instructions issued to Medina Sidonia and Parma

*29 April* Duke of Guise agrees to engineer Catholic rebellion in France

*9 May* Lisbon muster

*12 May* 'Day of the barricades': Guise takes Paris

*23 May* Anglo-Spanish peace talks moved to Bourbourg

*28/30 May* Armada sails from Lisbon

*3 June* English fleet concentrates at Plymouth

*19 June* Armada puts into Corunna after five days' wait for victuals; storm scatters fleet

*27 June* Council at Corunna advises Philip II to abandon Enterprise of England

*4 July* English navy sails for Spain (returns after two weeks)

*5 July* Parma inspects his fleet at Dunkirk; Dutch blockade fleet reinforced

*19 July* Council at Corunna decides to try again

*21 July* Armada sets sail against England

*25 July* Medina Sidonia sends first warning to Parma of his approach (arrives 3 August)

*29 July* Armada sights Lizard; council of war aboard *San Martín*; English sight the Armada and fleet puts to sea

*30 July* Armada enters Channel

| | |
|---|---|
| 31 July | First blood: loss of *Rosario* and *San Salvador*; Medina Sidonia sends second messenger to Parma (arrives 6 August) |
| 1 August | Armada re-forms into 'roundel' |
| 2 August | Second fight: off Portland Bill |
| 3 August | English council of war; division into squadrons; first letters from Armada reach Flanders |
| 4 August | Third fight: off Isle of Wight. Duke of Guise named 'lieutenant general of the kingdom' in France |
| 6 August | Armada reaches Calais; Parma receives news of Armada's approach; talks at Bourbourg broken off |
| 7/8 August | Fireships attack |
| 8 August | Fight off Gravelines; Parma starts embarking the Army of Flanders |
| 10 August | Army of Flanders completes embarkation; Medina Sidonia announces that Armada will return to Spain by northabout route; Seymour's squadron returns to Channel |
| 12 August | Armada off Firth of Forth; English abandon pursuit |
| 18 August | Elizabeth's 'Tilbury speech' |
| 20 August | Armada passes into Atlantic |
| 21 August | Medina Sidonia sends Don Balthasar de Zúñiga to court |
| 31 August | Parma stands down Flanders fleet |
| 12 September | Parma besieges Bergen-op-Zoom (to 30 October) |
| 14/16 September | Wrecking of *Trinidad Valencera* |
| 20 September | *Gran Grin, Santa María de la Rosa* and *la Rata Encoronada* wrecked; Medina Sidonia arrives at Santander |
| 24 September | Zúñiga arrives at court |
| 25 September | *Lavia, Juliana* and *Santa María de Visón* wrecked on Streedagh Strand |
| 28 September | *El Gran Grifón* wrecked off Fair Isle |
| 28 October | *Girona* wrecked off County Antrim |
| 5 November | 'Tobermory galleon' destroyed |
| 10 November | Philip II wishes he were dead |
| 12 November | Spanish council in Madrid votes to continue war with England |
| 24 November | Thanksgiving service at St Paul's in London |

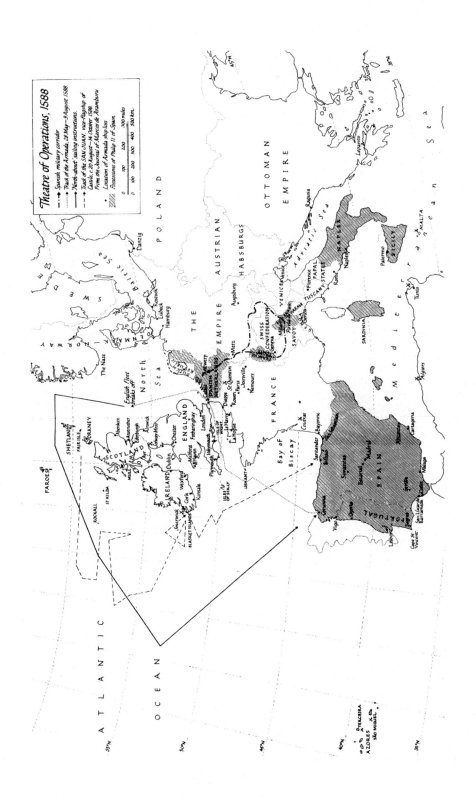

*Theatre of Operations, 1588*

→ Spanish military corridor
→ Track of the Armada, 28 May – 9 August 1588
→ North-about sailing instructions
→ Track of the SAN JUAN, vice-flagship of
   Castile, c. 20 August – 14 October 1588
   From the Journal of Marcos de Aramburu
• Location of Armada ship loss
▨ Possessions of Philip II of Spain

0    100   200   300 miles
0  100 200 300 400 500 km.

# INTRODUCTION

It was 10 August 1588 in the North Sea, and the late summer weather was unseasonably bad. Before a brisk south-westerly gale, with her storm-canvas set, ran the 800-ton English royal galleon *Victory*, scarred by recent battle. Her gaudily painted upper works were stained by gunsmoke; the royal standard at the mainmast and the flags of St George which whipped from the fore and mizzen tops were in tatters. The rigging showed signs of makeshift repair, the bowsprit and main mizzen had been splintered by shot, and the ship's longboat was missing. Although she was still seaworthy, the 39-gun *Victory* was in no condition to engage an enemy. Her shot-lockers, upon which her whole fighting capacity depended, lay empty.

Two days earlier the ship had been in the thick of the longest and fiercest artillery action which had ever taken place at sea. Somewhere to leeward the huge Armada from Spain against which she had fought, severely battered but with its formidable order and discipline still largely intact, was loose in the northern seas. Its ammunition stocks, though depleted, were not exhausted, while the massed companies of soldiers which it carried still rendered it invulnerable to any boarding attack. Worst of all, the English no longer knew where this fleet was, nor what it might yet do.

In *Victory's* great cabin her captain, Sir John Hawkins, treasurer of the English Navy, scrawled a postscript to the urgent report he had just completed, apologising for his poor handwriting: it was done, he explained, 'in haste and bad weather'. His dispatch, addressed to Sir Francis Walsingham, Queen Elizabeth's secretary of state, shows Hawkins to have been an extremely worried man. The Spanish fleet, he warned, was still:

> here, and very forcible, and must be waited upon with all our force, which is little enough. There should be an infinite quantity of powder and shot provided, and continually sent abroad; without the which great hazard may grow to our country; for this is the greatest and strongest combination, to my understanding, that ever was gathered in Christendom; therefore I wish it, of all hands, to be mightily and diligently looked unto and cared for.

Eight days later England's lord admiral, Charles Howard of Effingham, 'in haste and much occupied' aboard his flagship *Ark Royal*, remained anxious and uncertain about the Armada's movements and intentions, and in no doubt about its formidable strength. 'Some made little account of the Spanish force by sea', he confided to Walsingham on 18 August, 'but I do warrant you, all the world never saw such a force as theirs was.' Even by the month's end, the redoubtable

Sir Francis Drake was by no means confident that the threat had passed. Although the Armada might have been driven back towards Spain, a powerful army of invasion troops headed by one of the most determined and capable military commanders of the age still lay on the Flemish coast, poised to embark for England. From his flagship *Revenge* Drake warned on 20 August that the queen's ministers should not doubt that Alexander Farnese, duke of Parma, 'being so great a soldier as he is . . . will presently, if he may, undertake some great matter . . . my poor opinion is that we should have a great eye unto him'.

England's best-informed contemporary opinion was thus not disposed to underestimate the enormity of the threat which Philip II's great Armada had posed. But, as quickly as it had come, that threat had evaporated. It turned out that the Armada had no further tricks up its sleeve: intent only on a safe return home, it struggled on past the Northern Isles and into the Atlantic in an effort to gain sufficient sea room for the long run southwards to the ports of Galicia and Biscay. Most might have made it had they been more fortunate with the weather. But the autumn gales of that portentous year – the winds of God, as their Protestant detractors would have it – blew early and with unusual violence, driving many of the returning Spanish ships towards the Atlantic coasts of Scotland and Ireland. Perhaps as many as 40 were lost, often in cataclysmic circumstances, while those who survived the wrecks were hounded down with little mercy. For the Spaniards it was an unmitigated disaster, but one brought about more by the forces of nature than by the hand of their adversaries. In English and Dutch eyes, however, it was both an overwhelming victory and a clear demonstration of where divine sympathy lay. The anxious realities expressed by the English commanders in the campaign's immediate aftermath were thus quickly swamped, in the euphoria of deliverance, by a tide of patriotic fervour which saw the events as an affirmation of England's inevitable superiority over her Catholic foes. That fervour, and the misconceptions which it generated, have tended to dominate perceptions of the campaign ever since.

During the four centuries which have passed since that event, accounts of the Armada have proliferated. The story has a perennial appeal as the heroic and triumphant climax of a long maritime, military, economic and ideological struggle between England and Spain, and in many respects it is exceptionally well documented. On any reckoning it is a good yarn, and it has provided generations of historians with an abundance of fine material from which to spin it.

On the Spanish side, the three years of intensive planning and preparation which culminated in the sailing of the fleet generated a vast corpus of meticulous documentation. Dutch and English records are far less ordered or comprehensive, since the defensive efforts of 1588 were an *ad hoc* response to a sudden crisis, and much less was committed to paper (the poor record of Britain's preparations to resist invasion in 1940 provides a close modern parallel). But, even so, the documentary sources which have survived are still substantial.

Serious study of this material began in the late nineteenth century, with the calendaring and editing of a selection of the documents contained in both Spanish and English archives. These great works of transcription and condensation, together with their usually excellent commentaries, have formed the basis of most subsequent accounts of the Armada campaign. But although their value remains undiminished they are, as their editors were at pains to point out, no more than personal selections of those documents which were considered, in the light of late nineteenth-century historical perceptions, to be the most relevant.

For almost a century, in consequence, Armada studies tended to stagnate in the rich but unreplenished pond provided by their late Victorian progenitors. The calendared documents came to be regarded by most historians as the primary sources, while the archives from which they had been derived became almost totally forgotten. In the cases of the less comprehensive English and Dutch sources this confidence has largely (though not entirely) been justified. It has emphatically not been so with the Spanish ones.

Four distinct categories of primary evidence have survived. The first is the mass of reports, memoranda and letters concerning the complex processes through which the Armada strategy emerged, and the minutiae of putting that strategy into effect. Most of these are preserved among the state papers housed at Simancas Castle, near Valladolid, where Philip II created Europe's first public record office, and are relatively well known though still greatly underexploited. Some of the most important and intimate documents in this category, however, are to be found among the so-called 'Altamira papers' – the personal documents of Philip II – now scattered among half-a-dozen European collections. They reveal his close scrutiny of and reaction to every detail of the Armada's preparation, strategy and conduct; his deteriorating health as he pored over his papers; and his profound spiritual crisis when the magnitude of the enterprise's failure became clear. Few of these papers have previously been consulted for the crucial evidence they contain about the Armada's story.

A second category of Spanish material relates to the formation and execution of policy from the standpoint of the commanders in the field. This is contained in the archives of the two officers designated to lead the amphibious attack on England in 1588, together with some remarkable letters written by the fleet's vice-admiral during the heat of battle. Unfortunately the papers of the duke of Parma, who was both the army's leader and the supreme commander of the operation as a whole, have been seriously diminished – those at Naples by fire; those at Parma by termites and rodents; and those at Brussels by theft. But there is still enough to piece together, for the first time, the crucial importance of the Army of Flanders to the Armada plan.

The archive of the ducal house of Medina Sidonia, by contrast, still exists in excellent condition at San Lúcar de Barrameda, though some key original papers relating to the seventh duke's role in leading Philip II's fleet against England are now elsewhere. A few were acquired in the 1950s by the National Maritime Museum at Greenwich, and in the 1980s most of those for the crucial years 1587–9 were acquired by the Biblioteca March in Madrid and by the Karpeles Manuscript Library in Santa Barbara, California. They shed new light on important issues concerning the conduct of the Spanish campaign. Finally, in 1994, the campaign journal of the Armada's deputy commander, Juan Martínez de Recalde, and a selection of the lively letters he exchanged with Medina Sidonia during the campaign, were found by chance in a bundle labelled 'Curious papers' in a Madrid archive. They reveal major differences between the two men over both strategy and tactics throughout the campaign, as well as providing a host of details on incidents that had previously been obscure.

To these unconscious 'memoirs' of the principal commanders can be added the personal accounts of lesser men: commentaries and narratives contained in diaries, reports, or transcripts of interrogations. By combining these disparate personal impressions of events it is often possible to perceive the whole with greater clarity, particularly when trying to penetrate the chaos of battle, where each man's viewpoint and experiences are different, and recollection is clouded by violent activity, noise, weather, smoke, adrenalin-driven emotion and the pressing urgency of the moment.

Thirdly, a mountain of administrative papers survives on all sides concerning the acquisition and equipping of the ships, and the men, munitions and provisions which were loaded aboard them. For the fleets assembled in Spain and the Spanish Netherlands, these extensive and painstakingly detailed records, the routine output of numberless quartermasters, accountants, paymasters and filing clerks, have lain at Simancas in vast bundles, accumulating dust. They have never previously been systematically consulted by historians of the Armada. Through them we can reconstruct, often in extraordinary detail, exactly how individual ships were fitted out, armed and manned; how they performed in combat; and what finally became of them. Aboard some ships records were even kept of how many shots each gun fired, and on what date. If a vessel was subsequently wrecked, the king's bureaucrats later had to determine the precise location and circumstances of its loss – not for posterity, but simply to justify a final closing of that ship's accounts.

The English records are less plentiful. The 'Declared Accounts' of the treasurer of the Navy (preserved in two copies: one on parchment by the Exchequer, the other on paper by the Audit Office) provide much detail on the equipment and movements of the queen's ships, on the hire of other ships and on the wages of all who served at sea at the queen's cost. The accounts of the victualler of the Navy (preserved in the same series) record the cost of all provisions supplied to keep those aboard the ships at their posts. Unfortunately the naval accounts of the third institution concerned with naval administration – the Ordnance Office – have not yet been located for 1588. This is a pity, because those of later years show that Elizabeth's officials recorded every round of shot and every barrel of powder issued to each ship, the quantity 'spent at the sea' and the amount returned at the end of the campaign. The surviving administrative records for the Dutch fleet are even more fragmentary: a handful in the Algemene Rijksarchief, Admiraliteit section, and in the Rijksarchief Zeeland, Rekenkamer section, are all we have found to be useful.

All these documentary sources, together with many others in Belgium, France, Italy, the Netherlands, Portugal and the United States, have been examined and analysed to provide the narrative and analytical framework of our account. Moreover, the mass of surviving written evidence is now complemented by a fourth and previously quite unconsidered source which has allowed us, quite literally, to go on board the ships themselves and examine them and their contents at first hand.

In the terrible aftermath of the Armada more than 30 Spanish ships were lost off the western coasts of Scotland and Ireland. Underwater archaeological evidence from the Armada wrecks has, in many important respects, revolutionised our understanding of the reality of the events we have sought to chronicle, particularly when viewed in concert with the exhaustive documentary material. The sites of eight wrecks have now been confirmed by hard archaeological evidence, providing between them examples of many of the types of ship which sailed with the Armada. Off the coast of Antrim, during 1967–8, the remains of the Neapolitan galleass *Girona* were found and excavated by Robert Sténuit. In 1968–9 the remains of the *Santa María de la Rosa*, the Basque-built vice-flagship of Miguel de Oquendo's Guipúzcoan squadron, were found and excavated in the eye of a tide race off the south-west tip of Ireland. Between 1970 and 1983 the wrecks of the Rostock-built hulk *El Gran Grifón* off Fair Isle, and the Venetian troop carrier *La Trinidad Valencera* in Kinnagoe Bay, Donegal, were investigated in an extended series of excavation campaigns directed by Colin Martin. In 1985 the remains of three Levantine ships – the *Santa María de Visón*, the *Juliana* and the *Lavia* – were discovered in the surf off Streedagh Strand, Sligo. These remarkable wrecks, from which some material has been recovered, are now under a protection order by the Irish government. Yet another member of the ill-fated Levant squadron, the Ragusan *San Juan de Sicilia*, was wrecked in Tobermory Bay, Mull, though her remains have all but been obliterated by more than three centuries of determined hunting for her elusive (because illusory) treasure.

It should be emphasised that this new material in no way alters the broad outline of the Armada story, which is well known and incontrovertible. Philip II attempted to invade England, but his plans miscarried, partly because of his own mismanagement, and partly because the defensive efforts of the English and their Dutch allies prevailed. There is more to history, however, than broad outlines. With the evidence now at our disposal, much of it previously uninvestigated and all of it from primary sources, we can follow each stage in these processes with greater certainty than before and, perhaps more importantly, explain *why* events turned out as they did. Instead of basing our narrative on the pseudo-patriotic jingoism and speculative theorising which has characterised so many previous studies, we have sought to rest this account on a wide corpus of object-ive information drawn from contemporary documents and from the physical remains of the wrecked ships. All this evidence reinforces our belief that the Armada constituted a threat to England of overwhelming proportions, and con-firms that English commanders' anxious concerns about the menace it posed, quoted above, were not misplaced. We may reasonably conclude that Philip II's 'Grand Design' against England in 1588 might have been, in perhaps only slightly different circumstances, the crowning success of his reign.

At the time no one could have predicted the outcome, and Spain should no more be denigrated for losing than England's deliverance be regarded as a mani-festation of her inevitable superiority. Each nation demonstrated formidable strengths and serious weaknesses in the conflict, and both emerged from it with honour. We do not ourselves feel, more than four centuries after these stirring and terrible events, any predilection for one side or the other. The story stands on its own terms and the only bygones to be forgotten are the myths.

## Source notes and references

The principal printed collections are as follows. For Spain, *BMO* (which has now reached 15 February 1588), Duro and Oria, which print mainly documents from the state archives at Simancas; Maura, who printed documents from the Medina Sidonia archive (mostly letters now in the Karpeles Manuscript Library); and LCP, which provides a precis of the correspondence between the government of Philip II and the Netherlands. *CSPSp* provides an English precis for many Spanish documents, mainly from Simancas. For England, Laughton and the relevant volumes of the four *CSP* series: Domestic, Foreign, Ireland and Scotland, based on the corresponding series of State Papers in the PRO, provide most of the government's surviving papers. A number of subsequently destroyed documents from Naples and Parma were included in van der Essen, *Alexandre Farnèse, prince de Parme*.

The English printed material has been cited so often in books and articles concern-ing the Armada that we have felt it unnecessary to provide detailed references. Our notes therefore concentrate on those sources, most of them manuscript, which we feel will be less familiar to readers. Their characteristics are discussed, as appropriate, in the sources for each chapter. There is a good review of printed works in Rasor, *The Spanish Armada of 1588: historiography and annotated bibliography*: his survey of English material seems com-prehensive, but he includes little Spanish and virtually no Dutch or Belgian works.

The quatercentenary of the Armada generated many publications on the campaign and related topics. Most of the new narrative accounts are straightforward reiterations of the old story, though most are well illustrated and the best of them spiritedly told. Of the few with fresh material to add much the best is the National Maritime Museum's splendid *Armada*, edited by María José Rodríguez-Salgado, which is a lavish catalogue of its 1988 exhibition with linking commentaries by leading scholars. The most original of the crop is Felipe Fernández-Armesto's thought-provoking *The Spanish Armada: the experience of war in 1588*, which took revisionism to the point of claiming that in some respects the Spaniards won!

A number of more specialist studies have added important new material. Peter Pierson's *Commander of the Armada: the seventh duke of Medina Sidonia* not only provides a compelling biography of the man, based on previously inaccessible documents from the Medina Sidonia archives, but adds much detail on the conduct of the Armada campaign. As part of this Pierson made an ingenious set of reconstructions of the fleet at various stages in the battles (though these are, as he admits himself, largely hypothetical). Paula Martin's *Spanish Armada Prisoners* looks at the experiences of survivors incarcerated in England, and in particular examines the capture of the *Nuestra Señora del Rosario*, throwing new light on Drake's relationship with Don Pedro de Valdés. Tellechea Idígoras, in *Otra cara de la Invencible: la participación vasca*, published a magnificent series of documents, with linking commentary, about the Basques in the Armada, especially in the squadrons of Oquendo and Recalde. Geoffrey Parker published Recalde's 'political testament' – his journal and a part of his correspondence with Medina Sidonia during the campaign, both forwarded to the king just before his death: 'El testamento político de Juan Martínez de Recalde', *Revista de Historia Naval*. He also included much Armada material in his study *The Grand Strategy of Philip II*.

The proceedings of two international conferences held in the quatercentenary year provided rich veins of new material. A conference held in Sligo resulted in the publication of *God's Obvious Design*, edited by Gallagher and Cruickshank. Of relevance to our study are: Martin, 'The ships of the Spanish Armada'; Thompson, 'Spanish Armada gun policy and procurement'; O'Donnell, 'The requirements of the duke of Parma for the conquest of England'; Schokkenbroek, 'The role of the Dutch fleet in the conflict of 1588'; and Daultrey, 'The weather of north-west Europe during the summer and autumn of 1588'. In an appendix Gallagher and Cruickshank published a new transcription and translation of Francisco de Cuéllar's letter. *England, Spain and the Gran Armada*, edited by Rodríguez-Salgado and Adams, included 10 papers given at the Anglo-Spanish conferences in London and Madrid, several of them presenting English summaries of studies published in an important series sponsored by the Spanish Instituto de Historia y Cultura Naval: the individual volumes by José Luis Casado Soto (on the Armada's ships), Carlos Gómez-Centurión (on Spanish propaganda and on Philip II's policies in northern Europe), Manuel Gracia Rivas (on the troops aboard the fleet and on its medical services), Hugo O'Donnell (on Parma's army), Gonzalo Parente (on the published sources concerning the Army of Flanders) and Fernando Riaño Lozano (on Parma's fleet) are all discussed in the source notes to the relevant chapters below.

Little archaeological work has taken place on the Armada wrecks since 1988, but Colin Martin has published two articles on weaponry, both in the *International Journal of Nautical Archaeology*: 'A 16th-century siege train: the battery ordnance of the 1588 Spanish Armada'; and 'Incendiary weapons from the Spanish Armada wreck *La Trinidad Valencera*, 1588'.

# PART I

# THE FLEETS APPROACH

# 'The greatest and strongest combination'

Shortly after dawn the watchers on the cliff saw the first Spanish ships: fleeting shapes glimpsed far offshore through banks of mist and squally showers. The tar-soaked brushwood of the beacon burst urgently into flame, and within minutes a replying pinprick of light to the east confirmed that the alarm was passing along the chain to Plymouth and the waiting English fleet. From there the signal might be relayed to all parts of the kingdom.

It was Saturday 30 July 1588, and Philip II's long-expected and much feared Armada had arrived off the English coast.

The day before, within distant sight of the Lizard, the Spanish flagship *San Martín* had taken in sail and hoisted a flag near the great poop lantern to signal a council of war. As the fleet hove to, senior officers in their pinnaces began to converge on the flagship. On the *San Martín's* high after-deck a short, heavily built, bearded man of 38, simply attired, stood awaiting them. Around his neck hung the insignia of the Golden Fleece, Spain's most exclusive order of chivalry, of which Philip II himself was grand master. Don Alonso Pérez de Guzmán 'el Bueno' (the Good), twelfth señor and fifth marquis of San Lúcar de Barrameda, ninth count of Niebla and seventh duke of Medina Sidonia, was the king's captain-general of the ocean sea, and the 125 or so ships and 30,000 men of the Armada were under his sole command. Yet Medina Sidonia was a landsman, without previous experience of war afloat.

Now, with due ceremony, his officers came aboard. Beneath their cloaks flashed glimpses of sartorial splendour: garments of satin or silk laid with velvet and embroidery, gold buttons and lace, and the varied insignia of their knightly orders. Juan Martínez de Recalde had some difficulty in negotiating the *San Martín's* towering side, for he was 62 years old and suffered badly from sciatica. But despite his infirmity Recalde was the most experienced naval officer in the Armada, with a lifetime of sea service behind him. Steadfast, resourceful and immensely brave, he commanded the vice-flagship *San Juan*, had administrative charge of the Biscayan squadron and was second-in-command of the fleet. He also boasted important connections at court, having married the sister of Philip II's principal secretary of state. Recalde would not, however, lead the Armada in the event of Medina Sidonia's death. On the secret orders of the king that awesome responsibility would fall to another member of the council, the younger and more nobly born Don Alonso Martínez de Leiva who, like Recalde, was a knight of the Order of Santiago. Leiva commanded the Genoese carrack *La Rata Santa María Encoronada*, now rigged for war, aboard which sailed the cream of Spain's young nobility. A member of his crew later described Don Alonso as 'tall and slender, of a whitely complexion, of a flaxen and smooth hair, of behaviour mild and temperate, of speech good and deliberate, greatly revered not only by his own men but generally of all the company'. With his neatly trimmed beard and the simple cross of Santiago about his neck, he was the very epitome of a Spanish warrior-aristocrat.

Miguel de Oquendo, in charge of the Guipúzcoan squadron, was less nobly born but no less spirited: he was said later to have handled his flagship during the campaign 'like a lancer' – an extravagant simile, perhaps, for his lumbering 1,200-ton Basque merchantman *Santa Ana*, though not for Oquendo's personal panache. Of sterling calibre too was Martín de Bertendona from Bilbao, commander of the Levant squadron, whose family had served the crown at sea for generations. Medina Sidonia could also depend upon the commanders of his two non-combatant units – Juan Gómez de Medina of the supply hulks, and Agustín de Ojeda of the communications squadron, who had taken charge on his predecessor's death a week earlier. Both were solid, reliable men chosen for their experience and administrative competence.

As the members of the council came aboard the flagship they paid formal respects to the duke and his two principal staff officers, Diego Flores de Valdés, chief adviser on naval matters, and Don Francisco de Bobadilla, the general in charge of the fleet's strong military contingent. These two men were aboard the *San Martín* on the direct orders of the king – perhaps, some speculated, to make sure that the captain-general obeyed his orders to the letter.

Personal relationships within this select group of senior officers were not altogether harmonious. There was much envy of Bobadilla and Flores on the grounds that they had permanent access to Medina Sidonia's ear and used their advantageous position to discredit the other commanders. And Flores, despite his extensive naval experience, was of a touchy and quarrelsome disposition: in particular, he nurtured an implacable hatred for his haughty cousin Don Pedro de Valdés, commander of the Andalusian squadron. Ill feeling also existed between Medina Sidonia and the fiery Don Hugo de Moncada, who commanded the squadron of four heavily armed Neapolitan galleasses. Don Hugo considered himself, with some justification, to be an expert on oar-powered warfare (though this was now something of an anachronism, as events were to prove), and he seems to have resented serving under Medina Sidonia on professional grounds. These tensions were to erupt in a bitter clash later in the campaign.

These, then, were the councillors and commanders who filed into the *San Martín*'s great cabin and took their seats, surrounded by a bevy of staff officers and aides. Most of them were, by sixteenth-century standards, old men. Only Leiva, Moncada and the duke were under 40; Recalde was certainly the oldest but Diego Flores was almost 60 and most of the rest were around 50. Their collective experience was enormous. Both the Valdés cousins had played a lead-ing part in the reconquest of Florida in 1565–6, under the overall command of their uncle, Pedro Menéndez de Avilés. In 1575, together with Recalde, Don Pedro de Valdés had led a seaborne expedition from Spain to Flanders and, upon his return, the king gave him command of a small squadron to defend the Galician coast against pirates. These three men, like almost all members of the council, had also taken part in the Spanish conquest of Portugal and the Azores in 1580–3 (in 1581 Don Pedro's impetuosity caused an attempt to capture the island of Terceira to fail, which led to his court martial). Diego Flores had sailed with the fleet that took Philip II from Spain to England to his marriage with Mary Tudor in 1554. He had commanded a force of 23 vessels sent to the South Atlantic in 1581 and (like his cousin Don Pedro) had taken charge of several of the fleets that sailed annually between Seville and America, bringing to Europe, among other goods, the silver bullion upon which both the king and Spain's merchant community depended. Bertendona and Oquendo had commanded flotillas sailing from Spain into northern European waters and back. Recalde, however, could claim even greater experience of operations in the North Atlantic. In 1572, and again in 1575, he commanded fleets carrying troops from Spain to Flanders, and in between he participated in fierce naval encounters with the Dutch. In 1580 he led another expeditionary force to the west coast of Ireland. As they entered the English Channel in 1588, therefore, these men were sailing into waters which many of them knew well.

The soldiers were no less experienced. Don Francisco de Bobadilla had marched with the duke of Alba to suppress the Dutch Revolt in 1567, and served in the Netherlands for the next ten years; thereafter he held commands in Portu-gal, Italy and, again, Flanders. Don Alonso de Leiva had also served in the Low Countries and Portugal, although his most recent experience was in Italy, where he had distinguished himself in galley warfare against the Muslim raiders who constantly disputed control over the western Mediterranean with their Christian adversaries.

It was Leiva who, at the council of war now in session aboard the *San Martín*, pressed for an immediate attack on the main English base at Plymouth, just below the north-eastern horizon and only some 45 miles to leeward. There, he argued, they might with luck surprise the enemy fleet at anchor. He received strong support from Recalde who, even before sighting the English coast, had written to a relative at court that he wanted to 'ensure that the enemy comes out to fight, and to incite him to do so', and therefore advocated a surprise attack on the port of Plymouth: 'Although I am no friend of bravado, we should try it as we pass before the port [of Plymouth]', he wrote. Medina Sidonia listened carefully to these arguments and then, in the courteous but firm tone his officers had come to know well, proceeded to demolish them, pointing out that the entrance to Plymouth's harbour was narrow and difficult, and well defended by shore batteries. In any event, the duke continued, Plymouth was not their object-ive, nor, for that matter, was the destruction of the English fleet. The Armada was playing for much higher stakes than that.[1]

King Philip II, originator and absolute director of the scheme in which the Armada formed an integral part, had repeatedly laid down in unequivocal terms the fleet's goals, and Medina Sidonia took this opportunity to remind his officers of them. The fleet must sail up the English Channel and rendezvous in the Straits of Dover with the Spanish forces stationed in the Netherlands, known collectively as the 'Army of Flanders'. It would then escort a substantial part of that army, in specially prepared landing craft, to a beach-head in Kent. From this point the operation would come under the supreme command of the king's nephew Alexander Farnese, the duke of Parma. Parma's invasion force of 27,000 veterans would land and secure a foothold in the vicinity of Margate, where the Armada would off-load supplies, munitions, reserve troops and a train of heavy artillery. This hard-hitting army, well equipped to deal quickly either with oppos-ing field forces or static defences, would then launch a fast-moving assault on London, its flank supported by the fleet moving up the Thames estuary. Until that time the Armada would defend itself as necessary, although under no cir-cumstances at the expense of delaying progress towards its principal objective. In short, Medina Sidonia reminded his subordinates, the Armada was part of a co-ordinated plan which the king himself had devised – a plan which, if success-ful, would strike a mortal blow to the heart of Tudor England.

The duke had less confidence in Philip II's plan than his public assertions suggested. The following day, as he prepared to send the council's resolution by fast dispatch boat to the king, he felt obliged to add a coded addendum express-ing deep concern that he had so far received no communication from Parma in the Netherlands. Medina Sidonia had good cause for anxiety. There he was, at the entrance to the Channel, with a force of around 130 ships and nearly 30,000 men, 'and it amazes me [he wrote to the king in deep concern] that we have had no message from the duke of Parma for so many days, nor have we come across in our entire voyage any person or ship who has news of him'.

Communication between the two forces was difficult, but essential. Lack of it would not only set the whole complex operation at risk, but would also threaten the fragile security of the huge fleet for which Medina Sidonia bore sole responsibility. The duke continued by setting before the king his most immedi-ate worry, which was that 'in the whole coast of Flanders there is no port or place of shelter for great ships', so once the Armada reached its destination 'the first storm that comes along' would either scatter the fleet or drive it aground on the numerous offshore sandbanks. Medina Sidonia was counting on a swift and effortless junction with Parma, so as to minimise the awesome risks (which flew in the face of all military prudence) of effecting a complicated rendezvous in uncertain weather, at an inappropriate geographical location, and in the presence of a strong and aggressive foe.

'According to my instructions', Medina Sidonia reminded the king with thinly disguised unease, 'at the very moment when I arrive [in the straits], Parma's forces are to put out in their ships, without my having to wait for them a single moment.' But how could he be sure, as the Armada sailed on up the Channel, that Parma was ready? Until confirmation of this vital fact was received, the duke emphasised, 'to a large extent we are navigating in the dark'. Accordingly, he concluded, 'it seems best not to sail further than the Isle of Wight, until I have heard from the duke of Parma'. Subsequent events were to demonstrate that Medina Sidonia's strategic grasp of the problem was faultless, though circumstances quite beyond his control were to deny him a solution to it.[2]

The duke was no better informed about the movements of the English fleet than he was of Parma's state of readiness and, for the moment, this was the more acute of his growing catalogue of worries. On 30 July, as the Armada coasted eastwards and the beacon fires flickered along the Cornish coastline, Ensign Juan Gil (who spoke English) put out in the flagship's red-painted tender, its crew reinforced with 20 sharpshooters, to check on some unidentified sails which had been seen earlier, and to gather what intelligence he could on the whereabouts and intentions of the English fleet. That night he returned with a captured Falmouth fishing boat in tow. Her four terrified occupants were bundled up the side of the *San Martín* and their resistance to interrogation, if they made any, was short-lived. The English fleet, they said, had left Plymouth that afternoon under Lord Admiral Howard and Sir Francis Drake.

At this point the Armada was arrayed, in the military parlance still used by Spaniards at sea, in line of march. Ahead sailed the vanguard under Don Alonso de Leiva, followed by Medina Sidonia's main battle. Behind came Recalde with the rearguard. As dawn broke on 31 July, with the wind blowing from west-north-west, a large group of English ships was sighted to windward. This was Howard's main body, which had successfully cleared Plymouth during the night to cross the Armada's front, round its seaward side, and gain the commanding weather gauge at the Spaniards' rear. Shortly afterwards the remainder of the English fleet worked its way out of Plymouth and tacked close inshore to meet up with Howard to windward.

With action imminent, the *San Martín* hoisted the royal standard as a signal for the Armada to take up its prearranged battle formation. The manoeuvres which followed echoed the precision drill of an army in the field. On the signal the fleet transformed its line of march into line of battle by turning half-right. Leiva's vanguard fell back into an extended line on the left of Medina Sidonia's main battle, while Recalde's rearguard moved up to adopt a similar position on the right flank. The Armada was now arrayed in deep lines across a broad front, facing up the Channel for an advance towards its rendezvous with Parma.

Previous interpretations of the Armada's formation have made the assumption that its various squadrons were discrete tactical units which sailed as sub-formations under their respective commanders. In fact, the territorial fleets – those of Portugal, Biscay, Castile, Andalusia, Guipúzcoa and Levant – were primarily administrative groupings and, once at sea, their individual members became randomly dispersed throughout the Armada, and their nominal commanders exercised little control over them. This arrangement explains a number of apparent anomalies in the fleet's command structure. Diego Flores de Valdés, for example, though nominally the commander of the Castilian squadron, never set foot on that squadron's flagship San Cristobal during the campaign because his tactical function of chief-of-staff to Medina Sidonia demanded his constant presence aboard the San Martín. Similarly, Juan Martínez de Recalde, who on paper commanded the Biscayan squadron, in fact hoisted his flag on the Portuguese vice-flagship San Juan as Medina Sidonia's immediate subordinate within the senior squadron.

A diagram of the Armada's proposed formation, prepared at an earlier stage of the planning process, has survived as a copy made by an Italian diplomat (FIGURE I). This, plus various Spanish documents listing the detailed dispositions of the various ships, allows the fleet's battle order to be reconstructed with some confidence. It owed much to the precepts of galley warfare, in which precision manoeuvres and rigid formation-keeping were paramount. The core of the fleet, Medina Sidonia's main battle, accounted for rather more than a third of its strength, and included the flagship, a strong contingent of fighting galleons and the four galleasses, as well as non-combatant transports. The remaining ships were allocated to the extended flanks or 'horns' (cuernos) of the formation under Leiva (left horn or vanguard) and Recalde (right horn or rearguard). The strength of this highly regimented tactical disposition lay in the Armada's ability to defend itself without halting its advance. A force attacking from the rear could be flanked and ultimately surrounded by the horns, while any attempt to impede the Armada's progress from the front might be countered by swinging the horns forward.

Most of the responsibility for defending the formation, however, rested with a relatively small group of powerful vessels, no more than 20 in all, disposed in key locations throughout the fleet. These ships, all of them entrusted to senior or notably dashing commanders, were expected to break station on their own initiative in response to any attack on the formation as a whole. In this way Medina Sidonia could control the Armada's defence without compromising its overall order, simply by moving powerful and well-officered ships to any

Plan of the Armada, as laid down in orders

**a** Four Ships of the Vanguard commanded by Don Alonso de Leiva

**b** The Galleasses of Don Hugo de Moncada

**c** The Main Battle

**d** The *Pataches*

**e** The Galleys

**f** Eight Support Ships commanded by Don Pedro de Valdés

**g** Support Ships of the two Horns, the Right commanded by Don Gómez de Medina, the Left by the Vice-flagship of the Galleons [of Castile]

**o** The two Horns of the Main Battle, the Right commanded by Juan Martínez de Recalde, the other by Francisco de Bobadilla

1 The ship *Rata* commanded by Don Alonso de Leiva

2 The Galleass Flagship [*San Lorenzo*]

3 Galleon *San Marcos* commanded by Don Francisco de Bobadilla

4 The Flagship of the *Pataches* with Don Antonio Hurtado their commander

5 The Flagship of Juan Martínez de Recalde commanded by *Maestre de Campo* [Nicolas de] Isla

6 The Flagship of [Miguel de] Oquendo

7 Galleon *San Martín* commanded by the Duke [of Medina Sidonia]

8 Galleon of Diego Flores [de Valdés] General of the Galleons of Castile

9 Galleon *San Juan* commanded by Juan Martínez de Recalde

10 Vice-flagship of the Galleons of Castile

11 Flagship of the Hulks commanded by Juan Gómez [de Medina] General of them

12 Flagship of Don Pedro de Valdés

13 Galley Flagship, Juan Medrano

14 The Galleon of the Grand Duke of Tuscany, commanded by Gaspar de Sousa, Flagship of Portugal

15 The Ship *Regazona*, Flagship of the Levant ships, commanded by Martín de Bertendona

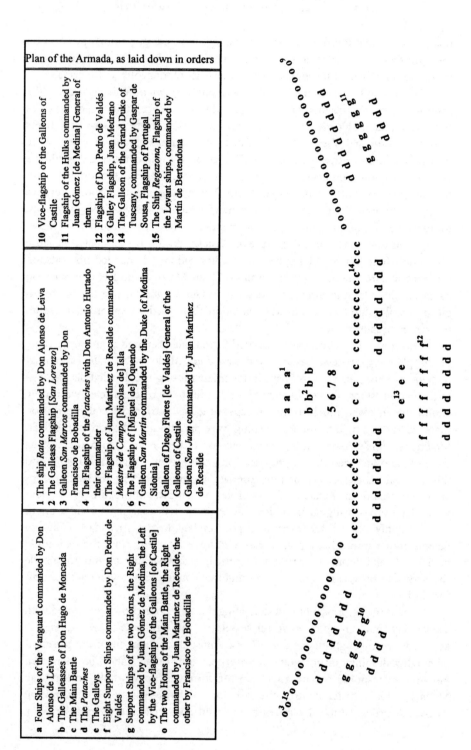

position he felt appropriate, and by giving them whatever discretion to act that he judged fit. Thus, for example, when Don Alonso de Leiva was put in charge of an augmented rearguard on 1 August, we do not later hear of him actually controlling the rearguard as an integrated force under his personal command. Most of the ships simply plodded on as before. But thereafter Leiva's great carrack *La Rata Encoronada* was to be found wherever the fighting around the rearguard was hottest, blasting away in concert with, but not commanding or commanded by, half a dozen or more of his fellow freelance troubleshooters who had moved from elsewhere in the fleet to support him, as Spanish gentlemen were honour bound to do.

Such movements normally took place within the formation and not around it, so the spacing between the ships was kept wide enough to permit free movement among them. As a group, the troubleshooters appear to have been vessels with a margin of performance over the progress of the fleet as a whole, which was naturally restricted to the speed of its slowest member. They could therefore fall back through the Armada, fight an action in its defence, and then regain station without slowing down the general advance.

This flexible and self-regulating tactical system neatly solved a less obvious but no less crucial problem of command. Medina Sidonia owed his unsought appointment, in part at least, to his elevated social position. He far outranked, in terms of nobility, every other officer in the fleet, so no one could object on social grounds (which were of extreme importance to Spaniards) to taking orders from him. But to have placed subordinates in positions of authority over their brother officers in a hierarchical structure of command would have created insuperable difficulties of precedence. The solution was, therefore, to create a system in which there were, in effect, no subordinate commands.[3]

While the ships took up formation, those on board prepared for action. From the poop of the *San Martín* Medina Sidonia, resplendent in half-armour and surrounded by his staff, watched as the battle drills he had personally laid down for the flagship went into effect. The ship's contingent of 202 arquebusiers and 100 musketeers, encouraged by the shouts of their officers, ran to their stations along the aftercastle bulwarks, in the waist and forecastle, on the two gundecks and high up in the fighting tops. A dozen were even arrayed along the

---

*facing]* FIGURE 1   The Armada's proposed battle-formation, based on a copy made by the Tuscan ambassador to Spain, Vincenzo Alamanni, from an original to which he had clandestinely gained access (ASF *Mediceo* 4919/340). It was sent to the grand duke of Tuscany on 25 March 1588. The total of 154 ships is 24 greater than that given in the Lisbon Muster of 9 May, though the excess is accounted for almost entirely by *pataches*. The remainder of the fleet is probably arrayed pretty much as it entered the Channel on 30 July. All of the numbered ships, together with Leiva's vanguard and Moncada's galleasses, may be identified as nominated 'troubleshooters'.

---

duke's private gallery at the stern. They presented a colourful sight (FIGURE 2). A list of the clothing taken from Armada survivors who later fell into English hands includes breeches made of cloth of gold, coloured cloaks with gold lace around the edges, 'a jerkin, embroidered with flowers, and laid over with gold lace' and, from the wardrobe of a Lieutenant Bermudo, 'a blue stitched taffety hat, with a silver band and a plume of feathers'.

The troops aboard the Armada came from all over the Mediterranean world and from all backgrounds – one company had even been raised among Christian converts of Muslim descent. No two soldiers looked exactly alike, and although some wore the cheaper clothes purchased in Lisbon for poor new recruits, many of the 6,000 veterans aboard the fleet were attired like dandies. In the words of a Spanish military expert, writing slightly later:

FIGURE 2 Spanish musketeers. This reconstruction by Ian Lowe is based on the recovery of weapons, clothing and accoutrements from the wreck of *La Trinidad Valencera*.

FIGURE 3 Wooden gunstocks from *La Trinidad Valencera*. The one on the top (from which part of the end is missing) is from an arquebus, which was a relatively light weapon. Its distinctive curved butt was designed to be held against the middle of the chest. The much heavier musket (below) has a straight butt, akin to modern firearms, so that it fitted snugly into the shoulder to absorb the stronger recoil.

> There has never been a regulation for dress and weapons in the Spanish infantry because that would remove the spirit and fire which is necessary in a soldier. It is the finery, the plumes and the bright colours which give spirit and strength to a soldier so he can with furious resolution overcome any difficulty or accomplish any valorous exploit.[4]

According to a general muster taken just before the Armada left Corunna in July 1588, the 19,000 soldiers aboard the fleet were organised into five Spanish and two Portuguese *tercios* or regiments, with some 'free companies' and a considerable number of unattached staff officers and gentlemen-volunteers. There were no cavalry units. Almost all the troops carried firearms – either muskets, which delivered a one-and-a-half-ounce lead ball, or the lighter arquebuses, of half-ounce calibre (FIGURE 3). The 3,000 musketeers, whose weapons were so heavy that they had to be fired from a forked rest, were something of an elite, distinguished by their elaborately feathered broad-brimmed hats. Four times as many men aboard the Armada carried arquebuses, which perhaps reflects the perceived suitability of lightly armed troops for the kind of close-quarter naval action anticipated by the Spaniards. Even the pikemen had been re-formed as arquebusiers. The individual weapons, though their calibres were for the most part standardised, had been fashioned and decorated to suit a variety of personal preferences. The 1,500 officers sported ceremonial halberds, with shafts cased in studded velvet, as marks of rank.[5]

The preponderance of close-combat weaponry reflects the central fact that the Armada's main offensive potential lay in the troops on board its ships. 'The aim of our men', Philip II had instructed Medina Sidonia shortly before the fleet sailed, 'must be to bring the enemy to close quarters and grapple with him.' It was held that the fleet's most effective way of defeating an adversary was to close with him, cripple and confuse him, and finally take him by boarding. All other weapons were subordinate to, and supportive of, this underlying aim.

The ships' armament included fearsome incendiary devices which, in unskilled hands, could be as dangerous to friend as to foe, and only properly qualified men were allowed to use them (FIGURES 4 and 5). One kind consisted of a ceramic pot filled with a mixture of gunpowder, spirits, and resin. It could be thrown, with lighted fuses tied round its pinched-in waist, onto an enemy's deck, where it would burst and scatter its fiercely burning, napalm-like charge. The other type was a wooden tube mounted on a long handle. This contained a series of gunpowder- and shrapnel-filled charges which, when ignited, would go off in a quick succession of flames and scattering projectiles. Weapons such as these were used when storming a breach, or launching a boarding assault.[6]

The main pre-boarding weapon carried by each ship, however, was her complement of artillery. Some of the San Martín's 48 guns were light swivel pieces mounted on the upper works for anti-personnel use, either against the crew of an enemy vessel or, should she herself be boarded, to bring down enfilading fire across her own decks. But the bulk of her artillery was ranged along the ship's two continuous gundecks. On the main deck, close to the waterline, were 17 or so bronze muzzle-loaders firing solid iron shot of up to 30 pounds. A similar number, but of generally lighter calibre, were placed on the upper deck; these included several stone-throwing pedreros which, though only effective at short range, could inflict formidable damage when their shot shattered on impact.

The 1,000-ton San Martín was one of the powerful galleons acquired by Philip II when he annexed Portugal in 1580. Others were constructed, at the king's command, in the following years to protect the maritime trade on which depended Portuguese prosperity and the tax revenue thereby derived. By 1588 the squadron numbered nine heavily armed battleships, supported by two smaller vessels. With them sailed the flagship of the Tuscan navy, the San Francisco (sometimes referred to as the Florencia, after her owner's principal city), bringing the combined firepower of the squadron up to 360 guns.

Eight escort galleons detached from their normal duty of protecting the transatlantic treasure fleets provided the Armada with the nucleus of a second group of royal warships, the squadron of Castile. Their 750-ton vice-flagship San Juan Bautista, though slightly larger than her seven sister galleons (all built in the early 1580s), was typical of them all. Low hulled and weatherly, she was designed to out-sail and out-gun Caribbean pirates or Protestant privateers (the Spaniards drew no distinction between the two), and to stay at sea for months on end. Even so, she was to prove no match for England's revolutionary royal galleons. During the fighting on 4 August Pedro Coco Calderón, an officer aboard the vice-flagship of the hulks, singled out 'the galleon San Juan' as the speediest vessel in the Armada. Unfortunately for the Spaniards the point of his story was that, in comparison with the English warship she was chasing, the San Juan 'appeared to be standing still'.

FIGURE 4   Ceramic firepots, as depicted by Cyprian Lucar in 1588 (left), and recovered from the wreck of *La Trinidad Valencera* (right).

This inferiority did not derive from any inherent weakness in her design, but rather from the purpose for which she had been built. The need to provide generous hold space to accommodate provisioning for long voyages affected the Indies galleons' sailing performance, and also dictated that their single gundeck should be placed well above the waterline. Stability considerations in turn restricted the weight of artillery they could carry. The *San Juan* herself boasted nothing larger than 7-pounder *pedreros*, of which she carried three, together with a hotchpotch of 20 light iron-throwing pieces of half-pound to five-pound calibres. Though excellent for the specialised task for which they had been designed, none of the Castilian galleons (and still less the five merchantmen and two *pataches* that sailed with them) could be regarded as front-line warships in a full-blown naval battle.[7]

In contrast, Hugo de Moncada's squadron of four galleasses from Philip II's kingdom of Naples were extremely heavily armed. These hybrid warships, with their 28 oars on each side, had been built some 10 years earlier to combine the mobility of a galley with the firepower of a galleon. For the Armada campaign their lateen-sailed Mediterranean rig had been replaced with a square-sailed configuration more suited to Atlantic conditions. With a displacement roughly four times that of a comparable galley, however, they were slow under oars, while their length and windage made them clumsy under sail. The galleasses suffered another chronic weakness which, in the weeks ahead, would prove fatal to two

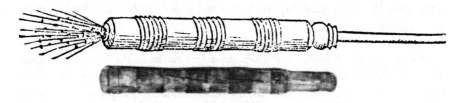

FIGURE 5   *Bombas*, or fire trunks, (top) as depicted by Girolamo Cataneo in 1571, and (bottom) an example from *La Trinidad Valencera*.

of them: their broad rudders, hung awkwardly on curved stemposts, were particularly susceptible to damage.

Nevertheless Moncada's galleasses presented an awesome sight. One English observer seemed particularly impressed by their vivid colour: 'The oars all red, the sails had upon them the bloody sword; the upper part of the galleass was also red – signs [he continued self-righteously] and manifest tokens of the bloody mind' that had sent them. Even the oarsmen – four convicts or prisoners to each oar – were dressed alike: in February 1588 each received a red jacket from the fleet's storekeepers. This was as near to a 'uniform' as the sixteenth century ever came. The working conditions of these 1,200 rowers (900 oarsmen and 300 reserves) were scarcely enviable, but they could have been worse. They were provided with straw-filled cushions and, for reasons of propulsive efficiency rather than humanity, were given high-energy rations and monitored by special medical teams.[8]

The role of the galleasses was to bring devastating firepower to bear at points which a conventional sailing warship might not reach, and they were armed accordingly. Moncada's flag galleass, the *San Lorenzo*, mounted six heavy pieces in her bow, ranged directly forwards, and four firing aft at the stern. The largest of these were 50-pounders. A further 20 pieces of 4- to 12-pound calibres occupied the restricted space within her castleworks (because of the rowing banks she could have no continuous gundecks). The raised catwalks above the benches on either side bristled with 20 swivel-mounted *esmeriles*, their octagonal bronze barrels protruding between gaudily painted protective screens. Beyond the bow of the galleass extended a massive ram, shod with iron. The *San Lorenzo*'s sister galleasses *Zúñiga*, *Girona* and *Napolitana* were virtually identical to the flagship, and together they constituted an apparently formidable battle group. Great things were expected of them.

Great things had also been expected of the four galleys which had sailed from Corunna under Diego de Medrano, but they had all gone missing. Bad weather in the Bay of Biscay had forced them to seek shelter in the nearest ports, and they failed to rejoin the fleet. These craft were not intended to take part in open-water fighting, for which they were known to be unsuited, but, together with the galleasses, as close-support units during the link-up with Parma and the subsequent landing in England. Their loss had added to Medina Sidonia's growing catalogue of worries.

Nineteen big merchant vessels commandeered in Spain's Basque ports made up the squadrons of Biscay and Guipúzcoa (a twentieth, the Biscayan flagship *Santa Ana*, also became separated from the fleet and never returned). These ships had been built in the shipyards of Cantabria and the Basque country: stout, ocean-going workhorses which plied the trade routes of north-west Europe or the whaling run to Newfoundland. Typical of their number was Guipúzcoa's vice-flagship, the 945-ton *Santa María de la Rosa*. This ship had been built the year before at San Sebastián by a prominent merchant, but before she could embark on her maiden voyage she was embargoed by Miguel de Oquendo, who was on the point of taking his Guipúzcoan squadron to Lisbon. When the *Santa María* arrived there her own light armament of 12 iron pieces was inventoried. Most were wrought-iron guns of antiquated design, of which the largest was a 7-pounder. To bring the vessel up to warship standard she was given four 18-pounder bronze *medios cañones* (cast some 40 years earlier by the German master-founder Gregorio Loefer), six 10-pounder *medias culebrinas*, also of bronze (manufactured in the 1550s at Malines, near Antwerp, by Philip II's master-gunfounder Remigy de Halut), and three swivel guns. These additions all belonged to the king. By the following March the *Santa María's* ordnance had been further augmented by the addition of a *pedrero* and a *media culebrina* from the Lisbon foundry. Even so, Oquendo had indented for a further 17 pieces to bring the *Santa María's* armament up to strength, for he considered his squadron to be seriously under-gunned. It was a complaint current throughout the Armada.[9]

Unlike most of his colleagues, who regarded artillery as a secondary and somewhat ignoble arm, the commander of the Andalusian squadron, Don Pedro de Valdés, took a close technical interest in his guns. Don Pedro, like Oquendo, wanted more and heavier guns for his squadron, and had lobbied the king directly to get them. He seems to have met with some success, particularly in respect of his flagship *Nuestra Señora del Rosario* (1,150 tons). In April 1588 he obtained a *culebrina* in exchange for a much smaller *medio sacre*, and the following month, just before the Armada set sail, added 10 more guns, including 4 *medios cañones* and 2 *cañones pedreros*, to his ship. At some point, too, he managed to swap 6 *sacres* for 6 heavy stone-throwing *pedreros*. By the time she set sail for England the *Rosario* carried 46 guns, overwhelmingly of short-barrelled heavy-shotted types. Don Pedro clearly subscribed to the 'close and board' school of tactical thought, and in this respect at least he was in accord with his less artillery-conscious brother officers.[10] His squadron included 10 great ships and one *patache*, all built in Cantabria in the 1580s for the American trade.

The ships of the three remaining squadrons were support rather than combat vessels. Ten big merchant vessels commandeered from Italian ports made up Martín de Bertendona's Levant squadron. Most of them had been grain carriers, with capacious holds suitable for bulk cargoes. But they were still expected to fight. Their overbearing magnificence, combined with the heavy armament and strong contingents of troops which they carried, would give them, thought Bertendona, an overwhelming tactical advantage in close-quarter battle. Some optimists even claimed that each could 'give battle to ten or twelve Englishmen'. One of the largest, the 1,100-ton *Trinidad Valencera*, from Venice, apparently boasted a particularly heavy armament. In addition to the complement of 28 bronze guns she had carried as a Mediterranean merchantman, the ship had four great battery cannons. One was a Turkish piece, perhaps captured at Lepanto

17 years before, while the other three were a matched set of *cañones de batir* (siege cannon) cast in 1556 at Malines by Remigy de Halut. These 2.5-ton monsters, which carried Philip II's royal arms combined with the English ones of Queen Mary Tudor, threw a solid iron shot weighing more than 40 pounds (FIGURE 6). Their effect against a ship at close range, it might be supposed, would be devastating.

But Master Remigy's *cañones de batir* were not intended for use at sea. They had been shipped, as the Spanish inventories of the fleet make clear, as part of a 12-strong battery of similar pieces. Eight, together with their field carriages and other accoutrements, were carried by the Levantine ships. Packed into the *Valencera's* hold were the dismantled components of six such carriages and their limbers – two full sets for each gun, to allow for breakdowns in the field (FIGURE 7). They formed part of the heavy siege train that would support Parma's march on London.[11] With it the *Valencera* carried a multiplicity of associated stores and munitions: 100 rounds of ammunition, and an appropriate amount of gunpowder, for each gun; a tripod gun-hoist (which could be folded for transport) for mounting the heavy barrels on their assembled carriages; and spare spokes, felloes and naves for the massive iron-shod wooden wheels, each five feet in diameter. There were also planks and baulks for the construction of gun platforms; gabions (basketwork cylinders which could be filled with earth to make defensive emplacements); esparto matting for consolidating earthworks; young fir trees with their branches trimmed to short spikes for making defensive entanglements; palisade stakes and woodcutters' axes; rollers and sledgehammers; wedges and handspikes; and screw-jacks for changing wheels in the event of a breakdown. Specialist tools were provided for the teams of farriers, blacksmiths, carpenters, wheelwrights and pioneers attached to the train. So too were tents (for the munitions, not the men), buckets, lanterns, handcarts, rope-soled sandals, earth-baskets and wooden shovels. Like her fellow-Levanters, *La Trinidad Valencera* was not a true warship. She was an armed invasion transport.[12]

*El Gran Grifón*, the 650-ton flagship of Juan Gómez de Medina's squadron of hulks, was, like most of the other 22 vessels in her group, also a commandeered merchantman. These ships were of northern European origin, either from the Netherlands or from the Baltic. The *Grifón* herself had been built at Rostock, and with her bluff bows and broad beam she typified the slow but roomy cargo ships that formed the staple of northern Europe's seaborne trade. She had been

---

*facing, head*] FIGURE 6    The escutcheon on a bronze *cañón de batir* from the wreck of *La Trinidad Valencera*, cast by Remigy de Halut of Malines in 1556. The shield shows the full arms of Philip II impaling those of his wife Mary Tudor, queen of England.

*facing, foot*] FIGURE 7    A Spanish land carriage, similar to those on which the Armada's siege train was to be mounted, from a technical drawing of 1594.

---

embargoed at San Lúcar early in 1587, when she arrived with a cargo of Baltic timber. To bolster her merchantman's armament of 27 iron guns, none of which was larger than a 6-pounder, eight newly cast bronze pieces were issued to her at Lisbon. Four were light 3-pounders, but the others were *medias culebrinas*, long 10-pounders which should have given the *Grifón* a capability of inflicting serious damage to an enemy's hull. The rest of the hulks, most of them somewhat elderly vessels, carried only light armament and sailed with the Armada as fleet auxiliaries. They carried additional troops, a field hospital, some 300 horses and mules, and general supplies. One, known to the fleet as 'the ship of the women', carried the wives of 32 married soldiers.[13]

Most of the 22 vessels in Agustín de Ojeda's squadron of light *zabras* and *pataches* specialised in dispatch-carrying and communication within the fleet. Apart from three large vessels – the flagship *Nuestra Señora del Pilar de Zaragoza* and (a bizarre touch) two embargoed British merchantmen, the *Charity* from England and the *St Andrew* from Scotland (Hispanicised as *Caridad Inglesa* and *San Andrés Escosés*) – they were all small pinnaces and caravels. Most had lateen-rigs and could use auxiliary oar-power when needed. It was with ships such as these that Columbus had discovered America, and their speed and sea-keeping qualities were outstanding. A *patache* sent by Medina Sidonia from Corunna to seek out units dispersed by the storm of 19 June arrived off the Devon coast within three days, and made the return journey in even better time. The inter-fleet communications support provided by these small vessels, by the pinnaces attached to individual squadrons, and by some other unassigned caravels and feluccas (*falúas*), formed one of the few unqualified successes of the campaign.

Such, then, was the Grand Fleet which on 31 July 1588 swung into line of battle within sight of the English coast. It numbered, according to the muster held some weeks earlier, more than 130 ships (although five of these had dropped out since leaving Lisbon). Altogether they carried 2,431 guns, 123,790 rounds of ammunition, almost 19,000 soldiers and 7,000 seamen. There were, in addition, almost 1,000 supernumeraries: gentlemen-adventurers with their retinues, and junior officers without commands.

Room had also been found for over 200 embittered English and Irish exiles, and 180 eager clerics.[14] Religion underpinned the fleet's morale and regulated much of its daily routine. The brooding presence of the Catholic Church and of its self-appointed champion, Philip II, pervaded the entire fleet:

> The principal reason which has moved his Majesty to undertake this enterprise [Medina Sidonia stated in the preamble to his General Orders] is his desire to serve God, and to convert to His Church many peoples and souls who are now oppressed by the heretical enemies of our holy Catholic faith, and are subjected to their sects and errors. In order that this aim should be kept constantly before the eyes of all I enjoin you to see that before embarking, all ranks be confessed and absolved, with due contrition for their sins.

The orders went on to prohibit blasphemy, swearing, gambling, feuding and the illegal embarkation of women – the latter being regarded as an 'evident inconvenience' as well as an offence to God. Medina expected each ship's company to attend full service at least once a week, while at daybreak and dusk the ship's boys sang the *Salve* and *Ave María* at the foot of the mainmast. Daily watchwords were chosen for their religious significance, and the Armada's standard was blazoned with the royal arms between the Virgin Mary and the Crucifixion, and crossed with the blood-red diagonals of holy war. Beneath was embroidered the battle cry 'Arise O Lord and vindicate Thy Cause!' Medina Sidonia's chaplain carried a letter of authority from the general of the Dominicans to repossess all the houses of that order in England which had been secularised at the Reformation.

Those who participated in the Armada unquestionably saw it as a crusade. They also knew that the pope had declared a plenary indulgence to all who sailed on the Armada (and even to those who simply prayed for its success). In the Netherlands, copies of *An admonition to the nobility and people of England and Ireland, concerning the present wars made for the execution of his holiness' sentence, by the high and mighty King Catholic of Spain* rolled from the presses, calling on all English Catholics to offer every assistance to the 'liberators' when they arrived and to abandon their allegiance to Elizabeth. It was to be distributed by Parma and his troops once they had crossed to England. Its author was William Allen, a Lancashire-born Oxford academic who fled into exile at the beginning of Elizabeth's reign and became superior of the seminary at Douai that trained English Catholic priests. The pope created him a cardinal in 1587. Following the Spanish conquest, Allen was to administer the new Catholic state under the joint authority of the pope and Philip II.[15]

The commanders of 'the greatest and strongest combination in Christendom' thus knew exactly what they were expected to achieve, and why they had been chosen by the king as God's principal instrument against Protestant heresy and English wickedness. Rather less certainty existed as to precisely how Philip's Grand Design should be put into effect. Quite apart from the ignorance which prevailed about Parma's state of preparation, there was the uncomfortable fact that Elizabeth's navy was already at sea, watching and waiting. The duke of Medina Sidonia cannot have been the only man aboard the fleet to find himself wondering, when he caught sight of the distant sails, what would happen next.

## Sources

It seems remarkable that so much has been written about so many relatively minor Elizabethan 'sea dogs', whereas so little is known of even senior commanders aboard the Armada. Vázquez, III, 361–443, and Duro, I, 209–16, provide a few details, but none has been honoured by biographies apart from its unhappy commander, on whom see Pierson, *Commander*, and more recently Alvarez de Toledo, duchess of Medina Sidonia, *Alonso Pérez de Guzmán, General de la Invencible*. Both rely extensively on the resources of the ducal archive at San Lúcar, but whereas the duchess looked in few other places and failed to provide full citations to the family papers that she used, Pierson's research was exhaustive and his scholarship meticulous. Maura, *Designio*, published many of the key documents from the Medina Sidonia archive for 1587–8.

Some surviving papers of three squadron commanders have been published. For Recalde, vice-commander (*Almirante General*) of the fleet, see Parker, 'El testamento político'; for Oquendo, see Tellechea Idígoras, *Otra cara*, chapters 2, 4, 5 and 7; and for Valdés, see Martínez, *Cartas de Felipe II*. For relations between the Valdés cousins, and their relative Recalde, see Lyon, *The Enterprise of Florida*, appendix III. The Lilly Library at Bloomington, Indiana, possesses a fine collection of Martín de Bertendona's papers. Although almost every previous account of the Armada states that Don Antonio Hurtado de Mendoza commanded the squadron of *zabras* and *pataches*, in fact he died before the fleet left Corunna, and was replaced by Captain Agustín de Ojeda (AGS *CS* 2a/286 fos 48off). Neither Ojeda, Gómez de Medina nor Moncada seem to have left surviving documents. Those of Diego Flores de Valdés may be in the archive of the counts of Revilla Gigedo, along with the papers of his cousin (and heir) Don Pedro published by Martínez (see above).

An analysis of the Armada's various ship types, based on documentary, pictorial and archaeological evidence, is contained in Martin, 'Ships of the Spanish Armada'.

## Notes

1 Tellechea Idígoras, *Otra cara*, 340–1, Recalde to Don Martín de Idiáquez, 29 July 1588, evidently written before the council of war held that day. Two sources independently reported that Leiva argued most strongly at the council for an immediate assault on Plymouth: see Duro, II, 374, 'Relación' of Alonso Vanegas, and PRO *SP* 12/214/51, testimony of Dr Góngora, after his capture on 1 August.

2 AGS *Estado* 455/492, Medina Sidonia to king, 30 July 1588, decrypt.

3 In March 1588 the Florentine ambassador secured a clandestine copy of the Armada's battle order, and sent it to his government, AS, Florence, *Mediceo del Principato* 4919/340. On 4 June the papal nuncio did the same, and on 12 July the Venetian ambassador enclosed a copy of a later plan 'from the original which lay on his majesty's table'. Filippo Pigafetta, evidently working from similar sources, gave further information about the fleet's formation in his *Discorso sopra l'ordinaza del'armata catolica*. See the brilliant reconstruction in Pierson, *Commander*, 134 and 235–43.

4 Details from Laughton, II, 209–10, 'Note of certain plunder' (individual garments); Deleito y Piñuela, *El declinar de la monarquía española*, 177–8 (quotation, from 1610); and Gracia Rivas, *Los tercios*, 109–11 (mass-produced clothes), 150–1 (the Morisco company raised by Francisco Melo, formerly mayor of Fez, Morocco) and 175 (number of veterans).

5 Gracia Rivas, *Los tercios*, 169–71, provides details on the 17,083 soldiers mustered at Corunna on 13 July 1588, noting that some 1,191 others still lodged in other Cantabrian ports. These figures, as he notes, differ significantly from those of the 'Lisbon muster' on May 1588, published just before the Armada first put to sea, but they represent the military disposition of the fleet as it sailed against England. See also the data on pp. 261–8 below.

6 Martin, 'Incendiary weapons'.

7    Details from the inventories of the 'Squadron of Castile' in AGI *Sección* III, *legajo* 2934; AGS *GA* 221/147–56, *relaciones* of March 1588; and Casado Soto, *Los barcos*, 208–9.

8    Reliable specifications for the galleasses are hard to find. The relevant archives in Naples (*Archivio militare* and *Giunta del Arsenale*) are fragmentary before 1600 and we have found no documents in Simancas that give the tonnage of the galleasses, and only one, AGS *GA* 202/148, that gives their age. However the 1589 'Addicioune' to John Mountgomerie's 'Treatise concerninge the navie of England', Pepys MS 1774, gave the weight as between 700 and 800 English tons. Since Mountgomerie's other facts about galleasses were correct, perhaps his estimate of their displacement is also accurate. The red colouring is recorded in BL Sloane MS 262/66v, and the issue of matching red uniforms is recorded in AGS *CS* 2a/274, unfol., order of 18 February 1588 to B. de Navarrete. Casado Soto, *Los barcos*, 233, considers the *Florencia* essentially another galleass, and gives her measurements.

9    AGS *GA* 221/41 lists the guns on board the seven *naos* and four *pataches* of Oquendo's squadron on 31 October 1587. See also Oquendo's indent for more guns, AGS *GA* 221/82, and the *Santa María's* receipt of ordnance dated 14 May 1588, AGS *GA* 221/153.

10   AGS *GA* 222/41, Valdés to the king, 5 March 1588, requesting more guns for his squadron. Later that month he apparently complained that although he had enough guns they were too light, Duro, I, 436. For his success in obtaining 6 *pedreros* in exchange for 6 *sacres* see Colin Martin, 'The equipment and fighting potential of the Spanish Armada', 437. Don Pedro also swapped a *medio sacre* for a *culebrina* from the *Duquesa Santa Ana*, AGS *CMC* 2a/1210, and a final issue of 10 guns was made just before the fleet sailed.

11   Martin '16th-century siege train'.

12   See the inventory of arms and munitions loaded aboard Bertendona's squadron, 14 May 1588, in AGS *GA* 221/156; and the bundles of accounts concerning the ships' equipment on departure in AGS *CS* 2a/280.

13   See the list of arms and munitions issued to Gómez de Medina's squadron, 14 May 1587, in AGS *GA* 221/147; and the bundles of accounts concerning the *Grifón's* equipment on departure in AGS *CS* 2a/280 fos 1931ff. On the *urca de las mujeres*, the 600-ton *Santiago* (built in 1551 and thus almost the oldest ship in the fleet), see Gracia Rivas, *Los tercios*, 164–7, and Casado Soto, *Los barcos*, 219.

14   The 'Lisbon muster' of 9 May 1588 has been reprinted several times (e.g. Laughton, II, 376–87, with annotations, translating Duro, II, 60–82); but the best edition is Oria, 384–435. A few additional vessels – the *falúas*, some support caravels and also at least one galleon (the *San Juan Bautista de la Esperanza*, which joined the fleet on 13 June: AGS *CMC* 2a/905) – seem to have been omitted. It may seem curious that this compendium of information, which would today be classified as top secret, was published and apparently disseminated by the Spanish government. But that was not Philip II's intention. On first seeing the document he was furious and complained that it would give advance warning to England of what to expect (see HS 143/77, the king to Mateo Vázquez, 3 June 1588). The idea of publishing the fleet's statistics apparently came from Medina Sidonia.

15   The proposed role of Cardinal Allen as interim governor of England is made clear by AGS *Estado* 165/176–7, the king to Parma, 5 April 1588. Philip II paid the salaries of 24 Jesuits stationed in Flanders who, in addition to the clerics aboard the fleet, would carry out the spiritual conquest of England (AGRB *SEG* 11/54v, order, 30 August 1588).

# 2

# 'A fleet to impeach it'

The fleet which had so laboriously warped out of Plymouth Sound during the night of 29/30 July was all that stood between England and defeat. To be sure, a few hundred regular soldiers were scattered in garrisons along the kingdom's coasts and militia forces were on standby – the beacon fires had been lit to alert men as well as ships. But they were far from ready. Many were not even familiar with the terrain upon which they might have to fight. Although military surveys of the geography and defensive arrangements for most coastal regions had been prepared in 1587–8, many remained inaccurate and incomplete. One harassed surveyor finished his map of part of the Norfolk coast in May 1588 in such haste that he had to omit a vital finishing touch, explaining in a note that 'Reason would a scale, but time permits not.'[1]

Last-minute haste and confusion similarly dogged the mobilisation of troops. Even in London, the government only issued orders to arm 10,000 citizens in mid-March, and then could not find nearly enough modern or serviceable equipment to go round. Many men received bows and arrows, but no instructions for their use, and in any case only continuous training from boyhood could produce an effective archer. No further military preparations followed until 6 July, long after the Armada had left Lisbon, when the Privy Council decided to establish a reserve army near London. This, however, could only be done by depleting forces elsewhere. In every shire of southern England, officials received instructions to divide the already stretched county militia into three parts:

> Some to repair to the sea coast, as occasion may serve, to impeach the landing . . . of the enemy upon his first descent; some other part of the said forces to join with such numbers as shall be convenient to make head to the enemy after he shall be landed (if it shall so fall out); and another principal part of the said trained numbers to repair hither to join with the Army that shall be appointed for the defence of Her Majesty's person.

For the moment, the troops designated to protect the queen were simply to stand at readiness to go wherever directed 'upon an hour's warning'. But on 2 August the government decreed full mobilisation: 'Her Majesty's pleasure is that you should forthwith send [them] into Essex, unto the town of Brentwood.'

From there the men were directed to Tilbury, where a small fortress was under construction to serve as a secure headquarters for Robert Dudley, earl of Leicester, 'General of Her Majesty's forces in the South'.

It was all in vain, for the Spaniards had no intention of landing in Essex. Their target lay in eastern Kent, where in the past Roman legions, Saxons and Danes had all stormed successfully ashore. The Armada might easily have done the same, and without serious opposition, for despite the urgent and often ingenious improvisations by Elizabeth's hard-pressed commanders, south-east England lacked an integrated defence system capable of withstanding a sustained assault by a professional army equipped with heavy artillery.

Some, indeed, regarded these panic-stricken preparations by land as a wasteful farce. As Sir Walter Raleigh was to write some years later: 'an army to be transported over sea . . . and the landing left to the choice of the invader . . . cannot be resisted on the coast of England without a fleet to impeach it . . . except every creek, port, and sandy bay had a powerful army in each of them to make opposition'. England's only defence, concluded Raleigh, lay in her 'many movable forts' – the galleons of the queen's navy – and the wisest strategy was therefore to 'employ . . . good ships on the sea, and not to trust to any intrenchment upon the shore'.

Elizabeth possessed few enough of these vital 'movable forts', but the ones she had were unquestionably the best in the world. The roots of a standing English navy lay in the reign of her father, Henry VIII, who had created a permanent defence establishment against the threat of Catholic attack following his excommunication by the pope in 1535. In 1546 he created a full-time Navy Board which, among other things, administered procedures for building, arming, victualling and maintaining the royal ships on a permanent basis. The illustrated inventory completed in that year by the Dutch artist Anthony Anthony allows us to glimpse Henry's 'navy royal' in frozen review, while the remains of one of his 'great ships', the 600-ton *Mary Rose*, are on display and under study at Portsmouth, close to the dock in which she was built in 1510 and not far from where she sank in action against the French in 1545.

The *Mary Rose* had been extensively rebuilt and re-equipped in 1536, and her wreck throws sharp light on the weapons technologies and tactical thinking of Henry's new professional navy at the close of his reign. For most of the time such ships were laid up on a care-and-maintenance basis to minimise cost to the crown, but in an emergency they could rapidly be mobilised for service in home waters. Since they were not designed to endure long periods at sea, or for extended voyages, the problems of victualling remained minimal. All they needed to make them operational was a full complement of seamen and troops which, in the case of the *Mary Rose*, amounted to some 100 and 600 men respectively. Virtually the full capacity of the ship was given over to the accommodation of weapons and men, who remained on board only long enough for a foray across the Channel, an expedition to Scotland, or (as in 1545) to repulse an enemy invasion attempt in home waters. Such ships were therefore designed for a mode of fighting that was short, sharp and – it was hoped – decisive.

Their tactics resembled those adopted by the Spanish Armada a generation later. Soldiers formed the primary weapon. On the *Mary Rose* they were predominantly archers, men trained from boyhood in the use of the yew longbow, who could cast a barrage of armour-piercing missiles from ranges of more than 200 yards, firing at a rate of up to six per minute. For the final stage of a successful engagement – the physical boarding and capture of an adversary – 300 pikes and bills were provided. Unlike the capital ships of the Armada in 1588, however, the *Mary Rose* seems to have carried few incendiary weapons (a single fire arrow was found in her wreck). Both for the preparatory bombardment intended to immobilise an enemy, and for the short-range salvoes designed to create confusion and alarm in the vital seconds preceding a boarding assault, she relied almost entirely on her guns.

Throughout his reign Henry had taken a close personal interest in the skilled and almost mystical art of gunnery, and with the help of foreign experts the gunfounders of England had become renowned throughout Europe. Even at the beginning of his reign, as a contemporary put it, the king possessed 'cannon enough to conquer hell', and by its close Henry's store of ordnance was truly formidable, including almost 200 guns of 9-pounder calibre and above. Many of these artillery pieces, especially the largest, were to be found on the gundecks of his big warships.

According to both contemporary documents and recent archaeological discovery, the *Mary Rose* carried an impressive armament. In addition to iron anti-personnel pieces, mostly quite small, she mounted 15 bronze guns, including 2 cannons royal, 2 demi-cannons, 2 culverins, 6 demi-culverins, 2 sakers, and 1 falcon. By the standards of their time these weapons were powerful and up to date, while the design of their carriages – examples of which have been recovered from the wreck – show that the English had already come to grips with the two main operational problems posed by the repetitive firing of heavy artillery at sea. The first was how to recharge a heavy muzzle-loading gun in combat, and the second was how to manhandle the gun and its carriage in a confined space and fire it through a gun-port. The solution to both problems was to abandon the use of heavy field-type carriages with trails and two large spoked wheels (or cheaper solid ones) upon which early shipboard artillery was frequently mounted. In there place a compact box-shaped carriage with stepped sides and four solid wheels was developed or trucks (FIGURE 8). A gun mounted on a truck carriage could be handled and adjusted with relative ease, while the whole assembly occupied far less deck space, so making it easier to run the gun back after firing and reload it inboard.

In spite of its widespread use aboard English ships as early as 1545, the Spaniards were still apparently eschewing this simple device in 1588, for they had not abandoned the 'close and board' mode of naval warfare rooted in medieval tradition. The navy that Henry bequeathed to his successors, while still composed of troop-filled battleships designed for use in the 'Narrow Seas', thus carried the seeds of a revolutionary concept which would flower under Elizabeth: the idea of a warship as a weapons platform whose offensive capacity lay not in her soldiers but in her guns. The presence, or absence, of truck carriages may therefore be regarded as a clear indicator of the kind of artillery tactics a ship intended to employ.

By 1547, the year of Henry's death, the navy royal consisted of 53 well-gunned warships totalling some 10,000 tons. But it was not a navy which England could afford to maintain. In a cost-cutting exercise of a kind all too familiar with modern peacetime navies, ships were sold off or scrapped, until by 1555 only 30 remained, most of them in poor condition. But then came one of history's great ironies. Philip II, king consort of England since his marriage to Mary Tudor, took a keen interest in English affairs. Even when he was absent, the Privy Council sent him Latin summaries of their deliberations, which he returned with comments and suggestions. In September 1555 the Council reported that most of the queen's ships were unseaworthy and should be brought to the Thames dockyards for repair. Philip was appalled.

> Since England's chief defence depends upon its navy being always in good order to serve for the defence of the kingdom against all invasion [he warned the Council] it is right that the ships should not only be fit for sea, but instantly available. And, as the passage out of the river Thames is not an easy one, the vessels ought to be stationed at Portsmouth, from which they can more easily be brought into service.[2]

As a result three capital ships of 500 tons or above were laid down. In 1588 all three, rebuilt and updated, would serve against the man who had assisted at their birth (one was even called the *Philip and Mary* until in 1584 Elizabeth changed her name to *Nonpareil*). So, thanks to Henry VIII and, to a lesser extent, Philip II, the navy inherited by Elizabeth Tudor when she came to the throne in 1558 was very much a force to be reckoned with.

By 1588 that fleet had 34 ships in commission. This might seem only a modest advance on the 30 Elizabeth had inherited at her accession, but while several were quite old (6 dated to the reign of Henry VIII) no less than 11 had been constructed since 1584 and 12 of the rest had been rebuilt to the same standards as the newer ones. Elizabeth's programme of naval development began under William Winter, surveyor of the navy, who started re-equipping the queen's fleet with new ships of medium tonnage, although the idea that they

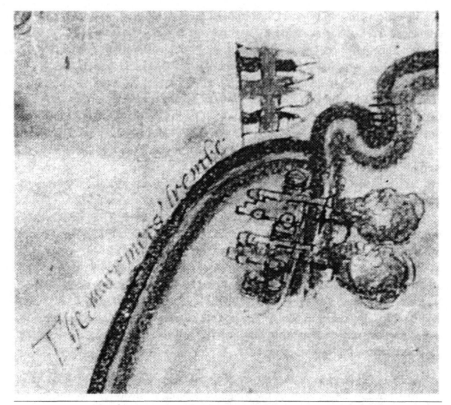

FIGURE 8  Detail from a manuscript map of 1580 showing English naval guns positioned on shore to bombard the Hispano-papal fortifications at Smerwick in south-west Ireland. The guns, which are protected by 'The marriners' trenche', are mounted on four-wheeled truck carriages with their distinctive stepped sides.

should be troop carriers as well as gun platforms was not immediately discarded. The 'Fighting Instructions' drawn up by Winter in March 1558 clearly envisage bombardment as a prelude, not an alternative, to boarding.[3] Thirty years later, however, this approach had been entirely abandoned in favour of prolonged bombardment at close range (FIGURE 9).

This critical change occurred in the 1570s, when the queen's shipwrights introduced a new design, known as 'race-built', which involved a reduction in the 'castles' fore and aft, sleeker lines – 'the head of a cod and the tail of a mackerel' claimed contemporary shipwrights – and a longer gundeck. The ships now carried fewer soldiers and a far larger complement of seamen, so their rigs and sail-plans could be made more complex and efficient. These changes produced two important advantages. First, they effected a revolution in armament, for the loss of the castles reduced the number of anti-personnel weapons which

FIGURE 9   Another detail from the Smerwick map showing Elizabeth's galleons attacking the Hispano-papal position from seaward. The ships (reading from the top) include the *Swiftsure*, the *Aid*, the *Marlyon*, the *Revenge*, the *Achates* and the *Tiger*. Many of these vessels fought against the Armada in 1588. Note their low 'race-built' appearance, and the mobile gunnery tactics which they are clearly employing.

could be mounted, while the longer gundecks permitted a significant increase in the weight of the main broadside. Second, the sleeker lines gave the English warships a distinct edge over their competitors, allowing them to sail faster and to manoeuvre – and bring their guns to bear – with (for the time) remarkable dexterity. The first of the faster 'all-big-gun battleships' of the Tudor navy was called (like the similarly innovative capital ship of the Edwardian navy in the early twentieth century) *Dreadnought*. Launched in 1573, she displaced 700 tons and carried 2 full cannons, 4 culverins, 11 demi-culverins, 8 sakers and 10 smaller pieces, a total of 31 tons of ordnance (not counting the weight of the gun carriages and tackles).[4] The ability to carry heavy artillery equivalent to almost 5 per cent of the total displacement was unprecedented. Besides supervising the construction of new ships of the *Dreadnought* class, John Hawkins (treasurer of the Navy from 1577) introduced an ambitious programme to rebuild all the older vessels in the queen's fleet to the new race-built design. Each year, one or two of the serving capital ships went into dry-dock and emerged (in Hawkins' phrase) 'reformed'.

Charles Howard of Effingham, Elizabeth's lord admiral, was unstinting in his praise of the new galleons. 'I protest it before God', he enthused after an inspection, 'were it not for her Majesty's presence I had rather live in the company of these noble ships than in any place.' He reported that his new flagship, the 800-ton *Ark Royal* (built in 1587) looked so majestic that she attracted 5,000 visitors a day on a visit to Flushing early in 1588, and he had this to say of her outstanding sailing performance: 'I think her the odd ship in the world for all conditions . . . We can see no sail, great nor small, but how far soever off they be we fetch them and speak with them.' He expressed scarcely less enthusiasm for the rest of the royal fleet: 'I have been aboard of every ship that goeth out with me, and in every place where any man may creep . . . There is none that goeth out now but I durst go to the Rio de la Plata in her.'

Of these glowing statements we may accept at face value all but the last: Elizabeth's galleons, like Henry VIII's warships before them, were not designed for long oceanic voyages. The shape and performance of any warship is conditioned by a range of conflicting factors which must be compromised. If one quality is to dominate, a penalty must be exacted from the others. Carrying capacity – whether of provisions for long voyages, of troops, or of armament – cannot be achieved except at the expense of speed and sailing ability. It was the requirement to carry all of these, in abundance, that so disadvantaged the Spanish ships which sailed against England in 1588. The English galleons, by contrast, were geared by the defensive requirements of an island nation to speedy and short-term mobilisation in home waters. It was not a high seas fleet which had to carry provisions for sustained voyages far from base, and so its ships were not encumbered by the need to carry heavy and bulky loads below decks.

The shipwrights of England therefore faced only one other major problem of design: how to combine a fast and agile ship with a heavy armament. They balanced this fine equation with a precision bordering on genius. The sleek lines of the new English galleons are seen to advantage in Matthew Baker's fine technical drawings of the 1580s, and contemporary observers – on both sides – agreed that the performance of these vessels far exceeded that of the best of Spain's fighting ships.

At the same time they were able to mount a formidable armament. Information about the guns aboard individual English ships during the campaign is sketchy, but the armament carried by two of the queen's galleons three years earlier is probably indicative. The 600-ton *Elizabeth Bonaventure* mounted, in all, 51.5 tons of ordnance (excluding carriages, ammunition and equipment), amounting to more than 8 per cent of her rated tonnage, while the smaller *Aid*, of 250 tons, had 27 tons of artillery aboard – nearly 11 per cent of her total. When in 1591 the Spaniards captured the queen's galleon *Revenge* of 500 tons (Drake's flagship against the Armada), after an epic battle off the Azores, they estimated that her 42 guns had a combined weight of 40 tons, or 9 per cent of the total, with 2 demi-cannon, 4 cannon periers, 10 culverins and 4 demi-culverins on her lower deck, with 4 more demi-culverins, 10 sakers and 8 more lighter breech-loading guns on her upper deck. Even without these powerful weapons, the total of heavy guns (9-pounders and above) possessed by Elizabeth's navy in the 1590s exceeded 600.

The ability to carry loads of this magnitude well above the waterline demonstrates the exceptional strength and stability of Elizabeth's race-built galleons. That these characteristics were combined with a sailing performance far superior to that of the best of their rivals further emphasises the success of late sixteenth-century English warship design.

By contrast the 1,050-ton Portuguese galleon *San Juan*, one of the most heavily gunned ships on the Spanish side, carried only 4 per cent of her tonnage in armament, while the 700-ton Castilian flagship *San Cristobal* could account for only 3 per cent of her rating in the weight of her guns. Moreover the largest of the *San Juan*'s guns threw only a 20-pound ball, and only nine of her 46 pieces fired a shot larger than 16 pounds. In exchange for their provision-filled holds and massed companies of troops, the Spaniards thus suffered heavy penalties both in firepower and in performance.[5]

What of the men who manned these splendid English galleons? In Henry VIII's day, as with the Spanish Armada of 1588, most of a warship's complement were soldiers, and the command structure included separate military and naval hierarchies in which the military authorities always prevailed. The naval reorganisation of Elizabeth's reign, however, and especially the highly individual genius of Francis Drake, gave rise to the more practical if socially revolutionary system of unified command under a single sea captain. The people aboard a ship, insisted Drake, must 'all be of a company' and his celebrated dictum that the gentlemen should 'haul and draw' with the mariners had evidently become normal practice aboard English warships by 1588. The Lord Admiral himself, as described above, took pride in inspecting 'any place a man may creep' inside his ships. He made himself familiar with the work of his seamen, 'namely sheet, halliard, bowline, tack and helm', and took pains to display his concern, 'specially for the poor toiling and continual labouring mariner, himself daily making enquiry how they did, and calling to them by name to know in what case they stood, and what they did lack'.

Lord Henry Seymour, who commanded the eastern squadron of the queen's navy, was also prepared to lend a hand on deck when needed. In June 1588 he dispatched a report to Walsingham from his blockading station aboard the *Rainbow* off Dunkirk, with a postscript apologising that it was not written in his own hand, which he had strained 'with hauling on a rope'. No Spaniard with pretensions to gentility, however modest, could have countenanced the menial task which Lord Henry lustily performed as a matter of routine.

Thus manned, and in a spirit of comradely teamwork under a single commander who was first and foremost a seaman, the new ships could exploit their technical advantages to the full. Their sailing superiority allowed them to gain the most advantageous position during a fight and, having gained it, to bring down sustained gunfire on the enemy. Moreover, in doing these things the English held yet another inestimable advantage over the Spaniards. Their ships were normally manned exclusively by seamen. Even though the men detailed to work the guns might still be officially listed as 'soldiers', they were no longer military personnel in the Spanish sense, but specialist naval ratings. On average, the English fleet had a seaman for every two tons of shipping. Each Armada sailor, on the other hand, was responsible for seven tons. To some extent the Spaniards made good this deficiency by employing soldiers to carry out general duties aboard the ships, and to serve the guns in action. But the English system, in which each seaman could turn his hand to working the ship or the guns as occasion demanded, was clearly much better. As the English artillery expert William Bourne put it, his sea-going compatriots were 'handsome about their ordnance in ships, on the sea'.

No such unity was to be found among Spaniards afloat. William Monson, a veteran of the Armada campaign, later provided a graphic critique of the shortcomings of his erstwhile opponents' command structure. They had, he wrote:

> more officers in their ships than we; they have a captain for their ship, a captain for their gunners, and as many captains as there are companies of soldiers; and, above all, they have a commander in the nature of a colonel above the rest. This breeds a great confusion, and is many times the cause of mutiny among them. They brawl and fight, commonly, aboard their ships as if they were ashore.

Medina Sidonia, it is true, had anticipated such troubles, for in his General Instructions to the Armada he sternly enjoined that 'there should exist perfect good feeling and friendship between soldiers and sailors . . . [that] there should be no possibility of quarrels among them, or other causes of scandal. I therefore order that no man shall carry a dagger, and that on no account shall offence be given on either side.' Despite these precautions, the underlying tensions nevertheless remained and could easily erupt in times of crisis. During the *Santa María de la Rosa*'s final desperate moments off Ireland a bitter altercation broke out between the seamen and soldiers, in which one of the military captains precipitately slew the ship's unfortunate pilot, Francisco de Manona, 'saying he did it [i.e. caused the wrecking] by treason'. This was a far cry from the comradely 'haul and draw' philosophy of Francis Drake.

The English system offered numerous advantages in combat, especially in stand-off combat involving heavy artillery. First, came experience and familiarity. The men who worked the Spanish guns were mainly regular infantry. Few had fought at sea before and virtually none, except those attached to the galleasses and the squadron of Castile, were familiar with the ships on which they sailed (Medina Sidonia had dismissed many of the masters and crews manning the squadron of Portugal because he apparently doubted their loyalty). Their English counterparts, on the other hand, were well versed both in the weapons carried by their particular vessels and in the idiosyncrasies of handling them on shipboard.

These fundamental differences emphasise yet again the contrary approaches to gunnery adopted by the two sides. The Spanish gun-crews, as noted above, expected to fire only one salvo before boarding and so, having loaded their pieces, they dispersed to battle stations which might be far distant from their guns. English gunners, on the other hand, who worked without the encumbrance of military weapons and accoutrements (to say nothing of the Spaniards' refulgent dress), merely stayed where they were and operated their guns continuously. Few soldiers were needed, for the English had no intention of boarding or being boarded. When, during the heat of the Channel battles, the governor of the Isle of Wight tried to send some musketeers to the fleet, Admiral Howard sent them straight back with a curt message saying 'that he had as many men as he desired or could well use'.

Sir William Monson pinpointed a third social contrast in the organisation of the two fleets, with brutal frankness, in an essay uncompromisingly entitled *The ill-management of the Spanish ships.* 'Their ships are kept foul and beastly', he wrote, 'like hog-sties and sheep-cots in comparison with ours.' This was hardly surprising, he explained, for no one on board was responsible for swabbing down the decks, and there was no galley to feed the ship's company as a whole. Instead, wrote Monson, 'every man is his own cook, and he that is not able to dress his meat may fast'. This was an exaggeration: although they lacked a communal cooking facility of the kind provided on every English ship, the Spanish soldiers were grouped into squads of eight or 10 known as *camaradas* (comradeships). Each group drew its rations collectively under the watchful eye of the ship's notary, and prepared them in rotation in the main galley using its own cooking utensils and serving dishes. But this was scarcely conducive to good discipline. The confusion and risk to general health posed by up to 50 separate food stores, and hundreds of soldiers jockeying for their turn in the galley, can only be imagined. These problems were exacerbated by the fact that general hygiene, even by the lax standards of the day, seems to have been exceptionally poor. English mariners (whose own shipboard habits were by no means exemplary) who came aboard Spanish vessels during the 1588 campaign all commented on the squalor and stench they encountered.[6]

England's naval defence in 1588 did not rest solely upon the queen's ships. As had been the case for centuries, the crown could draw upon a strong 'Volunteer Reserve'. Thirty private vessels which fought under Howard's command displaced between 200 and 400 tons, and carried up to 42 guns. They were warships in all but name. Several, indeed, had considerably more fighting experience against Spain than the carefully husbanded royal fleet. Only two of the queen's ships had sailed under Drake to the Caribbean in 1585, but all the 12 large merchantmen in that same fleet later served against the Armada. The raid on Cadiz two years later, again commanded by Drake, comprised six royal ships and 17 'civilians', almost all of which 'did their bit' in 1588. This should not surprise us, for many of these private ships belonged to prominent figures in the queen's navy, and the distinctions often became blurred. Howard himself owned seven vessels, which he normally used for privateering but in 1588 threw into the campaign against Spain. Hawkins owned three, and Drake two. All were commanded by their owners' relatives or commercial partners, thus creating a remarkably unified command structure among the fighting ships, whether royal or private.[7]

It would be misleading to dwell only on the strengths of the English fleet, however. Serious defects also existed. To begin with, the large fighting ships were not numerous. Ten of the 34 vessels of the navy royal were rated at 100 tons or less, and many of the 163 private ships involved at some stage of the campaign were small and of dubious value. According to Sir William Winter, they proved about as useful as Medina Sidonia's hulks. 'I dare assure Your Honour', he wrote later to Secretary Walsingham, 'if you had seen what I have seen of the simple service that hath been done by the merchant and coast ships, you would have said that we had been little helped by them, otherwise than that they did make a show.'

Nor were the past records of some of the privateers particularly inspiring. Two of the strongest galleons on the English side, the *Galleon Leicester* (42 guns) and the *Edward Bonaventure* (40 guns) had departed in 1582 on an expedition to sail to 'China and Cathay'. The enterprise quickly turned into a blackly humorous catalogue of incompetence and disaster. Off the coast of West Africa the fleet got lost. Its pilot, Mr Thomas Hood, who deprecated the use of books on navigation, declared '[I] will not give a fart for all their cosmography, for [I] can tell more than all the cosmographers in the world'. His confidence proved misplaced. Having inadvertently sailed in a circle back to where it started, the expedition had to sell one of its supporting ships in exchange for new provisions and better directions. The ramshackle fleet next departed for South America, where it ran into a flotilla under Diego Flores de Valdés (assisted by two other future Armada participants, Francisco de Cuéllar and Juan Gómez de Medina). Although the English managed to sink one of the Spanish ships, the action had to be terminated because the crew of the *Leicester* became too drunk to fight and the ship herself suffered such damage that she had to return to England. Another ship belonging to Sir Francis Drake and commanded by his nephew ran aground on the coast of South America, where John Drake and his hapless crew were either captured by the Spaniards, enslaved, or eaten by cannibals.

Such catastrophes, however, abounded during the 'age of discovery', and we should not make too much of them. A more serious disadvantage under which the English navy laboured in 1588 was the lack of commanders with experience of directing large fleets. The last full mobilisation of the country's maritime resources had taken place in 1545, and since then only small fleets had been deployed. Drake had led only 25 ships and pinnaces to the West Indies in 1585, and even fewer against Cadiz two years later, yet these were the largest fleets to have left England's shores in a generation. Winter, Hawkins and Frobisher had also held independent commands, but of even smaller squadrons.

The service record of Lord Howard, the commander-in-chief, was more limited still. During his long career (he was 52 in 1588) he had seldom taken a fleet to sea, having only been appointed lord admiral in 1585, and had never experienced naval combat. On the other hand, he came from a distinguished family of shipowners and seamen – he was the fourth of his family to hold the office of admiral under the Tudors – and he enjoyed excellent connections at court. He was a cousin of the queen, and was related by blood or marriage to most of the Privy Council. As with Medina Sidonia, no one questioned his right to command, and few criticised his skill in doing so. Again like Medina Sidonia, he possessed exceptionally gifted and supportive subordinates, whom he cultivated with sensitivity and tact. 'I confess my error', Howard graciously conceded on one occasion, 'but I did and will yield ever unto them of greater experience.' Where the duke could turn to Recalde and Oquendo, Howard could count on men like Hawkins and Drake.[8]

It was Drake who, after long argument, convinced Howard and the rest that their proper place in the early summer of 1588 was at Plymouth. Drake had correctly divined, unlike most other Englishmen, the grand strategy of Philip II: that the Armada would come from Spain to join with Parma and the Army of Flanders because Parma could not cross the Channel without the protection of a major fleet. Since that fleet could only reach Flanders via the Channel, Drake reasoned, it would be folly to concentrate the bulk of England's naval strength in the narrow seas, covering the Flemish ports. Instead, the main force should gather in a secure base as far to the west as possible, whence it might use the prevailing winds to gain the weather gauge of an enemy coming in from the Atlantic and then, from this advantageous position, harry it along the entire length of the Channel. 'The advantage of time and place in all martial actions', Drake presciently reminded his colleagues, 'is half the victory.'

Drake's argument prevailed. In February he brought a detachment of the main fleet to Plymouth, under his own command. On 3 June most of the remaining ships arrived, led by Lord Admiral Howard and accompanied by Hawkins and Frobisher, leaving only 15 galleons and their supporting auxiliaries under Lord Henry Seymour to guard the narrows. The western squadron now numbered 105 ships, including 19 of the queen's galleons and 46 large auxiliary vessels.

They were still at Plymouth on 29 July, despite several unsuccessful attempts to launch another raid on Spain. The main fleet was in the process of loading stores and munitions in the inner harbour when Captain Thomas Fleming of the 50-ton pinnace *Golden Hind*, one of the screen of pickets set to watch the Channel approaches, arrived with the momentous news that the Spanish Armada, in formidable strength and good order, had been sighted off the Lizard. Immediately the leading English ships began the tricky and laborious business of warping out of harbour with the ebb tide. Once the vital order had been given, the English commanders could do nothing until their ships had cleared port and were formed up, ready to sail, in Plymouth Sound. These few hours would have given Francis Drake, if the story is not apocryphal, ample opportunity to complete his game of bowls on Plymouth Hoe.

Not even Drake, however, could be sure how England's ships would fare in the battle which now seemed inevitable. Each side had, as we have seen, very different aims, equipment and tactical doctrines. Neither knew for sure the intentions, strengths and weaknesses of the other, or how best to respond to them. No one – least of all those involved – could predict the outcome.

## Sources

The standard account of the Tudor navy is now Rodger, *The Safeguard of the Sea: a naval history of Britain, I: 660–1649*; but see also Loades, *The Tudor Navy: an administrative, political and military history*; and the vintage study of Oppenheim, *A History of the Administration of the Royal Navy*, 45–183. Glasgow produced a valuable series of articles in *Mariner's Mirror* (all with slightly different titles) on 'The navy in the French wars of Mary and Elizabeth I'.

We have learnt much from a personal examination of the *Mary Rose*, now exhibited at Portsmouth dockyard; from Magdalene College, Cambridge, Pepys MS 2991 (the 'Anthony Roll'); and from Rule, *The Mary Rose: the excavation and raising of Henry VIII's flagship*. On the English leaders, see Kenny, *Elizabeth's Admiral: the political career of Charles*

*Howard earl of Nottingham*; Andrews, *Drake's Voyages: a reassessment of their place in Eliza-bethan naval expansion*; Kelsey, *Sir Francis Drake*; and Williamson, *Hawkins*. See also the most interesting document on the rotation programme presented by Adams, 'New light on the "Reformation" of Sir John Hawkins: the Ellesmere naval survey of January 1584'. On the development and performance of the race-built ships, see Parker, 'The *Dread-nought* revolution'.

On the defence of Elizabeth's realm by land, see Nolan, 'The muster of 1588', slightly revised in his *Sir John Norreys and the Elizabethan Military World*, 108–24. For an excellent documentary record of the 'muster', see the important collection of orders issued by the Privy Council for the defence of the realm in HMC *Fifteenth Report*, Appendix, part V (London, 1897): pp. 20–62 contain measures taken in 1587–8.

## Notes

1   The map is reproduced in Tenison, VII, plate 21. See also the description of this, and three other contemporary maps of coasts liable to be invaded, in Skelton and Summerson, *A Description of Maps and Architectural Drawings*, 51–2.
2   PRO SP 11/6/26, 'Memoria', August/September 1555. We have based our translation on the English version printed in Tytler, *England under the Reigns of Edward VI and Mary*, 485.
3   See Corbett, *Fighting Instructions, 1530–1816*, 42; and *Addenda*, 364–71.
4   Calculations of displacement (as opposed to the 'tons burden' normally used to denote the size of English ships) kindly supplied by Dr Jan Glete; weight of ord-nance calculated from the totals aboard each ship in September 1595 according to PRO WO 55/1672, 'A view and survey of all Her Majestie's Ordinnance'.
5   For the guns of the *Elizabeth Jonas* and the *Aid* see the indenture for the delivery of ordnance to Drake, 17 July 1585 OS, in Corbett, *Spanish War*, 27–32. Earle, *The Last Fight of the* Revenge, 181, provides the corresponding figure for the *Revenge*. The weight of ordnance aboard the *San Juan de Portugal* has been calculated from a list of the guns she had carried in 1588, drawn up in 1591 (two years after the ship's destruc-tion in Corunna harbour) as a guide to future policy, AGS GA 347/218, 'Las naves que fueron en esta última Armada', and for the *San Cristóbal* from AGS GA 221/147.
6   Quotation from Oppenheim, *The Naval Tracts of Sir William Monson*, 63–5. On the stench, see Laughton, I, 9 and 301, and II, 156 and 186.
7   Details from Keeler, *Sir Francis Drake's West Indian Voyage*, 12–16; and Andrews, *Elizabethan Privateering*, 89–94. The leading Spanish commanders (such as Oquendo and Bertendona) likewise owned their own ships, which they also hired out to the crown for the 1588 campaign.
8   Laughton, I, 199–202, Howard to Walsingham, 24 June 1588. The lord admiral could also rely on relatives in the fleet: among those commanding the queen's ships in 1588, Lord Henry Seymour was his brother-in-law, Lord Sheffield his nephew, Lord Thomas Howard his cousin and Sir Richard Leveson his son-in-law.

# PART II

## 'GOD'S OBVIOUS DESIGN'

South-east England and the Netherlands, 1588

Territories held by Dutch Republic

0        50        100 miles
0    50   100      150 km

North
Sea

ENGLAND

TEXEL

Alkmaar

Haarlem          Amsterdam
                    Naarden        Deventer
                 Leiden            Zutphen
                        Utrecht
                Gouda
        Brill
                      R. Waal

Brentwood
Tilbury
        Thames
        Estuary    North Foreland
                   ('Cape Margate')     Grave
Rochester
Canterbury              Flushing    Bergen-op-Zoom
Sandwich                    Ostend          Antwerp
        Dover  The Downs  Banks of  Sluys      •Lier
KENT          Goodwins  Flanders   Bruges   Ghent  •Mechelen
Rye                      Nieuwpoort
        Calais          Dunkirk
        Gravelines    FLANDERS     Aalst    •Brussels
        Boulogne   Bourbourg •Douai
                      R. Scheldt
                                 SPANISH NETHERLANDS
English
Channel                                      R. Maas

                   Cateau
                   Cambrésis

        P  I  C  A  R  D  Y

FRANCE

R. Rhine

N

# 3

# 'The great bog of Europe'

As the Spanish and English fleets manoeuvred off the Lizard, another confrontation was taking place 300 miles to the east. Along the coast of Flanders an expeditionary force of some 27,000 men commanded by Philip II's nephew, the duke of Parma, lay encamped close to its invasion transports, awaiting the approach of the Armada so that, under its protection, they might slip across the Channel to their assigned landing zone in eastern Kent. But without that protection they were helpless. In the shoal waters beyond the low coastline they could glimpse the sails of Justin of Nassau's 30 shallow-draught Dutch cromsters – well armed, deadly and pledged to destroy any of Parma's forces that put to sea. Just over the horizon, they knew, stood Queen Elizabeth's narrow seas fleet under Lord Henry Seymour, ready to intercept and annihilate the flotilla of open craft should it somehow evade the Dutch and make a sudden dash for England.

Most accounts of the Armada campaign concentrate upon the naval battles of the main fleets and pay scant attention to the vigil maintained by the forces in the straits. But their role in the defensive effort was just as important. And the Dutch risked everything too, for although the Armada was directed principally against England, it was also a bold attempt to counter a long-standing and deeply seated challenge to Spanish power in the Netherlands.

The 17 provinces of the Netherlands, which had been united under Habsburg rule by Philip II's father Charles V during the first half of the sixteenth century, formed the newest state in Europe. Some, including the prosperous western areas of Brabant, Flanders, Holland and Hainaut, had been familiar with firm government from Brussels for more than a century; but others, such as Friesland, Utrecht and Groningen, had not been absorbed until the earlier part of the sixteenth century. Gelderland, the largest province, was not annexed by the Habsburgs until 1543. And even when all these provinces were given a single administrative structure in 1548 they all nevertheless retained a lively spirit of independence which was accentuated by their different histories and traditions and by their different languages (French in the south; German and East Dutch in the east; West Dutch and Fries in the north and west).

The new Protestant faith, also born in the first half of the sixteenth century, found it easy to penetrate this patchwork of jurisdictions, customs and languages.

Before long Calvinism, Anabaptism and Lutheranism all had their devotees in different parts of the Low Countries. It was to counter the spread of these heresies that Philip II, who began to govern the 17 provinces in 1556, decided to increase the number of Catholic bishops in the Netherlands, to sharpen up the laws against Protestantism and to extend the scope of the Inquisition.

All these measures, however, required money; and money was in short supply. In 1564 the creation of new bishoprics was frozen, and two years later the enforcement of heresy laws and the activities of the Inquisition were suspended. These concessions prompted further agitation and more demands. In the spring of 1566 Protestants in the Netherlands began to organise open-air prayer meetings defended by armed guards. Their growing discontent led, in the summer and autumn, to a campaign of iconoclasm, in which they smashed Catholic religious images in wayside shrines and churches, and demanded the right to worship indoors as well as in the fields. By August 1566, according to the king's representative in Brussels, half the local population had gone over to Protestantism and 200,000 people were in arms against the government.

These events threatened Philip II's authority to an intolerable degree; they were a challenge to which he felt obliged to respond, whatever the cost. In Spain, the king and his advisers took the highly alarmist (and, as it turned out, grossly exaggerated) estimates of Protestant strength at face value and determined to meet force with force. It was resolved that Spain's most experienced general, the duke of Alba, should be sent to the Netherlands at the head of 10,000 Spanish veterans, with orders to raise whatever additional forces were needed to restore order and extinguish heresy. In the face of this overwhelming threat the king's opponents went to ground, and the Low Countries were effectively pacified before Alba's Spaniards arrived in August 1567.

However, the presence in the Spanish Netherlands of a professional standing army, commanded by perhaps the best general of his day, immediately transformed the international situation in northern Europe. The duke and his troops represented a permanent challenge to the security of neighbouring states: France, England and the semi-autonomous princes of Germany. All now felt sufficiently threatened by Philip II to offer support to the Protestant exiles and rebels led by William of Nassau, prince of Orange, when they invaded the Netherlands in 1568 and again in 1572. And although the first attempt proved a miserable and costly failure, the second achieved partial success, for the invaders managed to gain firm control over the heavily fortified coastal provinces of Holland and Zealand.

For four years the outcome lay in the balance. It was not only the impressive modern fortifications of the rebellious Dutch towns which complicated Spain's reconquest: there were geographical considerations too. The provinces in revolt, surrounded either by the sea or by broad rivers, were all islands or peninsulas, and communications within them were further complicated by lakes, marshes and waterways. In the words of an English traveller, Holland and Zealand constituted 'The great bog of Europe. There is not such another marsh in the world, that's flat. They are an universal quagmire. Indeed it is the buttock of the world: full of veins and blood, but no bones in't.'[1]

And this 'buttock' was defended by a fleet of small ships, able to operate close inshore, and capable both of blockading enemy ports and of preventing vessels sent from Spain from landing troops on Dutch territory. After the wrecking of one Spanish fleet on the Flemish coast in 1572, and the failure of another to reach the Netherlands at all two years later, no further naval attack on the rebels was attempted until 1588.

But Spain did not give up the struggle. Instead, the duke of Alba assembled a vast force of some 60,000 men, known to its contemporaries and to posterity as the 'Army of Flanders', and hurled it against one rebellious town after another: Malines, Zutphen and Naarden in 1572, Haarlem and Alkmaar in 1573. Those that they captured were sacked and a large part of their populations were massacred, irrespective of sex or age, and despite promises of clemency made beforehand. It was all to no avail. Alba's draconian policy only intensified the resistance of the towns still in rebellion, and the duke was recalled in semi-disgrace at the end of 1573. But this, too, failed to end the revolt. 'There would not be time or money enough in the world to reduce by force the 24 towns which have rebelled in Holland [and Zealand], if we are to spend as long in reducing each one of them as we have taken over similar ones so far', wrote Alba's dispirited successor in October 1574. 'No treasury in the world would be equal to the cost of this war', he repeated more ominously in November.[2]

His prediction came true within the year. In September 1575, crippled by the cost of supporting 60,000 soldiers for more than three years in the Netherlands, the Spanish treasury declared itself bankrupt and the flow of money to the Army of Flanders abruptly ceased. Within a few months Philip II's unpaid troops in the Netherlands either deserted or mutinied, while the Catholic political leaders of the provinces formerly under Spanish control made common cause with the Protestant rebels, still led by William of Orange. By May 1577 the prince of Orange was, in effect, the chief executive of a new 'government of national unity' established in Brussels and responsible to a States-General (parliament) representing all the provinces, languages and religions of the Netherlands.

This was the high point of the Dutch Revolt. The States-General demanded that Philip II accept them as his lawful government, and that crown officials be appointed only with their approval. Even more provocatively they insisted on freedom of worship for Protestants throughout the Low Countries. These were ultimata that no early modern monarch could accept with honour. As the king's advisers pointed out, concessions in the Netherlands would almost inevitably lead to a stream of similar demands from his other dominions. So, instead, Philip II determined on a systematic reconquest of his defiant provinces, and began to build up loyal forces in the far south-east of the Netherlands, closest to

FIGURE 10   Ian Lowe's reconstruction of
an Army of Flanders' arquebusier in field-
service order is based on contemporary
pictorial evidence and items recovered
from the Armada wrecks.

his possessions in Italy. A 700-mile military corridor, known to contemporaries
as 'the Spanish Road', conveyed troops and treasure from Lombardy to the Low
Countries at regular intervals to encompass, by sheer attrition and weight of
numbers, the defeat of the Dutch. From the autumn of 1578 these formidable
troops were moulded into a doggedly professional fighting force of supreme
quality and morale by that tough and energetic soldier Alexander Farnese, prince
(and later duke) of Parma (FIGURE 10).

Parma was an ideal choice for the command. In the first place, he was
Philip II's nephew. His royal blood entitled him to deal directly with sovereign
rulers, and gave him an effortless social status among the prickly Netherlands
aristocracy. Second, he had grown up at the Spanish court, where he had developed valuable contacts among the king's ministers, and at the same time
come to understand the complex processes by which policies were made (and
unmade) at the highest levels. Third, through his wide travels he had acquired a
penetrating appreciation of Europe's geography, and had come to know a large
number of influential people. In 1557 he visited England, and was even spoken of
as a possible bridegroom for the young and attractive Princess Elizabeth. Thirty
years later, on the eve of his planned invasion, he could still reminisce about the

excellence of the hunting around London.[3] In the 1560s he was introduced to the geography and history of the Netherlands as well as to its leading political figures, while his mother (Philip II's illegitimate elder sister) served there as regent. By the early 1570s he was a staff officer in the Spanish Mediterranean fleet, taking part in the great Christian victory of Lepanto in 1571.

Parma, although only 32 when he took command of the Army of Flanders in 1578, had thus already acquired extensive political and military experience. He also possessed huge personal resources. As the heir (and after 1586 as the ruler) of a major Italian state, Parma maintained his own diplomatic service, used his own credit where necessary to achieve his ends, and maintained a glittering court of around 1,500 people. In most years, 50,000 ducats were sent from his Italian estates to Flanders to support the duke's household, and he was able to raise far more (by 1592 almost one million ducats) in loans secured on his extensive properties.

Through these formidable sources of power and influence, Alexander Farnese was able to offer a wide range of rewards, bribes and promises at many opportune moments to advance his cause. In 1578–9 his subtle diplomacy drew the Catholics of the southern Netherlands back into the royalist camp, and throughout the 1580s his bribes secured the surrender of numerous fortified centres without a siege. As a Dutch commander bitterly remarked after one such reverse: 'Everyone knows that Spain's golden bullets made a greater breach in the heart of the traitor who commanded [the town] than their battery [did in the walls].'[4] But Parma was equally dexterous in the use of force. On the one hand, he was prepared to arrange the murder of those who refused his bribes: at Philip II's instigation he placed a price on the head of William of Orange, and an unsuccessful assassination attempt was made in 1582, followed by a successful one in 1584. On the other, thanks to the efforts of his 60,000 soldiers, Spaniards, Italians, Burgundians and Germans as well as native levies, Parma was able to starve one Dutch town after another into submission.

In January 1581 Parma's forces embarked upon a grand strategy that within four years would double the size of the Spanish Netherlands. Observing that Flanders and Brabant, the richest provinces involved in the revolt, depended for their prosperity upon water-borne trade, the prince realised that if his troops could occupy the Flemish coast and block the Scheldt below Antwerp the entire inland network of rivers and canals would be paralysed. Without access to the sea and the major rivers all the major towns caught within his net would be forced to surrender.

A complete Spanish reconquest, however, was a prospect that Parma's neighbours in north-western Europe viewed with grave dismay. The 'great bog' occupied a position of permanent strategic importance, since an army stationed there could with ease intervene in France and the Rhineland or even, given a fleet, in England and Scotland. The creation of the powerful Army of Flanders, first under Alba and then again under Parma, therefore caused a diplomatic revolution in northern Europe.

Looking back in 1589, England's chief minister of state, Lord Burghley, mused that 'The state of the world is marvellously changed, when we true Englishmen have cause for our own quietness to wish good success to a king of France and a king of Scots.' For the previous five hundred years Englishmen had generally been opposed to – and often at war with – the rulers of France and Scotland, and had usually found themselves allied with the rulers of the Netherlands. But now England's 'natural enemy', like France's, was Spain. The continuance of a rebellion which committed a large part of Spain's army to an enduring and expensive war in the Low Countries was therefore something that suited both England and France, not to mention the Protestant states of the Rhineland, very well. Their political advantage clearly lay in lending support to the Dutch rebels whenever they seemed to be in danger of succumbing. Thus in 1572 virtually all the Netherlands' neighbours had sent support to William of Orange's invasion; in 1574, when the rebel cause seemed to be faltering, France began to send subsidies; and in 1578, after a Spanish military success, France and England took the overtly hostile step of sending troops to fight for the Dutch.

In 1581, as Parma launched his master strategy, the Dutch Revolt once again seemed on the point of failing. Partly it was the religious divide, which made Catholic and Calvinist rebels uneasy bedfellows; partly it was the petty provincialism of the Netherlands, which made Hollanders reluctant to assist Flemings. But above all, it was the absence of a firm and universally accepted government. According to an English observer in the Low Countries, writing in October 1581, the rebellion was about to collapse 'for want of a good government; for there is a number that commands in the country, and few will obey'. In January 1582 he repeated: 'Every man will command, and few . . . will be commanded, so there is no order nor good government among them.'[5]

Deliverance, however, was at hand. The prince of Orange persuaded François de Valois, duke of Anjou and heir apparent to the French throne, to become 'prince and lord of the Netherlands'. In 1581 the States-General declared Philip II deposed from all his Netherlands titles, and Anjou arrived at the head of 10,000 troops to take over. Furthermore, he declared that the queen of England had announced her intention to marry him, and to place her resources alongside his in the defence of Dutch liberty. 'Froggy' therefore (as the contemporary English song had it) 'went a wooing', and spent the autumn of 1581 in England. The following February he returned to the Netherlands, claiming that he was engaged to Elizabeth and bringing with him as a token of this new attachment her favourite, Robert Dudley earl of Leicester, her cousin Lord Hunsdon, Secretary Walsingham and numerous other English courtiers. On 19 February, at Antwerp, they were all present when William of Orange, in the name of the States-General, invested Anjou with the regalia and dignities of the dukes of

Brabant. Representatives of the other provinces soon followed suit and the duke, now in receipt of funds and recognition from France and England, became in effect sovereign ruler of the provinces in revolt against Philip II.

But it did not last. First, in March 1582, William of Orange was severely wounded in an assassination attempt plotted by Parma and, while he was out of action, Anjou and the States-General fell to disagreement. Early in 1583, indeed, the duke's French troops attempted to take control of eight leading Low Countries towns, including Antwerp. Anjou was disgraced, and left the Netherlands in June. He died a year later. Meanwhile, amid the confusion, Parma's accomplished veterans advanced rapidly and captured most of the ports along the Flemish coast. In the summer of 1584 they struck inland and captured Bruges and Ghent, the key towns of Flanders, and in September the troops began a huge engineering project some 30 miles below Antwerp which would close the Scheldt and so cut off the metropolis from its vital access to the sea. It consisted of a great timber bridge 800 yards long, its central section floating on anchored pontoons defended by a complex of emplacements, containing almost 200 guns, with booms moored up- and downstream. Parma's blockade was completed at the end of February 1585. It was one of the wonders of the age, and the duke staked everything upon its success: it would be either 'his sepulchre or his pathway into Antwerp'.

Many contemporaries considered Antwerp, the great city on the Scheldt with a population of 80,000 and a three-mile circuit of powerful modern fortifications, to be impregnable. Certainly the States-General did very little to succour it, although this was due less to complacency than to the confusion and lack of leadership which followed the assassination of William of Orange in July 1584. Not until April 1585 was a major effort made to relieve Antwerp, when a fleet from Holland, commanded by Orange's illegitimate son Justin of Nassau, waited at the mouth of the Scheldt while, at Antwerp, a small flotilla of ships filled with explosives was released on the ebb tide down the river towards Parma's bridge. These floating bombs had been designed by an Italian, Federico Giambelli, with considerable ingenuity. Some were constructed to explode on impact, others were given a delayed fuse to ignite the charge as the ship neared the bridge, and others still were simple fireships filled with powder and shot which exploded when the heat reached them.

As Giambelli had intended, the subtle variety of his 'infernal machines' caused confusion and carelessness among the Spaniards. The whole idea of explosive ships was new, and the cataclysmic danger they presented was not fully appreciated. When the largest 'hellburner', which had been set to blow up almost harmlessly in the middle of the river just short of its target, spewed out its colourful pyrotechnics, the defenders of the bridge gathered by the water to watch the display. Even Parma came for a while. He had only just started back for his headquarters when one of the other vessels, primed to explode on impact, hit the bridge. At least 800 Spaniards were killed, many more were injured, and Parma himself was knocked down by the shock wave. But the stolid troops of the Army of Flanders soon recovered their discipline and their wits: they temporarily made good the damage, stood to their battle stations, and prevented Justin and his fleet from exploiting their advantage. A counter-attack was swiftly launched. The beleaguered cities of Brabant, including Antwerp, all now fell; but the terrible experience of the exploding ships was not easily forgotten. The 'hellburners of Antwerp' entered the vocabulary, and the irrational fears, of every Spanish soldier.

Parma and the Army of Flanders had achieved a great deal against heavy odds in a short time. Within four years they had driven those in revolt against Philip II's power into an enclave scarcely larger than they had held in 1572. After the capitulation of Antwerp, which was signed in August 1585, Parma was at last free to consider how best to complete the reconquest. He had no doubt of the ability of the troops under his command to achieve anything that was humanly possible. Some of his soldiers had been on active service for 30 years, and they were commanded by officers who had spent many years in action before rising to senior rank. In the words of one of Parma's staff officers, the Army of Flanders contained 'few soldiers who were raw recruits. They were powerful men, well armed and of martial aspect, highly trained and always ready to obey and to fight'; and Parma himself once boasted that his men were 'tough, disciplined, and born to fight with the people of the Netherlands'.

Those who had encountered Parma's troops in action could only agree. Sir Roger Williams, third-in-command of the army which awaited the Armada at Tilbury, held up the Army of Flanders as a shining example to others: 'To speak truth', he wrote, 'no army that ever I saw, passes that of the duke of Parma for discipline and good order.' And Sir Roger had good reason to know, since he had fought with the Spaniards in the Netherlands from 1574 until 1578, and thereafter against them. The earl of Leicester, commander-in-chief of Elizabeth's forces, was likewise filled with apprehension: the Army of Flanders contained, he noted with regret, 'the best soldiers at this day in Christendom'.[6]

In them, Parma held the tool to complete the recovery of the Netherlands. The Dutch were losing their nerve and their will to resist. They had failed to save any of the towns of Flanders and Brabant from capture, and now they were bankrupt. In 1583 interest payments on the state debt had to be suspended for lack of funds, and even the tomb of the prince of Orange was, according to an English visitor, 'the poorest that ever I saw for such a person, being only of rough stones and mortar, with posts of wood coloured over with black'. And the Dutch not only lacked money; now they had no leaders. Following the deaths of Anjou and Orange in the summer of 1584, no one in the young republic seemed capable of exercising effective authority. If the problem in 1581–2 had been too many commanders, by 1584–5 there were too few. The provincial assemblies, and even the States-General, lacked statesmen accustomed to command in war or experienced in the conduct of diplomacy. Orange's son Maurice, although accepted as governor by Holland and Zealand, was only 17, and many years would pass before he gained the skill and sagacity required to reconcile the differing interest groups within the Dutch state. Indeed, in the wake of Parma's victories, a vociferous peace party grew up within the rebels' ranks, anxious to make a deal with their former master while they still had something to bargain with. In July 1585, when the states of Holland proposed to levy another tax for the defence of Brabant, the town council of Gouda (in Holland) refused to consent and argued instead that the surest way to relieve beleaguered Antwerp was to start immediate negotiations with Spain for 'a good peace'. Only the dispatch of a large body of loyal troops brought Gouda to heel.

And yet, as he contemplated his next move following the fall of Antwerp, Parma noted with frustration that the rebels did not offer to surrender. Perhaps, he argued in a letter to the king at this time, he should simply continue his offensive and invade Holland and Zealand. The experiences of 1572–6, however, had already shown the dangers and difficulties of that course. After all, it had been difficult enough in Flanders and Brabant: time and again, in the bitter fighting around the besieged towns, victory had hung upon a thread. On every occasion, it is true, that thread had held, but one day, as Parma warned the king, 'God will grow tired of working miracles for us'.

And now, despite the miraculous fall of Antwerp, the Dutch 'show no sign of anything except renewed obstinacy'. Why? Parma was in no doubt about the reason. On 30 September 1585 he informed the king that 'English troops are arriving [in Flushing] every day, and already number four or five thousand men. And it seems that the queen of England wishes openly to take up their cause . . . for one can clearly see from the letter she has written to the rebels how much she is prepared to assist and encourage them.' It might be easier and more effective, he reasoned, to divert his forces from fighting the Dutch – who were certainly in no position to mount a counter-attack – to attacking their foreign supporters. Convincing evidence was to hand that, at several important junctions, the assistance of France and England had saved the rebel cause from collapse just when, militarily speaking, it seemed doomed. Now, with the death of Anjou and the outbreak of new civil dissension in France, further support from that quarter seemed unlikely; and, for the same reason, no French reprisals would be possible should Spain decide to deal with the Dutch rebels' persistent supporter on the other side of the English Channel.[7] But at precisely this moment, just as Parma was reaching the conclusion that war with England was the only way to break out of his impasse, Elizabeth of England declared war upon him.

## Sources

Our account of the Low Countries' wars rests mainly upon Parker, *The Dutch Revolt* and *Spain and the Netherlands*, and van der Essen, *Farnèse*. Details on Farnese's finances come from Romani, *Le corti farnesiane*. On English policy towards the Netherlands, north and south, see Wernham, *The Making of Elizabethan Foreign Policy* and *Before the Armada*, and Wilson, *Queen Elizabeth and the Revolt of the Netherlands*. On the intervention of France, see Holt, *The Duke of Anjou*, chapter 5.

Details on the collapse of public authority in the Dutch Republic immediately after the death of Orange may be found in van der Woude 'De crisis in de Opstand na de val van Antwerpen', and Hibben, *Gouda in Revolt*, chapter 7.

## Notes

1   Feltham, *A Brief Character of the Low Countries*, 1, 5.
2   Two quotations from Don Luis de Requeséns in Parker, *Spain and the Netherlands*, 48–9.
3   *CSPF*, XXI, part 4, 171: R. Spencer to Burghley, 15 March 1588.
4   Lincoln Record Office, *Ancaster Muniments*, X, fo. 1, Lord Willoughby to (?) Cristóbal de Mondragón, June 1586.
5   *CSPF* 1581–2, 346 and 406, Thomas Stokes to Walsingham, 22 October 1581 and 28 January 1582.
6   Paolo Rinaldi, one of Parma's household officers, quoted by van der Essen, *Farnèse*, V, 295; Williams, from his *Art of Warre*, by Evans, *The Works of Sir Roger Williams*, 14; Leicester by Brugmans, 284–6 (in a letter to Burghley, 15 November 1587 NS).
7   BNP *MS Espagnol* 182/212, Parma to (?) Don Juan de Zúñiga, 16 September 1585; AGS *Secretarías provinciales* 2534/212, Parma to the king, 30 September 1585; AGS *Estado* 589/120, same to same, 31 September 1585; and *Estado* 590/22–3, same to same, 28 February 1586.

# 4

# Armed neutrality, 1558–80

For the first decade of her reign, which began in 1558, Elizabeth made no change in traditional Tudor foreign policy. For 10 years she remained a fairly loyal friend of Spain and, like her father, seems to have done everything in her power to destabilise the governments of France and Scotland. To begin with, it is true, she had little choice, for she inherited a war as Spain's ally against France and Scotland by virtue of the fact that her elder half-sister Mary had married Philip II. This alliance soon miscarried, however, for although an English contingent took part in the great Spanish victory over France at St Quentin in August 1557, five months later the French retaliated by taking Calais, England's only continental possession. Then, in April, the heir to the French throne married young Mary Stuart, queen of Scots. The serious implications of this manifestation of the 'auld alliance' between France and Scotland soon became clear: the following year, by which time Mary's husband had become king of France, the two sovereigns began to quarter the arms of England with their own, and to style themselves 'Francis and Mary, rulers of France, Scotland, England and Ireland'. According to Elizabeth's appalled ambassador in France, the couple even had these presumptuous and outrageous insignia emblazoned on their dinner service.

These events would affect Elizabeth's foreign policy for decades, but to understand the reason for their significance it is necessary to consider some earlier developments. Perhaps the story – and hence the story of the Armada – began in the 1530s with the decision of Henry VIII of England to divorce his wife Catherine of Aragon in order to marry one of his court ladies, Anne Boleyn. It was easier said than done: the divorce led to a major breach with the papacy culminating in the separation of the Church in England from its mother Church of Rome, with Henry proclaiming himself its supreme head. These developments had international repercussions, both because Catherine was the aunt of Charles V, ruler of Spain and the Netherlands and Holy Roman Emperor, and because the breach with Rome opened England to the influence of the continental Reformation, which had already ended papal authority in much of northern Europe.

The Catholics soon struck back. They refused to acknowledge the validity of Henry's marriage to Anne Boleyn, and regarded the couple's only surviving child, Elizabeth, as a bastard; they rejected his claim to be supreme head of the Church of England; and, on these grounds, they plotted his deposition. In 1542 the Catholic James V of Scotland launched an invasion of northern England, and three years later the French sent an invasion force which entered the Solent and landed on the Isle of Wight. But Henry overcame both challenges. The English soundly trounced the Scots invaders at Solway Moss and James V, already ill, died on hearing the news. His week-old daughter, Mary Stuart, succeeded him. In the south, Henry himself was present (though ashore, at Southsea Castle) when his fleet engaged a French invasion force in the Solent: the affair was inconclusive, although one of the king's great ships, the *Mary Rose*, overset and sank during the action.

In 1547 Henry Tudor, king of England and Ireland, died peacefully. His crowns passed to his 9-year-old son, Edward VI, whose regents introduced a fully Protestant Church order in England and continued the war with France and Scotland. But Edward, a sickly youth, died six years later. In spite of attempts by his regents to continue the breach with Rome and secure a Protestant ruler, Henry's unilateral decisions of the 1530s were soon overturned, for the succession passed in 1553 to Mary Tudor, his daughter by Catherine of Aragon. In spite of prolonged harassment Mary had remained a determined Catholic, and she resolved to enforce her faith upon her new subjects. She also determined to ally England firmly with Spain. Within a month of her accession she opened negotiations with her cousin, Charles V, offering herself as the bride of his son and heir, Philip II. The couple were married at Winchester in July 1554, and a formal reconciliation of England with the Church of Rome took place in November. Three months later the first English Protestant heretics were burnt.

Mary's 'Spanish Match' was not a success. Despite the lavish distribution of pensions paid from his Spanish revenues, Philip remained unpopular, while the condemnation and execution of Protestants caused disquiet and unrest throughout the country. A major rebellion, led by Sir Thomas Wyatt, occurred in Kent in 1554. Most seriously, the queen, in spite of some false hopes, failed to conceive an heir. Philip's long absences from England (and therefore from his wife) between August 1555 and March 1557 and again after July 1557 were of course partly responsible; but probably Mary, 38 when she married, had already been rendered sterile by the cancer that killed her in November 1558.

Once again religion complicated the question of succession. Mary was survived by her half-sister Elizabeth who (although she had felt it politic to attend Mass after 1555) clearly nurtured Protestant sympathies. She was, moreover, the daughter of Henry VIII's (to Catholics) adulterous and illegal liaison with Anne Boleyn. Mary had regarded her as illegitimate. So too did Mary Stuart, queen of Scotland, the legitimate Catholic granddaughter of Henry VIII's sister, who consequently considered herself the rightful heir to the English and Irish thrones. Many Catholics agreed with her.

Philip II, however, was not one of them. Even though his authority in England ceased automatically with his wife's death, he still hoped to keep his late kingdom within the Habsburg orbit. Although several plots to overthrow Elizabeth in favour of Mary were submitted to him for approval, he rejected them all, for the last thing he wanted was a French princess on the English throne. Instead, Philip afforded Elizabeth every assistance, even offering at one point to marry her. But he did so with great reluctance. In a confidential letter of January 1559 to his ambassador in London, the count of Feria, the king explained that he had only made the offer 'to serve God and to stop that lady making the changes in religion that she has in mind'. He felt no personal enthusiasm for the match, and begged Feria to let him know Elizabeth's reaction to his proposal as soon as possible. 'Believe me', he explained to his ambassador, 'I shall be as happy with the one outcome as with the other!' Elizabeth Tudor rejected her lukewarm suitor in February, and within a month the king of Spain had announced his engagement to the 13-year-old French princess Elizabeth de Valois.[1]

Philip nevertheless did nothing to prevent the queen of England from reintroducing Protestantism in 1559, or from invading Scotland to support the Protestant faction there in 1560. In a sense he had no choice. Although he managed to make an advantageous peace with the French in April 1559, he failed to reach an agreement with the Ottoman Turks whose fleets continued to threaten Spain's Mediterranean possessions. By autumn 1559 the situation seemed so bad that, despite his growing anxiety about affairs in England and Scotland, he left the Netherlands and returned to Spain, there to devote most of his energies and resources to organising the defence of the Mediterranean. The affairs of northwest Europe were relegated, so to speak, to the back burner.

Philip retained no illusions about the probable future of relations between himself and his former sister-in-law. 'It grieves me to see what is happening over there [in England]', he wrote in a secret dispatch to Feria in London, shortly before leaving for Spain; 'and to be unable to take the steps to stop it that I want, while the steps I can take seem far milder than such a great evil deserves . . . But at the moment I lack the resources to do anything.' Later in his rather rambling letter Philip returned to the point in a more forceful and calculating way: 'The evil that is taking place in that kingdom has caused me the anger and confusion I have mentioned . . . but we must try to remedy it without involving me or any of my vassals in a declaration of war until we have enjoyed the benefits of peace [for a while].'[2] Philip II thus recognised, from an early point in his reign, the advantage of launching a pre-emptive strike against Elizabeth, even though it might, on the grounds of practical expediency, have to be delayed. In the event, Spain enjoyed the 'benefits of peace' with England for 10 years, but they did not long survive the arrival of the duke of Alba in Brussels in 1567.

The amicable if distant relationship between Elizabeth and her former brother-in-law came to an end as the result of two separate developments. The first concerned Spain's claim to a monopoly of all trade with, and all colonisation in, the American continent. This stemmed from a decision of the papacy in 1494, set out in the treaty of Tordesillas, which divided between the crowns of Castile and Portugal all lands discovered (and yet to be discovered) beyond Europe. Despite challenges by several French merchants this monopoly remained largely intact at the time of Philip II's accession. But in 1562 John Hawkins, a Plymouth merchant and shipowner who had been trading with the Canary islands (a Spanish possession off the Atlantic coast of Africa, and the staging post for all ships sailing from Spain to America), decided to set up a venture to take cloth and African slaves to the Indies, whence he would return to England with a cargo of hides and sugar. Although he made no application to the Spanish crown for a licence, Hawkins was careful to pay all the taxes due to Spain and to behave throughout, as he saw it, entirely within the law.

The voyage made a profit, and arrangements were made to repeat it on a larger scale in 1564–5. This time the queen invested in the venture, providing Hawkins with the 600-ton *Jesus of Lübeck*, an old warship from Henry VIII's navy which had been written off as unfit for front-line service. The second enterprise proved as profitable as the first, but the Spanish colonists became less open in their welcome of English merchants when officials in Madrid and Seville, anxious to exclude all interlopers, expressly forbade any trade with foreigners. Hawkins was obliged to underpin his trade with the threat of force, though the threat was (he asserted) simply a charade which allowed the colonists to claim, in their own defence, that they had only dealt with the English under duress. Meanwhile, a chilling example of Spain's resolve to keep all 'interlopers' out of the Americas occurred after news reached Philip II that a party of French Huguenots had settled in Florida. The king licensed a consortium of seafarers from northern Spain (led by Pedro Menéndez de Avilés and including, as already noted, Don Pedro de Valdés and Diego Flores de Valdés) to destroy them. In 1565 the powerful Spanish expeditionary force persuaded the French to surrender on the promise that their lives would be spared, and then slaughtered most of them. Those that remained were brought back to languish in prison.

On his third transatlantic voyage, which began in 1567, Hawkins took 10 ships, again including the *Jesus*, and another vessel belonging to the queen, the 300-ton *Minion*. At first things went well, and once more the Spanish colonists seemed glad to connive at the trade. As the fleet prepared for its homeward passage, however, it ran into a sudden storm in the Gulf of Mexico which severely damaged Hawkins' flagship, the crank and elderly *Jesus*. Seeking shelter, the battered ships limped to the small Spanish harbour of San Juan de Ulúa on the coast of Mexico. The sole function of this remote haven was to expedite the safe dispatch to Spain of the huge annual consignment of Mexican silver and other trade goods; at other times it was virtually deserted. It was so on this occasion. The English fleet met with no resistance, and after his customary courtesies to the few Spaniards in residence, Hawkins took the place over to set about repairing his ships and refreshing his men.

As fate would have it, however, two days later a fleet from Spain arrived off the port, under the command of Don Martín Enríquez, the newly appointed viceroy of Mexico. Hawkins protested his friendly mercantile intentions and, backed up by physical possession of the harbour and its defences, he obtained Don Martín's grudging agreement to complete his repairs and depart in peace. As the Spanish fleet entered San Juan and moored alongside the English ships, however, each side covertly prepared for action.

The viceroy considered no agreement with a pirate, as (with some justification) he regarded Hawkins, to be binding, and when he judged the moment right he launched a surprise attack on the English ships. A furious struggle ensued within the close confines of the harbour. The *Jesus*, after destroying two Spanish warships with her guns, was overwhelmed and captured, although Hawkins was able to transfer to the *Minion* with some of his men and escape, together with a 50-ton barque, the *Judith*, commanded by his young kinsman Francis Drake. Both ships eventually got home, although only 15 men remained alive on board the *Minion* when she entered Plymouth Sound in January 1569. Elizabeth had thus lost to Spain one of her royal warships, with another damaged, while a good part of the proceeds of the voyage (from which the queen looked to receive a return on her investment) had been confiscated. Many of her subjects, too, had been killed, and others remained in captivity.

News of this signal defeat arrived at a delicate moment. First, a minor diplomatic crisis already existed between Spain and England, for in March 1568 Philip had refused to grant further audiences to Elizabeth's resident ambassador, Dr John Man, on the grounds that he was a Protestant cleric and that he had insulted the pope in public (calling him 'a canting little monk'). At the same time Philip replaced his own urbane and accomplished envoy in England, Don Diego Guzmán de Silva (perhaps because he was a priest) with the intemperate and inexperienced Don Guerau de Spes. In the second place, the outbreak of a new civil war in France unleashed a fresh wave of Protestant aggression against Catholic ships on the high seas. In November 1568 Huguenot privateers came upon five ships carrying some £40,000 in cash from Spain to the Netherlands. The French attacked, and the treasure ships ran for shelter to England. Spes explained that the money belonged to Philip II's bankers and was being sent to Antwerp as part of a loan to pay the duke of Alba's army, and he asked for the queen's protection. She agreed and, since the privateers continued to threaten, most of the bullion came ashore. At precisely this moment, Elizabeth learned of the events at San Juan de Ulúa and immediately ordered the money to be taken to the Tower of London and the ships to be placed under temporary arrest.

The queen's intentions at this point remain unclear, but it is unlikely that she expected her actions to be construed as more than tweaking the Spanish lion's tail. But the lion did not roar. He sprang. Almost single-handed, Spes turned a crisis into a war. In December he asserted (wrongly) that Elizabeth had confiscated the treasure and urged Alba to embargo all English property in the Netherlands in retaliation, and he also asked the king to do the same in Spain. Both swiftly obliged. When she heard of it, the queen reciprocated. Spes was placed under house arrest and diplomatic intercourse, as well as trade, between England and Spain virtually ceased.

Other changes in the international situation, in the course of 1568, also placed new pressures on both Philip and Elizabeth. In the Netherlands the defeat of Orange's invasion left Alba and his victorious troops free to meddle in the affairs of neighbouring states; in France, the bitter civil war prevented the beleaguered government from pursuing any coherent foreign policy; in Spain, the need to suppress a major rebellion by the Moriscos of Granada forced Philip to divert many of his resources into a peninsular war for over two years; and, above all, the Scots deposed Mary Stuart.

The queen of Scots had been brought up at the French court from the age of 6; but when her husband, King Francis II, died at the end of 1560 – to the profound relief of both Elizabeth I and Philip II – Mary resolved to sail back to the land of her birth. It was a land she scarcely knew, and a society in which she had no close kin or established power base to sustain her. In 1566, after five years of moderately successful personal rule, her failure to build up a following in Scotland is reflected in the will she made on the eve of the birth of her son, the future James VI and I. She named fewer than 60 beneficiaries (a small number for a monarch) and few of them were Scots. All the first 7, and 10 of the first 12, were her Guise relatives. Mary Stuart had remained, in essence, a French princess in exile.

But although the queen could not forget France, France forgot her. When, in 1567, a group of Scottish nobles rebelled against her, imprisoned her and finally declared her deposed, she received support neither from her subjects, whom she had failed to cultivate, nor from her French relatives, who were too absorbed in their religious wars to spare any help. So in May 1568, when she escaped from her Scottish captors, she rode into England and threw herself upon the mercy of her only apparently friendly neighbour, Elizabeth. It proved to be the biggest mistake of her life. Many Catholics still believed Mary to be the legitimate queen of England, so Elizabeth could not afford to allow her either to take sanctuary with a sympathetic prince abroad or to remain at large among the numerous and restless Catholic population of northern England. Her only course, irrespective of its morality or legality, was to imprison the queen of Scots.

This outraged the Catholic world. From the summer of 1568 onwards Pope Pius V began to urge Philip II to invade England and depose Elizabeth in Mary's favour. When the king spurned his overtures, he turned in 1569 to the duke of Alba, going so far as to send him a golden sword, the symbol of a warrior of the faith, with its clear implication that Elizabeth should be struck down by force. Here too the pope met with a courteous but firm rebuff and so he adopted a new strategy. In February 1570, without informing Philip, he excommunicated Elizabeth and absolved her subjects from their obedience, sending copies to the duke of Alba a month later (also without telling the king) along with orders both to ensure their diffusion in England and to take steps to depose her.

By then Philip's patience had also run out. In January 1570 he angrily reminded Alba that Elizabeth had confiscated not only the treasure of his bankers but also the goods of his subjects in England; she had welcomed his rebels (perhaps 30,000 Dutch exiles, mostly Protestants and many of them implicated in the rebellions of 1566 and 1568, resided in England); she had broken off all trade; and she had licensed attacks on any ships sailing through the Channel under Spanish colours. 'By contrast, the damage which she, her kingdom and her subjects have received from us is so little that it hardly counts . . . so that one could justly say that she has declared war on us, but we are at peace with her.' This unequal situation, the king insisted, could not be allowed to continue: a way of harming Elizabeth, and thus of bringing her back to peaceful coexistence, had to be found. His letter also contained a 'messianic' element: Philip asserted that God's service 'required' him to intervene in order to liberate the Catholic queen of Scots and to restore Catholicism in England – especially since 'God has already granted that by my intervention and my hand that kingdom has previously been restored to the Catholic church once'. This confidence that God intended him to annex England made Philip ready, perhaps for the first but certainly not the last time in his reign, to throw caution to the winds. He informed Alba that:

> Even though human prudence suggests many inconveniences and difficulties, and places before us worldly fears, Christian certitude and the confidence that we must justly have in the cause of God will remove them, and inspire and strengthen us to overcome them. Certainly we could not avoid remaining with great guilt in our soul, and great regret, if because I failed that queen [Mary] and those Catholics – or, rather, the faith – they suffered and she was lost.

The king briefly reviewed several possible strategies for achieving these ends: an outright invasion by his various forces; a joint invasion with the French; and an assault on Ireland (representatives of the Irish Catholics had recently arrived in Spain to secure his support). He solicited Alba's assessment of these plans, and meanwhile ordered him secretly to provide both the English Catholics and Mary Stuart with money, arms and munitions, and to send military advisers to help train her supporters. To facilitate this, Philip enclosed a letter of credit for £75,000.[3]

Alba remained totally unconvinced by both the spiritual blackmail and the strategic alternatives. With heavy sarcasm (probably lost on his master) he drew up a detailed rebuttal: 'Even though the principal means must come from God, as Your Majesty very virtuously and piously suggests, nevertheless since He normally works through the resources He gives to humans, it seems necessary to examine what human resources would be needed to carry out your wishes.'

Alba began by ruling out an immediate invasion, with or without the French, on the grounds both of cost and of the troubled international situation. He also pointed out that, although the English Catholics begged for assistance, they had made it very clear that they did not want deliverance to come by means of a foreign army. Finally he noted that a rising by the Catholics of northern England the previous year had 'gone up in smoke'. The duke only approved of sending financial support to Elizabeth's disaffected subjects in Ireland and England, but anything beyond this would need to be arranged and funded from Spain.[4]

Despite this dash of cold water, Philip took two important steps to maintain the pressure on Elizabeth. He promised to send assistance to the Irish Catholics and he approved a suggestion from Spes (still in England, although closely watched by the queen's agents) that he should maintain contact both with discontented English Catholics and with Mary through a Florentine banker in London, Roberto Ridolfi, who enjoyed the pope's confidence and handled the funds secretly sent from Rome to England. Unfortunately for all of them, Ridolfi – virtually the only channel through which the various conspirators in England communicated – was almost certainly a double agent who shared all his information with Elizabeth's ministers.[5]

Philip's first ploy almost immediately produced excellent results. Early in 1571 Elizabeth sent a special envoy to Spain, urging the king not to support her Irish rebels, asking if she might send a new ambassador and declaring her willingness to negotiate a settlement to all outstanding issues.[6] Instead of using this as a bargaining counter, however, the king decided to support Ridolfi's plot to overthrow Elizabeth in favour of Mary queen of Scots. Two distinct – indeed incompatible – plans seem to have been under discussion. According to the subsequent testimony of Mary's ambassador at the English court, the Scottish queen would be spirited from her prison and taken to the coast, where a fleet manned by sympathetic Englishmen and led by John Hawkins (the same man who had been set upon and almost killed at San Juan de Ulúa scarcely two years before) would 'convey' her to safety in Spain. There she might marry Philip's brother, Don John of Austria, while her young son James would be betrothed to Philip's daughter Isabella. This Elizabeth later claimed she could have tolerated ('her Majesty thinks it no just cause to be offended with those devices tending to her [Mary's] liberty' according to Lord Burghley); what appalled her was clear evidence that Mary had also wished to dethrone her.[7]

Ridolfi left England in March 1571 armed with instructions, commissions and letters from his numerous contacts and, having visited Alba and the pope, arrived in Madrid at the end of June and met with the king, Feria (now leader of the 'interventionist' faction at Philip's court) and various other ministers. In July the Spanish council of state debated the English question and unanimously agreed with Feria's proposal that Elizabeth should be either captured or killed in the autumn while she was on her annual progress through the Home Counties. This, they anticipated, would unleash a general rising of English Catholics, to be led by the duke of Norfolk, whom Mary would marry. This in turn would serve as a signal for Alba to send a fleet, reinforced by a flotilla already standing by at Santander in northern Spain, to escort 6,000 troops drawn from the Army of Flanders across to England to assist Norfolk. Alba would be sent £50,000 specifically to prepare this task force. One week later, after carefully considering the recommendations and conversing further with Ridolfi, Philip wrote to apprise Alba of his plan.[8] A month later, however, the king introduced various significant refinements. First, Feria signed a contract with an agent of John Hawkins promising that Hawkins' squadron of 16 ships, then at Plymouth, would sail to the Netherlands in September and help ferry over Alba's troops. In return, Feria agreed that all surviving Englishmen captured at San Juan de Ulúa would be released from prison. Second, the king increased the number of Alba's troops scheduled for the expedition to 10,000 and designated Harwich in Essex as the landing zone. Third, he authorised Alba to send money to Scotland to help Mary's supporters there to create a diversion, although Philip specifically forbade him to send troops 'in order to avoid open war with the queen of England'.

These changes made the plan dangerously complicated, yet the entire initiative still remained with Norfolk and a bunch of assassins: until the latter killed the queen, and Norfolk brought his supporters out, the squadrons in Plymouth, Santander and Zealand could not join forces, let alone start embarking Alba's troops. Yet, apart from the documents circulated by Ridolfi, no reliable evidence existed either that Norfolk (who in any case was not a Catholic) wished to lead a rising against Elizabeth, or that any significant body of English Catholics would follow him if he did. As the scale of these problems dawned upon him, Philip changed his plans yet again. In August 1571 he informed Alba that, even if the plot to kill Elizabeth did not take place, or took place and failed, he must still invade. Realising that the duke would probably object strenuously to this (as he had to every other suggestion that force be used against Elizabeth) Philip fell back once again on messianic imperialism:

> No one can deny that this venture involves many and great difficulties, and that if it goes wrong we will incur considerable inconveniences (as you prudently pointed out [in a recent letter]) . . . In spite of all this I desire to achieve this enterprise so much, and I have such complete confidence that God our Lord, to whose service it is dedicated (because I have no personal ambition here), will guide and direct it, and I hold my charge from God to do this to be so explicit, that I am extremely determined and resolved to proceed and participate, doing on my side everything possible in this world to promote and assist it.

Such rhetoric left Alba unmoved. Upon receiving the king's letter he replied suavely but firmly that an invasion was at this stage out of the question because, 'as I have already told Your Majesty, I have not begun to make any preparations'. In any case he declared himself unwilling to hazard his troops in England unless they had guarantees of substantial local support.

In desperation, Philip played the messianic card one more time: on 14 September he again urged Alba to launch the invasion – even if Norfolk had been arrested, even if Hawkins failed to come over – because 'I am so keen to achieve the consummation of this enterprise, I am so attached to it in my heart, and I am so convinced that God our Saviour must embrace it as His own cause, that I cannot be dissuaded. Nor can I accept or believe the contrary.'[9] It was a poor substitute for strategy.

By then, unknown to either Philip or Alba, the plan had no chance of success. Thanks to the information supplied by Ridolfi (whether voluntarily or not) and by Hawkins (deliberately), by 5 September 1571 Elizabeth's ministers possessed enough incriminating information to arrest Norfolk and to order Mary to be more closely confined and prevented from speaking with anyone. A letter written by Lord Burghley late that night and sent to Mary's keeper 'haste, post haste, haste, haste for life, life, life' instructed him to 'have some good speech to the queen of Scots' both about her plans to escape and flee to Spain, and to 'provoke her to answer' about 'her labours and devices to stir up a new rebellion in this realm [of England] and to have the king of Spain assist it'.[10] Subsequent interrogation of the plotters soon provided most of the missing details: the complicity of Norfolk, of the Spanish ambassador and of Mary. Next, the servants of those implicated were brought in for rigorous interrogation. Faced with the full apparatus, legal and physical, of enquiry by torment, Mary's confidant, the bishop of Ross, became particularly eloquent, asserting that not only had Mary helped to murder her second husband, Henry Lord Darnley, but had also poisoned her first, Francis II, and was not a fit wife for any man. 'Lord!' exclaimed his interrogator. 'What a people! What a queen!' Eventually Elizabeth had Norfolk executed and Mary subjected to far stricter confinement. But she punished few others because – as Alba had always claimed – virtually no evidence existed that the Catholics of southern England harboured any wish to change their allegiance.

To a degree, the international situation in 1571 justified the king's dogged and apparently irrational insistence (so similar to his conduct in 1588) on pressing ahead with the venture, already code-named 'the Enterprise of England'. The Netherlands, from which the assault force would sail, were now obedient and free of dissidents; France, although again at peace, remained severely weakened after her recent civil wars; the Turks seemed fully occupied in the conquest of Cyprus, and in October 1571 their fleet suffered a resounding defeat by the combined forces of Spain, Venice and the papacy at Lepanto. But this remarkably favourable conjuncture did not last long, for the Dutch Revolt and the Turkish counter-offensive, both of which began in earnest in 1572, once more deprived Philip II of the resources with which to assault Elizabeth.

He could not, however, return to the harmony of the 1560s. The Ridolfi conspiracy – far more than the trade war or the 'perfidy' of San Juan de Ulúa – created a fatal rift between Elizabeth and her erstwhile suitor. She may not have been able to read (as we can) the minutes of the Spanish council of state, or the ciphered letters of the king authorising his forces in the Netherlands to invade, but the intelligence reports she received left her in no doubt that the king of Spain had tried to encompass her deposition and destroy her kingdom (although she may not have been aware of the assassination plan).

Henceforth Elizabeth never trusted Philip. She now openly welcomed and protected refugees from his 'tyranny', especially if they came from the Netherlands, for she wished to ensure that the Spanish regime in Brussels would never again be strong enough to launch an invasion against her. From time to time after 1572, therefore, she sent military and financial aid to keep the rebel cause alive. The queen also tolerated, and sometimes even directly supported, privateering expeditions against Spanish interests. Hawkins and Drake, still smarting from their humiliation at San Juan de Ulúa, needed little encouragement. Between 1572 and 1577 11 important English expeditions sailed to Spanish America, starting with a daring joint exploit by Francis Drake and his Devon men, some French Huguenots from Le Havre and a group of black slaves from Panama who had rebelled against their Spanish masters. Between them they seized a major treasure convoy near Nombre de Dios and raised the terrifying spectre for the Spaniards of white piracy allied with black rebellion. The series of raids culminated in the remarkable voyage of Drake through the Straits of Magellan and into the Pacific, there to harry Spanish colonies and shipping at will. The voyage, which turned into the first English circumnavigation of the globe, came to its triumphant end in September 1580. Drake brought back with him 100 tons of Spanish silver and 100 pounds of gold, and was knighted by the queen for his labours. His flagship, the *Golden Hind*, went on public display at Deptford as a national monument to England's achievements.

Philip II was incensed by the stream of reports that reached him concerning Drake's audacity, but for the moment he left England unpunished because, even though his agents had arranged a temporary truce with the Turks in 1577, the situation in the Netherlands continued to tie down his resources. Moreover, a successful effort against England would demand extensive maritime forces. Naval strength has always been notoriously difficult to build up, and even harder to maintain. Although in 1574 orders went out to assemble a fleet of 223 vessels (including 33 fighting ships and 34 Baltic hulks) at Santander, under the command of the redoubtable Pedro Menéndez, the conqueror of Florida, it never sailed because plague struck down the crews, delay decimated both the provisions and the ships, and no replacements could be found. Eventually its commander died and only 38 vessels (many of them small) managed to set sail for Dunkirk in 1575, carrying reinforcements for the Army of Flanders. Five of them ran aground on the sandbanks off the Flemish coast, while storms drove three others back to Spain and forced the rest (commanded jointly by Don Pedro de Valdés and Juan Martínez de Recalde) briefly to take refuge in the Solent. Perhaps Philip recalled, as he brooded over this costly reverse, the advice of his father, Charles V, concerning naval operations: 'Fleets at sea', the emperor had reminded his son as he groomed him for kingship, 'are as uncertain as the waves that bear them.'

In spite of this, Philip II sent another fleet against Elizabeth in 1580, albeit clandestinely. A year earlier a party of Irish exiles, with papal support, had returned home to instigate a general rebellion. The activists landed at Smerwick, a wide and remote natural harbour close to the westernmost tip of Ireland, and spent the winter in a temporary fortification (of which remains can still be seen) known as the *Castello del Oro*, the Golden Fort. From there they launched an appeal to the Catholic powers of Europe for reinforcement. In September 1580 some 800 volunteers raised in Italy and Spain under papal aegis were landed at Smerwick by a flotilla commanded by Juan Martínez de Recalde, who went on to survey the coasts of south-west Ireland before returning to Spain. Meanwhile the expeditionary force improved the defences at *Castello del Oro* and continued to await the general uprising. It never came. Instead, a small but powerful English naval squadron under Sir William Winter sailed into the bay and attacked the Hispano-Papal position, vulnerably perched like a stranded warship on a small peninsula jutting into the bay.

A contemporary map, sketched on the spot by one of the English participants, graphically shows Winter's ships in action (see FIGURES 8 and 9). Eight years later all of these vessels – *Revenge, Swiftsure, Aid, Tiger* and *Achates* – would encounter the Armada, and already we can see in action the mobile gunnery tactics that they would employ to such good effect in 1588. The big ships stand off in deep water, unanchored but with sails furled, bombarding the fort with their bow chasers, while the three smaller vessels take advantage of their shallow draught to run under full sail towards the enemy, firing as they go, and then coming about at the last possible moment to present first their broadsides and then their stern guns at close range. The simple device that made these quick-firing tactics possible is also clearly visible on the map: guns from the fleet have been landed to invest the fort from another angle and their carriages, tiny but unmistakable, are all naval-issue mountings of the efficient four-truck design.[11]

A few days later troops under the queen's lieutenant in Ireland, Lord Deputy Grey, assisted by Sir Walter Raleigh and others, joined Winter's force. The *Castello del Oro* was doomed: after three days' bombardment its defenders surrendered on being promised fair terms. All but 15 of them were promptly massacred in cold blood.

Although Philip II and his lieutenants failed in the Netherlands and in Ireland, in compensation they triumphantly conquered Portugal and gained its extensive overseas possessions, so creating the first empire in history upon which the sun never set. The last legitimate male in the direct line of the Portuguese royal house died in January 1580, leaving the king of Spain, whose mother had been a Portuguese princess, as next of kin. There were other claimants, but none could match Philip II's power. The first phase of the conquest was the invasion of the Algarve in July by a small army commanded by the duke of Medina Sidonia, the most powerful Spanish grandee in neighbouring Andalusia. It was supported by a fleet of 87 galleys and 30 ships commanded by the marquis of Santa Cruz, a veteran of Lepanto and many other galley encounters, which worked its way along the coast from Cadiz to the Tagus. There Santa Cruz joined up with Philip II's main invasion army, which had marched through the heart of Portugal to meet him, led (for the last time) by the ageing duke of Alba. In a brilliant combined operation the two commanders captured Lisbon on 25 August. Within two months the entire country was under Spanish control.

There was also a new empire in Africa, Asia and Brazil to secure and in 1581 the king (now resident in Lisbon) decided, for the first time since the Florida expedition in 1565, to reassert his control over the Atlantic. He dispatched another veteran of the 'pacification' of Florida, Diego Flores de Valdés, with 23 ships and 3,500 men to clear all intruders from the Atlantic coasts of South America and to establish a fortress at the Straits of Magellan to prevent any repetition of Drake's progress into the Pacific. Long before its ill-fated garrison arrived, however, another challenge to Philip II's power had developed much closer to home.

## Sources

On Philip and Mary, see Loades, *Mary Tudor*, chapters 6–7. The best account of the first decade of Elizabeth's reign is to be found in MacCaffrey, *The Shaping of the Elizabethan Regime*. See also, however, the penetrating analysis of Simon Adams, 'Eliza enthroned? The court and its politics'; and Rodríguez-Salgado, *The Changing Face of Empire*. Among the many studies of Mary queen of Scots, the works of the late Gordon Donaldson stand supreme: see in particular *All the Queen's Men: power and politics in Mary Stewart's Scotland*. See also the important collection of essays, Lynch, *Mary Stewart: queen in three kingdoms*.

Our account of the events of 1568–9, which led to the fateful breach between England and Spain, is based upon Williamson, *Hawkins*, chapters 8–9; Andrews, *Trade, Plunder and Settlement*, chapter 6; and Read, 'Queen Elizabeth's seizure of the duke of Alva's pay-ships'. On the delicate international situation of these years, see also the judicious remarks of Kouri, *England and the Attempts to Form a Protestant Alliance in the Late 1560s: a case study in Elizabethan diplomacy*. On the complex history of the Ridolfi plot, see Edwards, *The Marvellous Chance: Thomas Howard, fourth duke of Norfolk, and the Ridolfi plot, 1570–2*.

## Notes

1   The letter offering marriage is relatively well known, *CSPSp*, I, 22–3, Philip II to Feria, 10 January 1559. Previously unknown, however, is the king's secret holograph letter of the same date. He felt, he told Feria, 'like a condemned man awaiting his

fate' and begged the ambassador to let him know as soon as possible what Elizabeth decided. On 28 January 1559 he again assured Feria that 'If it was not to serve God, believe me, I should not have got into this . . . Nothing would make me do this except the clear knowledge that it might gain the kingdom [of England] for His service and faith', Archivo de la Casa de Medina Celi, Seville, *caja* 7, *legajo* 249, nos 11–12.

2   *Ibid.*, Philip II to Feria, 21 March 1559.

3   *BMO*, I, 42, Philip II to Alba, 22 January 1570: a most remarkable letter which, in the original, covers 22 sides of paper.

4   *BMO*, I, 43–7, Alba to Philip II, 23 and 24 February 1570.

5   Whether or not Ridolfi was a double agent, he certainly betrayed all the conspirators. First, from the start, Ridolfi, his English contacts and Spes all used the same cipher (*CSPSp*, II, 111, Spes to Alba, 29 February 1569), so that once Elizabeth had acquired the key from one of Ridolfi's servants, she could read everybody's mail. Second, Ridolfi regularly wrote unciphered letters to Mary as he moved from Brussels to Rome and Madrid, keeping her up to date on the progress of the plot, and thereby (since all Mary's mail was intercepted and read) keeping Elizabeth up to date too. On the probability that Ridolfi had been 'turned', see Edwards, *The Marvellous Chance*, 86.

6   *BMO*, I, 52–3, Elizabeth to Philip II, 20 March 1571, and 54–5, account of a meeting between Elizabeth's envoy (Sir Henry Cobham) and Feria, 8 June 1571. These documents make clear that Cobham had been authorised to arrange a new exchange of ambassadors, and to pave the way to a settlement of the trade dispute; the account in Wernham, *Before the Armada*, 308, seems too harsh.

7   Quotations from Collinson, *The English Captivity of Mary Queen of Scots*, 42–3, Burghley to Shrewsbury, Mary's custodian, 5 September 1571; details of this aspect of the plot from *CSPScot*, IV, 30–2, bishop of Ross to Burghley, 9 November 1571. If Mary had somehow managed to reach Hawkins, he would presumably have 'conveyed' her back to gaol.

8   AGS *Estado* 823/150–8, *consulta* of the council of state, 7 July 1571 (a remarkable document which records the substance of each councillor's views at two meetings of the council, and of a further interview with Ridolfi, all on the same day); and Archivo de la Casa de los duques de Alba, Madrid 7/58, Philip II to Alba, 14 July 1571 (ordering immediate invasion and the capture or killing of Elizabeth, just as the council had recommended the previous week).

9   *BMO*, I, 57–64, Philip II to Alba, 4 August 1571, the duke's reply on the 27th, and Philip's final effort to get action on 14 September. See also ARA *Staten Generaal* 12548, *loketkas* 14B/14, Philip II to Alba, 30 August 1571, and to Spes on the same day, summarised in *CSPSp*, II, 333–4.

10   Collinson, *The English Captivity of Mary Queen of Scots*, 42–3, Burghley to Shrewsbury, 5 September 1571, a most important document. It may have been written upon receipt of Hawkins' letter of the previous day, enclosing a copy of his 'contract' with Feria: see the text in Williamson, *Hawkins*, 185–6.

11   The importance of this contemporary sketch was first brought to our attention by Dr Tom Glasgow. See also his article, 'Elizabethan ships pictured on Smerwick map, 1580'. Much has been written about the Smerwick campaign, but the best study is the well-documented account of O'Rahilly, *The Massacre at Smerwick (1580)*.

# Cold war, 1581–5

Amid all the excitement of the Portuguese conquest an important enemy of Philip II had been allowed to escape: Dom Antonio, prior of Crato, an illegitimate scion of the ancient Portuguese royal family. Before the Spanish annexation Dom Antonio had been a principal ornament of the court at Lisbon. One of the richest men in the kingdom (his priory of Crato alone yielded 120,000 ducats a year), and fluent in Latin and several other languages, the 50-year-old prior was a charismatic figure who found many supporters for his claim to be the next lawful king of Portugal. In 1580 he had organised the defence of Lisbon and the opposition of Oporto to the Spaniards, while the following year he was in northern Portugal, directing a resistance movement until a large manhunt (co-ordinated by the duke of Medina Sidonia) forced him to flee abroad. But he still had friends. Above all, his supporters had secured control of eight of the nine main islands of the Azores archipelago, 1,000 miles west of Lisbon. Only the largest, São Miguel, recognised the authority of Philip II and when, in the summer of 1581, a small expeditionary force under Don Pedro de Valdés was sent to attack Terceira island, the main opposition stronghold, it failed ignominiously – largely through the impetuous carelessness of Valdés. Dom Antonio, then in France, at once set about gaining foreign assistance for a full-scale invasion of the Azores, which might serve as a springboard for his reconquest of Portugal. To Elizabeth of England he promised a fort in west Africa in return for support; to Henry III of France he offered Madeira, Guinea and Brazil.

In the event Elizabeth decided to remain neutral in the face of the threats conveyed by Philip II's ambassador, Don Bernardino de Mendoza, that open English aid for Dom Antonio would be regarded by Spain as a declaration of war – although she warned Mendoza that 'if he spoke to her again like that, she would put him in a place from which he could not speak at all'. Moreover, although she allowed Dom Antonio (referred to by English sources as 'the king of Portugal' but by most other diplomatic sources as 'the Pretender') to issue letters of marque to several of her privateering merchants, she felt obliged to banish him from her court. So he went to France, where 11 English privateers (including two ships owned by Drake) joined him and sailed under his flag to the Azores in the summer of 1582. Most of the rest of the Pretender's fleet of

58 vessels and 6,000 men came from France, collected and commanded by a former colonel of the French guards, Filippo Strozzi.

In order to dislodge Dom Antonio's forces from the Azores Philip II clearly needed to mount a major amphibious operation. There was nothing intrinsically novel about this: his armed forces, and those of his father, had done it many times before – against Tunis in 1535 and 1573, against Algiers (a spectacular failure) in 1541, to relieve Malta in 1565 and to capture Lisbon in 1580. Such operations were extremely complex affairs involving large fleets of galleys, often working in conjunction with land forces. Efficient logistics, precision fleet drills, and the fine balancing of complex and subtle variables, therefore constituted the essential preliminaries to a successful outcome, and Spanish galley commanders, of whom the most outstanding in the 1580s was Don Álvaro de Bazán, marquis of Santa Cruz, held a formidable and well-deserved reputation in such matters.

Galleys seldom ventured outside the Mediterranean, beyond which by the late sixteenth century the artillery-carrying sailing warship reigned virtually supreme. Until 1580 Spain did not possess an effective sailing navy in the Atlantic. Her only warships under sail were the relatively lightly armed escort galleons attached to the convoys of merchantmen that sailed annually between Spain and America and these, although extremely effective in their assigned role, were no match for heavy battleships of the type now developing in northern Europe, especially England. The 12 Portuguese galleons, powerfully built and powerfully gunned, captured (save one that sank) by Santa Cruz at the fall of Lisbon, changed all this.

With them Santa Cruz also captured a superb naval base. The narrow approach at the mouth of the Tagus, already defended with forts, was strengthened with heavy artillery to create, in the wide roadstead beyond, a safe and sheltered haven sufficient for the largest fleet. No other port on the Atlantic seaboard of the Iberian peninsula could offer this combination of almost unlimited capacity with total security both from enemies and from the weather. Lisbon would provide an ideal springboard should it ever prove necessary or desirable to mount a seaborne invasion of France, the Netherlands, or England, and in 1582 it offered the perfect base from which to intercept Dom Antonio's fleet and mount an operation to recover the Azores.

Santa Cruz's fleet of 60 ships and 8,000 men duly left Lisbon and made contact with Strozzi's ships off the island of São Miguel. After several days of sparring for position, on 26 July 1582 the two sides clashed in a close-range contest of attrition. Spanish tactics were simple: individual captains, having singled out an enemy ship, delivered a short-range broadside before grappling and boarding. Santa Cruz in his flagship *San Martín* sought out Strozzi's ship amid the smoke and chaos and, having found her, pounded her with gunfire until she was close to sinking. At the close, the Pretender's fleet had lost 10 ships sunk or captured, and well over 1,000 men, including Strozzi, who died of his wounds shortly after his ship's capture. Five days later Santa Cruz summarily executed most of the remaining prisoners.

Some thought that Strozzi had been unlucky to lose. His ships had proved nimbler than those of Santa Cruz and, like Hawkins at San Juan de Ulúa, they had used their artillery well, operating in mutually supporting groups of four 'to charge, and assail each of them one of the great vessels of the enemy'. This they did with considerable effect. When the galleon *San Mateo* dropped out of formation Strozzi's ships surrounded her, battered her with their artillery and finally boarded her. Several other vessels in Santa Cruz's fleet, including his own flagship, also suffered severe damage. Philip II's commemorative mural in the Escorial's Hall of Battles correctly depicts extensive shot damage on the Spanish side. The *San Martín* barely managed to tow the captured enemy flagship back to port.

All the same, Santa Cruz had won a great victory, and jubilation at his triumphant return seems to have gripped the whole of Spain. The French ambassador at Philip II's court sourly reported that some Spaniards went so far as to claim that 'even Christ was no longer safe in Paradise, for the marquis might go there to bring him back and crucify him all over again'. Later some of this pride and passion turned against the vanquished: according to the same ambassador, by October 1582 the Spaniards had 'taken to spitting in the faces of any Frenchmen they happened to meet in the street'.[1] Nevertheless Terceira remained in the Pretender's hands, and in the spring of 1583 he managed to reinforce his garrisons there with 800 fresh French troops.

Santa Cruz, who now enjoyed total command of the sea, reacted swiftly. Secure within his Lisbon base he prepared an amphibious invasion of overwhelming force: 15,372 men and 98 ships, including 31 big merchantmen converted as troop transports, small vessels and landing craft, 5 fighting galleons, 12 galleys and 2 galleasses. This time his aim was not to fight a fleet but to land an army: the task force could certainly defend itself if necessary, but its primary role was to put troops, together with their supporting equipment and supplies, on a selected beach-head and then to back them up until the military objectives had been gained.

Surprise formed an essential element in the plan. The Terceirans expected the Spaniards to land at the harbours of Angra and Peggia, and had disposed their forces accordingly. On the basis of local information and personal reconnaissance, however, Santa Cruz decided to deliver his main thrust at Mole, a beach 10 miles from Angra defended only by light earthworks occupied by infantry with some artillery support. Santa Cruz's own report of the landings has a strikingly modern ring:

> The flag galley began to batter and dismount the enemy artillery and the rest of the galleys did likewise . . . the landing craft ran aground and placed soldiers on the flanks of the fortifications, and along the trenches, although with much

difficulty and working under the pressure of the furious artillery, arquebus, and musket fire of the enemy. The soldiers mounting the trenches in several places came under heavy small-arms fire, but finally won the forts and trenches.

Dom Antonio and a handful of his supporters were lucky to escape with their lives.[2]

The Atlantic thus no longer barred Spanish expansion. Philip's monarchy had become a truly oceanic power: its armies, carried by sea, could strike with surgical precision at any point on its enemies' coasts. All it required was money, and a fleet. A bowl commemorating the Terceira landings (found among the wreckage of one of the 1588 Armada ships, and almost certainly belonging to an officer who had taken part in the 1583 operation) shows Spain's warrior patron saint, St James, with new attributes. He is depicted, as before, mounted on a charger, his cloak flowing in the wind and his sword-arm raised to strike down his foes. But these foes are no longer cowering infidels. They are the swirling waves of the Ocean Sea itself, waves now conquered along with the human enemies who sought refuge among them.

Beyond the swirling waves, and behind the defeated enemies, lay England. Elizabeth and her advisers viewed the rising tide of Spanish victory in 1583, with the conquest of Terceira in the south and of the Flemish coast in the north, with trepidation; and the events of 1584, with the deaths of Anjou and Orange and the fall of Ghent and Bruges, foreshadowed worse. The likelihood of a full Spanish reconquest of the Netherlands, restoring the situation of 1570 and 1571 (and thus the chance of repeating the Ridolfi strategy) had to be faced. Yet England now possessed few allies: Dom Antonio was a spent force, his cause in Portugal (at least temporarily) lost; the Netherlands, leaderless, seemed likely to go the same way.

Worse still, France clearly stood on the brink of civil wars even more terrible than those she had already endured. Until 1584, the conflict had pitted a Protestant minority, anxious to gain some official guarantees of toleration, against the Catholic government and its supporters. But the death of the duke of Anjou, heir presumptive to the French throne as well as elected ruler of the Netherlands, changed all that. King Henry III became the last of his line; his closest male relative was now Henry of Navarre, leader of the Protestant party. As such he was totally unacceptable to the Catholic faction led by Henry duke of Guise, Mary Stuart's cousin. Rather than see Navarre succeed to the throne, the French Catholics formed a paramilitary organisation, known as 'the League' and dominated by Guise, who entered into an alliance with the king of Spain. After three months of talks, Philip's agents signed a treaty at Joinville (Guise's headquarters), on 31 December 1584, that pledged mutual assistance for the Catholic cause in France and the Netherlands, recognised the Cardinal of Bourbon (an ally of Guise) as heir to Henry III and promised a Spanish subsidy to the League of £125,000 a year.

Even before news of the treaty of Joinville leaked out in March 1585, the authority of the French government had clearly declined, thereby increasing the prospect of Spanish success in the Netherlands. Many in England now believed that unless the queen acted at once to halt the rising tide of Catholic success it would be too late. In the words of Secretary Walsingham: 'the peril would be so great in case Spain should possess the said countries as, whether France concurs in the action or not, yet doth it behove her Majesty to enter into some course for their defence'.[3]

How could this be done without precipitating full-scale Spanish retaliation? Already in October 1584 Elizabeth's leading councillors had held a series of extended discussions on what England should do to stem the tide of Spanish victory. Everyone present seems to have accepted as inevitable that Spain would try, sooner or later, to make another attempt to topple the Tudor regime, but there unanimity ended. One group of councillors argued that the best response to this threat was to concentrate on domestic defence: strengthening the fleet, fortifying the coasts, organising supporters of the regime to fight more effectively in their own defence, but offering no offence to Spain abroad. 'So would England become impregnable', they concluded, 'and she on every side be secure at home and a terror to her enemies.' Other councillors argued that this was not enough. If Philip II ever reconquered the whole Netherlands, they stressed, his power would be 'so formidable to all the rest of Christendom as that Her Majesty shall no wise be able with her own power nor with the aid of any other, neither by sea nor land, to withstand his attempts'. In such an eventuality Elizabeth would become a prey to Philip's 'insatiable malice, which is most terrible to be thought of, but most miserable to suffer'. For 'Little England' to survive, action to halt Spain's reconquest of the Netherlands had to be taken sooner, while at least one committed continental ally (the Dutch Republic) remained, rather than later, when England would have to stand and fight alone.[4]

Which faction would the queen support? Her dilemma resembled that facing the British government in the later 1930s: whether to appease or to threaten the dominant continental power. Whereas it is possible to trace the steps from the Munich agreement of September 1938 to the Ultimatum of September 1939 through surviving Cabinet and Foreign Office papers, however, few surviving documents reveal the process whereby between October 1584 and September 1585 Elizabeth Tudor and her ministers led their country into a war with Spain that would last for 18 years.

The central difficulty lies in the mercurial personality of the queen herself: vain, secretive and shrewd, Elizabeth believed that she was her own best mentor, and over the years she had learned how to play off her various advisers in order to leave herself the greatest freedom of manoeuvre. Her councillors may have been an unusually talented group of men, almost entirely united in outlook and closely linked by a network of intermarriage and family connection (they were almost all cousins): even so they usually failed to impose their policies upon an unwilling queen. She rarely attended council meetings, and instead tended to seek the opinion of each councillor individually and then to 'leak' it to the rest – a practice surprisingly similar to Philip II's style of government. If the council nevertheless persisted in pushing a policy of which she disapproved, Elizabeth would stage a series of tantrums until they dropped the matter.

One chink in the queen's armour was her highly emotional reaction to the discovery of plots aimed against her. Evidence of any attempt (especially one conceived abroad) to murder her and destroy her regime might make the queen throw caution to the winds. In the event, the discovery of a series of international conspiracies, coinciding with the attempts on William of Orange's life, finally secured Elizabeth's support for those of her councillors who favoured an open war with Spain.

Elizabethan England boasted a highly efficient secret service, and in 1582 a bizarre stroke of fortune gave its chief, Secretary of State Francis Walsingham, the breakthrough he needed. Early that summer an English patrol apprehended a stranger in 'an old gray cloak' on the Northumbrian fells close to the Scottish border. He refused to give his name (it was later suggested that he might have been a Jesuit), and eventually bribed his way out of trouble, but not before he had been relieved of a bag containing his few possessions. They included a breviary, dental instruments and a mirror with a secret compartment in the back containing a coded message, which was duly dispatched to court. Walsingham's cryptographers at once got to work and the information they found eventually enabled them to penetrate Mary Stuart's secret pipeline to France. From then on, Elizabeth became privy to most of her captive rival's plots.

The first, hatched by an English Catholic, Francis Throckmorton, aimed to eliminate Elizabeth and replace her with Mary, who would then marry a prince favourable to Spain. Ambassador Mendoza, with Philip's full support, became deeply involved in the plot. Late in 1583 Walsingham had sufficient evidence to arrest and torture the leading conspirators. Some confessed, and a few were executed. The government placed Mary under closer guard, and in January 1584 expelled Mendoza. Later that year, a Jesuit priest travelling from Flanders to Scotland was found to possess a paper which revealed the existence of another plot to overthrow Elizabeth and replace her with Mary. Again, the conspirators were rounded up, tortured until they admitted the complicity of Mary and Philip, and then executed. If the queen intended their fate to deter others, she failed. In February 1585 yet another scheme to assassinate Elizabeth came to light, this time sponsored by the pope. It was the third foiled plot against the queen's life in two years.

Events abroad also threatened Elizabeth. In March 1585 the French Catholic League mobilised an army and demanded that Henry III join them in extirpating Protestantism from the kingdom. In July, by the treaty of Nemours, he reluctantly ceded a number of important towns to the League's control and promised to join them in making war on Henry of Navarre. The king of France had become, at least for the time being, the cat's paw of Spain's allies. Meanwhile, in the Low Countries, Parma tightened his blockade of Antwerp.

The dilemma facing Elizabeth and her council now deepened. In March 1585, in the light of recent developments, many councillors again argued that England's security required a pre-emptive strike against Spain before Philip II acquired enough strength to overwhelm England. Underhand aid to the Dutch and a little Caribbean piracy clearly no longer sufficed: only full-scale military and naval action could stop Spain now.

In August 1584, upon learning of Orange's assassination, Elizabeth had agreed to sponsor another semi-private naval attack on Spanish overseas interests, creating a special fund 'to be issued from time to time' on the orders of a commission consisting of Burghley, Walsingham and Lord Admiral Howard. The money went to Sir Francis Drake who, by the end of November 1584, had assembled a fleet of 15 ships (2 of them the queen's warships) and 20 pinnaces, with 1,600 men (500 of them soldiers) for an expedition to the East Indies. The total cost was estimated at £40,000, of which the queen agreed to contribute almost half in cash and ships.[5] The following month, however, she changed her mind and suspended the project, although she did allow a small colonising expedition to sail to America (a precarious settlement briefly took root at Roanoke in North Carolina) and permitted Drake to keep his force in being.[6] In April 1585, upon receiving news of the treaty of Joinville, Elizabeth's ministers began to negotiate with envoys sent by the Dutch Republic to secure a formal alliance and, as a gesture of support, she suspended all English trade with the Spanish Netherlands. As yet she dared do no more, believing that open aid for the Netherlands would lead England inexorably to a dangerous war, condemned abroad and unwelcome at home.[7]

Meanwhile, in Madrid, Philip and his ministers discussed how best to support the efforts of Parma and his troops in the trenches around Antwerp. Some argued that the sudden seizure of all Dutch shipping in Spain and Portugal, followed by a prohibition of the rebels' lucrative trade with the Iberian peninsula, might bring the revolt to a swift end. 'In my opinion', wrote one experienced minister, 'Holland and Zealand could easily be reduced if we deprive them of the trade with Spain and Portugal; and I am sure that in the end, when everything has been discussed, we shall have to do it.' The ideal time, he suggested, was either the autumn, when the Iberian ports would be full of Dutch vessels coming to collect wine, olive oil and other newly harvested crops, or the spring, when they brought Baltic grain; and he recommended the blanket seizure of all foreign vessels, except for those of Catholic states: 'I would arrest all of them, and afterwards we can discuss which should be released and which should not'.[8]

Elizabeth's prohibition of trade with the Spanish Netherlands in April 1585 played right into the hands of such 'hawks', and the following month Philip ordered the embargo of all foreign ships in Iberian ports, save only the French (on account, he claimed, of their small size). Characteristically, however, he carried it out in a suspiciously complex and clandestine manner.

> Do it [he told his agents in the ports] in such a way that, for the present, it will be understood that ships belonging to the rebels of all my states, and those from Hanseatic [ports] and Germany, and from England, will be embargoed on the grounds and with the pretence of wanting to create a great fleet. Having done this, once they have been embargoed and detained, we will know what we have in all areas [of the peninsula] and can better ordain what should be done.[9]

In the event, in July the king ordered the release first of all German and Hanseatic vessels (with compensation for the period of detention) and later of the English, leaving only the Dutch, whose vessels he eventually either incorporated into royal service or else sold by auction.[10]

In one respect the gambit worked extremely well. Dutch trade with the Iberian peninsula temporarily collapsed as scores of Holland and Zealand vessels suffered arrest and the republic immediately halted further sailings to Spain and Portugal. The total of Dutch ships leaving the Danish Sound – most of them bound for Iberian destinations – fell by 30 per cent and stayed low for three years. The decision to embargo non-Dutch ships as well proved a disaster, however, for when a party of Spanish officials came to arrest the English vessel *Primrose* near Bilbao, her master decided to fight his way out, taking with him to England not only the Spanish boarding party but also a copy of the embargo decree and the magistrate who had attempted to enforce it.

Elizabeth's ministers lost no time in studying the exact wording of the embargo decree served on the *Primrose*. They immediately noted that it affected only ships from Protestant lands (since it expressly exempted the French), which suggested a Catholic crusade. They also interrogated the Spaniards captured aboard the *Primrose*, who offered little reassurance on Philip's intentions: one of them informed his captors that 'hearing that the Hollanders seek aid in England and fearing lest they shall be aided', the king of Spain 'means by this arrest to fear [=deter] the English from aiding them'. Moreover an intercepted letter from a Spanish merchant in Andalusia to his partner in Rouen spoke unequivocally of 'the state of war that now exists with England'.[11]

Feelings in England were reciprocal. Following the Throckmorton plot (in which Spain had been deeply involved) and Orange's assassination (which everyone knew had been carried out at Philip's behest) the Privy Council had made contingency plans for an interim administration should Elizabeth die, and drafted a 'Bond of Association' that pledged that, should she perish by violent means,

Mary Stuart would automatically and immediately be executed. Meanwhile military and naval preparations went ahead apace, and Walsingham put forward 'A plot for the annoying of the king of Spain' which involved seizing all Spanish vessels off Newfoundland and unleashing Drake once more on the West Indies.

For the first time a clear majority of Elizabeth's council now favoured war. Philip's embargo had played into their hands, and the queen now began to follow their advice consistently. In June 1585 she invited Dom Antonio to return to England (he arrived in September), and the next month signed a treaty that bound Scotland, through its pliable and ambitious young king, James, more tightly to her side. She also commissioned a small squadron to sail to Newfoundland with orders to attack the Iberian fishing fleet (it later returned to England with many boats and about 600 captive mariners). Shortly afterwards the Privy Council drew up regulations for the issue of licences for any subjects affected by the embargo, allowing them to make good their losses by plundering any ship sailing under Philip's colours, as if a state of war existed between the two countries. At the same time Drake received permission to purchase more stores and press men for his voyage 'into foreign parts'.

News of Philip's decision to release all English ships affected by the embargo failed to change the queen's mind. On 20 August, at her palace of Nonsuch, she signed a formal treaty with the Dutch envoys which, together with a supplementary treaty three weeks later, undertook to provide over 6,000 regular troops for their army, to pay one-quarter of their defence budget (estimated at £125,000) and to supply an experienced councillor to co-ordinate government in the rebel provinces and to lead their army. In return the republic promised to surrender the strategic ports of Flushing, Brill and Ostend to England, as sureties until the queen's expenses could be repaid once Spain had recognised their independence.

Although the treaty of Nonsuch came too late to save Antwerp, which fell on 17 August, within a month (as Parma angrily noted) over 4,000 English troops had arrived at Flushing, one of the three Dutch ports ceded to Elizabeth by treaty. Meanwhile, on 24 September, Drake's squadron of 25 ships (2 of the queen's warships still among them) and 8 pinnaces, carrying 1,900 men (1,200 of them soldiers), sailed from Plymouth. The commanders included veterans of Drake's circumnavigation and of the Azores battles, as well as several men prominent at court – Christopher Carleill (Walsingham's step-son), Francis Knollys (Leicester's brother-in-law) and, for a time, Sir Philip Sydney. The main connection between the fleet and the court, however, lay in the ships: apart from the queen's 2 battleships, 4 others belonged to John Hawkins, 2 to Leicester, and 1 each to Lord Shrewsbury, Lord Admiral Howard and Sir William Winter. On 7 October 1585 they arrived off Galicia and for the next 10 days launched raids on several villages in the vicinity of Bayona, desecrating churches, collecting booty and taking hostages.[12]

Why exactly Drake chose to raid Galicia remains unclear, for neither his commission nor his instructions seem to have survived. Perhaps he needed to take on stores following a hasty departure from England; perhaps, as one of his officers later wrote, he wished to undertake some initial act of bravado 'to make our proceedings known to the king of Spain'.[13] Either way, no sovereign state could overlook such an act of naked aggression – especially taken in conjunction with Elizabeth's other manifest provocations: kidnapping the Iberian fishing fleet, welcoming Dom Antonio, issuing letters of marque, and sending soldiers and subsidies under treaty to assist rebellious subjects. As even Burghley admitted, all this meant that England was about 'to sustain a greater war than ever in any memory of man it hath done'.[14]

Although Elizabeth issued a justification for her actions in several languages, claiming that she merely wished to retaliate against Philip's support for plots directed against her, and against his embargo on English shipping, few believed her. As soon as he heard of Drake's actions in Galicia, the Imperial ambassador in Madrid warned his master that 'with this act the English have removed their mask towards Spain'. Two weeks later his French colleague reported that the English had killed some clerics and done damage 'approaching 300,000 crowns' in Galicia; while the Venetian ambassador, having described the same outrages, also forwarded a list of the 26 ships captured by the 'English pirates' off the coasts of Spain.[15] All three diplomats concluded that Elizabeth's actions amounted to a declaration of war. The question was no longer whether Philip would counter-attack, but when and how that counter-attack would take place.

## Sources

Read, *Mr Secretary Walsingham*, and more recently MacCaffrey, *Queen Elizabeth and the Making of Policy*, include excellent accounts of the making of English foreign policy, albeit (like Wernham, *Before the Armada*), they rest almost entirely upon English sources. On French developments during this period, see Chevallier, *Henry III*, 559ff, and Constant, *Les Guise*, chapter 7. On Dom Antonio, see McBride, 'Elizabethan foreign policy in microcosm', and Durand-Lapié, 'Un roi détrôné réfugié en France: Dom Antoine Ier de Portugal (1580–95)'.

The struggle for the Azores in 1581–3 is well covered by Tenison, IV, 175–213, and Fernández Duro, *La conquista de las Azores en 1583*. On the disastrous Valdés expedition of 1581 see Duro, *La conquista de las Azores en 1583*, 11–17: Philip II had Valdés court-martialled and imprisoned for insubordination. Details on the much-disputed English participation may be found in Andrews, *Elizabethan Privateering*, 202–3. The significance of the São Miguel battle for the revolution in naval tactics was first made clear by Waters, *The Elizabethan Navy and the Armada of Spain*.

For recent accounts of the coming of war, see Rodríguez-Salgado, 'The Anglo-Spanish war', and Adams, 'The outbreak of the Elizabethan naval war'. For Drake's role, see Kelsey, *Sir Francis Drake*, 245–9, and the documents in Keeler, *Sir Francis Drake's West Indian Voyage*.

## Notes

1 BNP *Fonds français* 16,108/365 and 425–7, Ambassador St Gouard to Catherine de Medici, 20 August, and to Henry III, 7 October 1582.

2 Quotation from Guilmartin, *Gunpowder and Galleys*, 216–17.

3 Quotation from Read, *Mr Secretary Walsingham*, 75. News of the treaty of Joinville reached Ambassador Stafford on 29 March 1585 NS (*CSPF*, XIX, 361–2).

4 Quotations from MacCaffrey, *Queen Elizabeth and the Making of Policy*, 338–9, citing Camden's *Annals*. The memoranda of the Council meetings in October 1584 are worth consulting *in extenso*: see *CSPF*, XIX, 95–8, and *HMC Salisbury*, III, 67–70. See also Burghley's formulation in a memorandum to the queen at this time: 'If he [Philip II] once reduce the Low Countries to absolute subjection, I know not what limits any man of judgement can set unto his greatness' (Scott, *The Somers Collection of Tracts*, 164–70).

5 PRO *SP* 12/46/159, 171 and 178 (with copies in PRO *AO*1/1685/20A) document the issues of money in 1584, starting with £3,500 paid to Drake in August 1584. See also BL Lansdowne MS 43/11, John Hawkins' 'project for distressing Spain', 20 July 1584 OS, and 41/5 Burghley's memorandum entitled 'The charge of the voyage to the Moluccas', 20 November 1584 OS.

6 By May 1585 the Spanish government knew of Elizabeth's plans to send another expedition to the East Indies: see *CCG*, XII, 58, Granvelle to Margaret of Parma, 29 May 1585. For details on the preparations, see Adams, 'The outbreak of the Elizabethan naval war', 50–8.

7 BL Harleian MS 168/102–5, 'A consultacion . . . touchinge an aide to be sent in to Hollande againste the king of Spaine', 18 March 1585 OS.

8 *CCG*, XI, 367–8, Granvelle to Charles de Mansfelt, 27 October 1584.

9 *BMO*, I, 476–7, Philip II order of 25 May 1585. It is worth stressing those words 'with the pretence [*con color*]', because several scholars have argued that the embargo was indeed intended to provide ships for naval operations (like the embargoes of vessels ordered by Philip in 1582, 1583 and 1586–8), but this does not appear to have been the case. For alternative views, see Rodríguez-Salgado and Adams, *England, Spain and the Gran Armada*, 6, 56 and 241.

10 *BMO*, I, 490–1, order of 3 July 1585; and AGS *GA* 80/125, 'Copia del apuntamiento que Antonio de Erasso dió a Don Cristobal de Moura', 20 July 1585.

11 PRO *SP* 12/179/36–8, examination of the well-informed Bilbao merchant Pedro de Villareal, 13 June 1585 OS (he also confirmed that Spain sent regular subsidies to the French Catholic League: someone later underlined all information in his testimony concerning France); and PRO *SP* 12/180/59A, captured letter from Juan del Hoyo, merchant, 5 July 1585 NS.

12 For details see *BMO*, I, 518–19 and 539, Pedro Bermudez to the court, 7 October 1585, and Licenciado Antolinez to Philip II, 14 November 1585.

13 See the discussion of motives, and the citation of sources, in Rodríguez-Salgado and Adams, *England, Spain and the Gran Armada*, 59.

14 *CSPF*, XIX, 705, 'Certain things to be considered', 23 July 1585.

15 See 'A declaration of the causes moving the queen of England to give aid to the defence of the Lowe Countries', October 1585, in Scott, *Somers Tracts*, 410–19; OÖLA *KB* 4/137, Khevenhüller to Rudolf II, 13 October 1585; Mousset, *Dépêches diplomatiques*, 192, letter to Henry III, 28 October 1585; *CSPV*, 123, Gradinegro to Venice, 25 October 1585.

# 6

## The Grand Design and its architect

Why, man, he doth bestride the narrow world
Like a Colossus, and we petty men
Walk under his huge legs

Shakespeare's lines on Julius Caesar might well be applied to Philip II, for after 1580 he governed one-fifth of the land of western Europe and one-quarter of its population. His global dominions embraced the Philippines, Mexico and Peru, the Iberian and Italian peninsulas, and the Portuguese outposts in Mozambique, Ceylon, Malacca and Macao, dwarfing those of the Roman empire at its apogee. Beneath his sceptre lay the bustling cities of Antwerp, Naples, Seville and Mexico, and subjects as diverse as the learned Benito Arias Montano, the painter El Greco, and the saint and mystic Teresa of Avila. And that sceptre dispensed absolute power: King Philip, as one of his courtiers irreverently observed, was like Christ, for he could make and break men as if they were clay.

Who was the man at the hub of such immense power? Although far more of Philip II's papers survive than those of any other early modern statesman, his personality remains elusive. As Robert Watson, Principal of St Andrews University, wrote in his *History of the Reign of Philip the Second* in 1777: 'No character was ever drawn by different historians in more opposite colours than that of Philip.' Considerable unanimity existed among those living in the years before the Armada, however. The famous portrait of the king by Sofanisba Anguisciola, painted about 1579, shows an austere face, with thin hair and neat beard almost entirely white, but steel-grey eyes that are clear and stern. He is dressed simply in black, his only decoration the emblem of the Golden Fleece hung on a light cord around his neck. In his hands he holds a rosary: it is as if the painter has surprised the king in a private moment, at prayer (FIGURE 11).

The king almost always dressed in black: he felt uncomfortable in anything else. He hated wearing coronation robes when he went to Portugal to be crowned (or so he wrote to his teenage daughters); and, although his household accounts show that he purchased a new suit of clothes every month, it was always made in the same simple style and the same plain colour. Even when he attended the wedding of his daughter Catalina to the duke of Savoy in 1585, everyone was

FIGURE II  Philip II by
Sofanisba Anguisciola,
about 1579.

richly attired 'except the king, who looked very ordinary, dressed in black just
like the citizens'. Philip ate the same food as his subjects and relished the same
enjoyments. In Valencia some fishermen offered him their day's catch, as an act
of homage, and the royal party went out on to the balcony of the house in which
they were staying and ate their supper in public, so everyone could see how
much they enjoyed the local fish. In Zaragoza, some years later, the king happened to be walking through the streets when he met a religious procession
coming the other way. At once he stepped back into the crowd and fell to his
knees, bareheaded, and remained there in the midst of his subjects in prayer
and reverence.

Perhaps this desire to blend with the rest of humanity, to avoid being identified as the man with supreme power and supreme responsibility, is significant.
It certainly contrasts sharply with the pomp and ostentation which Elizabeth
Tudor used to project herself as a being different from other humans. But the
contrast is easily explained. Elizabeth had been brought up in the unstable household of Henry VIII and his wives (of whom no less than four came and went

after Elizabeth's mother had been executed). As a girl she had been proclaimed a bastard; as a young woman she had spent part of her half-sister's reign under arrest. Philip, by contrast, had from birth been groomed for government with meticulous care. In 1543, at the age of 16, his father made him regent in Spain, an office he discharged intermittently over the next decade, and with considerable success. In 1554 he was created king of Naples, shortly before becoming king consort of England, and gradually most of his father's lands fell under his sway. But Charles V set no ordinary standards for his son to emulate. A successful statesman and soldier, an experienced traveller fluent in five languages, a master of the regal gesture and apposite phrase, a natural leader of men: he set a hard standard to follow, and Philip's long years of apprenticeship in the art of government only served to heighten his awareness of the elusiveness of success and the disgrace of failure.

The king had few other mentors within his family on whom he could rely absolutely for advice. Two aunts, his second wife (Mary Tudor) and his father all died in 1558; of his siblings, one sister lived in Vienna and the other became something of a recluse; his half-brother, Don John of Austria, the fruit of a brief affair between the ageing Charles V and a young girl in Regensburg, was only 11 when his father died; and his elder half-sister (also illegitimate) lived all her life in the Netherlands and Italy, never visiting Spain. Although Philip married Elisabeth de Valois in 1560, she died in childbirth in 1568 aged only 22. In 1570 he made his fourth and last marriage, to his niece Anna of Austria, but she too died in childbirth 10 years later, when she was only 31. Of his children, the eldest, Don Carlos, died insane in 1568, and his other sons all died young except for the future Philip III, born in 1578. Of his two daughters who survived childhood, Catalina left for Italy in 1585 and never saw her father again, leaving her sister Isabella (born in 1566) as the king's only family intimate.

Philip II seems to have filled the gap between these great expectations and his stunted family life with religion. There can be no doubt about his deep personal piety. Religious works made up a large section of his great library at the Escorial (which eventually numbered more than 14,000 volumes), and the notes kept by his librarian show these items in frequent use: one evening in 1572, for example, he called for a Concordance to the Bible because he wanted to check a reference before going to bed. Of the 42 books in the king's bedside bookcase, all but one (a serious historical tome) concerned the Christian faith. He attended Mass daily, heard a sermon at least once a week, and confessed and received Communion four times a year. He went on a retreat each Lent, as well as at times of severe emotional strain (for instance, after the death of his wife Elisabeth de Valois). The monks at the Escorial noticed that on occasion, when he was at prayer or in contemplation, tears would roll down the king's cheeks; and deeply religious people, including St Ignatius Loyola and St Teresa of Avila, detected in the king a piety of profound and unusual intensity.

Some found it obsessive. From the 1560s onwards, Philip's correspondence with churchmen began to deal increasingly with religious relics, above all with the recovery of relics from Protestant countries and their safe dispatch to Spain. By the end of the reign the relic-keeper at the Escorial, Friar José de Sigüenza, could boast that 'We only know of three saints of whom we do not have some part or other here', and the meticulous inventory of the collection enumerated a grand total of 7,422 authenticated items, including 12 entire bodies, 144 heads and 306 complete limbs. For a Catholic, one relic is a sign of admirable devotion, and a few relics may pass as exemplary piety; but 7,422 suggests unbridled obsession. Indeed, from 1587 onwards the king had 'his' relics brought out for veneration with meticulous regularity. Before long he insisted that all of them, displayed on different altars in the Basilica at the Escorial, should be placed on view at the same time. 'The king went up there, sometimes alone and sometimes accompanied by his children' to see them, Sigüenza noted. 'When he arrived, the king asked me many times to show him this or that relic; and, when I took them in my hands, before I could cover them with a cloth or veil, the most pious king bent down and, having removed his hat or bonnet, kissed them in my hand.' And, 'because some of them were so small', the friar added, with an understandable shudder, 'I too received a thousand kisses'.[1]

With such godliness in his heart and mind, it is not surprising to find that Philip II was unshakably convinced that he and his government enjoyed divine favour – in short, that God was on his side. In 1583, when news of the conquest of Terceira arrived, the king's personal secretary, Mateo Vázquez, reflected that

> The care, zeal and resources with which Your Majesty attends to matters affecting the service of Our Lord ensures that He looks after those affecting Your Majesty. To have the sea under our control is most important . . . but more important still is the promise of more fortunate successes which we may expect from God's hand in return for the care with which Your Majesty has sought the honour of God and of His religion.[2]

The king enthusiastically agreed. Time and again he pressed his policies upon unwilling subordinates, or upon taxpayers, on the grounds that his work was God's work. Philip once loftily urged a dispirited subordinate to take better care of his health 'because you are engaged in God's service and in mine – which is the same thing'; and throughout his reign, the king believed profoundly that God would provide whatever lay beyond human powers of prediction or execution, and he repeatedly counted upon miracles to bridge the gap between intention and achievement, to fill the interstices in his strategic plans.[3]

We have already seen Philip II use spiritual blackmail against the duke of Alba in 1571 concerning the invasion of England, and he deployed similar techniques frequently during the Armada campaign. When Parma objected to the king's plan for launching the invasion of England in the winter of 1587,

Philip blandly replied (as he had already told Santa Cruz), 'We are quite aware of the risk that is incurred by sending a major fleet in winter through the Channel without a safe harbour, but . . . since it is all for His cause, God will send good weather.'[4] When, somewhat later, Medina Sidonia tried to persuade the king that the contrary winds that had driven his fleet back to Corunna might be a divine warning, the king haughtily replied that, since the entire operation had been mounted for God's greater glory, such an interpretation simply could not be correct. And although the eventual destruction of his fleet, and of his hopes, temporarily shook the king's faith that God was on his side, his only public reaction was to order that the weekly prayers for the Armada's success be suspended, and to send a circular letter to his bishops asking for special services to be held in all churches to thank God that not everything had been destroyed, 'entrusting to Our Lord most sincerely all my deeds, so that His Divine Majesty may guide and direct them to whatever end may be to His greatest service'.

After the Armada, the king continued to justify his costly wars in France, in the Netherlands and against England on precisely the same grounds: they were necessary, and they would succeed, because he fought in God's name. Thus in 1591, when his private secretary (the same man who had crowed over the Terceira victory eight years before) argued that 'If God had meant Your Majesty to remedy all the troubles of the world, He would have given you the money and strength to do', Philip's reply was firm. 'I know you mean well', he wrote to Mateo Vázquez, 'but these are not matters that can be abandoned.' The king's various crusades abroad could not be dropped 'because the cause of religion takes priority over everything'.[5]

That the ruler of a global empire should have found it necessary to write such things to a trusted adviser, working literally in the next room, may seem surprising. But that was how Philip II preferred to govern. He abhorred personal interviews, preferring to transact all business in writing. In 1576, for example, he scribbled the following refusal to the request of a senior military adviser for an interview: 'I would be glad to see him, but in all honesty I have very little time. And anyway', he added for the benefit of his secretary, 'I forget so much of what is said to me at audiences . . . well, at most of them anyway, although you must not tell him that.' It was a strange but revealing admission. A few years later, when the duke of Medina Sidonia asked for an audience to discuss his plans on how to carry out the king's orders to invade southern Portugal, the king wrote back to him: 'If you happened to be close to court, it might be useful to hear the details from you in person; but since your letters will be delivered to me in complete secrecy, I think it would be best if you wrote.' Such a procedure may have saved the king time, and minimised his contact with other human beings, but it was a strange way to run a war.[6]

So instead of governing face-to-face, Philip II ruled from his desk by pen, usually working for eight or nine hours a day on his papers in a tiny office. He insisted that all orders should be issued over his personal signature, and he alone took the final decision on all major matters. He also solicited and read innumerable papers of advice from experts, and he received assessments on all incoming letters from ministers and courtiers; but once again the king always took the decision himself. The 'Diurnal' of the king's private secretary in the 1570s shows that Philip received 30 to 40 memoranda or reports daily, each one requiring a decision, and on one occasion he claimed to have signed 400 documents at a single sitting. By 1587, according to the Venetian ambassador:

> I am informed by someone who frequents his private apartments that he is never idle, for besides his desire to read himself all the incoming and outgoing correspondence of all areas, and from all the ambassadors and ministers of his vast dominions . . . and besides the many prayers which he says, he covers every day with his own hand more than a ream of paper, between memoranda, recommendations and orders, which he constantly sends to his councillors, judges, secretaries and ministers in this way, and countless other secret business that he handles with other individuals. It is hard to believe how much time he spends in signing letters, licences, patents and other affairs of grace and justice: on certain days they amount to 2,000 [items].[7]

Long before the typewriter, the photocopier and the word-processor, Philip was thus drowning in a sea of paper. 'I have 100,000 papers in front of me', he began one frenetic note to a secretary, and at times the pressure of work drove him to despair. One night in 1578 he complained to a minister:

> I have just been given this other packet of papers from you, but I have neither the time nor the strength to look at it. I will not open it until tomorrow. It is already after ten o'clock and I have not yet had dinner. My table is full of papers for tomorrow because I cannot cope with any more today.

A few months later he lamented that so many 'matters have come up that cannot be neglected, I do not believe that any human resources would suffice to deal with them all – especially not mine, which are very weak and getting weaker every day with all the things that have to be done'. Occasionally the number of pending decisions caused him to lose his temper. In 1581 he told his secretary:

> Some things are going to have to wait, because everything cannot be done at once. Try and do something to hold them up because I cannot take any more. Anyone who looks at how I spent today will see that just two men detained me for more than two hours and left me with more papers than I can manage in many more [hours]. So I am shattered. God give me strength and patience.[8]

To be sure, maintaining a system of 'confuse and rule', in which no one knew as much as the king himself, offered Philip a number of advantages. First, it enabled him to retain the initiative in government and prevent any serious abuse of power by his subordinates. Second, it allowed him to avoid having to take decisions on the spur of the moment, or under pressure from court factions. To a large extent, the king could resolve problems at his own pace, and in his own way. But herein lay a catch, for this could lead to putting off, or overlooking, really difficult choices until it was too late. The weaknesses as well as the strengths of Philip II's system of government all played their part in planning the 'Enterprise of England'.

Throughout Philip's reign there had been courtiers – many of them English Catholic exiles – who had urged an invasion to topple the Tudor state; and as early as 1559 (as we have seen) the king recognised that such action was both desirable and, perhaps, inevitable. But he always put off the fateful confrontation. Except for Ridolfi, until the 1580s no conspirators against Elizabeth received open support from Spain. Admittedly the troops who left for Smerwick in 1579 and 1580 departed from a Spanish port and in Spanish ships, but the king could (and did) disavow them when things went wrong. He seems to have felt that, until the Netherlands had been pacified again, England should be left alone.

The conquest of the Azores kindled a new a flicker of interest. 'After the taking of the island of Terceira', wrote a contemporary Spanish observer, 'the captains who accompanied the marquis of Santa Cruz . . . said openly that now we have Portugal, England is ours; and little by little we shall gain France also.' In 1583 Santa Cruz himself impressed upon Philip II the feasibility of a maritime expedition against England, and the king commissioned a series of 'position papers' concerning the best way to invade England and reviewing past amphibious operations, from the successful landings of the Romans and Saxons, through those of the Lancastrians in the fifteenth century, to the more recent plans of the French (against the Isle of Wight in 1545), the papal adventurers (at Smerwick) and Ridolfi (involving naval forces from Spain and an army from the Netherlands). The balance of evidence suggested that any future Spanish invasion should aim for London, since it was the seat of government and was easily accessible from the sea. In addition, once the expeditionary force from Spain landed in the Thames estuary, reinforcements would be readily available from the Army of Flanders.[9]

On receipt of Santa Cruz's proposal in September 1583, Philip II also sought the advice of the duke of Parma, commander of his forces in the Netherlands. 'In order to terminate [the Dutch struggle] once and for all', he informed his nephew, 'it might be advisable to take steps to ensure that the war there is not sustained from England.' He asked Parma bluntly whether he could prepare and launch an invasion that would eliminate Elizabeth and replace her with Mary Stuart. The duke did not rule out the possibility, although he preferred a surprise attack across the Channel by the Army of Flanders to a direct invasion from Spain; but, given his insecure military position, he suggested that it might be better to complete the conquest of the Netherlands before turning upon England.[10] With this the plan temporarily lapsed. The election in May 1585 of a new pope, Sixtus V, who burned with the desire to achieve some great triumph for the Catholic Church, changed everything. Within the month he had mentioned twice to the Spanish ambassador in Rome, the count of Olivares, his zeal to commission 'some outstanding enterprise' for the faith, specifying either the reconquest of the Moorish stronghold of Algiers or the invasion of England. The ambassador dutifully passed these details back to his master, but the king angrily scribbled on the back of the letter, 'Doesn't [the reconquest of] the Low Countries seem "outstanding" to them? Do they never think of how much it costs? There is little to be said about the English idea; one should keep away from such distant things.' For a time after this outburst the pope obligingly shifted his attention to the possibility of recapturing Geneva, formerly possessed by the dukes of Savoy and now the citadel of Calvinism; but in August he again proposed that Spain should invade England as a prelude to the final reduction of Holland and Zealand. Once more Philip rejected the idea: the war in the Netherlands, he pointed out, was so expensive that no further commitments could be undertaken until all the rebellious provinces had been regained. He also called attention to the fact that the Low Countries' wars were 'fought so that there should be no concessions over religion' and 'to maintain obedience there to God and the Holy See'. He therefore invited the pope to contribute to the costs of maintaining his army and so facilitate a speedier victory there.[11]

Sixtus V proved surprisingly tenacious and resourceful: he did not merely badger the Spanish ambassador but also worked through his own agent in Spain, Luigi Dovara, a courtier of the grand duke of Tuscany. Dovara promised that, should Spain attack England, both the papacy and Tuscany would contribute to the costs; but discussions with royal ministers throughout July and August proved inconclusive, and Dovara had practically abandoned hope when news arrived of Elizabeth's dramatic change of policy.[12]

Information about Drake's impudent outrages in Galicia between 7 and 17 October reached the king directly from Vigo and Bayona. The English had not acted with particular brutality, but they inflicted a great deal of damage on Church property, vandalising religious images and crucifixes, mistreated some clerical personnel and captured many Spanish ships in the area. Such acts of naked aggression and desecration, committed on Spanish soil, were highly provocative.[13]

The 'sack of Galicia' seems to have been the last straw for Philip II, the final proof that the English problem could no longer be deferred. On 24 October 1585 Philip dictated letters to inform both the pope and the grand duke of Tuscany that he accepted their invitation to undertake the conquest of England. He sounded only two notes of caution. First, 'Although His Holiness and His Majesty agree and are of the same mind about this enterprise, the lack of time (since putting the venture into effect requires extensive preparations) excludes the possibility of doing it in 1586, and so it will have to be delayed until 1587.' Second, because the total cost of the enterprise seemed likely to exceed three million ducats, at a time when the war in the Netherlands was already stretching Spain's finances to the limit, the king declared himself 'happy to contribute what he can, but states that it cannot be more than a third – or at the most a half – of the cost. The rest will have to come from [Rome and Florence].' In all other respects, however, Philip's response seemed positive, even enthusiastic, and he eagerly awaited the reaction of his Italian allies.[14]

When assurances of their continued commitment duly arrived, Philip dictated and signed further letters which committed him not only to carry out the conquest of England but also, as intended in 1571, to employ the Army of Flanders to achieve it. On 29 December 1585 he invited the prince of Parma, fresh from his triumphant reconquest of most of Flanders and Brabant, to propose a suitable strategy for invasion. Four days later he authorised Olivares to discuss with the pope certain political implications of the operation – how would the invasion be justified to the world; what role would his holiness and the grand duke play; who would rule England after the death of Mary Stuart (still the obvious successor to Elizabeth and explicitly recognised as 'my sovereign' by many Catholics). He also proposed that Parma should command the expeditionary force.

It was, of course, one thing to decide that England must be invaded, and quite another to make it happen. Nevertheless nine English governments had been overthrown or seriously undermined by seaborne invasions since the Norman Conquest of 1066, with several other successful landings of major forces and many more lesser raids (as well as seaborne assistance against England sent to Scotland or Ireland). Philip II and his ministers studied these various operations, and concluded that three strategies offered a reasonable prospect of success. The first consisted of a simultaneous combined operation by a fleet strong enough both to defeat the opposing English navy and to shepherd across the Channel an army sufficient to accomplish the conquest, just as William I had done in 1066 with spectacular success. The second possible strategy involved assembling an army in secret near the Channel while launching a diversionary assault on Ireland which would draw off most of England's defenders, leaving the mainland relatively open to invasion by the main force (the Smerwick operation of 1579–80 seemed to show the way). Finally, a surprise assault might be essayed (as, most recently, Edward of York had done in 1471 and Henry Tudor in 1485). That all these possible strategies received consideration in 1586–8 reflects great credit on the vision and competence of Philip and his 'national security advisers'; that they tried to undertake all three of them at once does not.

Confusion began to arise in January 1586 when the king invited Santa Cruz to assess how many ships and men would be needed to protect the coasts of

Spain and Portugal from further humiliating raids by 'pirates' like Drake. The marquis obliged the following month, but accompanied his list with an eloquent plea that the best way to defend the peninsula against the threat from England would be to attack England itself, and (somewhat presumptuously) offered 'to serve Your Majesty myself in the enterprise in the firm hope that, being so much in Your Majesty's service, I will emerge just as victorious from it as in the other things that I have done for you'. The proposal met with an enthusiastic reception, and Philip invited the marquis to prepare and send 'a paper showing the way in which you believe this could be effected, should circumstances permit'.[15]

This marked a radical departure in Spanish strategic thinking towards England, because all previous plans had involved an invasion launched from the Netherlands, not from the Iberian peninsula. Nevertheless Santa Cruz seized his opportunity and, aided by the provisioner-general of the navy, sent a detailed proposal in March entitled: 'The fleet and army that it would seem necessary to assemble for the conquest of England'. Unfortunately for us, Santa Cruz never specified the precise strategy envisaged, either in the proposal or the letters that accompanied it, because 'the business is such that it is absolutely impossible to deal with or discuss it in writing'; but the immense quantity and nature of the materiel specified, from capital ships down to the last pair of shoes, made his intentions perfectly clear. He evidently aimed to emulate William the Conqueror, leading an invasion in overwhelming strength.[16]

Predictably enough his scheme envisaged a vastly scaled-up version of the successful Terceira campaign. The task force would assemble at Lisbon and set out from there as a single amphibious operation under the marquis's direct command. It would then land an army sufficiently strong, with all the supporting services it required, at a point on the enemy coast from which it could speedily achieve a decisive victory. The strategic plan contained four main elements, starting with transport. Santa Cruz estimated that 150 ships totalling 77,250 tons would be needed to bring the projected 55,000 invasion troops (together with equipment, munitions and supplies) to their destination. They would include 40 large merchant vessels from Ragusa, Venice, Sicily, Naples and the Mediterranean coast of Spain; 25 Spanish royal galleons and other vessels currently based at Lisbon and Cadiz; 20 ships, including the fighting galleons, of the Portuguese crown; 35 Basque merchantmen from Biscay and Guipúzcoa; and 30 German hulks already under contract to Spain for the transport of naval stores from the Baltic. An additional 400 support vessels of various sizes and types would be needed for the mustering and preparation of the great fleet.

The second element in Santa Cruz's plan concerned the defence of this massive force as it advanced towards the disembarkation point. The role of the Armada, while at sea, would be wholly defensive. The engagement off São Miguel had demonstrated the futility, from the Spanish point of view, of a naval battle of attrition which achieved victory over an enemy fleet at the expense of the capacity to exploit that victory ashore. The fleet would therefore sail in such a way that rigid formation discipline coupled with vigorous self-defence would bring it to Elizabeth's shores, if not unscathed, then at least sufficiently intact to put the third phase of the operation into effect: to land and secure a beach-head for the army. To this end 200 specially designed landing craft would be built. This would doubtless prove the most difficult and crucial part of the whole enterprise, but it was one of which Santa Cruz and many of his subordinates had recent and successful experience. It would be little different from the Azores landings, though on a far larger scale, and Santa Cruz took care to specify those ingredients which had previously brought him victory at Lisbon and Terceira. The 40 galleys and six galleasses he called for would now come into their own. Unsuited they may have been to open-water combat with armed sailing ships; fragile they certainly were in heavy weather; but in sheltered waters close to land, screened from seaward by the main fleet, they would prove deadly. As swift and manoeuvrable destroyers they could operate right up to the beaches, bringing down fire on shore positions, while as support landing craft they could rapidly transfer heavy loads – particularly field and siege artillery – from the fleet to the beach-head. Finally, once the initial landing had been consolidated, and the land campaign begun, the galley force would support the army's flank as it broke out from its beach-head, probing the rivers and harbours as required, just as Santa Cruz's galleys had done for Alba in the Tagus six years before.

Once the troops and their equipment had been brought to the beaches, the operation would move into its fourth and final phase: the conquest of a considerable part of Elizabeth's kingdom, though Santa Cruz did not precisely define its limits. For this the army would require everything necessary to ensure quick success, since speed would be of the essence. A swift blow at some vulnerable yet important part of the Tudor state would provide the most certain solution to the English problem, and perhaps the cheapest one too. To put the issue beyond doubt, Santa Cruz reckoned he would need 55,000 front-line troops, many of them veterans. They would be supported by a large siege train organised into four batteries of 12 40-pounder *cañones de batir* and four 25-pounder heavy *culebrinas*, plus 16 heavy field guns, 24 lighter guns and 20 swivel pieces. An appropriate number of draught and pack animals, wheeled transport and specialist craftsmen would be attached to the artillery train, together with a 3,000-strong corps of pioneers, equipped to construct field fortifications and siegeworks and to clear obstacles.

Santa Cruz's general staff would include administrative officers, a medical service and a contingent of military police. Although the planning document made no mention of it (perhaps Santa Cruz felt that this was something the king would like to attend to himself), there would certainly have been a strong chaplaincy department to maintain the crusading zeal of the troops and add spiritual conversion to the temporal subjugation of English heretics. The whole prodigious undertaking would cost, by Santa Cruz's meticulous reckoning (calculated down to the last earthenware platter), 1,526,425,798 *maravedíes*, or about four million ducats (roughly £1 million).

Santa Cruz, like most commanders when asked by their political masters to draw up a plan of action, no doubt deliberately overestimated his requirements, to allow for the probability that they would later be scaled down, and worked on the assumption that a smaller force might also be able to do the job (albeit with less certainty of outright success). Be that as it may, work began almost immediately to prepare the task force he had called for. On 2 April 1586, after a high-level policy meeting at the Escorial, the king authorised naval preparations in three places: Santa Cruz (who had attended the meeting) would return to Lisbon and create a fighting fleet to be called 'The navy for the defence of my realm, and for the destruction and punishment of the pirates who threaten its coasts'; shortly afterwards the duke of Medina Sidonia received orders to raise troops and concentrate supply vessels in the ports of Andalusia; and, in the north, eight large merchantmen and four pinnaces in the Cantabrian ports were embargoed to form a new squadron under the command of Spain's most experienced Atlantic seaman, Juan Martínez de Recalde.[17]

Because the leading figures in the enterprise had been personally involved, the Armada's destination was not committed to writing at this stage and remained a closely guarded secret. One may speculate, however, that the ultimate target was Kent, as it would be in 1588, with a preliminary descent on the south coast of Ireland (perhaps Waterford or Wexford, since many subsequent strategic papers designated these areas for attack).

Santa Cruz's strategy differed radically from that proposed by another formidable strategist in the service of Philip II, the duke of Parma, whom the king had also asked for his views on a military solution to the problem of England. The duke dispatched his appreciation of the situation from Flanders just as the plans to create a fleet in Spain were finalised, on 20 April 1586. It consisted of a 28-page letter, examining each of the various possibilities open to Philip II, and further details were entrusted to an Italian confidant of the duke, the engineer Giovanni Battista Piatti. Parma began by regretting the lack of secrecy surrounding the king's intentions: even ordinary soldiers and civilians in the Netherlands, he asserted, had begun to discuss openly the best way to invade England. Nevertheless, he believed that three basic precautions might still save the Enterprise. First, the king of Spain must have sole charge 'without placing any reliance on either the English themselves, or the assistance of other allies'. Second, the French must be prevented both from sending assistance to Elizabeth and from intervening in the Netherlands. Third, sufficient troops and resources must remain behind to defend the reconquered Netherlands against the Dutch once the assault force had left.

After meeting these conditions, Parma suggested detaching a force of 30,000 foot and 500 horse from the Army of Flanders and ferrying it across the Channel aboard a flotilla of sea-going barges to launch a surprise attack on England. Provided his precise intentions and destination remained a secret – 'given the number of troops we have to hand here, and the ease with which we can concentrate and embark them in the barges, and considering that we can ascertain, at any moment, the forces which Elizabeth has and can be expected to have, and that the crossing only takes 10 to 12 hours without a following wind (and 8 hours with one)' – the duke felt sure the invasion could be undertaken with a fair chance of success. 'The most suitable, close and accessible point of disembarkation', he concluded, 'is the coast between Dover and Margate', which would permit a rapid march on London. In essence, this represented the third alternative invasion strategy: a surprise assault.

Only two paragraphs of the letter addressed the possibility of naval support from Spain, and even then only in the context of 'the worst-case scenario': that somehow details of the plan had become known in England. In that case, Parma suggested, since Drake's exploits had forced the king to mobilise a fleet to protect the Atlantic, perhaps this new navy might 'either sail suddenly up here in order to assist and reinforce the troops who have already landed [in Kent] and keep open the seaway between the coasts of Flanders and England; or else – if your fleet is large, well-provided, well-armed and well-manned – it could create a diversion which will draw the English fleet away [from the straits of Dover]'. This corresponded to the second alternative strategy for invading England, the one later favoured by Napoleon: a naval decoy to facilitate an attack by a relatively unprotected invasion army.[18]

To some extent, the long delay before Parma's proposal arrived at court reduced its appeal. The king had asked for it in December 1585; yet Parma only complied four months later, entrusting it to a special messenger who travelled to court by a circuitous route via Burgundy and Italy. It therefore did not reach the royal cipher clerks until 20 June and four more days elapsed before the king's advisers had debriefed the messenger about the exact amount of shipping available in the ports of Flanders to ferry a major army across the open sea, and about the possible advantage of seeking a landing place closer to London. Then the king turned the dossier over to Don Juan de Zúñiga, already responsible for co-ordinating the preparations advocated by Santa Cruz, and he in turn seems to have consulted Bernardino de Escalante.

The archives of Philip's government are full of letters and memorials written by men like Escalante, who lived and worked far outside government circles. Born in Laredo, the son of a prominent naval captain, he had sailed to England with the king in 1554 and spent 14 months there before enlisting as a soldier in the Spanish army in the Netherlands. He later returned to Spain, went to university

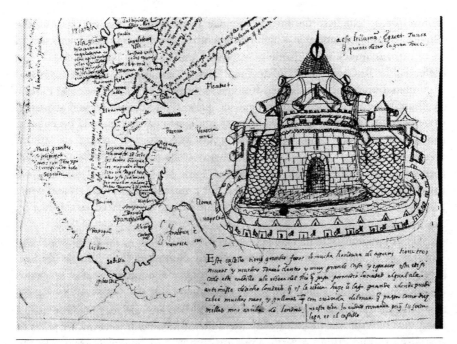

FIGURE 12   Suggestions as to how England might be invaded, presented in a memorial to the court in June 1586 by the priest and former soldier Bernardino de Escalante as a 'campaign map'. He dismisses the idea of expeditions via either Scotland or the Irish Sea, favouring instead a landing in southern Ireland to draw off the English navy while Philip's troops made a surprise landing in Kent before marching on London. The latter, Escalante avers, was defended only by 'E Greet Tuura' (the Tower of London).

and evidently studied geography as well as theology, for he later wrote an excellent treatise on navigation. After his ordination, he served as an inquisitor until in 1581 he became major-domo to the archbishop of Seville. Over the next 20 years, Escalante sent over 20 papers of advice, most of them concerned with the war against England, directly to the king's desk, as well as meeting with senior ministers to discuss his suggestions.[19]

In June 1586 Escalante reviewed the various alternative invasion strategies in detail and even drew a campaign map to illustrate them – the only cartographic effort concerning the Enterprise of England to survive (FIGURE 12). First (on the left of the map) he noted that a fleet from Lisbon might undertake a daring voyage through the North Atlantic directly to Scotland, where it would regroup before launching its main attack. 'The seas are high and dangerous', Escalante warned, 'but through Jesus Christ crucified everything is possible.' An attack into the Irish Sea might offer a second potential strategy, although the English navy, whose forces (labelled 'the enemy') appear in the map at the entrance to the English Channel, made this a high-risk operation too. No less dangerous would be a surprise attack from Flanders to Dover, and so on to London, which was defended by 'E Greet Tuura' (The Great Tower). Escalante therefore suggested a combination of the two distinct strategies advanced by Santa Cruz and Parma. A Grand Fleet of 120 galleons, galleasses, galleys, merchantmen and pinnaces, together with an army of 30,000 infantry and 2,000 cavalry, should be concentrated in Lisbon and launched against either Waterford in Ireland or Milford Haven in Wales. At the same time the Army of Flanders should be reinforced, first to tie down the English expeditionary force in Holland, and then to cross the Channel in small ships in preparation for a surprise march on London while Elizabeth's forces attempted to deal with the distant bridgehead established by the Armada.

This ingenious scheme, backed up by a wealth of detail on the political and physical geography of the British Isles, clearly convinced Don Juan de Zúñiga, because his own letter of advice to the king largely reiterated the plan proposed by Escalante. Zúñiga added only a few refinements. On the one hand, he argued that once the two beach-heads had been established and the seas made secure, a fleet of supply ships concentrated by the duke of Medina Sidonia in the ports of Andalusia should bring up further reinforcements and replenishments. On the other hand, he made some suggestions about Parma's options after the invasion. If London fell, the duke should create an interim administration pending the investiture of a suitable new ruler. 'Because of the cost of defending it' Spain would gain no advantage from the direct annexation of England, and so the newly conquered realm should be bestowed upon a friendly Catholic monarch. Zúñiga suggested Mary Stuart – but recommended that she should marry a dependable Catholic prince, such as Parma himself. If English resistance proved stronger than anticipated, however, the duke should use his presence on English soil to secure three key concessions. First, there must be complete toleration and freedom of worship for Catholics throughout the kingdom. Second, all English troops must be withdrawn from the Netherlands, and the places they garrisoned surrendered directly to Spain. Finally, England must pay a war-indemnity, and the invasion force should remain in Kent until it was received. With such high stakes, Zúñiga concluded, and with such a complex operation, it would be futile to attempt anything during the present campaigning season, so he suggested that the Enterprise of England should be launched in August or September 1587.[20]

The king seems to have made only one significant change to these suggestions when on 26 July 1586 he sent a 'master plan' to both Brussels and Lisbon commanding the concentration of forces for a dual assault on the Tudor state. Although this document has unfortunately not so far come to light, its contents can be deduced from subsequent correspondence between Brussels, Madrid,

Lisbon and Rome. A formidable Armada would sail from Lisbon in the summer of 1587 – one year later – carrying all available troops together with most of the equipment (above all a powerful siege train) needed for the land campaign, directly to Ireland. There it would put ashore assault troops and secure a beach-head (probably at Waterford), thus drawing off Elizabeth's naval forces and neutralising their potential for resistance. After some two months, however, the Armada would suddenly leave Ireland and make for the Channel. At that point, and not before, the main invasion force of 30,000 veterans from the Army of Flanders would embark on its secretly assembled flotilla of small ships and, under Parma's personal direction, leave the Netherlands for the coast of Kent while the Grand Fleet cruised off the North Foreland and secured local command of the sea. Parma's men, together with reinforcements and the siege train from the fleet, would then land near Margate, make a dash for London and seize the city – preferably with Elizabeth and her ministers still in it.[21]

One wonders whether Philip realised the enormous dangers posed by his hybrid plan. In retrospect, Santa Cruz's proposal contained much merit. The events of 1588 proved that, once they got their Armada to sea, the Spaniards experienced little difficulty in moving 60,000 tons of shipping from one end of the Channel to the other, despite repeated assaults upon it. And the Kinsale landing of 1601 showed that they could also secure and fortify a beach-head in southern Ireland. Likewise, Parma's concept of a surprise landing in Kent had much to recommend it: time and again, his troops had shown their mettle under his leadership, and the largely untrained English forces, taken by surprise, would probably have failed to withstand the Army of Flanders once it got ashore. The Armada's undoing ultimately arose from the decision to unite the fleet from Spain with the army from the Netherlands as an essential prelude to launching the invasion.

Why did he do it? Philip had participated in planning many victorious campaigns in the past, most notably the conquest of Portugal and the Azores between 1580 and 1583, and had seen active service in the campaigns of 1557 and 1558. He also possessed direct experience of the sea routes involved: in July 1554 he had sailed from Corunna to Southampton, his journey taking just one week, and five years later he had sailed back relatively easily from Flushing to Santander. He had also sailed three times between the Netherlands and England. But he remained essentially an armchair strategist: technical, tactical and operational considerations all remained a closed book. Moreover Philip refused to move closer to the action: he ignored suggestions that he should return to Lisbon in order to supervise the assembly of the fleet in person, so it took at least a week before Santa Cruz received a solution to each problem referred to the king (and between four and six weeks in Parma's case). More seriously, Philip normally remained ignorant of the problems that his commanders chose not to refer to him, or brought up later. Worse still, he declined to brief either of them properly: both received the master plan of July 1586 by mail (albeit Parma's copy went with the same messenger, Piatti, who had brought the duke's own suggestions to court). Neither could thus ask Philip to explain precisely how two large and totally independent forces, with operational bases separated by over 700 miles of ocean, could attain the accuracy of time and place necessary to accomplish their junction, or how the vulnerable and lightly armed troop transports to be collected in Flanders would be able to evade the Dutch and English warships stationed offshore to intercept and destroy them. Zúñiga, the only minister who possessed the authority and the knowledge to raise such objections, died in the autumn of 1586.[22]

Nevertheless Spanish public opinion at this time overwhelmingly supported the invasion of England as the only sure way to preserve the security of Spain, the Netherlands and the Americas. The duke of Medina Sidonia, who had spent most of his adult life superintending the departure of the convoys sailing from Seville to America, considered the solution to be self-evident. In a 10-folio memorandum, covering such basic matters as the urgent need for improved defences around the Caribbean ports and better-gunned escort vessels for the trading fleets, the duke (who little thought that he would eventually lead the Armada himself) believed the creation of a powerful navy to be indispensable for the nation's prosperity and security and urged 'that this should be set in hand at once, and in earnest, and let it be understood that it will not suffice simply to oppose what the English send: [our fleet] will need to go into the Channel'. The duke also recommended that 'in all parts – in Italy, as in Vizcaya, Guipúzcoa, Portugal and Andalusia – preparations and activity should be undertaken, because it will become known in England and will make them draw in their horns'. Spain's commercial community entirely agreed: the correspondents of the prominent banker Simón Ruiz all welcomed the news that a major fleet was being prepared against England, for they saw it as the only way to restore security to Spanish overseas trade; while the president of the council of the Indies, the minister responsible for New World affairs, likewise argued that only a direct strike against England would safeguard the Americas.[23]

The king agreed, and a stream of commands flowed from his desk to set in motion the plan adopted in July 1586. Orders went out for the new defensive squadrons raised in northern Spain to sail to Lisbon, and for troops to be raised all over Spain to man the new Armada, and for Naples and Sicily to send soldiers both by land along the 'Spanish Road' to reinforce Parma and by sea to Lisbon to join Santa Cruz. To transport the latter, and to convey stocks of artillery and munitions to Lisbon, Philip also commanded the embargo of suitable merchant ships and the addition of sundry galleys and four heavily-gunned galleasses from Naples to serve as escorts. He also began a diplomatic offensive designed to ensure that, at the crucial moment, no foreign power would raise a finger to save Elizabeth Tudor from his combined assault.[24]

## Sources

The early part of this chapter draws heavily upon Parker, *Philip II*, and Estal, 'Felipe II y su archivo hagiográfico de El Escorial', based on the 'Libros de entrega' of relics donated to the monastery by Philip II and his son. The genesis of the master plan for the Enterprise of England is taken from Parker, *Grand Strategy*, 179–92. On the troops sent to Flanders, see O'Donnell, *La fuerza de desembarco*; on those sent to Lisbon, see Gracia Rivas, *Los tercios*.

## Notes

1  Details from Estal, 'Felipe II', 207–9.
2  IVdeDJ 51/105, Vázquez to the king, and reply, 22 August 1583.
3  BPU MS Favre 30/73v, Philip II to Don Luis de Requeséns, 20 October 1573, copy of holograph original: 'Spero en Dios . . . que os dara mucha salud y vida, pues se empleara en su servicio y en el mío, que es lo mismo.'
4  *BMO*, III, 1006–7 and 1069–70, the king to Parma, 4 and 14 September 1587; *ibid.*, 1067–8, royal Instruction to Santa Cruz, 14 September 1587.
5  Quotations from Maura, 278–9; IVdeDJ 51/1, Vázquez to the king, and reply, 8 February 1591; and IVdeDJ 45/452, same to same, 5 February.
6  Quotations from IVdeDJ 53 *carpeta* 5, fo. 15, the king to Vázquez, 27 January 1576; and Maura, 38, the king to Medina Sidonia, 29 October 1578.
7  AS, Venice, *Senato: Dispacci Spagna*, 20/68–72, Lippomano to Venice, 14 April 1587 (partial precis in *CSPV*, 266).
8  IVdeDJ 61/130, Philip II to Pedro de Hoyo, April 1567; IVdeDJ 51/162, 180 and 181, Vázquez to Philip II and reply, 11 April and 15 October 1578, and 26 January 1581.
9  At least three documents associated with this early phase of the Enterprise of England have survived, entitled 'Razones que tratan de algunas cosas tocante al gran negocio de Inglaterra'. They are discussed in Lyell, 14–25. We cannot, however, accept Lyell's argument that the documents date from 1586–7: they must have been written before July 1584 because William of Orange is spoken of as still alive. See also the similar documents in *BMO*, I, 412–13 and AHN *OM* 3512/27–8.
10  *BMO*, I, 405–6, the king to Parma, 12 September 1583; and *ibid.*, 420–1, Parma's reply, 30 November 1583.
11  *BMO*, I, 478 and AGS *Estado* 946/85–8 and 103–4, Olivares to the king, 4 June and 13 and 28 July 1585; and 229, the king to Olivares, 22 August 1585.
12  The documentation is complex. AS, Florence, *Mediceo del Principato* 2636/123–4, Instruction to Luigi Dovara, 28 February 1585, sent to secure support from Pope Gregory XIII for a Spanish invasion of England. The initiative thus came from Tuscany but papal support formed the critical element.
13  See the report in *BMO*, I, 539, Licenciado Antolinez to the king, 14 November 1585; one man's belligerent reaction in AGS *GA* 176/160, Don Jorge Manrique to the court, 25 March (1586); and the sources on page 81 n. 12 above.
14  *BMO*, I, 536–7, 'Lo que se responde a Su Santidad'.
15  *BMO*, I, 566–7, Philip II to Santa Cruz, 26 January 1586; *ibid.*, 564, Santa Cruz to Philip II, 13 February 1586 (not 'January': see *BMO*, II, ix–x); *BMO*, II, 11–18, 'Relación de navíos' and letters from Santa Cruz to Philip II and Zúñiga, 13 February 1586; and

*BMO*, I, 566, Idiáquez to Santa Cruz, 26 February 1586 (again, not 'January': see *BMO*, II, ix–x).

16  *BMO*, II, 44–74, Santa Cruz to Philip II and to Idiáquez, enclosing his great *Relación*, 22 March 1586. The marquis showed commendable wisdom in keeping the proposed target to himself, for copies of his *Relación* fell into the hands of several foreign agents – including those of Venice, Urbino, France and, most dangerous of all, England: see Parker, *Grand Strategy*, 209–10.

17  *BMO*, I, 450–8, Santa Cruz's patent and instruction as Capitán-General del Mar Océano, 23 June 1584. The ships forming the squadron of Biscay were embargoed between 10 April and 7 May 1586 (AGS *CMC* 2a/1208) and Recalde was appointed to command them on 8 June (*BMO*, II, 179–80). Medina Sidonia's role in raising 6,000 troops to sail with Santa Cruz's Armada can be followed in Maura, 145–59.

18  *BMO*, II, 108–11, Parma to Philip II, 20 April 1586, and II, 195–6, 'Lo que dixo Juan Bautista Piata de palabra'.

19  See Casado Soto, *Discursos de Bernardino de Escalante*, 110–27, for Escalante's *discurso* of June 1586, composed at the Escorial; and 52, 79–80, 82, 147 and 157 for evidence of his 'hot-line' to the king and his ministers.

20  *BMO*, II, 212, *Parecer* of Don Juan de Zúñiga (June/July 1586). Zúñiga may, of course, have considered other papers of advice too, for several other 'experts' sent their opinions to the king: see, for example, the copies of four anonymous discourses written in 1586 'Sopra l'impresa d'Inghilterra' preserved in BAV UL 854/225–57v, 258–85, 286–8v and 289–303.

21  Although no copy of the master plan has yet come to light, its existence is clearly indicated in *BMO*, II, 333, Philip II to Parma, 1 September 1586: 'On 26 July I replied at length and in detail to the letter brought by Giovanni Battista Piatti, as I believe you will have seen before receiving this'; and *ibid.*, 387, Parma to Philip II, 30 October 1586, replying to 'your royal letter of 26 July which he [Piatti] brought me'. In its absence, the *traza* (plan) has been reconstructed from the following: *BMO*, II, 387–8, Parma to Philip II, 30 October 1586; 471–2, royal reply of 17 December 1586; 535–6, Parma to Philip II, 17 January 1587; and 624, Idiáquez to Medina Sidonia, 28 February 1587.

22  In their defence, others besides Philip and his entourage at this stage also advocated a junction between a fleet from Spain and troops from Flanders as the prelude to invading England, and saw no problem: see, for example, BAV *UL* 854/286–8v, 'Discorso sopra la guerra d'Inghilterra' (in Spanish), and *BMO*, II, 438–9, Juan del Águila to Philip II, 29 November 1586.

23  Library of Congress, Manuscript Division, Sir Francis Drake Collection #3, Medina Sidonia to Philip II, 25 October 1586, minute, point 13; Lapèyre, *Les Ruiz*, 422–3; and *Reivindicación*, 308, two letters written by the president of the council of the Indies to the king in March 1586. See also the bellicose views of Jean Richardot in the Netherlands, *CCG*, XII, 161, letter to Granvelle, 30 March 1586.

24  AGS *Estado* 1261/87, the king to his governor of Milan, 7 August 1586, ordering him to send Spanish troops to Flanders. The king ordered the towns of Spain to raise troops on 7 October 1586 (AGS *GA* 189/119 and replies fos 120–68), and the viceroys of Naples and Sicily to dispatch galleasses, artillery and troops 'to chase the pirates from the coasts of Portugal and make safe the seas around us' on 12 November: *BMO*, II, 414.

# 7

## Phoney war

In the event, Elizabeth herself removed a major diplomatic obstacle from Philip's path, for on 18 February 1587 her officials executed Mary queen of Scots.

Perhaps they had no alternative. Since 1580 conspiracies against Elizabeth had become almost incessant, each aimed at placing Mary Stuart on the Tudors' throne. A vicious circle became established: with so many plots afoot, Mary was too dangerous for Elizabeth to set at liberty; and yet, in captivity, plots offered Mary her only chance of freedom. The exiled queen, detained by her cousin in a succession of draughty castles with little opportunity for exercise, entertainment or outside recreation, gradually allowed intrigue and conspiracy to become her principal pastimes. In the summer of 1586, when Anthony Babington, a young English Catholic who had once served in Mary's household, hatched a new plot she rashly expressed her support in writing. Babington's plan involved the assassination of Elizabeth as a prelude to the invasion of a liberating Catholic army. From the first, Mary's correspondence had been intercepted and copied; Babington was unequivocally implicated and arrested in August. Soon after, Mary was herself placed under arrest, moved to the castle of Fotheringhay near Northampton, and there tried for treason. The verdict was inescapable.

In assessing the tangled sequence of events that followed, it is important to remember the fundamental insecurity of the Elizabethan regime. The queen, now over 50, could not be expected to live for ever, and she had no heir except Mary. It is true that in theory parliamentary statutes barred a Stuart succession, but similar statutes had once excluded both Mary Tudor and Elizabeth herself. In each case they had been overthrown without difficulty upon the death of the monarch who passed them. Most of those who influenced English politics in 1586 could still remember these earlier events. Some, indeed, had fled the country during the reign of Mary lest their Protestant sympathies led them to the scaffold. They could not have expected to fare any better under a new Catholic regime.

A few took a yet more pessimistic view. Some of Elizabeth's advisers had always believed in the existence of an international Catholic conspiracy dedicated to the extirpation of Protestantism in England. After the Ridolfi plot their opinion gained greater credence, sometimes even from the queen, and every new setback suffered by the Protestant cause abroad and every new plot detected by Elizabeth's spies at home increased the fears of the alarmists that a concerted assault by the Catholic powers was imminent. In 1586 no one could be sure how much (if any) foreign support Babington had secured. In August, as a precaution, John Hawkins took 18 warships to reconnoitre the coasts of Spain and Portugal, where naval preparations were reported to be afoot. During his three-month cruise Hawkins took prisoners who confirmed the worst: Spain was actively gearing up for a huge invasion.

Playing upon these fears, fanned by rumours (possibly invented) of a new plot against Elizabeth involving the French, the queen's ultra-Protestant councillors eventually persuaded her to sign a warrant condemning Mary Stuart to death. But she would not agree to send it to Fotheringhay. At last her worried advisers boldly took the decision out of her hands, and dispatched one of their number, the militantly anti-Catholic William Davidson, to ride to Northamptonshire with the signed warrant and personally supervise the immediate execution of his mistress's 'bosom-serpent'. Mary died with dignity on 18 February and the plots expired with her.

Some considered that Mr Davidson had done a good day's work for the Protestant cause, but it was less apparent at the time. As soon as she heard the news, Elizabeth's thoughts turned to the potentially catastrophic repercussions of the deed. She had encompassed the death of a former queen of Scotland and France who was not her subject, an anointed ruler who was the mother of James VI of Scotland, the cousin of Henry duke of Guise, leader of the French Catholic League, and the sister-in-law of both Henry III and Philip II (through his third wife, Elisabeth de Valois, who had also been Mary's playmate). The initial French reaction to news of Mary's death was alarming. In Rouen, angry mobs seized English ships and goods; in Paris, outraged clerics delivered inflammatory sermons calling for revenge, and exhibited pictures outside their churches luridly portraying the atrocities committed against English Catholics by the Elizabethan regime. In an attempt to appease these passions, the queen had William Davidson tried, clapped in the Tower, fined heavily and threatened with death, though in the event he remained in prison for just 18 months and the fine was waived. Elizabeth also forbade her principal minister, Lord Burghley, to come to court for four weeks and for the next four months shouted abuse whenever she caught sight of him. Other councillors involved in Mary's execution had a difficult time.

It was not an atmosphere conducive to the rational formulation of foreign policy, yet never had diplomatic dexterity been more essential to England's survival. Philip II's agents were everywhere, capitalising to the utmost upon the 'illegal' execution of Mary Stuart, and using it to justify their master's maturing plans to extirpate the tyrannous 'English Jezebel'. In February 1587 the Venetian ambassador in Madrid noted in wonderment that 'the Spaniards are moving towards their great object in various ways and from many sides, no less by diplomacy than by preparations for war, and even by a union of the two'.

At first not everything went Philip II's way. In the Mediterranean his possessions lay exposed to attack from the forces of Islam while Spain's army and fleet were tied down in the Atlantic theatre. So Spanish envoys duly travelled to Istanbul, capital of the Ottoman empire, with orders to negotiate an extension of the armistice between the Turks and Spaniards. English diplomacy swiftly rose to the occasion. The queen's unofficial ambassador in Istanbul, William Harborne, persuaded the sultan that nothing would be gained from a deal with Spain and Philip's agents went away empty-handed. So, although the Turks did not launch another attack in 1587 or 1588, the government in Madrid remained fearful that they might.[1]

Elizabeth's statesmanship also succeeded in Scotland. Matters here were severely complicated by the phantom will of Mary queen of Scots, who in May 1586 had written to the Spanish ambassador in Paris that she intended to 'cede and grant by will my right to the succession of this crown to the king, your master'. In all probability she never made the will (although Philip II ransacked the archives of Rome, Paris and Simancas to find some trace of it), but Elizabeth's agents intercepted Mary's letter describing it and sent a copy to James VI. That young man, now aged 20, realising that his mother's action threatened to disinherit him from his Scottish kingdom and undermined his expectation of succeeding eventually to the English crown, made clear his support for Elizabeth. Even Mary's execution failed to alienate him. Although he made a flurry of protests he continued to pocket his annual English subsidy of £4,000, and later imprisoned a Spanish envoy sent to woo him.

The loyalty of some of James's subjects seemed less sure, however. Rumours of pro-Spanish sentiment in Scotland alarmed Elizabeth so much that in September 1587 she created an army of 6,000 foot and 400 horse on the border and kept it there for almost a year. In spring 1588 the Catholic Lord Maxwell began a rebellion in south-west Scotland with the declared intention of providing the Spaniards with a base (King James rode out to suppress it in person); and in August, with the Armada off the Firth of Forth, alarming reports reached York that some Scottish border lords 'have said openly [that] so soon as they shall hear that the Spaniards be landed in any part of Scotland, they will ride straight into England, though the king say no'.[2]

English and Spanish diplomats also clashed in France. Following the treaty of Nemours, the Catholic League took possession of several strategic towns with Henry III's permission. Their leader, the duke of Guise, also held numerous strongholds in the provinces of Champagne and Burgundy. All these places lay in the east of France, however. So in April 1587 Guise's cousin, the duke of Aumâle, seized three towns in Picardy, near the frontier with the Netherlands, and replaced the royal garrisons with League troops; but he failed to capture the principal objective, the port of Boulogne. Earlier in the year a royalist spy in Guise's household had overheard a conversation about the need 'for some way to take the town of Boulogne, which was said to be necessary for them to receive and shelter the reinforcements they were expecting from Spain'. He passed the information on and alerted the garrison of Boulogne, which refused to admit Aumâle and his men. In June, to encourage this welcome spirit of independence, Lord Howard led part of the English navy to Boulogne and offered any necessary assistance.

Elizabeth also provided financial support to the Huguenots, sending money to raise German troops to fight for Henry of Navarre in France. All through the spring of 1587 rumours of their approach circulated, detaining both the duke of Guise and a detachment of the Army of Flanders in the east to resist them. When 11,000 German mercenaries finally crossed the Rhine in August, the Catholic army easily outmanoeuvred them and inflicted a sharp defeat before they could join forces with Navarre. However, their distracting presence kept Guise away from Picardy, and although he retained control of the places seized in April his troops again failed to take Boulogne. So in spite of spending over £50,000 in subsidies to the League in 1587, and sending a small army in its support, Philip II failed to gain a safe Channel port as a potential refuge for his fleet. It proved a crucial defect. Had the Spaniards possessed Boulogne in 1588, the Armada campaign might have had a very different outcome.

The cost of this, and of all the other preparations required for the invasion of England, severely strained Philip II's treasury, forcing the king to introduce stringent economies elsewhere. He turned down a plan by the council of the Indies in September 1586 to improve the defences of the Caribbean on the grounds that: 'As you can imagine, no one resents the damage [done by the English] more than I do, and no one desires more to repair it, if only there was a way to execute it as we wish; but your plans create a lot of problems, and the biggest one is the lack of money with which to pay for it all.' The king concluded with the hope that future plans would be accompanied by concrete suggestions about how they might be financed. The council of Portugal, for its part, called off a planned attack on the troublesome sultanate of Atjeh in Sumatra and a proposal to build a fortress at Mombasa in east Africa: the reason given for both was the need to concentrate all resources on the 'Enterprise of England'.[3] In March 1586 Santa Cruz had put the total cost of the 'Enterprise' at four million ducats (roughly £1 million), but the decision to involve Parma's army as well virtually doubled this figure. By the beginning of 1587 a group of the king's senior advisers estimated that 'seven million ducats will be needed to implement plans made, and to be made, for this year'. In the event, all this money and more was spent: as the king observed with justifiable pride to Parma in October 1587: 'as for money, you will see that the five million that has been sent you this year exceeds anything that has been sent in living memory'.[4]

The rising cost of the venture increased the king's anxiety to secure the financial contribution promised by Sixtus V. By the spring of 1586 the wily pontiff had already come to regret his earlier offer to pay one-third of the total, and he argued to the Spanish ambassador in Rome that the papal contribution was superfluous since the king would have to invade England anyway 'in order to avenge the insults done him; on account of the advantage this would provide in dealing with Holland; and because he cannot by any other means safeguard his trade with the Indies'. Ambassador Olivares later speculated that it was the pope's Neapolitan upbringing which made him always see 'vengeance and insults' as the mainspring of international affairs. Eventually agreement was reached on a figure of one million ducats, although the pope expressed misgivings that, if paid in advance, the king might use it for some other purpose. He finally agreed that the papal bounty would become payable as soon as confirmation reached Rome that the Armada had landed in England.[5]

This distrust seems to have aroused the king's own suspicions: on the back of the letter Philip ruminated on the risk that should Sixtus die unexpectedly, his successor might refuse to honour the commitment. In November 1586 these doubts became demands: he instructed Ambassador Olivares that all the cardinals must forthwith swear that, in the event of Sixtus's death, should they be elected pope they would honour his promise to pay. The king acknowledged the risk that this involved: 'Even though my desire to arrange this may lead to a breach of secrecy, because it may require a meeting of the college of cardinals, nonetheless it is a point of such importance that it should not be forgotten. Because if we are not protected, we may find ourselves deceived.'

Eventually Olivares resolved all the difficulties and the papal secretary of state signed an absolute undertaking to pay one million ducats to Ambassador Olivares once the Armada had landed. On 29 July 1587, two Roman bankers received a special deposit of one million ducats in gold from the papal treasury, payable as soon as a public notary verified that the invasion had taken place. On the same day, Sixtus also agreed on the terms for the government of England after the conquest: Philip would nominate, subject to papal approval and investiture, a ruler pledged to restore and uphold the Catholic faith. Until then, the administration of England would be entrusted to Cardinal Allen, superior of the English College at Douai, assisted both by the members of the various religious orders aboard the Armada and with Parma's army, and by local Catholics. Together they would superintend the restoration to the Church of all lands and rights lost at the Reformation.

No doubt the pope felt unenthusiastic about these arrangements, but he now had no choice. With Mary Stuart dead, and France paralysed by civil war, a Catholic restoration in England depended utterly upon the good offices of Philip II. For the king, too, the battle of wills with Sixtus involved losses as well as gains. He had devoted countless hours to these tortuous negotiations – his correspondence with Rome bears far more holograph annotations than his correspondence with Flanders – yet, even so, the deposited money was only available for a limited time. If no news had been received by November 1587, all would go back to the papal vaults.[6]

In other ways, too, the limited credit thus obtained did not offset a corresponding debit. Negotiations with the papacy had publicised the whole matter and, within a matter of weeks, much of the secrecy about the Armada evaporated when the Dutch captured and interrogated Oda Colonna, nephew of one of the cardinals who (thanks to Philip's anxieties) had been given full details of the plan. Colonna speedily revealed everything he knew about the Armada: its detailed financing, its organisation, and above all its general destination and its timing.

Incredibly, nobody believed him. Although the Dutch sent a transcript of Colonna's interrogation to England at once, no one at Elizabeth's court seems to have grasped its significance until May 1588 – five months later – when Walsingham at last ordered further questioning.[7] Part of the explanation for this strange oversight lay in the dilemma experienced by all governments in all ages: how to distinguish true from false intelligence. In Colonna's case the problem was exacerbated by the fact that his information expressly contradicted the data gathered by Elizabeth's ambassador in Paris, Sir Edward Stafford.

On the surface Stafford boasted superb qualifications, both social and professional, for England's foremost diplomatic posting: his late step-mother, Mary Boleyn, had been Elizabeth's aunt; his mother served as lady-in-waiting to the queen; his brother-in-law, Howard of Effingham, was both admiral of England and a Privy Councillor. Furthermore he had cut his diplomatic teeth in France during the negotiations for the queen's marriage to the duke of Anjou. His appointment as ambassador to the French court in 1583 therefore came as no surprise. Stafford's only real disadvantage lay in his poverty. He complained several times that he lacked funds to discharge his responsibilities properly and asked the queen to lend him money even if she could not afford to pay his salary; but she gave him no satisfaction and he ran up huge debts. He squandered not only own money but also a substantial sum sent to him by the queen to distribute among her French supporters. In January 1587, desperate for money, Stafford approached Don Bernardino de Mendoza, now Philip's ambassador in Paris, and declared himself ready to serve Spain in any way possible short of conniving at the queen's death in return for cash.

For the next 18 months he proved as good as his word, repeatedly revealing to Mendoza confidential information received from England and sending a stream of false information on Spain's pacific intentions back to London. In May 1588 he suggested that the Armada was aimed at Algiers; in June he told Walsingham that he thought the Armada would sail for the Indies; in mid-July he asserted that bets of 6:1 were being made in Paris that the Armada would never reach the

Channel; and on 31 July, with the Grand Fleet off the Lizard, Stafford still insisted that it remained at Corunna, too damaged ever to leave!

Elizabeth thus had to balance the reassuring news received from Stafford against the alarmist revelations of Colonna, and against the more sober – but equally alarming – reports of Philip's military, naval and diplomatic preparations sent by Walsingham's spies in Portugal, Spain and Italy. Even though few besides Colonna asserted unequivocally that the sole target was England, enough suspicion existed to justify a number of defensive measures. Between 1585 and 1588 the Navy Board built or purchased 16 new vessels and repaired the rest, until 'there is never a one of them that knows what a leak means', and also embargoed all ships in English ports. From these, special commissioners chose 64 armed merchantmen, 33 supply vessels and 43 private pinnaces to serve with the queen's ships in case of need. At the same time repairs to the fortifications along the south coast resumed, and orders went out to disarm known Catholics.

To hedge her bets, Elizabeth also opened negotiations with Philip II through the duke of Parma. No sooner had the queen signed the treaty of Nonsuch in August 1585 than she sent an envoy to Flanders explaining her action and exploring the possibility of reaching some accommodation, and from the summer of 1586 she allowed informal talks to take place at the duke's headquarters.[8]

Then, early in 1587, for reasons that remain obscure, Elizabeth changed her mind and decided upon a far more aggressive measure. For some months Sir Francis Drake had been seeking backers in England and the Netherlands for a new naval expedition 'to employ in a voyage to assist the king of Portugal, Dom Antonio, or on some other service'; now, on 25 March 1587, the queen ordered him to take his fleet to sea 'for the honor and safety of our realms'. What exactly did this mean? No written orders appear to have been issued for the voyage, but Drake's subsequent actions suggest that he had been told to attack the ports where Philip's fleet was being assembled, to do as much damage as he could and to keep the various parts of the Armada from joining forces. To this end Elizabeth provided six warships to reinforce the vessels already held in readiness by Drake, his friends (including Hawkins, Winter and the lord admiral) and the London merchants.

Drake galloped straight to Dover and sailed immediately for Plymouth with the queen's ships, joining the contingent from London *en route*. On 12 April, less than three weeks after receiving his commission, he led his fleet of 16 ships and seven pinnaces out of Plymouth Sound. As his sails filled with a welcome 'Protestant wind', Drake's parting message to Burghley maintained the ambiguity of his purpose: 'The wind commands me away: our ship is under sail, God grant we may so live in His fear as the enemy may have cause to say that God doth fight for her Majesty as well abroad as at home.'[9]

He left in the nick of time. In the first place, the simultaneous arrival in London of a soothing message from Stafford and an official negotiator from

Parma led the queen to change her mind only a week after Drake had sailed. Now she expressly forbade him to 'enter forcibly into any of the king's ports or havens, or to offer violence to any of his towns or shipping within harbouring, or to do any act of hostility upon the land'. A pinnace bearing the message sped after the fleet. In the second place, in spite of every attempt to prevent the news leaving England, Ambassador Stafford in Paris got wind of Drake's intended destination and immediately told Mendoza. Neither message arrived in time: the queen's pinnace never caught up with Drake, and although Mendoza's courier completed the journey from Paris to Madrid in only 11 days, he did not arrive until 30 April. It was too late. The previous evening, as the population of Cadiz watched an acrobat perform in the main square, Drake and his powerful fleet entered the harbour.

Preparations for the Armada had by then reached a critical stage. Long-term stockpiling of provisions was in a particularly delicate state, for sixteenth-century Europe enjoyed few food surpluses, and supplies of the magnitude required might be difficult to obtain at any price should the notice given be too short. This consideration was balanced by the fact that, in an age without tin cans or freezers, all types of food enjoyed a short shelf-life. Orders for biscuit and salt meat had been placed with contractors at Alicante, Cartagena and Malaga: to meet them 40 new biscuit ovens had to be built at Malaga alone. A contract was signed with Milan for a large consignment of rice, while grain purchases in Spain, which was already experiencing a shortage, drove up market prices. Nearly 200 tons of cheese came from the Baltic, transported in 20 Hamburg hulks. Other vessels from northern Europe brought essential naval supplies – pitch, cordage, timber and sailcloth – via the 'northabout' route around the British Isles, to avoid interception by the queen's ships in the English Channel.

Meanwhile Philip's agents were negotiating bulk contracts for the supply of military equipment. In Seville the duke of Medina Sidonia ordered a large number of campaign tents, and 12,000 sets of shoes, leather canteens and knapsacks for the invasion troops. The same town later supplied picks, shovels and gabions for the pioneers. The new forces received so many weapons that, according to the secretary of state for war, 'not a single arquebus, pike or musket is left in all Spain' and new supplies had to be ordered from Italy. Troops, too, were withdrawn from the trained garrisons of Naples and Sicily, and raw recruits were sent by galley from Spain to take their places.

The preparation of the fleet itself was also proceeding apace. To reinforce the royal flotillas already assembled at Cadiz, the Basque ports and Lisbon, the king's officers embargoed private merchantmen throughout the Iberian world. The viceroy of Sicily commandeered the *Trinidad Valencera* from Venice, the *Rata Santa María Encoronada* from Genoa, the *Anunciada* and *San Juan de Sicilia* from Ragusa, and the *Juliana* in December 1586. The duke of Medina Sidonia embargoed the *Gran Grifón* from Rostock, along with other Baltic hulks, in March 1587. The *St Andrew* of Dundee, a Scottish trader suspected of carrying contraband, was confiscated at Malaga at the same time, as was the English *Charity* at Gibraltar.[10]

The Armada had not yet become a coherent force, however, and most of its scattered component parts remained highly vulnerable to attack. Moreover, the need to keep the main fleet together in Lisbon seriously compromised the ability of all other coastal regions to defend themselves. No one knew this better than Drake. He also knew that, although the Armada would eventually sail from Lisbon, the main activity for the time being centred on Spain's great southern port, which possessed extensive facilities for equipping and victualling the Indies fleets. With its wide entrance, Cadiz may have been less secure than Lisbon, but it boasted forts, artillery and a squadron of nine galleys. Trusting in their protection, ships lay crowded at anchor between the seaward peninsula, upon which the town stood, and the mouth of the Guadalquivir, whence supplies could be brought down from Seville. By the end of April 1587 nearly 60 vessels lay in harbour: hulks and coasters loading for Lisbon, the tuna fishing fleet, and merchantmen of all types from small caravels to a 700-ton Genoese carrack about to depart for Italy with a cargo of cochineal, leather and wool. This motley and disorganised collection of ships and stores was the target, on 29 April, of England's pre-emptive strike.

Drake's fleet, flying no colours until the last moment to escape identification, entered the outer haven and in less than a day looted or destroyed two dozen Spanish ships, some of them large and powerful, together with considerable quantities of food, munitions and stores destined for the Armada. Only the prompt arrival of the duke of Medina Sidonia with a strong body of militiamen prevented the English from advancing into the inner harbour of Cadiz and capturing the town (as they would do in 1596). By the afternoon of 30 April the duke commanded some 6,000 troops in defence of the town, and set up new shore batteries which began to engage the intruders, though only the English vice-flagship *Lion* seems to have suffered much damage. Having liberally resupplied his fleet with provisions taken from the enemy, Drake led his fleet safely out to sea again on 1 May, a remarkable navigational feat, given the hazards of Cadiz Bay.

Its next destination at first remained a mystery, and Medina Sidonia sent off fast caravels and dispatch riders to warn his compatriots elsewhere of possible danger: to the Canaries, to Lisbon, to the king. He even sent one of his own ships to the Caribbean with orders for the treasure fleet, which was assembling for the Atlantic crossing back to Seville, to remain in Havana until further notice. Drake had other plans, however. After an unsuccessful attempt to catch Recalde's Biscayan squadron on the high seas, and an abortive landing at Lagos on the Algarve coast, the troops aboard his fleet captured the castle and harbour of

Sagres, near Cape St Vincent, on 5 May, desecrating churches and again replenishing their supplies.

Drake now interdicted the Armada's supply route between Andalusia and Lisbon, capturing or sinking virtually all shipping that tried to run the gauntlet of the English blockade. 'It hath pleased God', he informed Walsingham smugly on 27 May:

> that we have taken forts, ships, barks, carvels and divers other vessels more than a hundred, most laden, some with oars for galleys, planks and timber for ships and pinnaces, hoops and pipe-staves for cask, with many other provisions for this great army . . . All [of this] I commanded to be consumed into smoke and ashes by fire, which will be unto the king no small waste of his provisions, besides the want of his barks.[11]

At this point Drake apparently intended to stay off Cape St Vincent until ordered to do otherwise, and begged for reinforcements; but disease suddenly began to decimate his crews and a few days later he decided to abandon his station and head for the Azores instead. Many of the merchant ships, and also the damaged *Lion*, seized the opportunity to return home – much to Drake's fury – but on 19 June, off the island of São Miguel, the rest of his fleet captured the royal carrack *São Phelipe*, which had wintered in Mozambique and was travelling home alone. Drake brought her, and her cargo later valued at £140,000, triumphantly into Plymouth on 7 July.

It was a bitter blow, but the government of Philip II worked hard both to assess and to limit the effects of all this damage. Certainly the loss of 24 ships was a serious matter – many of the vessels that eventually sailed with the Armada were inferior in quality to those lost at Cadiz – and the destruction of stores (especially, as Drake had noted, the barrel hoops and staves) also proved tiresome. Nevertheless, more than enough of everything already existed to supply a formidable navy, and the build-up of ships, men and munitions continued apace. Recalde brought the 12 big vessels of his Biscayan squadron into Lisbon in May, while the veteran *tercio* of Sicily, stranded at Gibraltar by the English presence off Cape St Vincent, marched overland to join the fleet in July.

Philip and his advisers nevertheless could not help wondering whether Drake's raid might not form part of some larger enterprise. They therefore ordered the immediate construction of fortifications along the coasts of Spain and the Caribbean, and decided to raise 20,000 more troops. Once they heard of his departure for the Azores, their concerns turned to the security of the fleets scheduled to arrive from Asia and America. Medina Sidonia had warned the New World convoy to stay put, but the king desperately needed the treasure it carried to pay for his military and naval preparations, and in any case the ships due to arrive from India still knew nothing of Drake's presence. Philip therefore reluctantly decided that the attack on England would have to be postponed.

Instead, Santa Cruz and Recalde were ordered to lead their ships to the Azores and wait there until the transatlantic *flotas* arrived. On 16 July they led an impressive fleet of 37 fighting ships and 6,000 men down the Tagus. Three days later, a convoy of 106 vessels left Havana carrying treasure and trade goods worth 16 million ducats, and reached the safety of Santa Cruz's protective escort on 26 August. The marquis promptly brought them back to Seville, leaving Recalde with his squadron to assist any stragglers. In the event, Santa Cruz did not return to Lisbon until 28 September; Recalde with one more carrack not until 10 October.

The rejoicing occasioned by these impressive feats of co-ordination ended the panic that had gripped much of the Iberian peninsula during the summer. The foreign ambassadors at the court of Spain had filled one report after another with rumours about the exploits of 'el Draque', speculation on what he might do next, and criticisms of the government's ineffective response. According to the Mantuan ambassador, on one occasion the king 'swore by the life of the prince his son that he would be revenged, and having heard how people talked in Madrid about his delay in getting his fleet to sea, exclaimed "So now they have lost respect for me even in Madrid, and say that all the harm that Drake has done and is still doing arises from my slothfulness"'. Meanwhile, Lisbon erupted with anti-Spanish sentiment. Many Portuguese complained that their new masters 'wanted to take away the cream of all that was good in Portugal', noting that no such disaster had occurred under Philip's predecessors, and muttering that the Spaniards in Lisbon seemed completely unaffected, 'going to their bull-fights and playing their games as if nothing had happened'.[12]

This anecdote, even if true, reflected no more than an attempt to put on a brave face. Everyone realised that Drake's raid had changed the nature of the conflict with England. On the tactical level, since a state of war now clearly existed with Elizabeth, Philip decreed that English seamen captured by his ships should no longer be treated as pirates (until this point their captains, masters and pilots had been beheaded, and their crews sent to the galleys).[13] On the strategic level, the need for a direct assault on England seemed more pressing than ever. In the words of Philip's senior foreign policy adviser, 'with the English established in Holland and Zealand, together with their infestation of the Americas and the high seas, it seems that defensive measures cannot deal with everything. Rather, it obliges us to put their house to the torch' in order to force them to withdraw from 'the Netherlands, that voracious monster which gobbles up the troops and treasure of Spain.' Meanwhile a prominent councillor of war delivered a similarly belligerent message to the papal nuncio in Madrid in the wake of the Cadiz raid: the 'Enterprise of England', he asserted, remained essential to assure the safety of the fleets sailing between Spain and the Americas 'and also for [the king's] reputation, to avoid being subjected every day to similar accidents like this one'.[14] But how could these goals now be achieved?

## Sources

Parker, *Grand Strategy*, chapters 5–6, offers an overview of Philip II's foreign policy during the 1580s. For more detail on events in France, see Dickerman, 'A neglected aspect of the Spanish Armada'; and de Lamar Jensen, 'Franco-Spanish diplomacy and the Armada' in Carter, *From the Renaissance to the Counter-Reformation*. For the diplomatic contest in Istanbul, see Pears, 'The Spanish Armada and the Ottoman Porte'; Rawlinson, 'The embassy of William Harborne to Constantinople, 1583–8'; and Skilliter, 'The Hispano-Ottoman armistice of 1581'.

Read, *Mr Secretary Walsingham*, chapters 12–14, still provides the best account of the plots against Elizabeth. On Philip II and the Stuart claim, see de Lamar Jensen, 'The phantom will of Mary queen of Scots'; and Rodríguez-Salgado, 'The Anglo-Spanish war'. On Spain's leading Scottish supporter, who had actively sought foreign aid for his designs since 1583, see Brown, 'The making of a *politique*'. On Elizabeth's mobilisation, see Pollitt, 'Bureaucracy and the Armada'; Nolan, 'The muster of 1588'; and Gerson, 'The English recusants and the Spanish Armada'. For her biggest security risk, see Leimon and Parker, 'Treason and plot in Elizabethan England'.

*BMO*, III, xxix–xlvi currently offers the best description and evaluation of the Cadiz raid, though see also Kelsey, *Sir Francis Drake*, chapter 10. Corbett, *Spanish War*, 97–206, prints a useful selection of English documents; William Borough's chart of Cadiz Bay shows the shore batteries and their damage to the *Lion*: PRO *MPF* 318.

## Notes

1  See the fears of the Knights of Malta, who had been on 'red alert' against a Turkish threat throughout the spring of 1588, in AGS *Estado* 1089/288, grand master to the king, 16 June 1588.

2  Owen, *Calendar of the Manuscripts of the . . . Marquess of Bath*, 84–5, Elizabeth to Shrewsbury, 3 November 1587; and Huntington Library, San Marino, HA 30881/87v–88 and 120, Lord Huntingdon to Privy Council, 23 June and 11 August 1588 OS.

3  Heredia Herrera, *Catálogo de las consultas del consejo de Indias*, 597, royal apostil to a *consulta* dated 3 September 1586; Cunha Rivara, *Arquivo Português Oriental*, 130–1 and 146, Philip II to viceroy of India, 23 February and 14 March 1588.

4  The grand duke of Tuscany, when he first raised the idea of an 'Enterprise' early in February 1585, estimated that the cost to the king (above his normal expenses) would be 3.25 million ducats (AS, Florence, *Mediceo del Principato* 2636/124, Instruction to Dovara). The figure of seven million (two million for the fleet and the rest for the Army of Flanders) was given two years later by a special committee appointed by Philip II: IVdeDJ 101/99–104, papers dated 31 January – 5 February 1587. By 1588 the Armada cost 30,000 ducats a day and the Army of Flanders a further 15,000: see Parker, *Grand Strategy*, 198.

5  *BMO*, II, 26–7, 329 and 345, Olivares to Philip II, 24 February, 29 August and 9 September 1586. The pope had offered Philip a choice on the 'trigger' for payment: confirmation *either* that the Armada had left Lisbon, *or* that the army had landed in England; the king opted for the latter, evidently believing it more likely that Parma would get ashore somehow than that Santa Cruz would ever leave port again (*BMO*, II, 420, Philip to Olivares, 18 November 1586). His error cost him one million ducats.

6   *BMO*, II, 420–1, Philip II to Olivares, 18–19 November 1586; and AGS *Estado* 949/86, declaration of G. A. Pinelli and G. Gentili, 29 July 1587. Meyer, *England and the Catholic Church under Queen Elizabeth*, 520–3, printed the treaty of the same date from the copy in the Vatican archives. The majority of the correspondence in AGS *Estado* 946–9 concerns the 'Empresa', and many letters bear lengthy comments or corrections by the king.

7   See PRO *SP* 84/19/151–2v, Colonna's confession, forwarded by Maurice of Nassau to Walsingham on 9 December 1587 (and the summary of this letter at *CSPF*, XXI, part 3, 448–9); and BL Cotton Vespasian Cviii/95, Walsingham to Leicester, 5 May 1588.

8   Details in *CSPF*, XIX, 671–3 (mission of Sir John Smyth to Parma); and XXI, part 4, 145ff ('Compendium' of Andrés de Loo).

9   Drake's original commission to command the fleet, dated 15 March OS, is at West Devon County Record Office, Plymouth, PCM 1963 37/15. No copy of his Instructions seems to have survived, if indeed the queen ever committed them to paper, but their contents can be deduced from her subsequent letter countermanding them: see Hopper, *Sir Francis Drake's Memorable Service against the Spaniards in 1587*, 28–9, Elizabeth to Drake, 9 April 1587 OS.

10  Details from the records in AGS *CS* 2a/280 for each ship hired for the Armada. On the *Caridad Inglesa* and the *San Andrés Escocés*, see also AGS *GA* 203/123–4.

11  Corbett, *Spanish War*, 131, Drake to Walsingham, 17 May 1587 OS.

12  AS, Mantua, *Archivio Gonzaga* 600a, unfol., Cavriano to the duke, 27 May 1587; Roiz Soares, *Memorial*, 238. Apart from Mantua, good examples of the ambassadors' fixation with Drake during the summer of 1587 may be found in *CSPV*, AS, Genoa, *Archivio Segreto* 2418/3, and AS, Florence, *Mediceo del Principato* 4918.

13  *BMO*, III, 380 and 411, *consulta* of the council of war on 19 May 1587, royal resolution on the 23rd.

14  Maura, 167, Idiáquez to Medina Sidonia, 28 February 1587; ASV *NS* 19/256, Novara to Rusticucci, 6 May 1587, quoting Don Hernando de Toledo.

# 8

# The Armada takes shape

Drake's raid on Cadiz compelled Philip II to revise his entire strategy for the Enterprise of England. His plan, of course, had never been popular with Parma. As early as April 1586, even before the king first sent him detailed instructions, the duke complained that everybody knew about Spain's intentions, so the enterprise lacked the vital element of surprise. The delivery of the papal sword in September, the same symbol of crusading virtue accorded to the duke of Alba 15 years before, also symbolised the unwelcome publicity and lack of security that now surrounded the entire operation.

For three months – a measure, it would seem, of his disapproval – Parma held back his comments on the king's master plan of 26 July. Then, at the end of October, he enunciated all his doubts in a long letter. First he asked the king bluntly whether Spain could afford the operation, since the cost of building up sufficient forces in Flanders to defend recent conquests, as well as to conquer Ireland and England, would be crippling. 'And I shall be bold to say', wrote the duke, 'with the freedom your Majesty allows me, that if you find yourself without adequate resources to undertake such a great enterprise as this . . . I incline to the view that it would be better to defer or drop it'.

If the king still wished to persist with his plan, Parma continued, he should consider a second point: 'It seems to me that it would be most useful if the Armada from Spain were to be ready for action at the same moment [as the invasion from Flanders], because I am afraid that the Irish dimension may do us some mischief.' On the one hand, argued the duke, Elizabeth might deduce that there would be a second attack and raise troops abroad for her defence; on the other, the Armada might well be unable, through adverse winds or other unforeseen circumstances, to move as precisely as the king's plan demanded.

Philip II's reply, dated 17 December 1586, oscillated between uncertainty and irritation. He pointed out that he had scheduled the invasion of Ireland to take place only two months before Parma's assault, so that Elizabeth would scarcely have time to recruit foreign mercenaries. Instead, he predicted, she would withdraw troops from south-east England for service in Ireland, thus reducing opposition to Parma's cross-Channel attack.

The reservations of his outspoken subordinate nevertheless seem to have shaken the king's confidence. At one point in his letter he asked his nephew to consider whether it might be better for the Armada to land on the Isle of Wight instead of Ireland, and in a holograph comment he explained rather forlornly: '[you] must appreciate that . . . we cannot avoid building up the Armada we have here, because of the need to defend Portugal and for other things; and that, having thus created it, at so much cost, it would be best not to lose the chance of doing something with it'.[1]

This display of vacillation provoked Parma to make an even stronger criticism of the royal master plan. In January 1587 he unequivocally condemned both the seizure of an Irish springboard and the idea of a prior landing on the Isle of Wight. The king (his nephew boldly suggested) should concentrate on one thing at a time: if there must be an Armada, then let it sail straight for the Flemish coast and make the narrow seas safe for the Army of Flanders to effect its crossing.[2]

Once again the king wavered. He reviewed his nephew's many criticisms and complaints one by one but stumbled upon a devastating objection which, in the event, he later forgot. In a remarkably convoluted sentence he expressed his anxieties about:

> the need to make the Channel safe, because of the risk of sending a fleet like ours to sail between France and England at the appointed time (which often sees very bad weather in the Channel) without having a safe port in either, nor in Flanders (except for Dunkirk, which apart from being the only one available is not suitable for ships of large draft), forcing it to face the weather; leaving aside the general advantages, and the more detailed knowledge of those coasts, that the enemy fleet will have. All these are points of substance, and I am looking into them.[3]

Either his illness in the spring, or the trauma of Drake's raid, or the intractability of the issues themselves seems to have prevented further consideration of these 'points of substance'. In the meantime, therefore, despite Parma's arguments, the king left his Grand Design unchanged, and preparations both for the prior landing of the Armada in Ireland and for the invasion of Kent from Flanders continued simultaneously.[4]

Philip nevertheless tinkered with his chosen strategy. In February 1587 he asked the duke of Medina Sidonia, in charge of collecting the fleet that would sail from Andalusia as a second supporting wave, whether the escort galleons of the Indian Guard, now at San Lúcar, might be spared to reinforce the Armada instead. The prospect of imperilling the annual rhythm of the American silver-fleet appalled the duke, who pointed out that 'the link between the two continents is the foundation of the wealth and power we have here' since the treasure from Philip's transatlantic possessions formed the lifeblood of the entire empire.

The duke only changed his mind after Drake's raid on Cadiz, at which he had enjoyed a ringside seat. Now he favoured adding to the Armada several armed Indies merchantmen, as well as the galleasses from Naples and the ships embargoed to carry troops and munitions from Sicily to Lisbon. At Lisbon, the duke suggested tentatively, all the separate units should be formed into a single Grand Fleet which would operate together at all times. The king agreed and issued the necessary orders.[5]

Before long, however, Philip changed his mind again: perhaps Ireland was indeed a bridgehead too far. Now, he informed his nephew:

> Because the Armada here must first deal with meeting and protecting the fleets coming from the Americas, I do not think it will be possible for it to reach the Channel before your own crossing. This should not matter, but rather conforms with what is already arranged, because neither the person you sent here [Giovanni Battista Piatti], nor you after his return, asked for the Armada to come before, but only after . . . The best course seems to me that, almost at the same time, or as close to it as possible, we attack in three directions: an invasion by you and your forces; a diversion via Scotland, thanks to the men and money that the Catholics of that kingdom have requested; and an attack by this Armada on the Isle of Wight or Southampton.[6]

That was at the beginning of June 1587. Then, for almost a month, the king fell relatively silent. Historians have found it hard to explain this hiatus, but the reason is simple. Philip II's health suddenly collapsed. On 6 February 1587, long before Drake's raid, a note of deep weariness crept into the 60-year-old king's orders to his secretaries: 'You can send me a memo about these matters', he wrote, 'so that I can look at it along with the rest; although, the way things are these days, I don't know when that will be.' The next day, the king felt worse: 'I cannot handle any further business just now, because I have a terrible cold – which I already had last night – and I certainly cannot read or write . . . So you can see from this how impossible life is just now.' But the king soldiered on. On 9 February, at 10 p.m., he complained that papers were still being brought for him to read and sign – 'Look what I get to cure my cold!' – and by the 14th he clearly felt overwhelmed: 'I have been here, working on my papers for a long time . . . but while I've been at it, 10 or 12 more dossiers have been brought. The rest will have to wait until tomorrow.' With increasing frequency the king sent papers back unread because he 'had no time', or 'could not face them'.[7]

Finally, just after news reached him of Drake's destruction at Cadiz, Philip became seriously ill. By 26 May he could cope only with the most urgent papers, and by 14 June not even that – a pressing letter from Mateo Vázquez had to wait two weeks before it could be read out to the ailing king. On the 20th, Philip's valet regretted that the king was so restless 'that I can no longer take advantage of that hour after he wakes up, which is the best time to read him state papers, because then he is alone and has the leisure [to listen]'. Ten days later, the same valet lamented that 'the king's eyes are running all the time, his legs are very weak and his hand still painful; and the world is waiting'.[8]

It was indeed. Part of the problem lay in Philip II's obsessive desire to supervise every decision for himself. Admittedly he had come to trust Don Juan de Zúñiga, who had drafted the Armada master plan; but Zúñiga died in November 1586. This left a gap at the centre of power which, for some time, no one could fill. In May 1587, at the beginning of the king's illness, his secretary of state for war vented to a colleague his frustration at 'the considerable time wasted in consultation, for His Majesty is slow in replying and time is lost that cannot be regained'. He expressed the hope that more responsibility might be laid upon the council of war, whose membership had increased to six by May and rose to nine by August.[9]

The council's first major attempt to influence policy seems to have been made towards the end of the king's long illness, when news of Drake's outrages impressed upon the government the need to take action of some sort. On 23 June its members had insisted that Santa Cruz should put to sea with his entire fleet in order to protect the approaching treasure ships; as we have seen, the king agreed. Then on 13 July they took up Medina Sidonia's earlier suggestion that all the ships mustered in Andalusia should sail to Lisbon, so that when the marquis returned from the Azores he would have at his disposal a single fleet of irresistible force. Later that same day the king agreed again.[10]

Three weeks later 86 ships under Don Alonso de Leiva sailed into the Tagus, firing off their guns with such exuberance that (according to an eyewitness) one could not see the sea for smoke. They included the great-ships of the future Levant and Andalusian squadrons, together with 28 hulks and the four Neapolitan galleasses. For several weeks, the crews and embarked troops on the fleet were required to sleep on board their ships, in order to be ready to sail for England as soon as a contingent of Guipúzcoan ships under Miguel de Oquendo came down from the north, and the squadrons commanded by Santa Cruz and Recalde returned from the Azores.[11]

The last of these vessels, however, did not return to the Tagus until 10 October. To set sail for England in late autumn, even if the whole fleet had been in a seaworthy state, posed grave problems because of the high risk of storms: some recalled the fate of Charles V's expedition against Algiers, which had set out against all advice in October 1541 and ended with the loss of most of the fleet. The council of war (which included some men with long naval experience) realised all along that sending Santa Cruz to the Azores to protect the returning convoys against Drake would jeopardise the attack on England:

In view of the uncertainty concerning the time at which the marquis and his fleet may return, bringing the treasure ships with them, and without knowing the strength in which they will return (whether because they have encountered and fought the enemy, which would cause some damage, or because of storm damage or sickness among the crew, which are all things that often occur), we cannot predict or plan what may happen after the ships get back.

One councillor went even further: 'It is already clear', he warned the king, 'that we cannot undertake any other major enterprise this year beyond escorting home the fleets.'[12]

Philip, his health now restored, vigorously rejected these views. Instead, on 4 September, perhaps in response to Don Alonso de Leiva's boast that his part of the Grand Fleet was fully prepared for action, he issued yet another detailed set of instructions for the Enterprise of England. Once again he said nothing about invading Ireland – indeed he devoted two whole clauses of the instructions to explaining that, because of the delays caused by Drake's raid and the need to escort the treasure fleets, there was no longer time to secure a base in Ireland before going on to invade England. He also ruled out a descent on the Isle of Wight. The purpose of the enterprise, the king emphasised, remained unchanged: to restore England to the Catholic Church and to end English attacks on Spain's interests. But he had critically modified its strategy.

Santa Cruz, together with Leiva's fleet of auxiliaries assembled in Andalusia, Recalde's Biscayan ships and Oquendo's newly arrived squadron from Guipúzcoa, must now 'sail in the name of God straight to the English Channel and go along it until you have anchored off Margate head, having first warned the duke of Parma of your approach'.[13] Then came a crucial ambiguity in the king's instructions. 'The said duke', Philip continued, 'according to the orders he has received, on seeing the narrow seas thus made safe by the Armada being either anchored off the said headland or else cruising in the mouth of the Thames . . . will immediately send across the army that he has prepared in small boats, of which (for transit alone) he has plenty.' The king went on to insist that, until Parma and his men had made their crossing, the Armada 'must do nothing except make safe the passage, and defeat any enemy ships that may come out to prevent this'. He also loftily asserted that 'from Margate, you can prevent any junction between the enemy warships in the Thames and the eastern ports, with those in the south and west, so that the enemy will not be able to concentrate a fleet which would dare to come out and seek ours'.

All this left important questions unanswered. To begin with, would the fleet go across to the ports of Flanders to meet the army, embarked in advance and ready to go, or were the invasion barges expected to put out to meet the fleet in open water? In the former scenario, how would the deep-draught ships of the Armada negotiate the shallows and sandbanks which fringed the Flemish coast; in the latter, how could a fleet cruising far offshore protect the exposed barges from the shallow-draught Dutch or English blockade ships when they sallied out?

The parallel instructions sent to the duke of Parma shed scarcely more light on these vital matters. 'I have decided', the king told his nephew:

> that as soon as the marquis of Santa Cruz gets the treasure fleet safely to Cape St Vincent, which we hope to hear about from one hour to the next, and surrenders them there to the care of the galleys of Spain, he will go straight to Lisbon. There he will pick up the rest of the fleet which awaits him and they will all sail directly, in the name of God, to the English Channel, proceeding along it until they drop anchor off Margate head.

The king promised Parma that the fleet would send advance warning of its approach, and continued, 'you will therefore be so well prepared that, when you see the narrow seas thus secured, with the Armada riding off the said cape or else cruising off the mouth of the Thames . . . you will immediately send the whole army over in the boats you have prepared'. The king, once again, offered the assurance that, until the army had safely crossed, the Armada would concentrate solely on maintaining a clear passage; he commanded Parma, for his part, not to stir from the Flemish coast until the fleet arrived. But on precisely how the army and the fleet were to meet, or how Parma would cross the vital 40 miles that separated Dunkirk from Margate head, the king wrote not a word.[14] It was, to say the least, an unfortunate oversight.

Now that the king's mind was made up again he wanted no further delays or objections. He sent instructions to both Lisbon and the Netherlands by courier rather than with a special messenger briefed to answer questions about the plan. He also told Parma in no uncertain terms to cease his complaints:

> I cannot refrain from reminding you [wrote the king] that, apart from the initial idea of this enterprise and the selection of yourself to command it (which were my decisions), everything else connected with your end of the plan, including the resources and plan prepared, were according to your own instructions of which you alone were the author. Moreover, for its preparation and execution, I have given you in great abundance everything you have asked me for.

All further criticism of the plan must now cease, and the duke must put it into effect at once.[15]

After a perfunctory word of thanks for delivering the treasure galleons safely to Seville, the king also began to bombard Santa Cruz with orders from the moment he brought his storm-battered fleet back into Lisbon. One such missive (on 10 October) ended: 'and so there is no more time to waste in requests and replies; just get on with the job and see if you cannot advance the agreed departure date [25 October] by a few days'. On 21 October, as the deadline approached, the king bewailed that 'so much time has been lost already that every further hour of delay causes me more grief than you can imagine. I charge and command you most strictly to leave before the end of the month.' Letters of exhortation, wheedling and hectoring by turn, left the king's tiny office in the Escorial for Lisbon almost daily. When the marquis sent one excuse after another for the unpreparedness of his ships – from the perennial problems of logistics and maintenance to the damage wreaked by a cyclone on 16 November – the king dismissed them out of hand.

The Venetian ambassador at court, Hieronimo Lippomano, obtained a copy of Santa Cruz's measured refutation of one of these unrealistic tirades and paused to speculate on why the king refused to believe his most experienced admiral. He suggested three reasons: first, it was 'difficult for him to change plans, once he has decided on something'; second, Philip's knowledge of international affairs led him to see operations in each theatre as part of a wider context, increasing his anxiety to act before the overall favourable situation changed; and finally, his supreme confidence 'in the course of his good fortune' led him to assume that God would reward his efforts if he only performed his own part to the full.[16]

In fact the king, who of course never saw this analysis, would largely have agreed with its content. He frequently impressed upon his subordinates that, although they might understand the needs of their own theatre of operations, he had to consider the 'big picture': 'next year we might find ourselves with a Turkish fleet attacking Italy, should the sultan make peace with the Persians', he once warned Parma, while the French might reconcile their differences and make peace in order to prevent Spain from annexing England.[17] In addition, the cost of his armed forces placed a tremendous strain on Philip's finances: the gathering together of the Armada was costing 30,000 ducats every day, and Parma's army a further 15,000. By March 1588 the king had to sell his late wife's jewels in order to raise funds, and throughout the year he asked for weekly statements of the amount of money in the treasury and personally determined which obligations should be met and which must wait. In June Philip told his councillors that 'finding money is so important that all of us must concentrate only on that and on nothing else, because whatever victories we may win, I do not know what will come of them (unless God performs a miracle) without money'.[18]

The king had another reason for his obsessive behaviour. On 30 September 1587, after regretting that he had heard nothing from Parma for six weeks, the king informed his nephew of Santa Cruz's belated return from the Azores and advised him that, if the English should move their fleet down to Plymouth, leaving the Thames estuary unguarded, he might slip across the Channel alone and launch a surprise attack. Just possibly exploiting the knowledge that his co-commander was still not prepared, Parma at first accepted this further change of plan and boasted to the king on 14 November that:

Everything here will be ready and in being by the 20th, and . . . I am entirely resolved, in the name of God and with His holy assistance, to put to sea myself on the 25th . . . Unless we hear that there is an [enemy] fleet in the Channel that might prevent us from crossing, and if God is pleased to bring us safely to land and favour us . . . I hope we shall be able to give a good account of ourselves to Your Majesty.[19]

Now the king panicked lest Parma should undertake his solo venture and then become stranded in Kent without the fleet from Spain. He therefore fired off another barrage of letters urging Santa Cruz to put to sea even if he could lead only 48 seaworthy ships (10 December), and finally even if he had only 35 (21 December).[20] Parma, for his part, received a stream of royal letters enquiring whether he was already in England, and, if not, why not. Eventually, the duke lost his temper. 'Your letters seem to infer', he wrote back furiously to the king, 'that I may have done what Your Majesty emphatically ordered me not to do': to cross before he knew that the marquis of Santa Cruz and his fleet were ready to protect the operation. He warmed to his theme:

> Your Majesty is perfectly well aware that, without the support of this fleet, I could not cross over to England with the boats I have here, and you very prudently ordered me in your letter of 4 September not to attempt to do so until the marquis arrived . . . Your Majesty has the right to give absolute orders, which I receive as special favours and execute; but for you to write to me now with a proposal that runs so contrary to the previous express orders and command of Your Majesty, causes me great anguish. I beg you most humbly to do me the very great favour of telling me what to do next.

The letter – perhaps the most disrespectful and critical that the king ever received from one of his subordinates – remained uncharacteristically free of annotation from the royal pen.[21]

After this interlude of order, counter-order and disorder which confused everyone – foreign ambassadors and spies as well as the king's own ministers – the king calmed down. He simply reverted to the 4 September plan, with its fatal requirement that the invasion could take place only after two commanders had linked up in the narrow seas: Parma must not stir until the fleet from Spain arrived off Margate; the Armada should attempt nothing against England until it had 'joined hands' with Parma.[22]

The anxiety of these weeks seems to have taken its toll on the king's health again. At Christmas 1587 he took to his bed once more. He was unable to get up to eat until 17 January 1588, and not until the 20th did his valet pronounce him capable of governing his empire – and his Armada – once again. But the four weeks' convalescence seems to have gone some way towards restoring the king's legendary prudence, and he now began to take more rational steps to save both the Armada and the enterprise for which it had been created. Although on 16 January Santa Cruz wrote from Lisbon to say that the Grand Fleet would be ready to sail by the end of the month, the king no longer believed him. To check the true state of affairs he dispatched to Lisbon the late duke of Alba's tough and resourceful nephew, the count of Fuentes, with orders to ascertain what was really happening. Fuentes carried with him the authority, if need be, to dismiss Santa Cruz from his command.[23] When Philip's hatchet man arrived at Lisbon on 30 January he found a state of utter chaos. Santa Cruz was both seriously ill and in deep mental despair, feebly trying to direct the fleet's preparations from his sickbed. Even at the height of his powers, the marquis had been a fighting admiral rather than a staff officer; he got things done by a combination of bombast, ruthless energy and a lifetime's experience of war. The Armada was now beyond such simple cures, and in any case Santa Cruz had lost the physical stamina and the will to apply them. As he lay dying, the whole enterprise lay on the verge of collapse.

Months of bad management, compounded by bad luck, had inflated even simple problems out of all proportion. The preparation and embarkation of the task force's siege train offers a case in point. It had turned out that the field carriages of the eight cañones de batir which were to be shipped aboard the Levant squadron were in poor repair and of an outdated pattern, so it was decided in October 1587 to replace them before embarkation. Two full sets of new-pattern carriages were ordered for each gun. But seasoned timber could not be obtained, and so green wood was used in its place. Then the ship carrying the specially made iron fittings for the carriages was wrecked. The work was not completed until January.

Further difficulties arose when the time finally came to embark the heavy guns and their awkward accoutrements. On 2 January 1588 the captain-general of artillery, Don Juan de Acuña Vela, wrote to Philip II from Lisbon urging that the guns should be put aboard the ships at once, despite Santa Cruz's assurances that the matter could wait: clearly the ailing marquis was losing both his grip and his energy. On 30 January, still struggling with the problem, Acuña Vela wrote again to the king explaining that in the course of the previous week he had only been able to stow five of the cañones de batir aboard the Levantine ships: he had hoped to get the remaining three aboard that day but the galleys, which were the only craft capable of slinging heavy loads, were otherwise employed. The Levanters' big tenders, which were also required for the operation, were not available either, for they were working flat out distributing biscuit among the fleet. Four days later Acuña Vela reported that two more cañones were aboard, and only one now remained ashore.[24]

Similar difficulties apparently beset almost every aspect of the fleet's preparations, from the maintenance of the ships down to the supply of cheap eating utensils for the troops. Over the winter months, Fuentes discovered, the Armada had been reduced to a shambles of 104 unseaworthy ships and rotting supplies and – more critical because less easily cured – of dispirited and disillusioned men. The strength of the tercios assembled in Lisbon fell by 500 men a month; of the

500 or so sailors from Guipúzcoa who perished aboard Armada vessels, over 200 died at Lisbon before the fleet set sail.[25]

Among the dead was Santa Cruz himself, carried off by typhus like so many of his men. He was little mourned: according to a Lisbon chronicler the marquis had been proud, avaricious and cruel, so that although he was worth over half a million ducats, only four people accompanied his coffin to the tomb, 'and his death was regretted by no one'.[26] But it enabled the king to take one of the few wholly sensible decisions of the entire unhappy venture. What the Armada needed, if it were to sail at all, was not another fighting admiral but a determined and practical man with the kind of personal qualities and administrative skills needed to turn the muddle at Lisbon into a coherent fighting force. Such a man was Don Alonso Pérez de Guzmán 'el Bueno', duke of Medina Sidonia.

Medina Sidonia's qualifications to succeed Santa Cruz were impeccable. He had taken part in the Armada's planning from the outset, overseeing with great efficiency the outfitting and dispatch of the units assembled in the ports of Andalusia. They had all arrived at Lisbon in good order, and on time. This was perhaps not surprising, for the duke's administrative talents had been proved year after year, whether in governing his own vast estates or in fitting out, arming and manning the great transatlantic convoys which sailed annually from Andalusia to America. Nor did Medina Sidonia lack naval knowledge, at least on a theoretical level: his father had been taught by Pedro de Medina, the leading Spanish expert on navigation, and the ducal library was strong in nautical items.[27]

Though he lacked combat experience, Medina Sidonia could also boast a respectable military record. He had led an army during the Portuguese campaign of 1580, and commanded the relief force whose expeditious arrival had saved the town of Cadiz from being sacked during Drake's 'beard-singeing' exploit in 1587. His effective response to the attempted English landings had earned the praise and gratitude of Philip II and his ministers: the Venetian ambassador at Madrid went further, and opined that the duke had been the only man who kept his head in the crisis.[28] Finally, and in some respects most important of all, he headed one of Spain's most ancient and aristocratic families. None of the senior officers already serving in the Armada – not even the fiery Moncada, nor even Recalde and Leiva, each of whom had proposed himself as the successor to Santa Cruz – could feel any resentment or injustice in serving under a duke of Medina Sidonia.

The duke was already exceptionally well briefed. He was one of the few men outside the king's inner council who had been privy to the initial decisions about the Enterprise of England, as well as becoming involved in many of its administrative and technical aspects. In autumn 1587 he had spent some weeks at court, and took part in ministerial discussions on the conduct of the impending war with England.

In January 1588, when the king resolved to send to Lisbon 10 escort galleons and four large merchantmen of the Indian Guard, now repaired and renovated following their safe delivery to Seville the previous September, he instructed Medina Sidonia (now back at his ducal castle of San Lúcar) to expedite the move. It would be his last service to the Armada as a subordinate.

Not for one moment, it seems, had Medina Sidonia wished for or expected high military command. Suddenly, to his surprise and shock, he received a letter dated 11 February announcing that, since Santa Cruz was clearly too ill to lead the Armada, the king wished him to take charge. Understandably, given the current state of the Armada – and no one knew better than the duke the chaotic state that prevailed – Medina Sidonia felt most reluctant to assume command, and the reasons he advanced for being excused the appointment have often been used to discredit him. 'I have not good enough health for the sea', he wrote to the king's secretary, Don Juan de Idiáquez, on 16 February:

> for I know by the small experience I have had afloat that I soon get rheumatism . . . furthermore the force is so great, and the undertaking so important, that it would not be right for a person like myself, possessing no experience of seafaring or war, to take charge of it. I have no doubt that his Majesty will do me the favour which I humbly beg, and will not entrust me to do a task of which, certainly, I shall not give a good account; for I do not understand it, know nothing about it, have no health for the sea, and have no money to spend upon it.

It is now clear that Medina Sidonia's refusal arose from more than the reasons given in this uncharacteristically disorganised and rambling letter. The king simply dismissed the duke's excuses as misplaced modesty, and refused to consider them further; but he did not see a second letter written two days later, when the duke had had time to collect his thoughts and marshal his objections. This time he provided a damning assessment of the whole Armada venture, which he (like Parma and Santa Cruz) believed to be ill conceived and consequently doomed almost inevitably to failure.

These cogent arguments never reached the king. Philip's health remained poor throughout most of February and March, and he complained of pains in his stomach, of tiredness and of overwork. Piles of urgent correspondence accumulated on his desk – some unopened, others unread, most unanswered. In any case, Medina Sidonia's vital letter of 18 February was not among them. It had been intercepted and retained by the two councillors who inherited the mantle of Don Juan de Zúñiga: Don Juan de Idiáquez, a Basque whose family had long been prominent in the central government, and Don Cristóbal de Moura, a Portuguese whose diplomacy and duplicity had played a key role in the annexation of his native land in 1580. Now they attended continuously upon the king and handled the day-to-day receipt, filing and dispatch of the immense quantity of paperwork which the king's single-handed direction of the Enterprise of England generated. They resided at court throughout 1588, and nothing of consequence concerning the Armada bypassed them.

When, in the course of these duties, they opened Medina Sidonia's frank letter of 18 February, they were appalled. 'We did not dare to show his Majesty what you have just written,' they chided the unfortunate duke, and went on to rebuke his pusillanimity: 'Do not depress us with fears for the fate of the Armada, because in such a cause God will make sure it succeeds.' They also warned him of the consequences of refusing such a signal honour from his king. Everyone knew, they reminded him, that the offer had been made; to refuse it now would lead to accusations of ingratitude, selfishness, even cowardice. 'Remember that the reputation and esteem you currently enjoy for courage and wisdom would entirely be forfeited if what you wrote to us became generally known (although we shall keep it secret).' Here was a palpable threat, and it found its mark. Before the combined impact of moral pressure, special pleading and naked blackmail, Medina Sidonia crumbled.

He asked for an audience with the king, but was refused. So the new captain-general of the ocean sea reluctantly made his way to Lisbon. On his arrival – on the ides of March – he found a cheery letter from Philip that reassured him that 'If I were not needed so much here, to provide what is necessary for that [enterprise] and for many other things, I would be very pleased to join [the Armada] – and I would do so with great confidence that it would go very well for me.' The duke's reaction to this royal insight has not been preserved.[29]

With the Armada now in safe hands, the ailing king and his ministers turned their thoughts back to the diplomatic isolation of Elizabeth. The keystone of their policy, once again, was the paralysis of France. In spite of the defeat of the royal armies by the Huguenots at Coutras in October 1587, and the humiliation of Henry III by the duke of Guise, Spain still feared that the queen might receive some support from France. But at a meeting with the Spanish ambassador in late April, Guise agreed that he would engineer a general rebellion by the Catholic League the moment he heard of the Armada's departure. The immediate payment of 100,000 crowns in gold (£25,000) to the League's leaders clinched the deal.[30]

Guise, however, could no longer control the enthusiasm of his subordinates. The Paris Catholics began to agitate for a takeover of the city and when, on 12 May 1588, Henry III deployed his Swiss guards to preserve order, the entire capital erupted into violence, erecting barricades against the king's troops and forcing him to flee. The 'Day of the Barricades' made Guise the master of Paris and shortly afterwards he became 'lieutenant-general of the kingdom'. From Madrid, the French envoy warned his master that 'The corruption of these times and Spanish money will make a scar on the subjects of Your Majesty that will not easily be effaced, and a wound in your kingdom that will not heal.'

Philip had in fact intended that Guise should capture Henry and force him to make concessions (including free access to ports like Boulogne and Calais); but even without that crowning achievement the towns of Picardy, as well as Paris, remained under League control. As the Armada approached the Channel, the French economy ground to a halt: 'I never did see, nor no man hath seen it, since France was France, that ever money was impossible to be gotten as it is here now among all sorts, for all traffic ceaseth and for money there is none to be seen.' Neither Henry III nor the French Protestants could now save Elizabeth.[31]

Philip's diplomacy also ensured – rather more surprisingly – that the Dutch rendered precious little aid to England. In part it was an English 'own goal'. Leicester's government of the Netherlands had not been successful. The earl had proved unable to manage the prickly Dutch leaders as William of Orange had done: he was sworn in as governor-general in January 1586, but his powers were left undefined. He tried to create a strong central executive, to levy higher taxes for defence and to purge the provincial governments of those who opposed his policies. But his position soon crumbled. First, he failed to stop Parma, who in the 1586 campaign captured several towns along the great rivers that now separated the two sides. Second, early in 1587, two of Leicester's English subalterns betrayed his cause and delivered to Spain the strategic town of Deventer and a fort that dominated Zutphen. These misfortunes totally discredited the earl and 'there grew a wonderful alteration in the hearts and affections of the people against the English. They uttered lewd and irreverent speeches of his Excellency and the whole nation.' Far more serious, Elizabeth decided to resume the talks with Parma.

Meanwhile, on 12 June 1587 Parma laid siege to the deep-water port of Sluis on the Flemish side of the Scheldt. On the 24th bombardment began and, early the next month, the Spaniards managed to throw a bridge across the estuary below the town (as they had done at Antwerp), and cut it off from the sea. Elizabeth hurriedly sent reinforcements and money across to the Dutch, for not only was Sluis defended by English troops, it was a port from which England could be invaded. But she also indicated her willingness to reopen talks with Parma about a ceasefire. The siege continued until 4 August when, after 13 days of constant fighting around the walls (breached by some 14,000 rounds from Parma's guns), the English garrison ran out of powder and surrendered. Elizabeth, somewhat shaken, now begged her Dutch allies to join her in negotiating with Parma. When they refused, Leicester made a half-hearted attempt to seize a number of strategic towns in the republic, as Anjou had done three years before. Like Anjou he failed; and, again like Anjou, having failed he went home (December 1587).

The Dutch now seemed totally incapable of mobilising their own defence. They had 20,000 troops in garrison, with only 11,000 as a field army, plus the 6,000 men of the English 'secours': without the latter, their defence by land would collapse. Their naval strength was also poor. Although in 1584, a few months before his death, Orange had stated the urgent need for 10 'good ships' to patrol the coasts in case of Spanish attack, the States-General refused to comply. Instead of building warships of 300 and 400 tons, they brought a few converted merchantmen of 200 tons into service. When in May 1588 some Dutch vessels arrived at Dover to join the English fleet they were rejected on the grounds that they were too small to be of service. If the Armada's target had been a port in Zealand, or even Amsterdam, the Dutch could have done virtually nothing to resist. The reconquest of the Low Countries, and therefore the rebellion, might have been over in a matter of weeks.[32]

But, as Parma well knew, the Armada aimed at England. Nevertheless, continuing the talks with Elizabeth served his purpose: on the one hand they cast some doubt upon his intentions; on the other they called into question England's commitment to Dutch defence. On Philip II's orders the talks were continued, with hints of new concessions. The English accepted the bait – sending commissioners to Ostend (a town loyal to the States-General) in February; moving to Spanish territory at Bourbourg (near Dunkirk) in May. Parma's agents exploited divisions among the English commissioners, even encouraging one of them to break ranks and discuss terms for a complete English withdrawal from the Netherlands, and then made much political capital out of it with the suspicious Dutch. It is true that Elizabeth also gained something from the talks (above all an observation post in Flanders from which to monitor Parma's military preparations), but she lost far more by forfeiting the confidence and trust of the Dutch.

After the capture of Sluis most of Parma's energy went into concentrating sufficient troops for a successful invasion of England, and with obtaining transport vessels to convey them. The first proved easier than the second. Two thousand Spaniards marched from Lombardy to Luxembourg along 'the Spanish Road' in September 1586, and a further 9,000 Italians and 4,500 Spaniards followed them during 1587. An assault force of 27,000 men could thus be spared for England, while still leaving behind enough troops to defend the Spanish Netherlands.

The duke devoted far less time to finding sufficient vessels to transport this expeditionary force. In November 1587, when he assured the king that his forces were all ready for the crossing (pages 120–1), his own records reveal that only 67 vessels lay in Dunkirk harbour, and that they lacked 370 guns and 1,630 sailors. Nieuwpoort harbour contained a number of barges and other small craft, with some more in Sluis, but his biggest vessels – which included a flagship of 400 tons and three more of 300 – all lay at Antwerp, hemmed in by Dutch blockaders. Admittedly he made plans to strengthen the flotilla by hijacking 30 Scottish merchantmen with their six escort vessels as they sailed from Danzig to Aberdeen, and sent 10,000 ducats in gold to Catholic leaders in north-east Scotland to arrange it; but neither the gold nor the ships were ever seen again.[33]

Parma now became profoundly uneasy about his ability to get the army across. 'My vessels here', he warned the king in December, 'are no good for anything except transportation, because for the most part they are barges and cobs, which in a fight would be so small and frail that four warships would be able to sink every boat they met'. Far more than four warships now lurked off the Flemish coast: in that month, for the first time, Parma reported to the king the presence of a powerful Dutch blockade squadron, commanded by Justin of Nassau, and warned him that the Armada would need to clear the way for his forces to come out and reach the appointed place. From now on, his letters repeatedly drew attention to this problem. In April 1588, for example, he lamented that:

> The enemy have ... been forewarned and acquainted with our plans, and have made all preparations for their defence; so that it is manifest that the enterprise, which at one time was so easy and safe, can now only be carried out with infinitely greater difficulty, and at much larger expenditure of blood and trouble. I am anxiously awaiting news of the departure of the duke of Medina Sidonia with his fleet ... [to protect] my passage across, so that not the smallest hitch should occur in a matter of such vital importance. Failing this, and the due co-operation of the duke with me, both before and during the landing, as well as afterwards, I can hardly succeed as I desire in Your Majesty's service.[34]

It seems curious that none of these communications bears any holograph comment from the royal pen, for Philip II normally festooned all that interested him with notes and observations. The absence of such apostils does not, of course, mean that the king did not read these letters, but it does suggest that he may have failed to grasp their full significance.

Nor did he heed those in command of the fleet who questioned the wisdom of the Grand Design. On 15 February 1588 Martín de Bertendona reported to the king a conversation with Santa Cruz, just before the marquis died. They had agreed, said Bertendona, that the key problem was the lack of any deep-water ports between the Isle of Wight and Flushing, and had reviewed the sort of difficulties that could arise in the Channel when storms blew. 'But', Bertendona concluded serenely (and undoubtedly sarcastically), 'since it is Your Majesty who has decided everything, we must believe that it is God's will.' Perhaps it was also Bertendona who informed a papal agent in May 1588, that:

> Unless God helps us by a miracle the English, who have faster and handier ships than ours, and many more long-range guns, and who know their advantage just as well as we do, will never close with us at all, but stand aloof and knock us to pieces with their culverins, without our being able to do them any serious hurt. And so we are sailing against England in the confident hope of a miracle![35]

Between the death of Santa Cruz in February and this conversation in May, however, a minor miracle had indeed occurred. Under Medina Sidonia's firm but courteous direction, aided by his own prodigious capacity for hard work and a willingness to seek the opinions of his more experienced subordinates, the fleet became seaworthy. The ships already at Lisbon were repaired and they were joined by several new ones: some additional great merchantmen, including the *Lavia* and the huge *Regazona* (which became Bertendona's flagship), by embargo in February; the galleons and armed merchantmen of the Indian Guard – now named the 'squadron of Castile' – in April. One of the duke's lesser achievements was to invent the printed military form: he took over a press in the city, and ran off multiple copies of his General Orders, with blank spaces left for non-standard items.

Not all the problems could be solved by efficient paperwork, however. One outstanding worry was the lack of galleys. Both Santa Cruz and Bertendona had stressed that because of the amphibious nature of the operation these were even more essential than additional ships. At least 12 would be needed, they felt, for close support when Parma's army stormed the Kent beaches. Medina Sidonia clearly agreed. Within three days of his arrival at Lisbon he wrote to the king that the four galleys allocated to him were not enough, especially as three of them were so old. But his request apparently fell on deaf ears. Only four galleys eventually sailed, and none of them reached the English Channel.

The duke proved more successful in his efforts to rationalise the bewildering and totally unstandardised hotchpotch of guns which had been gathered together from the length and breadth of Europe, and to match them with the available ammunition. Medina Sidonia backed his own judgement that artillery would play a major role in the battles to come, and in this he was supported by Don Francisco de Bobadilla, the fleet's senior military commander, who later wrote: 'There was great scarcity of cannon balls . . . The count of Fuentes can bear witness how much I pleaded in this matter with Don Juan de Acuña, telling him that if the enemy did not allow us to board them and if the artillery fight lasted four days, he might tell me what we might do on the fifth if we carried so few rounds.' Acuña Vela, the king's captain-general of artillery, had estimated that 30 rounds per gun would suffice but, heeding Don Francisco's advice, the duke now insisted that quotas should go up to the unprecedented minimum of 50. He petitioned the king, and they did.[36]

Right up to the end Medina Sidonia and his commanders strove to obtain more guns. They even pressed trophies from former victories into service. A bronze gun bearing the royal arms of Francis I of France, perhaps captured at St Quentin in 1557 or even at Pavia in 1525 (when Francis himself was taken prisoner), was loaded aboard the Levanter *San Juan de Sicilia*. The *San Juan's* sister ship *La Trinidad Valencera* received a huge Turkish *cañón de batir*, possibly a prize from Lepanto 17 years earlier. Meanwhile, the seven bronze foundries at Lisbon worked flat out, and when Medina Sidonia arrived to take command an initial batch of 40 new pieces had just been delivered. Another 11 were in the process of manufacture. Under Medina Sidonia's regime, steps were taken to speed up production still further. All royal guns normally bore the king's arms (his full titles and escutcheon if the piece was of 20 quintals or above, just his name and a crown if they were lighter). But such embellishment took time, and so a special dispensation to omit it was obtained. This step was entirely sensible, but production pressures also took their toll on quality, and many corners were cut. Horrifying accidents occurred when inadequately baked moulds burst, or when guns failed their proofing tests. In one such incident a weak gun exploded, killing two gunners and taking off the arm of a third. Perhaps as a result, many pieces were not properly proofed, and on occasion sub-standard guns were evidently passed fit for service.[37]

Among the duke's other achievements in his first three months of office was to provide each ship with a printed set of pilotage instructions and a proper chart. Santa Cruz had obtained, on 25 September 1587, a 'careful relation of all the coasts of England with a note of the depth and size of the harbours' – almost certainly Waghenaer's *Mariner's Mirror* – and a chart of the coasts of England, Scotland and Ireland from the Lisbon cartographer Luis Teixeira. But these were single copies for his personal use. In January 1588 the king also provided a special itinerary for his fleet, which he had personally checked against his own maps; but once again only one copy was sent to the Armada. This was clearly of limited use, so Medina Sidonia arranged for the itinerary to be printed and ordered Ciprián Sánchez of Lisbon to prepare 85 identical charts of the coasts of Spain, England and Flanders, for distribution among the fleet. They were all aboard by 12 May 1588, when the cartographer was paid. Individual captains now had a practical guide to the waters in which they were expected to sail.[38]

By then the fleet had increased from the 104 ships of February to 130, and the troops from scarcely 10,000 to 18,973.[39] Many of those languishing in hospital were cured – even old Recalde, after being bled four times, came back aboard. Provisions and water were stowed according to a carefully planned turnover system, and the abysmal morale of the men gave way to a pious fervour to sail. In Lisbon Pedro de Ribadeneira, a leading Jesuit, composed an 'Exhortation to the soldiers and captains who sail on this campaign to England' which confidently asserted that 'We are not going on a difficult enterprise, because God our Lord, whose cause and most holy faith we defend, will go ahead, and with such a Captain we have nothing to fear.'[40] In Rome, the pope declared a special indulgence to all who sailed on the Armada and even to those who simply prayed for its success. In Madrid, while the population joined in massive religious processions every Sunday and holiday, and at other times followed a small published church-by-church guide to gain the Armada indulgence, the king's printer brought out a detailed 'True relation of the Armada' which listed all the ships, the guns and the officers aboard, sending copies for translation to Naples, Rome, Milan, Cologne and Paris. Philip intended the document both to intimidate his enemies and to impress his allies: all Europe would know that the conquest had been achieved by Spanish arms and treasure (perhaps rendering more acceptable the king's claim to choose England's next monarch). And in the Escorial, according to one source, the entire royal family spent three hours daily in relays before the Holy Sacrament, praying for the Armada's success.[41]

By the spring of 1588, thanks to his single-minded concentration on the mobilisation of the resources of his entire monarchy (and of most of his allies) Philip had managed to assemble 130 ships and 19,000 troops in Lisbon, with 300 more small ships and 27,000 veterans waiting in Flanders. At the same time, the strength of his enemies had dramatically decreased. The Dutch lacked the power both by land and sea to offer effective opposition, and Elizabeth's forces by land were stretched to the limit: all her veteran troops remained in the Netherlands and 6,000 soldiers she could neither spare nor afford guarded the Scottish frontier in case of an invasion. Although she eventually divined that Philip's fleet from Spain would need to join the Army of Flanders before trying to land, Elizabeth never grasped until it was too late that they planned to storm ashore in Kent rather than in Essex (see page 255 below).

After a series of parades in early April, and the consecration of the expedition's banner on the 25th, a general fleet muster was held at Lisbon on 9 May. Everything was now ready, or as ready as it would ever be. On 28 May 1588 the duke of Medina Sidonia led his great Armada down the Tagus towards the open sea.

The world held its breath. 'Things hang in the balance, and not just these affairs [of northern Europe] but of all areas,' wrote Philip II. 'Please God, let the events up there be for His cause, and may He assist us as is so necessary.' After all the crises, he felt calm again, confident that 'nothing on my part remains to be done': everything now depended on the careful execution of the plan he had conceived and shaped with such care over the previous three years – and on a few miracles to which, he felt, his prodigious efforts in God's cause entitled him.[42]

## Sources

Ill luck has dogged the archives of the men whom Philip II chose to execute his Grand Design. Virtually no papers concerning Santa Cruz's tenure of the office seem to have survived at Simancas: AGS *Secretarías provinciales* 1579, which is his Order Book for 1580–7, contains little of interest, and few copies of his correspondence with the fleet have been found. The duke of Medina Sidonia's papers for 1587–8 suffered a different fate. In the 1950s the National Maritime Museum at Greenwich, England, acquired a slim volume of important letters from the Armada campaign separated from the Medina Sidonia archive a century before (see Munby, *Phillipps Studies*, 109; and a translation of the documents in Waters, *Elizabethan Navy*, 53–67). Then, in the 1950s, the New York collector H. P. Kraus acquired a much larger collection of Medina Sidonia papers, including most of the seventh duke's correspondence with the king for 1587–9, as well as his administrative papers as captain-general of the coast of Andalusia. In 1986 the Biblioteca Bartolomé March in Madrid purchased a small part of this collection, consisting mostly of patents and autograph letters by celebrities. The rest is now splendidly lodged in the Karpeles Manuscript Library at Santa Barbara, California, except for a few items in the Library of Congress, Manuscript Division, Sir Francis Drake Collection. Many of the royal letters in these collections were published in Maura, *Designio*. The definitive biography of the duke is Pierson, *Commander*.

Parma's archives have also suffered grievous losses: German soldiers burned most of those in Naples in 1943; rodents and damp have attacked those in Parma; those left in Brussels at his death in 1592 have apparently disappeared (details in Parker, *Grand Strategy*, 374 n. 12, 399 and 405 n. 9). On the other hand, van der Essen, *Farnèse*, published many of the lost documents from Italian archives; while two important studies included material from the papers of Parma's subordinates, now preserved in the archives of Simancas: O'Donnell, *La fuerza de desembarco*, and Riaño Lozano, *Los medios navales de Alejandro Farnesio*.

The last two works form part of a series sponsored by the Spanish Institute of Naval History and Culture. Other important volumes include: Parente, *Los sucesos de Flandes de 1588*, reprinting in convenient form all the major histories of the 'Enterprise' written by Spaniards who served in the Netherlands in 1588; Gracia Rivas, *Los tercios*, tracing the history of each infantry regiment that sailed on the Grand Fleet; and Gracia Rivas, *La sanidad en la jornada de Inglaterra*, on the diseases that afflicted these men and on the measures (spiritual as well as medical) taken to cure them. Finally, Gómez-Centurión, *La Invencible y la empresa de Inglaterra*, examines the aims of the expedition and the propaganda that surrounded it.

On the Dutch, see the vintage studies of Motley, *A History of the United Netherlands*; Fruin, *Verspreide Geschriften*, 118–224; and the excellent modern account of Oosterhoff, *Leicester and the Netherlands*.

No satisfactory account exists of the talks at Bourbourg. The English perspective is covered by Read, *Lord Burghley and Queen Elizabeth*, 396–407, but see also the 'Diarie' of the English embassy in BL Sloane MS 262/41–86. For Parma's policy, see the correspondence of the Spanish commissioners in Haus-, Hof- und Staatsarchiv, Vienna, *Belgien PC* 43/1–77, and the letters to the king calendared in LCP. For the Dutch reaction, see Japikse, V, 501ff, 534–5, 565–7, 571–2, and VI, 56ff.

## Notes

1  *BMO*, II, 387–8, Parma to the king, 30 October 1586; and 471, the king to Parma, 17 December 1586 (draft and royal apostil). It should be remembered that Parma ceaselessly complained to the king that he lacked money for his army.

2  *Ibid.*, 535–6, Parma to the king, 17 January 1587.

3  *Ibid.*, 621–2, Philip II to Parma, 28 February 1587, in reply to Parma's letters of 24 December 1586 (apparently now lost) and 17 January 1587 (*ibid.*, 535–6). This was not the first time that the king had drawn attention to the lack of a deep-water port under Spanish control in the Netherlands. See *BMO*, I, 550, the king to Parma, 29 December 1585: 'And because of this [lack] it would be most useful to have some port there, somewhere like Enkhuisen, which faces Friesland, because nothing can be done without a port.'

4  *BMO*, II, 621–2, the king to Parma, 28 February 1587. But at this stage his plan still included a pre-emptive strike on Ireland, see Maura, 167–8, Don Juan de Idiáquez to Medina Sidonia, 28 February 1587. The first paragraph makes clear that the secretary had been commanded to reveal the king's secret intention: to get the English out of Holland and the Indies by 'putting the torch to their own house'. And 'since this cannot be achieved on the [English] mainland at the first stroke, we might start with Ireland, which we could use either as a pledge to exchange for the places they hold in the Low Countries . . . or as a springboard for a second strike against England'.

5  Maura, 163–74, Medina Sidonia to Idiáquez, 22 February 1587; Idiáquez's reply, 28 February; Medina Sidonia again, 5 March; and *BMO*, III, 474–5, the king to Medina Sidonia, 3 June 1587.

6  *BMO*, III, 479–80, Philip II to Parma, 5 June 1587. See also *ibid.*, 770–2, Parma's withering response of 20 July.

7  BL Additional MS 28,700 fos 147, 151, 155 and 156, Vázquez to the king, 6, 7, 9 and 14 February 1587.

8  BL Additional MS 28,363 fos 88, Juan Ruiz de Velasco to Vázquez, 26 May 1587; 112, Vázquez to Ruiz, 14 June and reply dated 30th; and 116–17, Ruiz to Vázquez, 20 June. The king began to transact business again on 1 July and got out of bed for the first time two days later (fo. 128).

9  BL Additional MS 28,376 fo. 336, Prada to Idiáquez, 17 May 1587. Some very similar observations about the king's tendency to run a one-man ship were made by the Venetian ambassador in Madrid: *CSPV*, 236–7, Lippomano, 12 January 1587.

10  *BMO*, III, 601–2 (*consulta* of 23 June 1587), 652 (same, 3 July) and 718–19 (same, 13 July). See also the notes of decisions taken, 628 (29 June) and 719 (13 July). It seems to us that these *consultas* mark a new departure for the council, for they deal with matters of policy rather than (as previously) administration. But it is nevertheless apparent that the councillors were not privy to the details of the Grand Design. They may, like several ambassadors, have heard vague rumours, but their recorded opinions reveal no certain knowledge.

11  Details from Roiz Soares, *Memorial*, 240. On 5 September, Leiva told the king that 'his' fleet was all ready to leave Lisbon: *BMO*, III, 1011–12.

12  *BMO*, III, 652, *consulta* of 3 July 1587. See also the pessimistic view of Prior Don Hernando de Toledo, reported by the Venetian ambassador on 5 August: *CSPV*, 302.

13  The location of the proposed landing place remains somewhat mysterious even today. In his letter of 20 April 1586, Parma had suggested 'the coast between Dover and Margate, which is at the mouth of the Thames' (*BMO*, II, 110), but he never seems to have been more specific on paper. Apparently only two participants wrote it down for posterity: Juan Bautista de Tassis, inspector-general of the Army of Flanders, stated unequivocally in his manuscript history that the invasion forces were intended to sail into the anchorage of the Downs and storm ashore at Margate (Tassis, *Commentarii de tumultibus belgicis*, 491); and Paolo Rinaldi, Parma's chamberlain, made a similar assertion in his still unpublished 'Liber relationum': BRB MS II.1155/216–216v. 'El cabo de Margat' appears in the king's instructions to both Parma and Santa Cruz in September 1587, and we would suggest that the choice of that precise location was made on the basis of Lucas Waghenaer's *Mariner's Mirror* (Latin edition 1586), which clearly showed Margate roads as the only safe anchorage at the

mouth of the Thames. The fact that some Armada ships almost certainly carried Portuguese manuscript maps of the area copied from Waghenaer strongly supports our interpretation.

14 *BMO*, III, 1006–7 and 1967–8 the king to Parma, 4 September 1587, and to Santa Cruz, 14 September 1587. It is clear that these document were conceived and prepared at the same time, because a particular phrase was recast by the king who added 'para lo de Portugal fue muy bien como está aquí'. (This phrasing would be fine for the one for Portugal.)

15 *BMO*, III, 1069–70, the king to Parma, 14 September 1587.

16 AS, Venice, *Senato: Dispacci Spagna*, 20, unfol., Lippomano to Venice, 14 November 1587, enclosing a copy of Santa Cruz's letter of the 4th (see a partial precis in *CSPV*, 320–3, 'undated').

17 *BMO*, III, 1069–70, Philip II to Parma, 14 September 1587, minute. See the papal nuncio's perceptive analysis of Spain's strategic dilemma should the enterprise not take place in 1587: *ASV NS* 19/283–4, Novara to Rusticucci, 10 August 1587.

18 See AGS *Estado* 594/192, *Relación* of the Army of Flanders, 29 April 1588 (monthly cost = 454,315 crowns); *Actas de las Cortes de Castilla*, 118 (Philip II claimed on 9 June 1588 that the Armada absorbed 900,000 ducats per month); IVdeDJ 55/XI/62–3, Mateo Vázquez to Philip II and reply, 31 March 1588 (selling jewels); and HS 141/160, Philip II to the count of Barajas, 18 June 1588, copy (concentrate on cash-flow).

19 *BMO*, III, 1146 and 1398–401, the king to Parma, 30 September 1587, and reply, 14 November 1587. Parma received a number of reports from his friends and agents in Spain concerning the state of the Armada (see, for example, AS, Parma, *Carteggio Farnesiano* 129, unfol., letters from Contador Alonso Carnero), so he must have known that it was far from ready at this stage. For evidence that Parma could not have 'put to sea' either in November 1587, see page 127 above.

20 *BMO*, III, 1391–2, 1536, 1579, 1616–17 and 1662–3, Philip II to Santa Cruz, 9 November, 10, 21 and 29 December 1587 and 4 January 1588. The bombardment only ceased when Santa Cruz pointed out that his spies in England had confirmed that Parma remained in Flanders.

21 *BMO*, III, 1538–9, 1594 and 1834, the king to Parma, 11 and 24 December 1587, and Parma to the king, 31 January 1588.

22 *BMO*, III, 1719–20 and 1732–3, *consultas* of the council of war, approved by the king, 15 and 17 January 1588; and Instructions to Parma and Medina Sidonia on 1 April in Duro, II, 5–18.

23 BL Additional MS 28,363 fos 175–9v, Vázquez to Juan Ruiz de Velasco and reply, 16–20 January 1588; but fo. 188, dated 12 February 1588, reported that the king was still under doctor's orders. For further health bulletins, see HS 143 fos 12–13 (23 January 1588), 29 (27 February), 41 (8 March) and 46 (16 March). An instruction to Fuentes, which includes the possibility of dismissing Santa Cruz, is at *BMO*, III, 1757.

24 *BMO*, III, 1255–7 and 1301–2, Juan de Acuña Vela to the king, 17 and 24 October 1587, pointing out the need for new field carriages and the difficulties of constructing them. Problems of embarking the siege train are chronicled in *BMO*, III, 1653–4, 1819 and 1865–6, Acuña Vela to the king 2 and 30 January and 3 February 1588.

25 Losses from the *tercios* recorded in Gracia Rivas, *Los tercios*, 172–3; deaths of sailors in Tellechea Idígoras, *Otra cara*, 397.

26 Roiz Soares, *Memorial*, 245.

27  The duke's role in preparing the *flotas* is evident from the numerous letters he exchanged every year with the Casa de La Contratación at Seville; see, for example, AGI *Contratación* 5108 (for 1586-7) or *Indiferente General* 2661 (for 1586).

28  See the king's praise in Maura, 208 and 214. Gabriel de Zayas, a veteran minister, suggested that the duke should be brought in to run the whole government ('si mi voto valiesse algo, mañana le dará la presidencia de Indias con el consejo de Estado'): BL Additional MS 28,363/50, Zayas to Vázquez, 10 May 1587. The praise of Ambassador Lippomano may be found in *CSPV*, 273ff. There was, however, one howl of rage: the admiral of Castile thought Medina Sidonia was no better qualified than he was, and told the king so (AGS *Estado* 165/212, letter of 23 February 1588).

29  KML *MSP: CR* 5/82, Philip II to Medina Sidonia, 11 March 1588. We have not located the letter of 18 February, but its contents may be deduced from the reply written by Idiáquez and Moura four days later: see Oria, 152. AS, Mantua, *Archivio Gonzaga: Spagna* 601, unfol., Cavriano to the duke of Mantua, 2 March 1588, records the royal rejection of Medina Sidonia's request to 'kiss the king's hands'.

30  AGS *CMC* 2a/23, 'Cuenta de Gabriel de Alegría', entry for 29 April 1588, at Soissons.

31  Mousset, *Dépêches diplomatiques*, 380, letter to Henry III, 5 June 1588; BL Additional MS 35,841/88-9v, Sir Edward Stafford to Walsingham, 7 July 1588 OS. The forces of the Catholic League tried to take Boulogne again in spring 1588, but once more they failed, see Constant, *Les Guise*, 164-5 and BL Additional MS 35,841/69, Stafford to Walsingham, 18 June 1588 OS.

32  Dutch strength by land taken from *CSPF*, XXI, part 3, 14-15; and by sea from ARA *Staten Generaal* 12561.3, fos 1-2, and Bor, *Oorspronck*, book 25, fos 6-7.

33  AS, Naples, *Carte Farnesiane* 1690, unfol., 'Relación de los baxeles que se hallan oy lunes 2 de noviembre en este puerto de Dunckerque' (recording only nine boats of 150-200 tons' burthen). See also the accounts of the paymaster of the 'Armada de los estados de Flandes', Thorivio Martinez, preserved in fragmentary form in AGS *CMC* 2a/1077, 3a/692 and 3a/713, and Riaño Lozano, *Los medios navales de Alejandro Farnesio*, 239. About the phantom Scots ships see AGS *Estado* 592 fos 49, Parma to Philip II, 22 March 1587, and 73, 28 April 1587; and AGS *Estado K* 1566/100, Parma to Mendoza, 13 April 1587; *K* 1566/128, Mendoza to the king, 20 May 1587; and *K* 1565/60, Robert Bruce to Don Bernardino de Mendoza, 2 October 1587.

34  *BMO*, III, 1579-81 and 1834-5, Parma to the king, 21 December 1587 and 31 January 1588, about the small boats; *BMO*, III, 1579-83 and 1617-19, Parma to Philip II, 21 and 29 December 1587 about the Dutch blockaders; *CSPSp*, IV, 261-2, and AGS *Estado* 594/79, same to same, 5 April 1588 (general demoralisation).

35  *BMO*, III, 1964, Bertendona to the king, 15 February 1588; the nuncio quoted by Mattingly, *The Defeat of the Spanish Armada*, 223 – Mattingly thought it might have been Recalde, but we believe the parallel remarks of Bertendona make him a more likely source.

36  Tellechea Idígoras, *Otra cara*, 581, Bobadilla to Idiáquez, 20 August 1588. For the decision to raise the shot quota to 50 per gun see Medina Sidonia to the king, 15 March 1588, AGS *GA* 222/12 and 26. For sub-standard weapons, see pages 194-5 below.

37  AGS *GA* 223/24, Acuña Vela to the king, 10 April 1588, about the production of utility ordnance without the royal arms. For regulations regarding the application of arms to artillery see AGS *GA* 206/295, same to same, 8 June 1587. Details of the

Lisbon foundries, and the extreme production pressures of early 1588, are noted in AGS *GA* 220/15, Acuña Vela to the king, 25 February 1588; AGS *GA* 222/53, same to same, 12 March 1588; AGS *GA* 222/22, Fuentes to the king, 12 March 1588.

38 The printed *Derrotero*, which contained excellent information on tides as well as coasts, was published by Oria, 155–80. However, Rodríguez-Salgado has shrewdly noted that the data came from outdated commercial sources: 'Pilots, navigation and strategy in the *Gran Armada*'. The maps are noted in AGS *CS* 2a/283, payment to Ciprián Sánchez; AGS *Estado* 2851, unfol., Idiáquez to Santa Cruz, 25 September 1587; and Cortesão and Teixeira de Mota, *Portugaliae monumenta cartographia*, plate 367 and pp. 81–2. The Armada also carried some excellent pilots. The one on the *Rosario* was said by the English to be 'as perfect in our coasts as if he had been native born' (Laughton, II, 186). All the Armada lacked, in navigational terms, were charts of the west coast of Ireland.

39 Data from Casado Soto, *Los barcos*, and Gracia Rivas, *Los tercios*.

40 Ribadeneira's *Exhortación* quoted, with many other fascinating illustrations of the Jesuit's attempt to 'sacralise' the enterprise, by Gómez-Centurión, *La Invencible*, 70.

41 Whitehead, *Brags and Boasts*, 58–78, on the published items; on the processions and on the royal family at prayer, see BAV *UL* 1115/199–206, 'Avvisi' of 28 May and 25 June 1588; AS, Modena, *Ambasciatori Spagna* 15, unfol., Bishop Ripa to Ferrara, 25 June 1588; and ASV *LP* 46/121, 'Breve instrucción para todos los que huvieren de ganar el Santíssimo Iubileo'.

42 AGS *Estado* 595/32, Idiáquez to Philip II and reply, August 1588.

## PART III

## 'IT CAME, WENT, AND WAS'

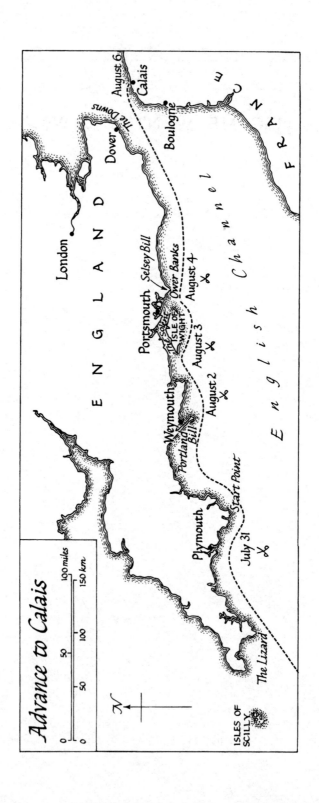

## Advance to Calais

ISLES OF SCILLY

The Lizard

July 31

Plymouth

Start Point

Portland Bill

Weymouth

August 2

August 3

Portsmouth

Selsey Bill

ISLE OF WIGHT

Over Banks

August 4

*E n g l i s h   C h a n n e l*

London

ENGLAND

Dover

The Downs

August 6

Calais

Boulogne

FRANCE

0    50    100    150 km
0    50    100 miles

# 9

## The advance to Calais

Great things were now expected of the Armada. The king and his ministers saw the 1588 campaign as the simultaneous means of preserving the lifeline between Spain and America, of protecting the Iberian peninsula from invasion and of ending the war in the Netherlands – that 'voracious monster which gobbles up the troops and treasures of Spain'.

Philip's instructions to Medina Sidonia on 1 April 1588 did not, however, entirely make clear how to achieve these momentous objectives. In part, they repeated the orders issued to Santa Cruz the previous September, and commanded the captain-general to lead his fleet directly to 'Cape Margate', there to 'join hands' with Parma and his army. But at precisely this point the instructions become bogged down in details about the conduct of the fleet, and the overriding need to curb immorality among its sinful human cargo on such a saintly enterprise. Theology and practical advice were inextricably muddled. There must be no blasphemy aboard the ships; the English fleet must be defeated if it tried to attack or halt the Armada; drinking, gambling, feuding or (God forbid!) womanising must be rigorously suppressed; the two dukes must co-operate fully on terms of equality and respect. The king's only detailed comment on the fleet's strategic options related to what should be done if, by some mischance, the rendezvous between the Armada and Parma proved impossible. Then, and only then, the king conceded, the fleet might return through the Channel, capture the Isle of Wight, and wait there until a second attempt to join Parma could be made. If, on the other hand, everything went according to plan, and Parma became firmly ensconced in southern England, the fleet might go on to accomplish the conquest of Ireland.

Philip's instructions contained two glaring omissions: the continuing absence of any detailed explanation as to how the rendezvous should be effected, and how the Armada could secure local command of the sea to cover Parma's crossing. A few sentences did indeed touch on these points, but their implications were more alarming than illuminating:

There is little to say with regard to the mode of fighting and the handling of the Armada on the day of battle . . . [but] it must be borne in mind that the enemy's object will be to fight at long distance, in consequence of his advantage in artillery, and the large number of artificial fires with which he will be furnished. The aim of our men, on the contrary, must be to bring him to close quarters and grapple with him, and you will have to be very careful to have this carried out . . . The enemy employs his artillery to deliver his fire low and sink his opponent's ships; and you will have to take such precautions as you consider necessary in this respect.

We may admire the king's tactical insight on this problem; but at the same time we must censure him – as no doubt his unfortunate commanders censured him privately – for his total failure to suggest a solution.[1]

For two more months, however, these difficulties remained academic because the Armada was still not ready to leave Lisbon. On 14 May the duke at long last pronounced it fit to sail, but with the weather 'as boisterous and bad as if it were December' and a north-westerly gale howling up the Tagus estuary, the ships remained at anchor for a while longer. At last, on 30 May, the Armada put to sea, but its northward progress proved tortuously slow because of contrary winds and the abysmal sailing qualities of the hulks. Some of these squat bulk carriers were over 20 years old, and all of them were notoriously clumsy. The big Levanters, designed as they were for the economic shipment of grain in the Mediterranean, proved little better.

Now that he could gauge the unsatisfactory performance of his fleet at sea, Medina Sidonia's old doubts returned, and he shared them with the king. Philip's response was sympathetic, but uncompromising:

I see plainly the truth of what you say, that the Levant ships are less free and staunch in heavy seas than the vessels built here, and that the hulks cannot sail to windward; but it is still the case that Levant ships sail constantly to England, and the hulks hardly go anywhere else but up the Channel. Indeed it is quite an exception for them to leave it to go to other seas. It is true that if we could have things exactly as we wished, we would rather have other vessels, but under the present circumstances the expedition must not be abandoned on account of this difficulty.[2]

Another serious problem also began to manifest itself. Despite the duke's careful preparations at Lisbon, the provisions started to run out. Some of the food was putrid, and had probably been so from the start. Considerable quantities were thrown overboard, and of what remained, as the English who went aboard the *Nuestra Señora del Rosario* after her capture in July observed, 'their fish [was] unsavoury and their bread full of worms'. Medina Sidonia's success in boosting the size of his forces had exacerbated the shortage. The 12,000 fighting men on the books in February had now swollen to almost 19,000, and they consumed provisions at a faster rate than had been anticipated. Orders therefore went out cutting rations to one pound of biscuit per day, and reducing the issue of meat. The Armada's unexpectedly slow progress intensified the problem still further, and with it the duke's forebodings.[3]

Medina Sidonia did what he could. He sent dispatches to Galicia almost as soon as the Armada put to sea, with orders for the provincial governor to send fresh food and water to the fleet as it came abreast of Cape Finisterre. On 10 June, as the wind at last turned southerly, he sent Captain Moresin back to Parma, noting three days later that 'The weather has been so good that I hope he will arrive in Flanders fifteen days before we do.' Every ship now cleared the decks for action and the senior infantry officers toured the fleet to make sure that each man had his weapons ready and knew exactly what to do when the time for action came.[4] Meanwhile, however, unknown to the duke, the victualling tenders waiting off Finisterre departed, for their fresh supplies had begun to rot.

Medina Sidonia faced a critical choice. Should he take advantage of the fair wind that had speeded Moresin northwards, or should he wait for the fresh supplies he had ordered? He decided on the latter, lingering in vain for five days. The new delay left the Armada with little choice but to put in somewhere for supplies, and the council of war decided that dwindling provisions made it imperative to head for Corunna to restock the fleet. By late evening on 19 June the flagship *San Martín* and 35 other ships had reached harbour but the remainder, including the galleasses, the hulks and the Levanters – all the most vulnerable vessels in the Armada – together with Recalde's entire squadron of Biscayans, stood off beyond the headland in the failing light, intending to make their entrance the following morning at daybreak. During the night a sudden and violent south-westerly gale scattered the waiting ships, and drove some as far afield as the Scilly Isles.

The duke's initial reaction to this disaster seems to have been one of total despair. On 24 June he composed a long and detailed appeal to the king, urging him to abandon the enterprise altogether. His arguments were marshalled under two headings, theological and practical, in that order. Medina Sidonia, it would seem, had got the measure of his master. He was moved to write, he began, by the unusual severity of the storm the Armada had just experienced which, he observed, 'would at any time be remarkable; but since it is only the end of June and since this is the cause of Our Lord, to Whose care it has been – and is being – so much entrusted, it would appear that what has just happened must be His doing, for some just reason'.

Perhaps, the duke speculated before turning to the practical issues, the Almighty had issued a warning that the Armada should not continue, for His own good if unfathomable reasons? Be that as it may, the fleet's present situation was perilous. Twenty-eight of its vessels, including some of the most powerful ones, were missing, along with the entire artillery train and around 6,000 men. Without them the forces under his command would be dangerously outnumbered by those of the enemy. Medina Sidonia could see only two options: either to press on regardless with the remaining ships, or to wait at Corunna for the missing vessels to return. Both would involve grave risks. Any attempt to carry out the Grand Design except in overwhelming strength, he pointed out, would prove counter-productive, for a depleted Armada would never be able to reach Parma's army, let alone shepherd it across the Channel. Yet further delay would mean sailing northwards during the season when navigation was most hazardous. Therefore, the duke humbly concluded, might it not be better to cancel the whole operation and make some honourable peace with Spain's enemies? At the very least, all these weighty considerations made it 'essential that the enterprise we are engaged in should be given the closest scrutiny'.[5]

The courier departed; the duke waited. He had risked his reputation, his job and perhaps even his life on two counts: first by suggesting that the king should make peace with his enemies, which came close to treason; and second, more seriously, by implying that perhaps Philip II no longer had God on his side which, in the king's eyes, might verge on heresy.

Medina Sidonia was not alone in his concerns. On 27 June he called another council of war to discuss the Armada's dilemma. After a lengthy examination of the alternatives a vote was taken and, to the duke's profound relief, nine of his 10 senior officers agreed that the Armada was too weak to proceed in its present condition. Only one, the impetuous Don Pedro de Valdés, argued vehemently for an immediate surprise attack. Things would never get better, he urged, and might well get worse: they must strike now, while they still could. His views were noted before the council signed its recommendation, and sent it to the king.

Meanwhile, irrespective of Philip's response, much practical work needed to be done. The great task of repairing and revictualling the ships began, and gradually the stragglers returned. 'The duke is working with great energy, as usual', Recalde told the king, for once again Medina Sidonia's tireless attention to detail and wide administrative experience paid rich dividends. Like Lord Admiral Howard, with whom he had much in common, the duke's style of command was not remote or aloof. July 10, for instance, found him in the bowels of the storm-damaged *Santa María de la Rosa*, supervising the stepping of a new mainmast. The task took six hours, and was accomplished with much difficulty. 'When it was finished', he reported with genuine modesty to the king, 'I thought we had not done badly.'[6]

Four days before this a courier arrived from the Escorial with a reply to Medina Sidonia's dispirited letter of 24 June. It had caught the king at a bad moment, in the midst of another bout of ill health brought on by pressure of work. 'I have to spend so much time on incoming papers', he lamented, 'that I believe it's making me walk badly . . . Please tell some of the ministers in Madrid to moderate the number of papers they send.' But he had nonetheless given Medina Sidonia's report, and the council of war's endorsement of it, his full consideration. The opening lines of his reply must have made Medina Sidonia blench:

> Duke and cousin [began the king]. I have received the letter written in your own hand, dated 24 June. From what I know of you, I believe that your bringing all these matters to my attention arises solely from your zeal to serve me and a desire to succeed in your command. The certainty that this is so prompts me to be franker with you than I should be with another.

After this uncompromising start the rest of the missive, although firm, was considerate and mild in tone. Each of the original reasons for the undertaking was restated, and each of the duke's objections systematically demolished by Philip's perverse logic. First the theology: 'If this were an unjust war, one could indeed take this storm as a sign from Our Lord to cease offending Him; but being as just as it is, one cannot believe that He will disband it, but will rather grant it more favour than we could hope.'

Then came the logistics and strategy. The English had no allies and the king was convinced that their forces, in spite of Medina Sidonia's fears, remained inferior to Spain's. With a following wind the fleet would be in the Channel within a week, whereas if it remained in Corunna the Armada could do nothing to compel Elizabeth to negotiate. Worst of all, now that England had mobilised her warships, the disorganised and dispirited fleet at Corunna represented a sitting target, liable either to be destroyed at anchor or blockaded in port while the English ravaged the unprotected Iberian coasts and captured the next treasure fleet.

To the king the logic of the situation was unarguable, and his captain-general of the ocean sea should need no further reminding of where his duty lay. 'I have dedicated this enterprise to God', concluded Philip, with a final thrust which brooked no further dissent. 'Pull yourself together, then, and do your part!'[7]

The delay at Corunna also allowed the king another opportunity to micromanage. He had received a copy of Medina Sidonia's letter to Parma dated 10 June reporting that he had 'consulted the pilots and other experts aboard this fleet who are familiar with the whole coast of England, and asked them to decide in which port this Armada might shelter' while he waited for news that Parma had his forces ready. Philip now took advantage of the fleet's unexpected return to Spain in order to overrule this proposed departure from his master plan. 'The main point [of the plan] was to go on until you could join hands with the duke my nephew', he chided, 'and proceed to the agreed location and make safe the duke's transit.' Parma, the king stated yet again, could not emerge with his flotilla until the Armada arrived in the narrow seas. There must therefore be no delays *en route*.[8]

A few days later, the king decided that Medina Sidonia needed 'minders' who could both keep his independence in check and augment his inexperience of naval affairs. He therefore appointed Diego Flores de Valdés, commander of the squadron of Castile, to serve on the flagship as principal naval adviser. He also sent a minister from Madrid to make sure the duke obeyed: Medina Sidonia must 'order those whom you, acting on my behalf, will direct, to go over to his galleon, together with those whom he may deem most useful and who may be least missed from the vessels on which they now serve'. The choice of Flores, whose naval career was long but not particularly distinguished, and who knew more about convoys than battles, would crucially affect the outcome of the Armada campaign.

For the moment, however, the king's firm stand seems to have made Medina Sidonia almost a happy man. On 15 July he reported jubilantly that 'God, since it is His own cause, and since He has not forgotten the great service that His Majesty wishes to offer with this enterprise, has been pleased to reunite the entire fleet, without the loss of a single ship, and with no loss for any of them. I hold this to be a great miracle.' The duke, like his master, now looked forward confidently to victory.[9]

In some respects, given the situation in which the Armada now found itself, the king's insistence that it should press on at all costs made sound strategic sense. Disbanding the fleet, which represented so much spent capital in both resources and prestige, before it had achieved any of its objectives, would achieve nothing: it could not even, as Philip observed, exert pressure on the English nego- tiators at Bourbourg. Moreover the English fleet might indeed easily descend on Corunna, just as it had done the previous year on Cadiz, wreaking havoc with the whole fleet as it lay helplessly at anchor.

In Plymouth, indeed, the English had contemplated just such a move. While the queen's commissioners continued to negotiate fitfully at Bourbourg, her admirals prepared another pre-emptive strike against Spain. On 1 June Howard left the Downs, and two days later he was at Plymouth, where he and Drake now commanded 60 fighting ships. For the time being the weather turned against them. 'God send us wind,' Howard later exclaimed, for 'if the wind had favoured us when we went out from hence . . . they [the Spaniards] should not have needed to come this far to have sought us'. On 4 July his prayer was answered, and the queen's ships sailed for Spain. But they never arrived. Storms off the Scillies, more storms off Ushant, and finally a flat calm when they were 60 miles off the Spanish coast kept the English away from Corunna. When at last the wind got up again, victuals had run dangerously low, and in any case it blew the fleet swiftly back to Plymouth where they urgently sought to replenish their ships.

As Howard later realised, 'the southerly wind that brought us back from Spain brought them out'. On 21 July, with almost all the stragglers reunited, Medina Sidonia led a refreshed and strengthened Armada to sea again.

After receiving the king's incisive letter of 1 July, the duke had taken several important steps. He re-emphasised the holy nature of the campaign and repeated his orders to avoid swearing, gambling and blasphemy, and for prayers to be said twice daily. In an attempt to improve spiritual motivation all the men of the fleet were landed in batches on the island of San Antón in Corunna harbour, where each was confessed, blessed, and issued with a pewter medallion showing the Virgin on one side and Christ on the other. Morale, understandably, had reached a low ebb, and the duke chose the island location for fear that his men might desert if allowed ashore. Some of the more privileged gentlemen-adventurers, who enjoyed less restricted access to shore leave, did take the opportunity to abscond: a medical officer aboard the *Nuestra Señora del Rosario* later reported that a number of them 'stayed in the Groyne [Corunna] and would not go forward'. These faint-hearts were probably no great loss. Recalde had already grumbled about commands being given to men simply 'because they are gentlemen'. Very few of them, he went on, 'are soldiers, or know what to do'.

When the fleet eventually sailed from Corunna it was in much better heart than before. Fresh provisions had been embarked, the loads more sensibly distributed, and special efforts made to sustain health and cure the sick. Some reinforcements of men had arrived, but Medina Sidonia had carefully rejected the unsuitable ones. When a contingent of 400 recently assembled levies arrived from Galicia the duke dismissed them outright, explaining to the king that they were so old, infirm and undernourished, and so lacking in military experience ('not one of them knows what an arquebus is') that, rather than have them die worthlessly aboard ship, he had succumbed to the 'lamentations of their wives' and sent them home.

On 19 July the duke convened another council of war to decide whether the Armada should put to sea and, if so, what tactics to adopt when it encountered the English fleet. All the commanders present voted to sail for England on the next favourable tide, and all but one of them advocated a battle formation based on that adopted at Lepanto, with an extended line of ships arranged in a main body with flanking 'horns'. The dissenter, once again, was Don Pedro de Valdés. He proposed that the fleet should be divided into three sections, with the 'weak and slow vessels in the centre so that with the fighting ships divided equally into a rearguard and vanguard around this, if the enemy should attack from behind the whole fleet can turn about. Thus the vanguard can support the rearguard or, should the attack come from the front, the rearguard can reinforce the van.' Don Pedro was clearly a difficult man, but on this occasion he was undoubtedly right: after the Armada's first encounters with the English it adopted precisely this more compact and defensible formation.[10]

Two days later the Grand Fleet was once more at sea, heading for England. On the 25th Medina Sidonia felt confident enough of his progress to send another pinnace to Parma, announcing his approach. Four more days of brisk southerly winds brought the Armada across the Bay of Biscay to the latitude of Ushant, beyond which lay the entrance to the English Channel. About this time they were spotted by a Cornish ship bound for France to load salt. Her captain noted with awe the great red crosses on the Armada's sails before fleeing homewards with his breathless story. But now the fleet suffered casualties. When dawn broke on Thursday 28 July, some 40 ships were missing. Storms had forced the four galleys to run for cover: one, the *Bazana*, was wrecked at the entrance to Bayonne; the convicts aboard another, the *Diana*, mutinied. The 768-ton Biscayan flagship *Santa Ana* also came to grief, losing one of her masts through a pilot's error. She sought shelter first at La Hogue, on the eastern side of the Cherbourg peninsula, and finally at Le Havre, where she was to remain immobilised throughout the campaign. Nevertheless the Armada continued under shortened sail until it sighted the English coast at about 3 o'clock on the 29th. Medina Sidonia now called a halt to allow the lost vessels to catch up and to hold his last council of war before entering the battle zone.

The Armada had caught the English at a disadvantage. The navy had only regained Plymouth Sound after its abortive attempt to raid Corunna on 22 July, its victuals all but consumed, and replenishing them in south-west England, an area unaccustomed to providing the huge quantities of victuals required by large fleets, proved slow. A golden opportunity thus existed for the surprise attack advocated by Recalde and Leiva at the council of war, but instead of driving towards Plymouth Medina Sidonia ordered the Armada to take in sail for the night again, and it only began its stately advance up the English Channel on 30 July.[11]

At dawn on the 31st the duke caught his first view of the English fleet. Over 100 ships had assembled in Plymouth Sound the previous day as the Armada approached and, under cover of darkness, the Lord Admiral skilfully led most of his ships across the front of the Armada to gain the weather gauge from seaward, while a decoy squadron, tacking close inshore on the Armada's left, left the Spaniards in confusion about English intentions until their entire fleet was arrayed against them to windward (FIGURE 13).

This formed a prelude to battle to which Medina Sidonia immediately responded. 'Our Armada put itself into combat formation' runs the entry in the duke's diary, and his fleet spread out, as agreed by the council of war, into its fighting formation: Leiva in command of the left wing (vanguard) with about 20 capital ships; Recalde in command of the right (rearguard) with some 20 more; and Medina Sidonia in the centre with the rest. The battle array spanned at least two miles from flank to flank, and it clearly presented an awe-inspiring sight. The English were certainly impressed by it, and deeply apprehensive. 'We never thought', observed one of them, 'that they could ever have found, gathered and joined so great a force of puissant ships together and so well appointed them with their cannon, culverin, and other great pieces of brass ordnance.' There was no question in English minds, either, about the calibre of the Spanish crews. Only trained and disciplined seamen could have adopted and maintained so large and

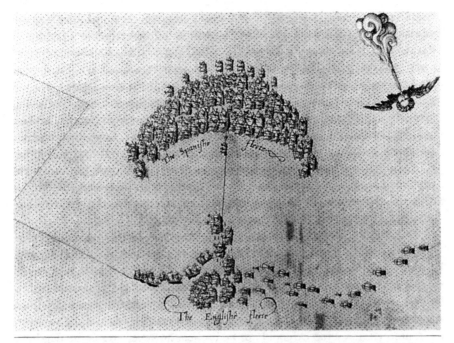

FIGURE 13   A detail from the second in a set of engravings made by Augustin Ryther in 1590, from drawings by Robert Adams, to illustrate Petruccio Ubaldino's narrative of the campaign which was in turn based on Lord Admiral Howard's personal record of the battles. It shows the situation off Plymouth on 31 July, after the English fleet had gained the Armada's weather gauge. The Lord Admiral's aptly named pinnace, *Disdain*, is shown darting forward to offer Howard's 'defiance' to the Spanish flagship.

complex an arrangement of ships, especially ones whose sailing qualities were so varied. Whatever its weaknesses might be – and, at this stage, Howard and his officers had no means of gauging them – it was clear that the Armada would be no soft touch.

War had not been formally declared between England and Spain, and before battle commenced the lord admiral deemed it proper to perform an old-fashioned act of etiquette. He issued the Armada a 'defiance', or challenge. From among the ranks of the English fleet emerged an 80-ton barque, appropriately named *Disdain*, which dashed on the wind to within hailing distance of the Armada's main battle before firing a derisory token shot into its towering midst. Then she deftly came about and beat back to the safety of the English fleet. Formalities complete, Howard then launched his first attack.

The lord admiral's opening tactics surprised and perturbed the Spaniards, whose tactical doctrine rested upon writers such as Fernando Oliveira of Portugal and Alonso de Chaves of Castile. Oliveira's influential treatise *The Art of War at Sea* (the first manual of naval warfare ever published) recommended 'a single and straight line' as the ideal combat formation, but nevertheless advised captains to carry heavy weapons only at the prow, like a galley, with lighter pieces, mostly muzzle-loaders, on the broadside. 'It is never safe at sea to allow opponents on your beam; rather you should always keep them ahead when you are fighting,' warned Oliveira. 'Never expose your broadside to them.' A trailing horns formation obviously secured this tactical goal. Chaves, for his part, advised battle fleets 'to sail in wings [*en ala*] because all [the ships] can see their enemies and fire their artillery without impeding each other. They must not sail in line [*en hila*], with one behind the other, because that would cause serious harm, since only the ships in the van can fight.'[12] Yet this is precisely what the English fleet seemed poised to do: the Spaniards were about to witness the first true line-ahead attack in the history of European naval warfare.

This tactic exploited the mobility and firepower of the broadside-armed sailing ship, and its effectiveness lay in its simplicity. One ship, usually the flagship, led the attack, while the rest followed in a line with the vice-flagship at the rear, bringing each broadside to bear in succession. No rigid formation had to be kept, for the leader could move where he willed with the rest of the force snaking behind him. So long as each ship kept behind the stern of the vessel to its front, the line's integrity could not be broken, however erratic the flagship's path might be. The whole line, moreover, could turn about on the flagship's command and, led now by the vice-flagship, recross the enemy and present its other broadside while the disengaged side reloaded. This movement could be carried out as often as was necessary, as Sir Walter Raleigh later put it, to keep the enemy 'under a perpetual shot. This you must do [he added] upon the windermost ship or ships.'

The 'windermost ships' of the Armada were those which lay at the outer ends of its trailing horns. So Howard's galleons stormed across the Spanish rear, engaging first Leiva's vanguard and then, more forcefully, Recalde's rearguard on the far wing. Some ships of the rearguard broke station in the face of this assault, and sought shelter among the main body, but Recalde in the *San Juan de Portugal* stood firm, and for some time most of the English fire was directed at his ship.

According to Recalde the English 'fired more than 300 rounds' at the *San Juan*, 'damaging key parts of the rigging, including the mainmast stay, and sent a ball through the foremast from one side to the other' before help arrived from the other troubleshooters. After a couple of hours the English withdrew to a safe distance, some four miles astern.[13]

Reactions to this first engagement varied. Drake merely commented that 'we had them in chase, and so coming up unto them there passed some cannon shot between some of our fleet and some of them', while Hawkins described the same incident as 'some small fight'. Clearly the disciplined formation of the Armada, and its evident strength, produced the effect for which it had been designed: the English were not prepared to come close even though, beyond point-blank range, their guns could inflict little damage. 'We durst not adventure to put in amongst them,' wrote the Lord Admiral of the first day's fighting, 'their fleet being so strong.' Henry White, captain of the 200-ton auxiliary *Bark Talbot* (later one of the fireships at Calais), put the matter more bluntly: 'The majesty of the enemy's fleet, the good order they held, and the private consideration of our own wants did cause, in mine opinion, our first onset to be more coldly done than became the value of our nation and the credit of the English navy.'

The Spaniards felt as critical of their own efforts. Captain Vanegas, the gunnery officer aboard the *San Martín*, estimated that the Spaniards had fired 750 rounds against 2,000 from the English. The damage inflicted upon the *San Juan* eventually forced Recalde to abandon his station while his crew carried out emergency repairs. Moreover, in his report to the flagship, Recalde warned that since the 'Levant ships do not carry as much heavy artillery as the enemy, the latter will get closer and cause them damage', and predicted that if Don Alonso de Leiva (who had taken temporary command of the rearguard in *La Rata Encoronada*) 'should receive the bombardment that I received yesterday he will not be able to resist, because he carries no heavy artillery with which to resist'.

Recalde blamed all these problems on the decision not to blockade Plymouth:

> I do not know why we never put into effect what we decided about going to the entrance of Plymouth harbour, and so allowed the [English] to gain the weather gauge – because otherwise they could not have managed it. There are some very experienced people out there and we were like novices and made the wrong call.

'Still,' he continued sourly, 'what's done is done, and there is no reason to keep on discussing it. But it is very necessary to make sure that in future they do not consume us little by little, and without any risk to themselves. We should rather put all our eggs in our basket, and the sooner the better for us.'[14]

As Recalde vented his feelings and struggled to repair his ship, two further disasters struck the Armada. First, the Guipúzcoan *San Salvador*, one of the most heavily armed ships in the fleet, and the headquarters of the Armada's paymaster, was suddenly rent apart by a tremendous explosion (FIGURE 14). Mystery surrounds its cause. One explanation blames sabotage by a German gunner, who was allegedly being cuckolded by a Spanish officer (what the lady was doing aboard in the first place is not made clear). Another more plausible version tells of 'the captain falling into a rage with the gunner and threatening to kill him if he shot no righter'. In a fit of professional pique, continues the story, 'the gunner cast fire into the powder barrels and threw himself overboard'. Quite possibly it was simply an accident. With so much gunpowder about, and so many lighted matches and linstocks on the decks, it is remarkable that such catastrophes were not more frequent.[15]

Whatever the cause, the damage to the *San Salvador* was extensive. The blast blew out two decks and the sterncastle and disabled her steering gear; half the 400 men on board were either killed or badly burned by the explosion, or drowned trying to escape it. The duke brought the Armada's progress to a halt, went himself to the stricken vessel's aid, and took energetic measures to limit the damage. His men extinguished the fire before it could reach the main magazine, which contained more than seven tons of gunpowder, and towed the vessel into the safety of the fleet. Many of the wounded – most of them dreadfully burned – were taken off. The following day, Medina Sidonia's advisers reluctantly concluded that they could not repair the burnt-out hull and restore her sailing rig, so the *San Salvador* would have to be abandoned. The 'principal persons' still aboard, and the paymaster's treasure, came off in small boats, but in the haste and confusion about 50 of the most seriously wounded were left, so that the ship, with its guns and powder aboard, could not be scuttled. They were still there when, later that same day, John Hawkins and a prize crew arrived, but finding 'the stink in the ship so unsavoury and the sight within board so ugly', they left abruptly and had her towed to Weymouth.[16]

The other casualty of the day was even more important. Don Pedro de Valdés in the *Nuestra Señora del Rosario*, one of the free-ranging 'troubleshooters' charged with the formation's defence, and also carrying 50,000 ducats from the king's treasury, collided with one of the Biscayans while coming to Recalde's rescue, damaging his bowsprit, and this relatively minor accident set in train an escalating series of mishaps. The temporary loss of her spritsail affected the *Rosario*'s steering, which led later to a more serious collision with her sister Andalusian *Santa Catalina*. This brought down the *Rosario*'s foresail and yard, and damaged the foremast rigging. Don Pedro and his men made strenuous efforts to make good the damage but late in the afternoon the unstayed foremast

---

*facing, head*] FIGURE 14  The *San Salvador* incident on 31 July, from a detail in No. 5 of the Ryther engravings. The stricken vessel is shown abandoned and on fire, while the crescent-shaped Armada continues its advance up-Channel. An oared vessel is coming out of the English fleet to take possession of her. Note the pair of galleasses bringing up the rear on each of the Armada's flanks.

*facing, foot*] FIGURE 15  This detail from No. 4 of the Ryther engravings shows the situation on the morning of 1 August, when Drake had abandoned his position at the head of the English fleet to capture Don Pedro de Valdés's crippled *Nuestra Señora del Rosario*. The *Rosario*, minus her foremast and bowsprit, is seen at the top right, with Drake's *Revenge* and two smaller vessels closing in. Note the flotsam of battle floating past at the top – a convincing touch.

---

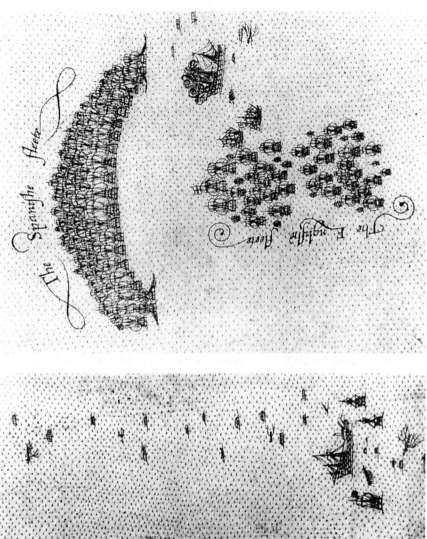

The Spanifhe fleete

The Englifhe fleete

The Englifh fleete

suddenly broke at deck level to fall in a tangle of shrouds and sails against the mainmast. The ship was now unmanageable, and Don Pedro sent a pinnace to ask the duke for aid. According to one of the messengers (the Dominican friar Bernardo de Góngora, who wrote a lively account of the campaign), 'the duke was willing to help and assist him, but Diego Flores de Valdés forbade him to do it, since it would put the entire fleet in jeopardy'. In view of this, according to Friar Góngora, 'the duke continued on his way and left the good Don Pedro and his company . . . in the power of the enemy, who were never more than a league behind us . . . God knows what happened to them'.

Don Pedro was furious. In his eyes he had been dishonourably abandoned in the face of the enemy by his commander. Recalde also fired off outraged messages to the flagship pleading for the fleet to wait while both the *Rosario* and his own *San Juan* could be repaired. Medina Sidonia agonised. 'If I could have remedied the situation with my blood', he later confessed, 'I would have gladly done so.' Instead he accepted the view of Diego Flores (who detested his cousin Pedro) that his overwhelming duty was to maintain the fleet's unimpeded progress towards its objective.[17]

The first English vessel gingerly to probe the abandoned Andalusian flagship's apparently formidable defences was the 200-ton *Margaret and John*, a merchant ship from the squadron provided by the City of London, which came up at about 9 p.m. and discharged her muskets into the *Rosario*'s towering bulk. Don Pedro responded with two cannon shots, and after further desultory skirmishing the *Margaret and John*, which was clearly incapable of taking the *Rosario* by force, left to rejoin the fleet.

At dawn the following morning Don Pedro found himself in the presence of a far more formidable foe: the sleek and gaudily painted galleon *Revenge*, carrying the flag of Sir Francis Drake (FIGURE 15). How precisely the vice-admiral of the queen's navy came to be there, all alone and far from his allotted station, has been a subject of dispute ever since. The night before, Drake had been ordered to set watch for the fleet by displaying a lantern on his stern for everyone else to follow, so that the English ships could remain in contact with, but at a safe distance behind, the Armada's ponderous advance. But, according to an irate Martin Frobisher, no lantern ever appeared – Drake's 'light we looked for, but there was no light to be seen'. Frobisher's explanation was simple, and deeply accusatory: Drake, he averred, had spotted the stricken *Rosario* and 'kept by her all night, because he would have the spoil'. Sir Francis scarcely bothered to argue. He claimed half-heartedly that he had glimpsed strange sails in the darkness and, apparently forgetting about the lantern, had gone to investigate, 'not knowing what they were'. When dawn broke he found, to his professed surprise, that 'we were within two or three cables of the *Rosario*'. 'Ay marry', retorted Frobisher, 'you were within two or three cables length, [because] you were no further off all night.'

Be that as it may, the morning of 1 August found Sir Francis and Don Pedro at the start of what would become an extraordinary relationship. At first the Spaniard had refused to surrender at all; then he refused to discuss surrender with anyone except Sir Francis in person. When at last Don Pedro came aboard the *Revenge* under a flag of truce, and Drake pointed out to him the hopelessness of his position, his defiance crumbled. He asked to be left alone for a few moments to make up his mind and then emerged, with his face all flushed, to announce his surrender.[18]

Pandemonium immediately broke out aboard the *Rosario*. Four of the seven or eight English renegades who had sailed with her had already prudently slipped away by boat, for they could expect no mercy from their countrymen. Curiously, however, the Spaniards made no effort to save the king's 50,000 gold ducats, many of which now disappeared. 'The soldiers merrily shared [the treasure] amongst themselves,' reported Richard Hakluyt, without specifying whether they were Englishmen or Spaniards. Some may have vanished during the transfer of specie to the *Revenge* in thin canvas bags: according to another contemporary account, 'there is great likelihood . . . that some of the treasure was purloined away'. But it seems unlikely that Drake would have been so naive or unobservant as to let any such irregularity take place, at least on the part of others. Don Francisco de Zárate, whose ship Sir Francis plundered in 1579 off Acapulco, noted with grudging admiration that 'when our ship was sacked, no man dared take anything without his orders: he shows them great favour, but punishes the least fault'.

In the end just over half the *Rosario*'s treasure actually reached the queen's exchequer.[19] How much of the rest was purloined by Drake is anyone's guess, but suspicion naturally fell on him, especially from Frobisher, who later furiously exclaimed that Drake 'thinketh to cozen us of our shares of 15,000 ducats; but we will have our shares or I will make him spend the best blood in his belly'.

That squabble lay in the future. Following the capture of the *Rosario* on 1 August no one was available to argue with Drake because the previous night, without his lantern for guidance, the English fleet had scattered. According to Howard, when dawn broke even the nearest of his ships 'might scarce be seen . . . and very many out of sight, which with a good sail recovered not his Lordship the next day before it was very late in the evening'. Drake's dereliction of duty had given the Spaniards a full 24 hours' grace and the Armada sailed on.

During the night of 1/2 August the wind fell, becalming both fleets some miles west of Portland Bill. Then, as dawn broke on the Tuesday, a fresh breeze sprang up from the east to give the Spaniards, for the first time, the weather gauge. Responding to the danger, Howard led his galleons, close-hauled, towards the north-north-east, attempting to place himself between the Armada and the

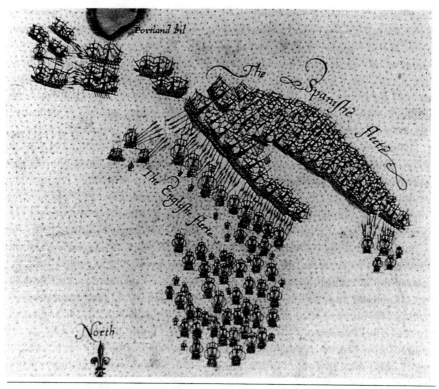

*Portland bil*

*The Spanyshe flecte*

*The Englysshe flecte*

*North*

FIGURE 16   The battle off Portland Bill on 2 August, from No. 6 of the Ryther engravings. The action between the galleasses and Frobisher's ships off Portland Bill is clearly shown.

shore. But Medina Sidonia used his advantage of wind to counter this attempt, forcing the English ships to come about in a reach towards the south-south-west.

These moves gave the waiting troubleshooters a chance to intercept. For the first time since the fighting began some of the larger ships now came to close quarters, and an artillery fight began. Bertendona's *Regazona* bore down on a large English vessel, intent on boarding, but his adversary prudently turned seaward and opened the range. This general melee continued for more than two hours, without clear tactics on either side beyond a strong Spanish desire to grapple and board and an equally strong English determination to stay clear and use their guns.

While this skirmish was taking place well to seaward of Portland Bill, a separate action had developed just to the west of it (FIGURE 16). When, at dawn, the English fleet abandoned its attempt to weather the Armada, the leading ships found themselves close inshore in a flat calm. Most were medium-sized merchantmen from the London squadron, but their leader was Martin Frobisher's powerful *Triumph*, the largest ship in the English fleet. The Spaniards sensed a golden opportunity to close and board. Medina Sidonia, who was by now fully engaged in the fight developing around his rearguard, therefore dispatched Don Hugo de Moncada with his four crimson-painted galleasses to deal with Frobisher's isolated force.

The galleasses, led by Moncada in the *San Lorenzo*, advanced towards the *Triumph* and one of her smaller consorts, which responded with a withering fire from her 'excellent artillery which fired with extraordinary speed, killing several soldiers'. The galleass replied with her cannon, however, until the smaller vessel seemed almost ready to surrender – some of her soldiers were seen taking to the boats ready to sail to the *Triumph*. The captain in charge of the musketeers in the fo'c'sle called on Don Hugo to increase speed so that they could reach the ship and take her. According to the captain, 'he replied that he was doing all he could, but that he had no orders from the duke to board'.[20] At this point, the wind suddenly rose, and the English escaped. The incident greatly displeased Medina Sidonia, who dispatched an officer to Moncada's flag galleass to 'say aloud to Don Hugo . . . certain words which were not to his honour'. Later that day the duke also sent a message to Moncada that began with this reproach: 'A fine day this has been! And if the galleasses had done their bit as I expected, it would have gone badly for the enemy.'

At first, however, Medina Sidonia had other things to worry about. Howard took advantage of a change of wind to disengage with a number of his more powerful galleons from the Spanish rearguard and make a thrust into the heart of the Armada. The lord admiral 'called unto certain of her Majesty's ships then near at hand and charged them straightly to follow him, and to set freshly upon the Spaniards, and to go within musket-shot of the enemy before they should discharge any one piece of ordnance'. And so they again attacked in line ahead, firing their guns only when they came into close range. In Howard's words 'the Spaniards were forced to give way and flock together like sheep'. Recalde agreed, complaining that he received 'no assistance from any other ship in the fleet, because they all seemed to want to take refuge one behind the others, so that they fled from the action and collided together. It is a disgrace to mention it.'[21]

Medina Sidonia also came under heavy bombardment, with the English 'firing at him ship by ship'. Although the *San Martin* discharged her own guns 'very well and quickly', according to the ship's gunnery officer, 'so that half the enemy's fleet did not come near, but fired from a distance', in return for about 80 outgoing rounds the flagship received 500, some of which struck the hull and rigging and carried away the flagstaff and one of the mainmast stays. A Spanish observer aboard another ship noted in wonderment that the *San Martin* was so enveloped in gunsmoke that for 'more than an hour we could not see her'.

Once the English disengaged, Medina Sidonia took some key decisions. First, he still had no word from Parma to confirm that his invasion force was ready, let alone to explain how he intended to join it with the fleet. He therefore dispatched another pinnace to Flanders, seeking urgent clarification of his plans for the proposed link-up. Next he reorganised the Armada's tactical formation. His initial assumption that the English fleet would lie ahead of him, attempting to block the straits, with only a small detachment at Plymouth, had proved totally wrong. Now he came to share Recalde's realisation that 'the English do not intend to fight a battle, but simply to delay us and prevent our voyage'. The duke therefore resolved:

> that the Armada should travel in two squadrons, vanguard and rearguard. The rearguard will be reinforced by the best ships in the fleet, one half under the command of Juan Martínez [de Recalde] and the other half under Don Alonso de Leiva. [Moncada] and the flag galleass, and two other galleasses, will go in the rearguard with Juan Martínez, and Captain Peruchio with the fourth galleass will go in the vanguard with me.

He also ordered Moncada to make sure that 'the three galleasses [in the rearguard] should be held in reserve, and that they should rally immediately to all opportunities that arise without the need for further orders' (no doubt another allusion to Don Hugo's reticence against the *Triumph*). The English sources subsequently referred to the new formation as a 'plump' or 'roundel'. It was precisely the battle plan that the unfortunate Don Pedro de Valdés had proposed at Corunna.[22]

Not that the extended formation had proved defective: on the contrary, in spite of two unexpected and serious accidents, and in the face of a strong English fleet to windward, Medina Sidonia had demonstrated during his first days of action both the tactical and strategic strengths of the Armada and his own skill in commanding it. Furthermore, remarkably little damage had been inflicted by either side upon the other, even though at times the ranges appear to have been point-blank. Captain Vanegas reckoned that the two fleets had expended a total of 5,000 rounds in the course of the day, yet the injuries sustained even by the heavily engaged *San Martín* remained minimal. Both commanders must have been surprised at the disappointing equation between the amount of precious roundshot expended and the damage it had caused.

This expenditure concerned the English far more than the Spaniards. The fight, as John Hawkins reported to Walsingham, had been 'sharp and long', and had cost 'a good part of our powder and shot'. It would not be wise, he thought, to engage the Spaniards further until ammunition stocks had been replenished. The English had reached a moment of acute crisis. It was one thing to have nimble ships which could take advantage of wind and tide, and thus keep the Spaniards at arm's length, but to defeat the Armada it was necessary physically to destroy its ships, not just run circles around them. On the one hand, Howard and his subordinates could see that their vaunted heavy artillery, despite the expenditure of so much shot at moderately close range, had not inflicted serious damage on the Spanish ships. On the other hand, if the English brought their ships much closer they would clearly run the risk of being boarded and over-whelmed by the Spanish troops.

In strategic (if not in tactical) terms, the Spaniards had thus proved them-selves to be the superior force. As soon as the gunfire stopped, with the English fleet temporarily neutralised by its ammunition crisis, the Armada simply shook itself back into formation, licked its minor wounds, and continued the eastward advance.

Spanish victory did not, however, depend solely on maintaining the Armada's progress. In order to succeed, the link-up with Parma still had to be achieved. The council of war aboard the *San Martín* on 29 July had recommended that until arrangements for the rendezvous were clear, and Parma's readiness as-sured, the Armada should proceed no further than the Isle of Wight. Otherwise the fleet would commit itself to plying up and down the narrow seas while it waited for Parma; and to beat back westwards in the teeth of the prevailing weather, with the English fleet to leeward, was unthinkable. There can be little doubt that by the evening of 2 August, with the Isle of Wight looming on his port quarter, Medina Sidonia seriously considered seizing the secure anchorage at Spithead. There, at least, he would have the option of a safe and defensible haven until contact had been made with Parma, and he might even be able to establish a beach-head on the Isle of Wight.

The English were equally aware of this possibility. But what could they do to prevent it? Their strategy, insofar as they had one, had been to cut out and disable individual members of the Spanish fleet, to 'pluck their feathers by little and little', as Howard put it. On the morning of 3 August, having obtained some meagre replenishment to its ammunition stocks (much of it from the two cap-tured Spanish ships), the English fleet was presented with an excellent feather-plucking opportunity. As dawn broke a large ship was observed trailing behind the seaward flank of the Armada, a few miles off the dangerous western en-trance to the Solent. The straggler was Gómez de Medina's wide-bellied flagship, the Rostock hulk *El Gran Grifón*. Although the hulks were generally regarded as non-combatants, the nobly officered *Grifón* was herself a gallant if clumsy member of the Armada's troubleshooting elite. She may have been left behind as a decoy, to tempt some English ships to board and thus precipitate a general engagement. Instead, as the English ships closest to her crowded on sail to catch the light morning airs, a powerful galleon, almost certainly Drake's *Revenge*, glided abeam the wallowing *Grifón* and gave her a broadside at close range, came swiftly about to give her another, and then crossed her stern to rake it with gunfire. It was a devastating example of the mobile artillery tactics that individual English captains were beginning to adopt. But the *Grifón* hung grimly on, struck by at least 40 roundshot, her decks still thronged with angry soldiers who remained firmly at their posts despite serious casualties, ready and eager to board and carry any English ship rash enough to clap sides. The incident neatly demonstrated the strength of the Armada as a whole: it might be battered but it could not be destroyed; and yet, unless it was destroyed, its underlying military potential remained as strong as ever.

As the fight around the *Grifón* developed, more ships became involved: Recalde's *San Juan* received another 200 incoming rounds and the *San Martín* 130. Now Medina Sidonia sent in the galleasses to extricate the damaged hulk and gave the signal for a general engagement; according to Captain Vanegas, the two fleets expended another 5,000 rounds. The mainmast of Drake's *Revenge* received a direct hit, but otherwise, once again, neither side reported any serious damage. The English then drew off, preferring to delay the Spaniards rather than precipitate an all-out battle. The duke therefore turned his ships about, and the Armada continued relentlessly on its way.

The next few hours of the campaign were crucial, for the Armada had now reached a commanding position close to the Solent's eastern entrance. Now, if ever, Medina Sidonia had the chance to put his alternative plan into effect. It was not an easy choice. The king's instructions on the matter had been repeated and explicit: alternatives to the main strategy could only be considered once an attempt to make the rendezvous with Parma had actually failed. But until he knew what practical arrangements for that rendezvous had been made by Parma, the duke's only sensible course was to find a secure anchorage in which to husband and if necessary defend the Armada until direct contact with his opposite number had been made. A seizure of the Solent, seen in this light, might be regarded as a wise precaution rather than a change of plan.

In the event, however, the English resolved Medina Sidonia's dilemma. The previous evening, in response to his fleet's sustained lack of success against the Armada, Howard had ordered a major reorganisation of his forces. Until then his fleet had been little more than a loose agglomeration whose members, apart from a general obligation to support the flagship, acted as individual circumstances dictated. But now it seemed necessary to pursue a wider strategic aim, and the immediate priority was to deny the Spaniards entry to the Solent. An urgent council of war was convened aboard the *Ark Royal* which decided to organise the fleet into four quasi-independent squadrons under the commands of Howard, Drake, Hawkins and Frobisher (FIGURE 17). These squadrons were given tasks which, if performed in unison, should force the Armada past Selsey Bill and clear of the Solent.

During the night of 3/4 August some units of the Armada again fell astern of the main body. They were the Portuguese galleon *San Luís* and the Andalusian hulk *Duquesa Santa Ana*. Like *El Gran Grifón* the previous day, they presented the

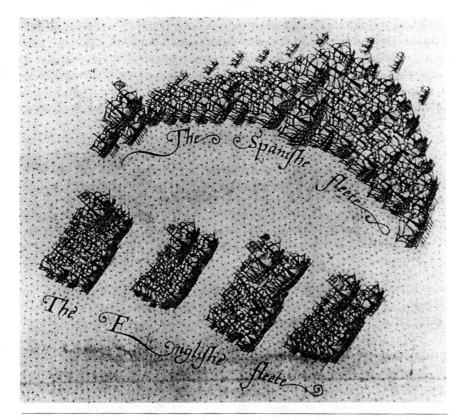

FIGURE 17   Another detail from No. 6 of the Ryther engravings shows the English fleet, having been reorganised into four squadrons on 3 August, continuing to shadow the Armada up-Channel.

English – again perhaps deliberately – with obvious targets. But this time there was no wind. Hawkins, whose squadron lay closest to the Spanish stragglers, lowered his ship's boats and moved to the attack under tow. Medina Sidonia responded by sending in the three galleasses now attached to the rearguard, one of them towing Leiva's *Rata Encoronada*.

As the ranges closed the guns began to fire, and soon the galleasses had become the main objects of the English attack. One was seen to list, another lost her lantern, and a third received some damage to her prow. Once again, however, no English ship attempted to close and board, and so the galleasses therefore took the *San Luis* and *Duquesa* in tow and drew them clear of the action. At this point a south-westerly wind sprang up, enabling the immobilised sailing ships on both sides once again to manoeuvre.

Meanwhile Frobisher, on the left wing, had taken his squadron into the difficult tidal seaway to the east of the Isle of Wight. Medina Sidonia, perhaps in an attempt to force a passage into the Solent, led a flotilla of powerful galleons towards them. Frobisher in his vast *Triumph* seemed to be in difficulties (quite possibly feigned). The ship's boats were lowered to tow him clear as the left wing of the Armada began to converge on him. Then a breath of wind filled the *Triumph*'s great sails, and her hull took on way. Medina Sidonia fired a gun to call off the chase.[23] Recalde, who had been closing in on Frobisher, was furious:

> We were gaining the wind, and some of our ships were gaining ground on many of the enemy's, and we gave them chase. And as we were thus harassing the enemy and pressing home our victory, our flagship fired a gun to call us back so we could resume our voyage . . . In [my] opinion we should not have desisted as our flagship did until we had either made them run aground or else followed them into a port. Nor was it wise to sail with our fleet beyond that anchorage, near to the Isle of Wight, until we had heard from the prince of Parma, because it was the best anchorage in the whole Channel for every circumstance.[24]

Recalde was doubtless right, but Medina Sidonia had little choice. While the principal ships of the Armada were thus occupied on the left wing, at the entrance to the Solent, a furious and unexpected English attack suddenly developed further down the line. This assault was delivered 'in such wise', according to a Spanish eyewitness, 'that we who were there were cornered, so that, if the duke had not gone about with his flagship . . . we should have come out vanquished that day'. The surprise attack had fatally unbalanced Medina Sidonia's dispositions, and drawn him away from any chance of forcing the Solent.[25]

At first this did not seem like a defeat. On the contrary, it brought considerable short-term gains to the Spaniards, for the Armada was left unmolested for three full days. Another 4,000 rounds had been fired on 4 August and, according to Howard's journal, 'Forasmuch as our powder and shot was well wasted, the Lord Admiral thought it was not good policy to assail them any more until their coming near unto Dover.' For the moment Howard had time to spare, and he used his privilege as commander-in-chief to confer well-deserved knighthoods on Hawkins and Frobisher.

The Spaniards, too, made the best use they could of their time. Medina Sidonia sat down to write again to Parma, bringing him up to date with the increasingly serious situation:

> The enemy's fleet has come to bombard me so that we have had to turn and face them, and most days they have bombarded us from morning until night, without ever letting themselves go alongside our armada, even though for my part I have done everything possible and given them every occasion – sometimes our ships have been in the middle of their fleet, all to the end that one of their ships should board and so bring on the battle.[26]

It occurred to him that a few more smaller but faster ships might assist in this process, and so he asked Parma to send him 40 or 50 from the Dunkirk flotilla at his earliest convenience.

On 5 August the fleets lay becalmed and several ships took the opportunity to carry out repairs. That night Recalde and his crew at last had time to repair the mainmast which had been damaged by shot in the first encounter, and to cover the bindings with pitch so that the English would not notice. The next day, however, the westerly wind returned, and the fleets got under way again. On the morning of 6 August Boulogne on the French coast came in sight. What should the Armada do now?

Philip II's instructions had specified 'Cape Margate' (the North Foreland) as the place where the fleet would 'join hands' with Parma; now, with the English in battle array three miles astern, this made no sense. And yet, with no word from Flanders, should the fleet go directly to Dunkirk, there to pick up the invasion forces directly, or should it hold back? The journal of the *San Martín* makes clear the dilemma facing the duke and his advisers as the fleet drew level with Calais:

> There were different opinions on whether to anchor in that roadstead, and most favoured going on; but the duke, understanding from the pilots he brought with him that if he proceeded further the currents would force him out of the Channel and into the North Sea, determined to anchor before Calais, seven leagues from Dunkirk, where Parma could come and join him. And so at 5 p.m. he ordered the whole fleet to drop anchor.[27]

Medina now wrote to ask Parma once again for 'forty or fifty flyboats' so that 'we can hold off the fleet of the enemy until Your Excellency can come with all the rest [of your forces] and we can capture some port [no doubt on the Kent coast] where this Armada can anchor in complete safety'.[28]

At this point, with his great task force substantially intact, and with the Army of Flanders only 25 miles away, in spite of all the anxieties and accidents Medina Sidonia might well have been forgiven for thinking that he had fulfilled his master's command and, against overwhelming odds, successfully 'done his part'.

### Sources

The major official source for the voyage of the Armada is Medina Sidonia's *Diario* or journal printed in Oria, 233–48 (a better transcription than Duro). There is an admirable English translation, juxtaposed with Howard's 'Relation of proceedings', in Clowes, *The Royal Navy*, 564–82. Duro also included a large number of 'Relations' by others on the Spanish side, and Laughton did the same for the English. See the useful list of surviving sources in Pierson, *Commander*, 267–8. Recently, Geoffrey Parker found and published a collection of documents sent to the king after the campaign by Recalde. It consists of seven *billetes* (memoranda) sent by Recalde to the flagship, and returned with comments (surely the earliest surviving exchange of opinions between commanders during a fleet action), a *Diario* kept on Recalde's ship and a cover note: see Parker, 'El testamento político'.

Nevertheless some gaps in the story remain. Most accounts are either silent or superficial concerning the fighting on 3 August (24 July OS) 1588. Our details come from Duro, II, 384–6, account of Captain Vanegas. They are also almost all silent about the fighting on the following day after the escape of the *Triumph*. The fortunate exceptions are the 'relation' of an anonymous officer from Seville aboard an Andalusian ship, *ibid.*, 275–6, and the account of Captain Fernando de Ayala, aboard the flag galleass *San Lorenzo*, BNM MS 5489.

Confusion also surrounds the inspiration for the Armada's famous crescent-shaped battle plan, described in Medina Sidonia's letter to the king of 28 May 1588 (Duro, II, 101–5). Where did he get this idea? There are two obvious precedents. On the one hand, this was the traditional formation for galleys in battle, from the battle of Salamis in 480 BC (where Herodotus describes the Athenian fleet as attacking in a semi-circle) to Lepanto in AD 1571. On the other, the Indies *flotas* also normally sailed with a centre of transports and two 'wings' of warships. Most historians, starting with Pigafetta in 1588, have considered only the Mediterranean parallel but, given Medina Sidonia's earlier experience with the *flotas*, and the acknowledged purpose of the Armada, it seems just as likely that he adopted the tactical formation whose worth had already been amply proved by the armed convoys on the Americas run. We are grateful to Professors Richard E. Mitchell and Peter O. Pierson for shedding much light on this problem.

Considerable uncertainty exists concerning the actual size of the fleet that Medina Sidonia led against England. The Lisbon muster of 9 May listed 130 ships, but several changes took place after that. A list of ships dated 13 July 1588 noted that the hulk *David* was too badly damaged to sail further, the *zabra Concepción* had already sailed to Flanders (with Captain Moresin), and another hulk, the *Casa de Paz Grande*, also stayed at Corunna. That brought the total down to 127, but this was compensated by the addition of a new armed merchantman (the *San Juan Bautista de la Esperanza*), 9 caravels to reinforce the communications squadron, and 6 oared *falúas* (or feluccas) hired at Lisbon as ship's tenders (details in AGS CS 2a/280 fos 3082–129). If all the caravels sailed with the rest of the fleet on 21 July, the duke would have commanded 137 vessels. Ten days later, without the galleys and the *Santa Ana* of Recalde, there would therefore have been 131. But since few of the caravels are mentioned by later sources, it may well be that some or all of them stayed behind. Perhaps it is best to retain the traditional figure of 125 ships for the strength of the Armada when it entered the Channel. The size of the English fleet which opposed them was reliably established by Laughton, II, 323–42.

Particular controversy has surrounded the number of Ragusan vessels in the Armada: de Courcy Ireland, 'Ragusa and the Spanish Armada of 1588', believed that perhaps eight Ragusan argosies sailed with the Grand Fleet; while Kostíc, 'Ragusa and the Spanish Armada', argued for only three or four. Individual ship files in AGS CMC 2a/1208 indicate that there were at least five: the *Anunciada, Santa Maria de Visón, San Nicolás Prodaneli, San Juan de Sicilia* and *Santa María de Montemayor*. Only the last survived the campaign.

For the battles in the Channel, see the impressive reconstructions in Pierson, *Commander*, 128–66; and on the overall strategy, and how it changed, see Adams, 'The battle that never was'.

# Notes

1   Quotations from *CSPSp*, IV, 245–50, which is an almost integral translation of AGS *Estado* 165/104–14 (but note that on p. 245 'my nephew' is the Archduke Albert, not Parma).

2   Duro, II, 150–4, the king to Medina Sidonia, 5 July 1588, replying to the latter's complaints about the laggardly sailing qualities of the Mediterranean merchantmen and the hulks. For a discussion on the construction of the Mediterranean grain ships, which made them excellent bulk carriers but poor warships, see Colin Martin, '*La Trinidad Valencera*'.

3   AGS *CS* 2a/278 fo. 617, 'Relación de los bastimentos podridos' thrown into the sea, 30 June 1588; AGS *CMC* 2a/772, papers of the *San Francisco*, printed ration orders of the duke, 9 July 1588. On the dramatic growth of infantry size under Medina Sidonia's command, see Gracia Rivas, *Los tercios*, 172–3.

4   KML *MSP: CR* 5/264–7, Medina Sidonia to Philip II, 10 and 13 June 1588, minutes.

5   Maura, 258–61, Medina Sidonia to Philip II, 21 and 24 June 1588.

6   On stepping the *Santa María*'s mast, see Duro, II, 169–70, Recalde to the king, 11 July 1588, and 175, Medina Sidonia to the king, 11 July. See also the praise of Oquendo to the king, 15 July, in Oria, 248.

7   The king's further bout of ill health is recorded in HS 143 fos 97 (the king to Mateo Vázquez, 18 June 1588) and 111 (28 June). The courier brought an interesting array of letters: Oria, 210–14, Philip II to Medina Sidonia, 1 July 1588 (quoted in the text); and KML *MSP: CR* 5/304 and 306, Moura and Idiáquez to Medina Sidonia, 1 July 1588, berating the duke for his pessimism, telling him to 'put on some weight and get some sleep' (Moura) and to pull himself together (Idiáquez).

8   AGS *Estado* 455/320–1, Medina to Parma, 10 June 1588, copy sent to (and annotated by) Philip II (see also KML *MSP: CR* 5/264–7, minute of the same letter, listing the various anchorages where the Armada could wait while Parma made his final preparations); and Oria, 202–3, Philip II to Medina, 21 June 1588, minute. Some have doubted that the duke ever received the last letter, originally sent to him by way of Flanders, but its presence among his papers settles the matter: see KML *MSP: CR* 5/278–9 (copy), 289 (Philip's note of 26 June, enclosing a copy of the preceding and again stressing the need to press on) and 319–21 (Medina Sidonia's reply of 6 July, acknowledging its receipt).

9   Pierson, *Commander*, 122–3 and 266 n. 34 proves that Flores, Bobadilla and the rest only came aboard the flagship permanently in Corunna; he also quotes Philip's instructions to Andrés de Alva, 9 July 1588, about adding even more advisers. The duke's epiphany appears in KML *MSP: CR* 5/353, Medina Sidonia to Archduke Albert, 15 July 1588, minute.

10   AGS *GA* 225/55–6, Valdés to the king, 15 and 19 July 1588.

11   The exact decision taken by the council of war on 29 July remains unclear. In two angry notes on 1 August, one to Medina and the other to Bobadilla, Recalde stated that the council had resolved to blockade Plymouth harbour and regretted that the resolution had not been put into effect. The duke replied: 'This was discussed by the council, but nothing was decided; nor was it advisable', Parker, 'El testamento político', 22–4; see also Recalde's critical diary entry for 29 July: *ibid.*, 29. A surgeon aboard the *Rosario* later told his English captives that the council had 'agreed that

IT CAME, WENT, AND WAS

if they could passe the haven with twenty ships abreast they would follow that advice', PRO *SP* 12/214/51, interrogation of Dr Góngora. Fernando de Ayala, aboard the flag galleass, heard that the council resolved to attack Plymouth only if the English fleet were still within: BNM MS 5489/112.

12 Oliveira, *A arte da guerra do mar*, fo. lxxii; Chaves, *Espejo de navigantes*, 'De la guerra o batalla que se da en la mar'.

13 Parker, 'El testamento político', 29, *Diario* entry. Some accounts claimed the *Gran Grin* stood by Recalde, but the admiral claimed at the time that the ship 'never took her place' (*ibid.*, 25, to Medina Sidonia, 1 August 1588).

14 Parker, 'El testamento político', 22–5, Recalde to Bobadilla and Medina Sidonia, 1 August 1588, holograph, with responses in the margin. The perception that the English were wearing down the Armada 'little by little' was confirmed, word for word, by Howard: 'we pluck their feathers by little and little' (see page 157 above).

15 In July the hulk *Paloma Blanca* experienced almost the same fate when a soldier dropped a lighted fire-pot near some cartridges filled with powder, causing a minor explosion: KML *MSP: CR* 5/325, 'Relación que haze el alférez Bezerra'.

16 Recalde criticised the decision not to clear the ship entirely and 'either burn or scuttle it', so that the English would not gain advantage from it, see Parker, 'El testamento político', 31. The following year the ship's owner, Joan de Aguirre of Tolosa, claimed 18,000 ducats' compensation from Medina Sidonia because, he asserted, despite the damage caused by the explosion, the ship could have been repaired and brought back to Spain, KML *MSP: CR* 5/492, Philip II to Medina Sidonia, 17 July 1589.

17 Houghton Library, Harvard, fMS Span 54, letter from Fray Bernardo de Góngora to Fray Martín de Los Angeles, 15 August 1588. Medina Sidonia's *Diario* gives broadly the same story. Nevertheless several observers, both at the time and afterwards, saw abandoning the *Rosario* as a critical error. Don Juan de Cardona, for example, writing to the king on 20 November 1588, denounced this as 'the origin and cause' of all later disasters because, afterwards, the 'rumour went round the fleet that no ship should take any risks; for if a flagship had not received any relief, who would rescue the rest from any danger in which they might place themselves', Oria, 352–3. See similar sentiments in Duro, II, documents 171 and 185, and Parker, 'El testamento político', 30.

18 Laughton, II, 134–6, interrogation of Valdés by his English captors. Here the squadron commander stated that Drake offered only 'the safety of our lives and courteous entertainment'. Years later, however, he assured the king that he had only surrendered 'after a day and a night of bombardment' and against a promise that he and his crew 'would be given free passage to Spain or Flanders, whichever they preferred, and they would receive back their arms and insignia', Martínez, *Cartas de Felipe II*, 117, Valdés petition of *c*. 1615.

19 PRO *E* 133/47/3, 'Drake versus Drake, 1605': depositions of George Hughes, Simon Wood and Evan Owen. See Paula Martin, *Spanish Armada Prisoners*.

20 BNM MS 5489/126v–130, from the 'Compendio' of Fernando de Ayala, who sets the story on 'the second day of combat, the 5th of August'. The second day of combat was 2 August, and the events included clearly relate to the fight on that day with the *Triumph*, which Ayala correctly described as the largest ship in the English fleet

(indeed he thought it might be the Portuguese carrack captured by Drake the previous year). Ayala also noted that some had accused Moncada of cowardice, and included this description as a defence of his late commander. Moncada's advance was also probably delayed because he had to cross the tide race which runs between Portland Bill and the Shambles reef towards which, no doubt, the wily Frobisher had purposely lured him.

21 Parker, 'El testamento político', 31, Recalde's *Diario* for 2 August, confirmed by Bertendona's account: Lilly Library, Bloomington (Indiana), Bertendona Papers, 171, 'Relación de servicios'.

22 PRO *SP* 94/3/11, Medina Sidonia to Moncada, dated 2 August 1588, copy (precis in *CSPSp*, IV, 359). See also Medina Sidonia's *Diario*: Oria, 236-7.

23 Recalde states that 'we noticed that the enemy flagship [presumably the *Triumph*] had lost its rudder, and so all our fleet gave it chase': Parker, 'El testamento político', 32. No English source mentions any squadron flagship experiencing problems with its rudder, and so this may have been a ruse to distract the Armada from what was happening on its right flank.

24 Parker, 'El testamento político', 32.

25 Mystery surrounds 'the Isle of Wight alternative'. Despite the king's repeated prohibitions on stopping anywhere before 'joining hands' with Parma, on 29 July Medina Sidonia and his council of war definitely resolved to wait in the eastern Solent, if by the time they arrived there they had still not heard from Parma, AGS *Estado* 455/492, Medina Sidonia to the king, 30 July 1588. The king was furious at this departure from his plan, and fired off another eloquent (if vain) protest, AGS *Estado* 165/146, the king to Medina Sidonia, 14 August 1588. The duke's *Diario* does not mention any desire or attempt to force an entrance to the Solent, and neither does any other Spanish source except Recalde: but his journal is explicit – Parker, 'El testamento político', 32. We can rule out the possibility that the Armada was swept involuntarily past Selsey Bill by natural forces. The tides off the Isle of Wight are complex (there is for example a double high tide in the Solent) but relatively weak: it is therefore highly unlikely that the tide swept the Armada past its eastern entrance against its will, as many authorities have claimed. The winds over the crucial period, too, were, by general admission, at first absent and then light and from the south. They, too, would hardly have driven the slow-moving fleet irresistibly eastwards. We therefore conclude that the Armada sailed on past Selsey Bill through human, not natural causes, either because the Spaniards took a positive decision to do so, or because English pressure forced them to, or both. We are most grateful to Alan Ereira for an illuminating discussion of these points.

26 AGS *Estado* 594/116, Medina Sidonia to Parma, 4 August 1588, copy.

27 Oria, 241, from the *Diario*. This document, although organised as a day-by-day narrative, was clearly revised before being sent to Philip II on 21 August 1588. In his first letter to Parma from before Calais on 6 August, Medina claimed only that 'the weather [*el tiempo*]' had forced him to drop anchor, AGS *Estado* 594/118. When did Medina Sidonia resolve to depart from the king's instructions to sail to 'Cape Margate' and await Parma? Most recently Adams, 'The battle that never was', concluded that Medina took the decision at the last moment, as a direct result of the close proximity of the entire English fleet and the absence of communication between the two dukes. This is confirmed by Recalde who, in notes sent to Medina Sidonia on 28 July

and again on 1 August, still wrote of 'las Dunas' (the Downs) as the fleet's destination, Parker, 'El testamento político', 19, 22.

28   AGS *Estado* 594/120, Medina Sidonia to Parma, 6 August 1588, copy (his second letter of the day). As pointed out by Adams, 'The battle that never was', 187, the duke can only have meant a port in England. Recalde was one of those who opposed anchoring off Calais, Parker, 'El testamento político', 33.

# 10

# The banks of Flanders

There can be few sets of military correspondence so unidirectional as that which passed between the dukes of Medina Sidonia and Parma as the Armada made its way from Lisbon to Flanders. On 10 June, as he approached Cape Finisterre and confidently anticipated that he would reach the rendezvous within a fortnight, Medina Sidonia sent a *zabra* to inform Parma of his progress, pointing out that because of the coastal sandbanks and the lack of a deep-water port in Flanders, there could be no question of attempting a link-up close to shore. His next letter, dated 25 July, simply provided confirmation that, after the delay at Corunna, he was again on his way. No acknowledgment arrived to either dispatch, but Medina Sidonia persisted. On 31 July, as the Armada approached Plymouth, he sent a plea for more pilots who knew the coast of Flanders, while four days later, after the first bouts of fighting off the Isle of Wight, he urgently demanded replenishments of powder and shot, and confirmed his imminent arrival at the rendezvous.

Still he received no reply. On 5 August, off Beachy Head, Medina Sidonia tried again. This time he sent a pilot to explain why the Armada was making such slow progress, and how much it needed reinforcements. In spite of all this, when the fleet reached Calais there was still no word from the shore. Medina Sidonia came close to despair. 'I have constantly written to your Excellency', he protested to Parma in yet another missive, 'and not only have I received no reply to my letters, but no acknowledgment of their receipt.'[1]

It was an extraordinary situation: the joint commanders of the greatest amphibious operation in European history to that date had no effective contact with one another. Much has been made in the past of Parma's silence, some (including many Spaniards at the time) going so far as to accuse the duke of deliberately trying to sabotage the enterprise. But this is either malice or fantasy. It assumes that travel by land or sea in early modern Europe was easy, rapid and regular. Of course it was not. In the sixteenth century a journey between any given points might take days, weeks, or months, depending entirely on the vagaries of the weather, the state of roads and bridges, the availability and mode of transport, the political situation, and the presence or absence of pirates or bandits along the route.

A letter sent from Brussels or Paris to Madrid, for example, might reach its destination in as few as 10 days; but in the summer and autumn of 1588 a combination of atrocious weather and sustained activity by Huguenot partisans south of Bordeaux meant that some important communications took three weeks or more. Others did not arrive at all. In normal times, it is true, communications by sea were often swifter and surer than those by land, but these were not normal times. Moreover, when one of the correspondents was on the move, like Medina Sidonia aboard the Armada, the situation became infinitely more difficult. Even if a messenger from the Armada found his way in due course to a fixed destination on shore, it would be far more difficult for him to find his way back, because the fleet by then would have moved on to a different, and unknown, location. To make matters worse, the English and Dutch fleets commanded the waters over which Medina Sidonia's messengers had to pass. That the duke appears to have expected rapid and reliable communications between himself and Parma once he had put to sea reveals a profound misunderstanding of the logistical limitations of his position. It was one of his few serious mistakes during the campaign but it proved fatal.

In the event, not one of the couriers dispatched from the Armada reached Flanders in time to do much good. The envoy sent from the Bay of Biscay on 25 July, in 'an armed pinnace with six oars', took only seven days to reach Parma, but the next messenger dispatched on 31 July, when the fleet was drawing level with Plymouth, could not make sail until the following morning, and only reached Parma's headquarters early on 6 August. Later that same day the messenger dispatched by Medina Sidonia off the Isle of Wight on 4 August arrived. Yet by this time the Armada was actually dropping anchor off Calais, just over the horizon, though it was another day before its arrival became known in Flanders. So although Medina Sidonia repeatedly expressed regret at his slow progress, and sought to increase his speed exactly as Philip II had exhorted him to do, from the perspective of the Army of Flanders he arrived much too soon.[2]

A reply from Parma finally reached the Armada on the evening of Saturday 6 August, as it lay huddled before Calais. At first the pinnace bearing it was mistaken for an enemy vessel, and fired upon, but it swiftly delivered its shattering message, which had been written three days earlier. The duke of Parma, it reported, 'had not embarked a barrel of beer, still less a soldier', and would not be able to join forces until the following Friday, at the earliest.[3]

On Friday? Another six days? Medina Sidonia was horrified, for the Armada had now been drawn into the situation he had dreaded all along. It had reached Calais, but without securing even localised command of the sea. The English fleet, now even stronger than before, was close to his rear, and still held the commanding weather gauge. Finally, the army he was to pick up 25 miles away across the Flemish shoals was not yet ready to embark.

What was to be done? As Medina Sidonia's next, despairing letter to Parma made accusingly clear, the Armada's position was perilous in the extreme. Just beyond artillery range stood the English fleet, and to leeward lay the shallows known to mariners as 'the banks of Flanders'. This natural hazard had been rendered even more treacherous by the Dutch, who cunningly removed all the navigation marks and buoys from the coast and rivers before the Armada arrived.[4] On the one hand, Medina Sidonia's cumbersome task force could get no closer to Parma's embarkation ports: it could only wait in its precarious position outside Calais and hope for the best. In other circumstances, perhaps the galleasses and a few of the smaller galleons could have been detached and sent to drive off the Dutch blockaders, but with the English fleet anchored in battle order just over a mile away Medina Sidonia dared not divide his forces. On the other hand, no one, least of all the duke, supposed that the English would allow the immobilised Armada to remain unmolested at anchor for a further six days.

The testimony of Don Diego Pimentel, one of the Armada's senior infantry commanders captured by the Dutch two days later, reveals that at least some of the fleet's high command remained entirely in the dark about the state of affairs in Flanders. Pimentel assured his captors that he had expected Parma to make a dash for the Armada with whatever forces he had ready. When asked if he did not realise that the Dutch had a powerful squadron outside Dunkirk which would vigorously oppose any attempt by Parma and his men to come out, Pimentel admitted that he and his peers had expected nothing less. But, he reiterated, 'it never occurred to them for a moment that the duke would not attempt a sortie'. Pimentel went on to wonder why Parma had not at least sent out his small warships to drive or draw off the Dutch fleet, even if they perished in the attempt. This way, reasoned Pimentel, at least the invasion barges could have slipped out to join the Armada.[5]

Pimentel's testimony probably reflects the thinking of Medina Sidonia at this point for, as his interrogators smugly noted, Don Diego was 'related to the principal families of all Spain', and he had no obvious reason to lie. If so, three distinct misconceptions become clear, which explain the failure to make the vital rendezvous envisaged by Philip II. First, Medina Sidonia assumed that news of the Armada's approach had preceded it. This, of course, had not been so. Not only did his own messengers fail to keep ahead of the fleet; so did everyone else. The first news of the Channel battles to reach the Netherlands came, remarkably, from English sources. At 3 p.m. on 6 August the English diplomats at Bourbourg received a letter from London announcing that the queen's ships had engaged the Armada off Plymouth. The delegation at once began to pack its bags, to the open amazement of the Spanish negotiators who, quite unaware of the Armada's progress, suggested to Parma that this might only be 'some subterfuge or cover' intended to secure diplomatic concessions from Spain. The truth only emerged some hours later.[6]

Medina Sidonia's second misplaced assumption stemmed from the first. He believed, quite wrongly, that Parma, being forewarned, would have his troops aboard the transports before the Armada reached the narrow seas, and would therefore be able to put out the instant its sails appeared on the horizon. There was more to this misjudgement than poor communications; it stemmed from a fundamental failure of comprehension.

Here Medina Sidonia must bear some of the blame, for the necessary information had been available to him before the Armada sailed. In mid-May Captain Francesco Moresin, a staff officer from the Army of Flanders, had arrived at Lisbon to brief the duke on the state of Parma's preparations. His news was not encouraging. First, losses among the troops in winter quarters had dangerously reduced the numbers available for embarkation. Second, the Flanders flotilla had few escorts for the unarmed low-freeboard landing craft and barges in which they were to be transported. Perplexed, Medina Sidonia turned to the king for guidance but received little help. The reduced number of troops, Philip replied, would be more than compensated by the increased number of soldiers aboard the fleet, of which 10,000 had been earmarked to reinforce Parma's forces once they landed in England. The king simply glossed over the lack of escort vessels, passing the responsibility for clearing the seas squarely back to Medina Sidonia. Parma's own vessels, stated Philip (quite accurately), were not of a kind 'that can put out and seek you at a distance, unless you have first cleared away all enemy ships from the straits first, because they are ships for transport and not for fighting'.

Medina Sidonia seems to have forgotten, or failed to have grasped, this vital fact. On 10 June, as the Armada sailed north from Lisbon, he revealed his misconception in a letter to Parma, which confirmed that he 'was coming towards your Excellency, and will write again to you when I enter the Channel so your Excellency will know where to come out and join us'. He dispatched the letter by fast pinnace, requesting Parma to send back news of 'how far your preparations are advanced, when you can put to sea, and where we can meet'. A copy of this letter in due course reached Philip II, who noted ominously in the margin: 'this cannot be, if Medina does not secure the seas first with his fleet'. Too late, it seems, the king had begun to recognise the deficiencies of his own plan.

Parma received Medina Sidonia's letter of 10 June, carried once more by Captain Moresin, only 11 days later – an extremely fast delivery from Finisterre to Flanders. He at once dispatched a note of protest to the king: 'Medina seems to believe that I should set out to meet him with my small ships, which is simply impossible. These vessels cannot run the gauntlet of warships; they cannot even withstand large waves.' Once again Philip perceptively but vainly annotated the margin of this letter, received only on 7 August, the very day that disaster struck his fleet. 'Please God', he scrawled, 'let there not be some slip-up [*embarazo*] here.'[7]

Parma now waited impatiently for the Armada to arrive, for he did not discover until 21 July (ironically, the day it set forth again) that it had been delayed at Corunna. Eventually he sent Captain Moresin on a second mission to Medina Sidonia, repeating his warning about the need for the fleet to gain local command of Flemish coastal waters before he could bring his forces out to join it. But a bizarre combination of shipwreck, storms and an encounter with the English fleet delayed Moresin: although he sailed from Flanders on 14 July, he did not reach Spain until 2 August. Consequently Medina Sidonia remained in sublime ignorance of the facts, and right up to the moment he anchored off Calais he continued his fruitless bombardment of Flanders with letters asking where the rendezvous was to be, and when Parma would reach it.[8]

These two serious misapprehensions were compounded by a third. The Armada's commanders clearly believed that, following the arrival of Lord Henry Seymour and his squadron off Calais, only a handful of enemy ships remained to blockade the Flemish coast. Once again they were seriously misinformed. Parma knew, as they did not, that the Dutch possessed, in addition to their small navy, a sizeable reserve of large but shallow-draught merchantmen capable of carrying large bodies of men and forward-firing heavy artillery. His main concern, therefore, was to keep the Dutch fleet divided, for once it was concentrated off Dunkirk or Nieuwpoort – from which it was possible to sail only at high tide – his own ships would be hopelessly blocked in.

To avoid this Parma had adopted three stratagems. First, he kept most of his troops well away from the Flanders coastline, deployed to give the impression that they might be preparing to invade Holland or Zealand. Second, the duke himself kept unpredictably on the move between his bases at Antwerp, Ghent and Bruges. Finally, he divided his invasion fleet among several harbours. About 70 vessels, including the 400-ton flagship and a large galley (specially built by a team of ship's carpenters brought from Venice), were at Antwerp. Another flotilla lay at Sluis, captured by Parma the previous year, and the duke devised a plan for the big ships to sail down the Scheldt from Antwerp, 'liberate' the flotilla confined in Sluis, and then proceed to Nieuwpoort and Dunkirk to embark the invasion army. Parma carried out a personal reconnaissance of the estuaries and channels along the north coast of Flanders but found that between 130 and 140 Dutch ships lay in wait in the Scheldt to forestall precisely this manoeuvre. He reluctantly concluded that none of the Antwerp ships could reach Sluis in safety by that route. Resourceful as ever, therefore, the duke decided to leave the larger warships where they lay, in order to pin down the Dutch blockaders, and move the rest to Sluis along the inland waterways. Pioneers worked to deepen the canals and to break some dikes in order to increase both the level and the flow of water until in March 1588 all the smaller craft from Antwerp and other ports along the Scheldt could move to Ghent. Thence over 100 ships (including the large galley) eventually reached Sluis. At the same time, some 200 seamen recruited in Hamburg and Lübeck arrived overland to reinforce the crews aboard the flotilla.

Inevitably the Dutch noticed these developments and almost immediately placed another blockade squadron before Sluis, ruling out any thought of a sortie from there too. So Parma set his pioneers to work again, this time to deepen the rivers and to dig new canals in order to link Sluis with Nieuwpoort. On 5 April they opened a 'cutt' 10 yards wide and almost two yards deep which, even though the larger and better-armed vessels had once again to be left behind, allowed the barges and other flat-bottomed craft to reach the coast.

Against heavy odds, by the beginning of June 1588, seven merchantmen and 173 flat-bottomed craft, divided into three squadrons, now rode in Nieuwpoort harbour, ready to join the warships and transports at Dunkirk. As soon as he received news of the Armada's arrival off Calais, Parma not only started to board his troops in the Flemish ports, but also ordered the ships in the Scheldt to move downstream in order to draw off more Dutch blockade ships.

The plan worked. Contemporary Dutch records show a complete failure to discern Spanish intentions. Some, dismayed by the continuation of the talks at Bourbourg and the absence of a decisive battle in the Channel, supposed that the Armada was bound for either Flushing or Amsterdam; others feared that even though the fleet was directed against England, the Army of Flanders might still take advantage of its presence to launch a surprise assault on the republic. On 12 July 1588, when Justin of Nassau, the Dutch admiral in charge of blockading the Flemish coast, suddenly realised that Parma's entire army could sail out from Dunkirk and Nieuwpoort at any moment, he commanded only 24 ships. By contrast, 32 ships cruised off Sluis, 135 blockaded Antwerp and a further 100 stood guard further north around the entrance to the Zuider Zee and the Eems. All suggestions by the Dutch federal government that more vessels should be concentrated off Flanders ran into bitter opposition from the political leaders of Holland and Zealand who, as late as 10 August – two days after the battle off Gravelines – still feared that Philip really intended to attack them. As Seymour, from his vantage point at the Downs, correctly remarked, 'I think they [the Dutch] desire more to regard their own coast than ours'; while Admiral Howard noted with irritation, as he closed with the Spanish fleet, that 'There is not one Flushinger nor Hollander at the seas.'[9]

Thus, in spite of all the charges that he had been unprepared, Parma achieved his vital objective: surprise. The Dutch did not know what he intended to do, and their forces remained widely dispersed as a result. Even the blockade of Dunkirk was not impassable: Parma managed to send out one ship on 17 February 1588, four on 1 March, one on 1 May, three on 7 June, one each on 30 and 31 July and 1 and 2 August, three on the 5th and three more on the 12th – all to seek out the Armada – while two Armada vessels entered Dunkirk to take on stores and left again shortly afterwards. Lord Burghley, upon reading a report about this, scribbled angrily in the margin: 'Wherefore serveth Justin and his ships of Zeeland?'

Nevertheless, to concentrate an army of 27,000 men at the two designated embarkation ports, to get them – along with the necessary horses, provisions, weapons and equipment – aboard the 270 or so vessels concentrated there, and then to get both flotillas to sea and to join them into a single force, presented a series of different challenges. It would require, Parma estimated, a lead time of six days. Therefore, since he only received confirmation of the fleet's approach on 6 August, Parma could not have his forces fully ready until the 12th. If, by then, the Armada could clear the seas and escort him across the Channel, he could be marching on London by the 13th.

At first it seemed that this might prove possible, for while the Armada waited anxiously off Calais, the French Catholic governor of the port proved to be unexpectedly helpful. He sent presents to Medina Sidonia and welcomed ashore a number of Spanish dignitaries from the fleet. They included Inspector-General Don Jorge Manrique, Paymaster-General Juan de Huerta, and many others. Better still, the governor allowed the Spaniards to purchase water, fresh vegetables and other food, and throughout that Sunday a stream of victuallers plied to and fro between the anchored Armada and the shore.

It may have been the warmth of this welcome that convinced the English commanders that they had to act without delay. With the arrival of further auxiliaries and, on the afternoon of 6 August, of Seymour's squadron from the Downs, their fleet now numbered around 140 sail (FIGURE 18). The situation was desperate. For all the English knew Parma might already be embarking his forces at Dunkirk, and the very survival of the Tudor state thus depended on preventing the Armada from reaching them.

At a council of war aboard Howard's flagship Ark Royal early on the morning of 7 August it was resolved to launch a fireship attack against the Armada that night. Conditions for the stratagem were perfect. The Spanish fleet was crowded together at anchor, and its commander seemed uncertain of his next move. To leeward lay the Flemish shoals, upon which the Spanish ships might be driven. Best of all, from the English point of view, the conjunction of spring tides and a freshening westerly breeze could be expected to bear the fireships swiftly into the Armada's heart.

Eight fireships were prepared at a cost (subsequently minutely calculated in order to compensate the owners) of £5,111 10s 0d. It was, as one naval historian has observed, 'perhaps the cheapest national investment that this country has ever made'.[10] The vessels were packed with combustibles, and their guns loaded with double shot which would discharge spontaneously as the fire took hold, adding a psychological dimension to the stratagem. No Spaniard could forget Giambelli's terrible 'hellburners of Antwerp', and it was known that the great pyrotechnician was now living in England. Howard was consciously playing on

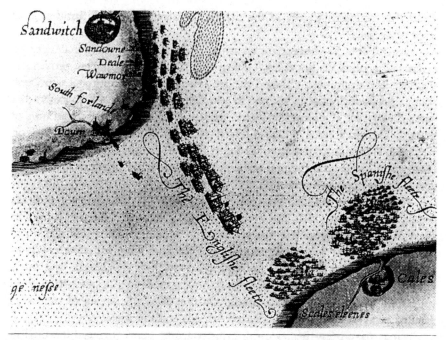

FIGURE 18   The situation in the narrow seas on 6 August, as shown in No. 8 of the Ryther engravings. The Armada is anchored off Calais, with the English fleet poised to windward. Seymour's eastern squadron is leaving its anchorage in the Downs to join in the final assault which will be precipitated by a fireship attack.

these fears, for it was clear that Spanish resolve was close to breaking-point, and his objective was therefore not so much to destroy ships as to create confusion and panic throughout the whole Armada. If that could be done, he and his officers reasoned, then the forces of nature, aided by the English fleet, might be expected to accomplish the rest.

So it transpired. Medina Sidonia had, of course, been acutely aware that such an attack was likely, and had done what he could to counter it. Before night fell he set a screen of small craft to windward of the Armada, with orders to grapple and tow clear any fireships that might approach. When, at midnight, the attack came, two of the fireships were indeed intercepted and dragged into the shallows – an act of considerable heroism on the part of the nameless pinnace crews. But the remaining six careered towards the midst of the defenceless Armada. Medina Sidonia had anticipated this eventuality, and sent out a felucca bearing one of his most distinguished staff officers, the prince of Asculi (thought by many to be Philip II's illegitimate son), together with his most experienced pilot, Marolín de Juan, with orders that any vessel that found itself in the path of a fireship should slip its cables and stand clear until the danger had passed, after which it should re-anchor.

It was a sensible enough stratagem, and in other circumstances it might well have worked. But, as the fireships came drifting closer, their pre-loaded guns discharging as the heat reached them, an already deteriorating situation degenerated into panic. Every ship in the fleet had two or even three anchors deployed, and almost every one of them was lost. Most captains simply cut or buoyed their cables and fled. The strong currents which prevail in the narrowest part of the Channel made it almost impossible for them to regain their positions and re-anchor, even had they wanted to. At a stroke the Armada had been transformed from a cohesive and still formidable fighting force to a scattering gaggle of panic-stricken ships.

Both of the clerical narratives of the campaign stress the magnitude of this disaster. Though they harped upon the value of the lost anchors – 500 ducats per ship, groaned Father La Torre; 100,000 ducats' worth in all lamented Father Góngora – both realised that the loss could not be calculated merely in financial terms. It would now be extremely difficult for the fleet either to re-anchor and wait for Parma, or indeed to approach any coast with safety. The immediate problem facing the Armada, however, was the loss of its tightly controlled formation, upon which both its effectiveness and its future security depended.

Panic apparently even gripped the flagship. When Asculi's felucca reached the side of Recalde's ship, which was already making sail, the prince shouted up a summons for the admiral to attend a council meeting. Recalde growled back 'that this was no time for him to leave his ship, and that his advice counted for nothing'. The prince replied that 'his vote too did not count', and complained about 'the confusion aboard the flagship *San Martín*'.[11] When dawn broke, however, the flagship and her loyal group of close supporters had apparently regained their composure. The *San Martín*, true to her own instructions, had immediately re-anchored after the fireship attack, as had Recalde's *San Juan*, the *San Marcos* and two other Portuguese galleons. At dawn on 8 August these five ships found themselves facing the entire English fleet. For the first time in the campaign Medina Sidonia had no doubt where his duty lay. At last he could stand firm as honour demanded, shoulder to shoulder with his comrades, and defy the enemy to his last breath. Even so, he did not neglect his responsibilities as a commander, and the ships' boats were sent scudding away to leeward to rally the scattered fleet. As they left the first English ships came within range, and heavy firing began.

At this point Lord Admiral Howard's attention was diverted from the lion-hearted quintet of galleons which stood between him and the dispersed Armada. In the confusion which followed the fireship attack Don Hugo de Moncada's flag galleass, the *San Lorenzo*, had been slow to cut her anchor cables and therefore collided with Don Alonso de Leiva's enormous *Rata Encoronada*, damaging her

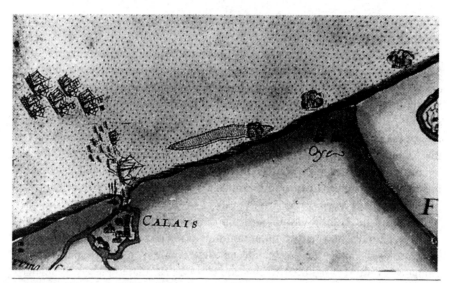

FIGURE 19   The aftermath of the fireship attack, from a detail in No. 10 of the Ryther engravings. The Spaniards have scattered to windward leaving the galleass flagship *San Lorenzo* grounded off Calais. Instead of pursuing the Armada, Lord Admiral Howard has paused to capture this tempting prize, and 11 rowing boats and a small sailing vessel can be seen descending on the galleass in an attempt to take her out. The situation is further confused by gunfire, apparently directed against the English, from the shore batteries at Calaies. Three Spanish ships are shown grounded and in flames along the coast further east, though in fact only two, the *San Mateo* and *San Felipe*, were lost here, and neither caught fire.

poop severely and breaking her rudder so that she could not steer. Seeing the fireships approach, many of her soldiers escaped up ropes cast down from the *Rata*, while the 'poor convicts at the oars began to cry out pitifully and to hammer at their chains and fetters in the hope of escaping by jumping in the sea, preferring to die by water than by fire'. All this confusion seems to have distracted Moncada. Even with the English bearing down on him and the Armada in full retreat, he refused to abandon efforts to re-sling the rudder and let the tide carry him to the safety of a Flemish port, and he rejected the offer of two French boats to tow him (for a price) into neutral Calais. Eventually the galleass grounded on a sandbank just off Calais, and as the tide fell her seaward guns pointed impotently at the sky as she heeled over. Howard could not afford to leave behind such a powerful vessel – one of the few capable of sailing to Dunkirk and driving off the Dutch blockaders – and so he sent an assault party in ships' boats to take her (FIGURE 19). After a ferocious hand-to-hand struggle, during which Don Hugo died with a bullet in his brain, the *San Lorenzo* was entered and sacked. The diversion only ended when a French boarding party, of technically neutral status in the conflict, was roughed-up by the rampaging English seamen. Not unnaturally, the French shore batteries responded by threatening to blow the galleass and everyone in her to pieces unless the English immediately withdrew.[12]

This prolonged sideshow brought little immediate profit to Howard, although he could now be sure that the galleass would never reach Parma, but it greatly assisted Medina Sidonia, who used the unexpected two-hour respite to mobilise an effective defence of his now rapidly re-forming fleet.

By now the troubleshooters had begun to take station on either side of the flagship, and soon a ragged but determined protective line shielded the Armada's rear. Sir William Winter, a member of Seymour's eastern squadron which had reinforced the English fleet off Calais, observed this regrouping with detached professional interest: 'They went into a proportion of a half-moon . . . Their admiral and vice-admiral, they went in the midst . . . and there went on each side, in the wings, their galleasses, armados of Portugal, and other good ships, in the whole to the number of sixteen in a wing, which did seem to be of their principal shipping.' It was the old trailing-horns defensive posture, this time composed almost exclusively of the troubleshooters, doggedly prepared to take whatever the English might yet throw at them.

The battle which followed lasted nine hours, and was fought along the fringes of the shoal waters between Gravelines and Ostend (FIGURE 20). It was fierce and very confused, but it may be summarised as a running fight in which the Spaniards strove to maintain a unified and compact defensive formation, and to keep as close as possible to Parma's ports of embarkation, while the English endeavoured to cut out the weathermost ships and force the rest leewards into the shallows. A vital factor was the wind, which veered steadily throughout the day from south-south-west to north-west, setting the Spanish fleet at an increasingly greater disadvantage as it did so. The weather too had deteriorated, with the sea now rough and the visibility poor.

Through the confusion, however, we can detect features which mark this battle as radically different from anything that had gone before. First, much of it was fought at very close range. 'Out of my ship', wrote Sir William Winter of the *Vanguard* afterwards, 'there was shot 500 shot of demi-cannon, culverin, and demi-culverin: and when I was furthest off in discharging any of the pieces, I was not out of the shot of their harquebus, and most times within speech of one another.' The fact that the protagonists were within hailing distance – which, amid the noise and chaos of battle, must have been very close indeed – is graphically borne out by what Pedro Coco Calderón of the hulk *San Salvador* saw from the Spanish side:

The enemy inflicted such damage upon the galleons *San Mateo* and *San Felipe* that the latter had five guns on the starboard side and a big gun on the poop put out of action . . . In view of this, and seeing that his upper deck was destroyed,

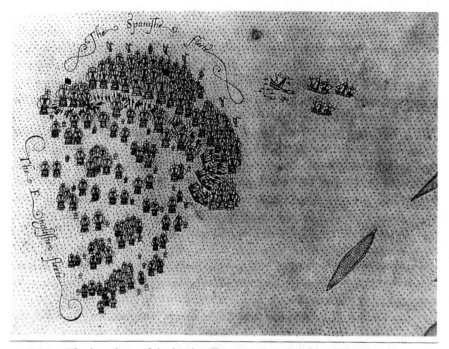

FIGURE 20   The last phase of the battle off Gravelines, on 8 August, shown in another detail from No. 10 of the Ryther engravings. The Armada has re-established its defensive 'half-moon' formation, after Medina Sidonia's draconian measures to restore discipline, and is fighting off a determined close-range attack by the English. To the right the Biscayan *María Juan* is shown sinking – the only vessel, so far as we know, actually to go down during the battle.

both his pumps broken, his rigging in shreds, and his ship almost a wreck, Don Francisco de Toledo ordered the grappling hooks to be got out, and shouted to the enemy to come to close quarters. They replied, summoning him to surrender in fair fight; and one Englishman, standing in the maintop with sword and buckler, called out 'Good soldiers that you are, surrender to the fair terms we offer you.' But the only answer he got was a musket ball which brought him down in sight of everyone, and [Don Francisco] then ordered the muskets and arquebuses to be brought into action. The enemy thereupon retired, whilst our men shouted to them that they were cowards, and with opprobrious words reproached them for their want of spirit, calling them Lutheran hens and daring them to return to the fight.

Some time earlier the *San Felipe*'s sister, the *San Mateo*, had experienced an even closer encounter with one of the English ships. As the two vessels passed one another their sides scraped together so closely that a single foolhardy

178

Englishman was able to leap across on to the Spaniard's deck. No one followed him, and he was instantly cut down.

The English were now, for the first time, pressing their attacks home at a range close enough to inflict real damage on the Spanish hulls. We have already seen the shambles to which the San Felipe had been reduced, and she was one of many. The aggressive and persistent troubleshooters, now fighting desperately to save the Armada from annihilation, naturally suffered most. The San Martín herself received '107 direct hits on the hull, masts and sails by cannon shot, which would suffice to destroy a rock'. Several of them penetrated her hull close to the waterline and only the heroic efforts of two naked divers with oakum and lead patches kept the leakage under control. Recalde estimated that over 1,000 rounds were fired against his San Juan. The San Mateo, which had been singled out by a hard-hitting pack of English galleons, fought until 'she was a thing of pity to see, riddled with shot like a sieve'. As well as damage received from the enemy she had suffered from the recoil of her own guns which, lashed directly to the hull frames, began to pull her whole internal structure apart.[13] She gaped open, and it was feared that she would sink, but in the evening the flagship sent a diver who managed to patch up some of the holes. Nevertheless the San Mateo, like the San Felipe, had been mortally stricken, and the two Portuguese galleons began to fall behind the rest of the fleet. That night they ran aground, the former in the shallow waters between Nieuwpoort and Ostend and the latter between Ostend and Sluis. The following morning, after a stiff fight, the Dutch captured both galleons, their commanders and most of their crews.

A group of English ships also battered the Levanter San Juan de Sicilia: 'so heavily with their guns that they completely shattered her . . . [we had to] repair the damage from the many shots which the ship had received alow and aloft and from the prow to the stern, and below the waterline in places difficult to repair'. Underwater damage was also sustained by the Santa María de la Rosa which, according to the sole survivor of her subsequent wrecking, 'had been shot through four times, and one of the shots was between the wind and the water, whereof they thought she would have sunk'. Both La Trinidad Valencera and El Gran Grifón sustained hull damage so severe that it eventually forced the crews to run them ashore; Oquendo's flagship, the Santa Ana, 'lay open through incoming shot, so that the pump was working night and day'; Francisco de Cuéllar's ship, the San Pedro of the Castilian squadron, 'was badly holed by very large cannon-balls which the enemy fired into her in several places'. According to Father La Torre, in the thick of it aboard the San Martín, it 'rained bullets on all the leading galleons'.[14]

Despite all this punishment, only one Spanish ship actually sank during the battle. She was the Biscayan María Juan, which was surrounded by English ships and battered to death: as she was 'in speech of yielding' to one of her assailants, 'before they could agree on certain conditions, [she] sank presently before their eyes'. Only a single boatload of her people escaped.

Human casualties aboard many other ships were high. No more than 127 of the 457 men who had embarked at Lisbon on the *San Felipe* ever came ashore again, and the death toll aboard the *San Mateo* was scarcely less. The Armada's overall losses at Gravelines were probably over 1,000 killed and 800 wounded. But the fighting spirit of the survivors remained strong. At one stage in the battle a great Italian ship, probably Bertendona's *Regazona*, was observed to be 'running with blood', with her main guns dismounted, though she was still to be seen at her station in the defensive rearguard three hours later.

The action began to wane between four and five in the afternoon, when English ammunition stocks started to run out. To escape, the Spaniards were now obliged to sail, without adequate pilots or charts, into the unknown shoal waters off the Flemish coast. According to Father La Torre, 'There was scarcely a man who could sleep that night; we were all wondering when we would run aground.' So the men prayed, or cried to the Virgin to save them, while the chaplains confessed them until dawn broke to reveal that a fortuitous shift of wind had carried them to the open sea.

But the Armada was no longer together. Yet again, the fleet had become scattered and 'the duke's ship, which was usually in the van, seemed to be the last of all'. This was deliberate and proper, for Medina Sidonia wanted to wait for Parma as long as he could. General morale among the Spaniards remained low. Some even speculated that the duke intended to surrender, and several sources state that some members of his council of war advised this desperate expedient. But according to La Torre 'there was no pinnace available [to handle negotiations with the enemy], which was a particular favour from God and, in any case, the duke did not want to follow this course, preferring to die like a knight'.[15]

Medina Sidonia and his officers confessed themselves, and prepared to continue fighting, while the guns of the *San Martín* fired three times as a signal for the fleet to re-form on the flagship. To Medina Sidonia's acute embarrassment and anger this evoked no response, so he sent out boats to the nearest ships with orders to bring their captains to him. La Torre has preserved the grim dialogue which followed when the recalcitrant officers came aboard:

'Did you not hear the gun?' demanded Medina Sidonia furiously.
They admitted that they had.
'Then why did you not rally?' he asked the terrified officers.
'We thought your flagship was sinking, and that we should all hasten away to safety.'

There was a short pause before the duke coldly delivered his verdict. 'Hang the traitors', he ordered.[16]

In the end only one captain was hanged at the yard arm and paraded around the fleet to re-establish its shaken discipline: Don Cristobal de Ávila, the captain of a hulk, who had been a close neighbour of Medina Sidonia's at San Lúcar. But although the duke might still rally his fleet with this salutary example, he no longer had an objective for which to fight. The wind had already carried the Armada, albeit once more in a semblance of disciplined order, away from the coast of Flanders and into the uncertain waters of the North Sea. And with that, as Recalde observed, 'the enterprise was over'.[17]

## Sources

The king had foreseen the importance of secure communications between Medina Sidonia and Parma, and devoted a paragraph to the subject in his 'Instructions' of April 1588, blandly stating that it would be possible either for a zabra to sail to Dunkirk, or a pinnace to row to 'some beach in Normandy'. What Philip failed to anticipate was both the time that this might take, and the total disruption of the postal system in 1588. On the problems posed by distance in the sixteenth century, see Braudel, *The Mediterranean and the Mediterranean World*, 354–94, and Parker, *Grand Strategy*, 47–75. On special conditions, see *CSPV*, 381; AGS *Estado* K 1567/110, Don Bernardino de Mendoza to the king, 20 August 1588; and many others. We are very grateful to the late Professor W. L. Warren for insights into this problem.

The principal sources for the events of 6–9 August remain Duro for the Spanish, augmented by Recalde's account (published by Parker, 'El testamento político'), and Laughton for the English. For Parma and the Army of Flanders, see Parker, *Grand Strategy*, 229–50; Riaño Lozano, *Los medios navales de Alejandro Farnesio*; and the chronicles reprinted in Parente, *Los sucesos de Flandes de 1588*. For the Dutch, see the vintage account in Bor, *Oorspronck*, book 25, which relied on interviews with survivors and on documents now lost; and the more recent studies of van Overeem, 'Justinus van Nassau en de Armada'; and Schokkenbroek, 'Wherefore serveth Justinus with his shipping of Zeeland?' See also the published documents in Japikse, VI; Brugmans; and *Notulen van de Staten van Zeeland 1588*.

## Notes

1   Parma sent copies of all Medina Sidonia's letters to the king, with unflattering annotations: see AGS *Estado* 594/114–22 (eight letters, 25 July to 7 August) and AGS GA 226/6 (7 August 1588). One original (also 7 August) survives, AS, Parma, *Carteggio Farnesiano: Spagna 6*.

2   See details in AGS *Estado* 594/113, Parma to the king, 7 August 1588; and *CSPV*, 382–3, Parma letter of 12 August 1588.

3   Considerable confusion surrounds the exact date given by Parma for his estimated departure time. His letter to Medina Sidonia seems not to have survived but, according to Medina's reply of the 7th, it was written on 3 August (AGS *Estado* 594/122). The account of Fray Gerónimo de la Torre (Duro, II, 402–3) notes the attack on Parma's pinnace but merely says its message was that the duke was not yet ready, being at Dunkirk 'seven leagues away, to which we could not go for fear of the sandbanks, and from which he could not come because he was not ready'. Medina Sidonia's *Diario* records the arrival of another message, sent by the duke's secretary

at Dunkirk, who asserted that neither Parma's men nor their munitions were yet embarked, 'and that it seemed to him impossible that everything could be done in less than 15 days', Oria, 242. Recalde's *Diario* claims that Parma's pinnace arrived at dawn on the 7th, with the news that nothing had been embarked, and that the process would take 15 days, Parker, 'El testamento político', 33–4. Both sources erred because, in the event, Parma's entire army was embarked by Tuesday 10 August. The most ingenious account of Parma's message to Medina Sidonia was recorded by the Dutch historian Pieter Bor, writing some 30 years later: Parma said he 'could not come out before Friday', but no one could be sure which Friday he meant! (Bor, *Oorspronck*, book 25 fo. 9v).

4 AGS *Estado* 693/30, Don Guillén de San Clemente (Spanish ambassador in Vienna) to the king, 13 September 1588, referring to a complaint lodged by the town of Emden.

5 From *Breeder verclaringhe van de vloote van Spaengnien: de bekentnisse van Don Diego Pimentel* . . . , Knuttel pamphlet no. 847 (The Hague, 1588). Most of this pamphlet, which was a transcript of Pimentel's interrogation, was later published in Bor, *Oorspronck*, book 25 fos 11–11v. Abbreviated translations into English, French and Spanish were made (see copies in PRO *SP* 84/6/5–12); Laughton, II, 75–6, published an even more abridged version.

6 BL Sloane MS 262/62 ('Diarie' of the English commissioners); and Haus-, Hof- und Staatsarchiv, Vienna, *Belgien PC* 43/1, Spanish delegates to Parma, 6 August 1588. Even the letters written from the fleet on 25 July, announcing its departure from Corunna, only arrived in Flanders on 2 August, see AGS *Estado* 594/113, Parma to the king, 7 August 1588, and AS, Parma, *Carteggio Farnesiano* 129: *Spagna 6*, Don Francisco de Bobadilla to Parma, 25 July 1588, endorsement.

7 AGS *Estado* 455/320–1, Medina Sidonia to Parma, 10 June 1588, copy with royal annotations. Philip's 21 June letter in Oria, 202, responded to this. Parma's letter of protest to Philip is at AGS *Estado* 594/79, dated 22 June 1588.

8 AGS *Estado* 594/107, Parma to the king, 21 July 1588, rehearses what Moresin had been instructed to say to correct Medina Sidonia's misconceptions; but he never arrived. See AGS *Estado* 165/271, 'Lo que refiere Don Rodrigo de Avilés', and AGS *Estado* 594/105, Parma to the king, 18 July 1588. Parma's letter to the king of 22 June only got through on 7 August, too late to be of use (see endorsement on AGS *Estado* 594/79, and also AGS *Estado* 2219/78, the king to Parma, 7 August 1588).

9 Laughton, I, 331 and 341, Seymour to the Council, 6 August, and Howard to Walsingham, 8 August 1588 NS.

10 Oppenheim, *A History of the Administration of the Royal Navy*, 163. Drake provided one ship, the *Bark Thomas*; three more (the *Barks Talbot* and *Bond*, and the *Hope*) had sailed with him to the Caribbean in 1585, Keeler: *Sir Francis Drake's West Indian Voyage*, 45–6.

11 Parker, 'El testamento político', 34. When dawn broke, Asculi and Marolín found their felucca far from the Armada, in the midst of the English fleet. They therefore took refuge in Calais, AGS *Estado* 594/182, Asculi to Philip II, 12 August 1588.

12 See the fascinating (albeit verbose) account of the galleass's final hours in the 'Compendio' written between 1589 and 1592 by Fernando de Ayala, one of the infantry captains on board, BNM MS 5489/120–31. For events through English eyes, see Richard Tomson's lively account in Laughton, I, 344–50, and the fine description (perhaps written by Valentine Dale) in BL Sloane MS 262/66v–67v. Also see BNP

*Fonds français* 5045/152–6, and AGS *Estado* 693/31, M. de Gourdan's reports to the French government, 10 August 1588. In the end, all the *San Lorenzo*'s guns and stores, along with many of the abandoned anchors, were salvaged and sent to Parma, see AGS *Estado* 594/152; AGS *CMC* 3a/1704, no. 45, account of Vicenzo de Bune; and *CSPF*, XXII, 228.

13 Duro, II, 405, account of La Torre; AGS *GA* 226/8, Don Jorge Manrique to the king, 19 August 1588. *El Gran Grifón* was also severely damaged by the recoil of her own guns, AGS *CS* 2a/280 fo. 1941, Philip II *cédula* of 5 June 1591: 'maltratada de la mucha artilleria con que . . . la armada inglesa la batio, y de la que ella asimísmo jugó contra ellas en 7 de agosto'.

14 Tellechea Idígoras, *Otra cara*, 359, on the *Santa Ana*; Gallagher and Cruickshank, *God's Obvious Design*, 224, on the *San Pedro*; La Torre in Duro, II, 405.

15 The possibility of surrender is mentioned by La Torre, Duro, II, 407; corroborated by Vanegas, *ibid.*, 393, and Don Orduño de Zamuzio, Oria, 325.

16 Duro, II, 407–8. According to the bitter account of the other captain, Francisco de Cuéllar, Bobadilla condemned them and the duke pardoned him: see Gallagher and Cruickshank, *God's Obvious Design*, 225.

17 Parker, 'El testamento político', 16, Recalde to Don Martín de Idiáquez, 8 October 1588: 'en saliendo al mar de Flandes era acavada la cosa'.

# Anatomy of failure

The Armada, wrote Emanuel van Meteren shortly afterwards, had 'vanished into smoke'. And it had also sailed into legend.

Practical men like Howard, Drake and Hawkins knew how close the call had been but, once the danger was past, their realistic appraisals lacked popular appeal. Elizabeth's government, with eager support from Protestant factions throughout Europe, could not ignore this unique opportunity for mustering popular opinion against Spain. The spin doctors had a field day. The very enormity of the Armada, and its blatant appearance off the coast of England, seemed to demonstrate Philip II's greed, tyranny and ambition for all to see. At the same time its dispersal and flight in the face of a gallant and (supposedly) tiny foe added incompetence and cowardice to Spain's catalogue of wickedness. To cap it all the Almighty had demonstrated, by sending His winds to destroy the proud and mighty Spanish fleet, exactly where His sympathies lay.

Thus was born the first and most persistent legend: the great size of the Spanish ships. They were so huge, reported the contemporary Englishman William Camden, that the winds grew tired of carrying them, and the ocean groaned under their weight. Some of the Armada's ships were certainly large, and the fleet contained 55 vessels of 500 tons and upwards, but many of these were not fighting galleons. They were invasion transports, whose wide hulls and heavy cargoes made them clumsy and vulnerable. All the 13 English ships over 500 tons, by contrast, were heavily armed royal galleons, and the largest of them, Martin Frobisher's 1,100-ton *Triumph*, was bigger than any comparable galleon in the Spanish fleet. Only four of the Armada's big converted merchantmen appear on paper to have been larger, but this may be illusory. The Spaniards and the English used quite different formulae for calculating tonnage, and it is probable that the Spanish method gave a rather higher figure.

Once the size of the Spanish ships has been reduced to realistic proportions, another of the legends can be demolished. Their guns, some claimed, were mounted so high on their towering sides that the balls flew harmlessly over the low English vessels, whose every shot, in return, told upon their huge adversaries.

This ludicrous view, rejected by serious historians since the late nineteenth century, now has few devotees. Subsequently, however, another erroneous and just as misleading hypothesis about the armament of the opposing fleets emerged. Although Cesareo Fernández Duro in Spain and Sir John Laughton in England both correctly concluded that the Armada's total firepower was much lighter than that of the English fleet ranged against it, this conclusion was turned on its head by an English historian, Professor Michael Lewis, in the 1940s. Lewis sought to extrapolate the numbers and categories of the Spanish armament from the only sources to which he had access: some very limited information culled from Simancas by Captain Fernández Duro in the 1880s, and the English inventories of the guns aboard the captured *San Salvador* and *Nuestra Señora del Rosario*.

In a most ingenious statistical exercise, Lewis used these figures as a sample from which to project a grand total for the entire fleet. But his argument is fatally flawed. Both the *San Salvador* and the *Rosario* were exceptionally heavily gunned, and therefore grossly unrepresentative of the Armada as a whole. We can be quite sure of this. Specific records of at least 75 per cent of the *actual* guns, including virtually all of the larger ones, are preserved in the documents at Simancas, and Professor I. A. A. Thompson has now made a detailed and perceptive analysis of this information. His conclusion is that, in reality, the total effective firepower of the Armada was little more than half of Lewis's *minimum* estimate and so, far from being nearly one-third greater than that available to the English fleet, it was almost exactly one-third less.

Nor can Lewis's other main contention now be sustained. He sought to demonstrate that the Armada was greatly superior in heavy close-range 'ship-smashing' types of the short-barrelled 'cannon' variety, while the English had concentrated on the lighter-shotted and much longer-barrelled members of the 'culverin' family which, it was thought, had a greater range. By employing guns of the latter category, Lewis argued, the English ships could exploit their better sailing characteristics and higher speeds to dictate the distance at which they fought, keeping beyond the effective range of the Spaniards' ship-smashing cannons but within the distance at which they could ply their lighter long-range culverins.

This erroneous view about the contrasting range capabilities of the two types of gun was widely held by artillery theorists in 1588 and has therefore, understandably, been followed by most historians. In practice, however, most sea-gunners, English and Spanish, were coming to realise that excessively long pieces offered no obvious advantage in performance and were exceedingly difficult to handle aboard ship. Moreover, it is now known that lengthening the barrel of a smooth-bore gun beyond a certain point, far from increasing the range, actually reduces it. A charge of black powder, when ignited, can only produce a set volume of gas, at a relatively constant rate of production, and when that is expended (or is not being produced quickly enough to maintain pressure behind the rapidly accelerating projectile) any further increase in barrel length will actually retard its velocity. The critical length is reached at a point roughly 24 times the diameter of the bore. In practice, however, quite wide variations of this length produce little noticeable effect, and a gun 15 to 20 times its calibre in length – the proportions of a cannon – would have had much the same muzzle velocity, and hence range, as a culverin 35 calibres long. The important point to note is that, in spite of the difference in length, the effective range remained much the same. And that range was very short. Although a projectile might carry as far as 2,000 yards, its accuracy and hitting power beyond about 200 yards was minimal. Real damage to a ship could only be inflicted at even closer ranges.

What mattered most was the weight of the projectile delivered, and the rate at which a gun could discharge it. Here the Spaniards were at a distinct disadvantage. Even the *San Juan de Portugal*, on which Recalde sailed, built in 1586 and reputed 'the best-gunned ship in the Armada', carried nothing larger than a 20-pounder, with eight more pieces throwing between 16- and 18-pound shot. Most of her other big guns were periers, and the majority of the *San Juan's* 46 guns fired 10-pound balls or less. Among the flagships of other squadrons, Oquendo's *Santa Ana* (Guipúzcoa) carried 47 guns, but only three fired 16-pound balls or more; Don Pedro de Valdés's *Nuestra Señora del Rosario* (Andalusia) carried 46 guns, of which nine threw 16-pound balls or more; and the *San Cristobal* (Castile) carried 32 guns, the largest of them two 12-pounder periers.[1] Thompson has estimated that the Armada as a whole carried only 138 guns of 16-pounder calibre or above, and of these the largest (12 of them) were siege pieces, unsuited to shipboard use. The corresponding English figure was 251, all of which were sea-service weapons. Although quite a high proportion of these were classed as 'culverins' – around 18-pounders – the majority were in fact short-barrelled weapons 20 calibres or less in length. A Spaniard would have called them *medios cañones*.

The misconceptions outlined above conditioned Lewis's subsequent interpretation of the battles, which has since become widely accepted. His scenario runs thus. During the initial engagements the English, wishing to keep clear of the heavy close-range batteries carried by the Spanish ships, kept the distance open and pounded the Spaniards with their long-range culverins. They scored numerous hits, but the projectiles were not heavy enough nor, at that range, of sufficient velocity, to do the Armada serious damage. The Spaniards, however, were goaded into returning fire beyond the effective range of their heavy guns to such an extent that, by the time all-out battle was joined off Gravelines, they had run out of ammunition. According to Lewis, this gave the English the chance, at last, to come really close to their adversaries without fear of being crippled by short-range 'ship-smashing' fire and subsequent boarding. And the English culverins proved, at these close ranges, to be capable of inflicting serious damage.

Certainly English gunnery achieved considerable success off Gravelines. Equally certainly the Spaniards meted out remarkably little damage in return. Apocryphal stories of the Spanish bombardment's supposed ferocity abound

– the best known, predictably, coming from sources close to Drake. In one version a gentleman 'lying weary' in the *Revenge*'s great cabin had the bed shot from under him by a saker ball; shortly afterwards (the bed having somehow been restored), a demi-culverin shot discommoded two other gentlemen, one of whom was the duke of Northumberland, while they were dallying in precisely the same place. But whatever superficial if spectacular damage of this kind may have been done to the upper works of Elizabeth's galleons, it is clear that they suffered little serious hurt, and there were few human casualties too. No more than 100 Englishmen seem to have been killed in the fighting.

No doubt the ships' carpenters carried out many minor repairs without need for comment after the action; as for substantial damage, several historians have noted that the English government's own 'Dockyard Survey' of the queen's ships in September 1588 recorded only a few unserviceable components, variously described as 'worn', 'cracked', or 'decayed', as requiring replacement. On occasion, perhaps, these were euphemisms for battle damage, although the frequency with which they occur is little greater than might be expected in any routine survey. Some damage, indeed, is directly attributed to enemy action: a smashed (or lost) ship's boat; the *Revenge*'s mainmast 'decayed and perished with shot'. But it is almost all relatively minor, and the entries are few. Of substantial combat damage to the hulls – the kind of damage sustained by so many of the Armada's ships – there is not a single mention.[2]

This absence is misleading, however, because the dockyards were responsible only for masts, sails and other fittings: repairs to the hulls of the queen's ships were arranged and paid for by the treasurer of the navy. The accounts of Sir John Hawkins, as treasurer, for the year 1588 show substantial expenditure on 'the grounding, graving, repairing and preparing at Chatham of all her highness' ships' after the Armada campaign. These structural repairs required over 12,000 feet of planking (ranging from 1 to 4 inches thick); almost 100,000 nails and 1,000 treenails; over 15,000 pounds of ironwork; 85 loads of oak and elm timber; and wages for 948 'shipwrights, sawyers and pulleymakers' who worked an average of 35 days each. This total represents the largest repair bill found in any of the accounts submitted by the treasurers of the navy during the entire period of the Spanish war, and it indicates that Elizabeth's warships returned to port after the Armada campaign in need of considerable repair.[3]

Nevertheless, these figures must be placed in perspective. First, the total cost only ran to £3,500 – the amount required to build or repair just one new warship – in a record naval expenditure for the year of over £92,000. Second, although Hawkins's account provides no detail about which ships received what repairs, something about the scale and nature of the operation can be deduced from the materials supplied. The majority of the planking required after the fleet's return was 1- and 2-inch (11,000 feet), which can only have served for the superstructures, while the 3-inch planks (1,500 feet) probably went into internal decks. Repairs to the ships' hulls would have required 4-inch planking, and of this Hawkins purchased only 500 feet. Likewise all the iron nails would have gone into the superstructures, because fastening the hull required treenails – of which Hawkins required only 1,000. Third, 85 loads of timber (roughly 85 tons) would not go far, since constructing an Elizabethan galleon required at least 500 loads. Furthermore, the same account reveals that far more repairs took place *before* the campaign against the Armada. Early in 1588, just for Howard's squadron, contractors supplied almost 29,000 feet of planking (almost 4,000 feet of it 4-inch), 9,000 treenails, 56 'great beams', and 262 loads of oak, elm and maple. In other words, the queen's ships required far more repairs before they fought the Armada than after. It therefore seems safe to affirm that Philip's ships failed to inflict serious damage on their adversaries in 1588, even though during the engagement on 8 August (at least) some of them had fired repeated artillery salvoes at very close quarters ('within speech of one another').

It was to explain this apparent contradiction that Michael Lewis put forward the theory that, by the time of the action off Gravelines, the Spaniards had expended all their ammunition, so their heavy guns were therefore no longer a threat at close range.

Here too he was wrong. We now know for certain that the Armada did *not* run out of shot. True, many of the participants remarked on the intensity of the artillery action on both sides. Spaniards who had also fought at Lepanto considered that, in comparison, the cannonading they experienced in the Channel was 20 times more furious. Lord Admiral Howard agreed: 'There was never seen more terrible value of great shot', he wrote, 'nor more hot fight than this was.' Petruccio Ubaldino, a Florentine resident in England who had close connections with both Howard and Drake, confirms this impression. 'The multiplied firing of the greater artillery . . . on both sides . . . [was] considered to be firing no less quickly than ordinary arquebuses in the hottest skirmish.' And, even before Gravelines, Medina Sidonia expressed desperate concern about his diminishing ammunition stocks, and urgently requested replenishment from Parma.

But a closer reading of his request reveals that he was not short of heavy-calibre shot. What he wanted from Parma was 4-, 5- and 10-pounder projectiles only. It would seem that the bigger guns had fired much less frequently. Yet these were the very weapons with which the duke might have hoped to cripple an adversary prior to boarding – the tactic which, above all else, the Spaniards sought to employ, for it exploited their single great advantage of overwhelming military manpower.

Nevertheless there can be no doubt that the big guns were not used to their full effect, or anything like it. In the first place, shot of all calibres, and especially the larger calibres, has been found in abundance on every Armada wreck so far investigated. All of these ships had been heavily engaged; most, indeed, had been leading members of the 'troubleshooting' elite. Furthermore the administrative

## Shot expended by ships of the Spanish Armada, 1588

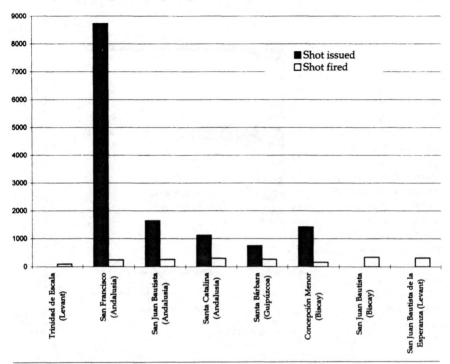

TABLE I  A graph showing the mismatch between roundshot issued to and fired by a number of hired ships for which detailed records of ammunition expenditure have survived. It shows that of the vast quantities of munitions supplied only a tiny proportion was actually used. Much of the exceptionally large amount of shot issued to the *San Francisco* of Andalusia was probably intended for distribution to the other ships of her squadron.

records at Simancas show that several of the Armada's hired ships brought large stocks of unexpended roundshot back to Spain.

While the royal warships had been issued with powder and shot which could be used and replaced with a minimum of formality, the embargoed vessels which sailed with the fleet were each issued with specific quantities of munitions by crown officials before the campaign began, and were expected to record every projectile and every pound of gunpowder which they subsequently expended. These meticulous chronicles are extremely informative, for they provide a detailed day-by-day breakdown of the gunnery performance of many individual ships throughout the fighting (TABLES I and 2). The figures show, for example, that the 22-gun Levanter *Trinidad de Escala* (*Trinidad de Scala*) fired 35 shots on 2 August (1.6 rounds per gun), 21 shots on 4 August (0.96 rounds per

## Roundshot recovered from the wreck of the flagship *El Gran Grifón*

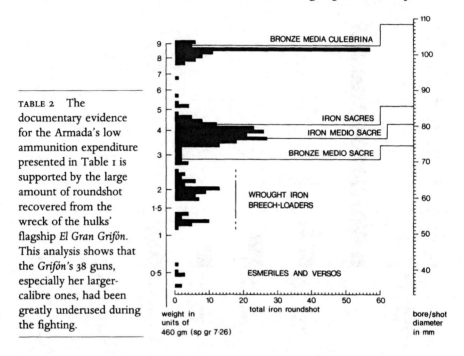

BRONZE MEDIA CULEBRINA

IRON SACRES
IRON MEDIO SACRE

BRONZE MEDIO SACRE

WROUGHT IRON
BREECH-LOADERS

ESMERILES AND VERSOS

total iron roundshot

weight in
units of
460 gm (sp gr 7·26)

bore/shot
diameter
in mm

TABLE 2 The documentary evidence for the Armada's low ammunition expenditure presented in Table 1 is supported by the large amount of roundshot recovered from the wreck of the hulks' flagship *El Gran Grifón*. This analysis shows that the *Grifón*'s 38 guns, especially her larger-calibre ones, had been greatly underused during the fighting.

gun) and 38 during the Gravelines engagement on 8 August (1.7 rounds per gun). Similarly the Guipúzcoan *Santa Bárbara*, which appears to have carried 28 guns instead of the 12 credited to her in the Lisbon muster, fired 22 shots on 31 July (1.1 rounds per gun), 28 on 1 August (1.4 rounds per gun), 47 on 2 August (2.35 rounds per gun) and 167 (56 of them stone shot) on 8 August (8.35 rounds per gun). Over the four days of actual fighting the Andalusian vice-flagship *San Francisco* (21 guns) discharged only 242 rounds, while her sister ship, the *Santa Catalina* (23 guns), fired only 300, an average of about 3 per gun per day. The Biscayan *Concepción Menor* fired 156 balls from her 20 guns, an average of under 2 per gun per day. These figures come nowhere near to accounting for the 50 or more rounds with which, according to the Lisbon muster and the ships' own records, each gun had been provided. Of the 1,421 cannon shot which had been issued to the *Concepción Menor* at Lisbon, she handed back no fewer than 1,256 on her return; while of the exceptionally large quota of 8,731 rounds issued to the Andalusian *San Francisco*, she returned 8,489.[4]

So here at last is a full and sufficient explanation for the Armada's remarkable failure to inflict serious damage on the English fleet. The Spaniards simply did not fire their guns, especially their few heavy guns, often enough. But why was this so?

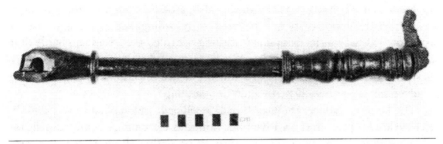

FIGURE 21    A gunner's linstock from the wreck of *La Trinidad Valencera*, in the form of a clenched fist. This device was used to hold the length of slow-match by which a piece of artillery was detonated.

The answer, it seems, lies in the highly specialised procedures and battle drills for which the Spaniards had equipped and prepared themselves but which, in the event, they could not use. We know from Medina Sidonia's instructions to the fleet, and from actual examples of Armada artillery and associated equipment recovered from the wrecks, that the guns were kept loaded at all times (FIGURES 21 and 22). Whenever battle was joined one salvo was therefore available for immediate use, and an operator holding a lighted linstock at the side of each gun was the only requirement for discharging the first round. This method characterised galley warfare, when a single forward-firing volley was unleashed

FIGURE 22    Roundshot and wadding in a loaded iron 4-pounder from the wreck of *El Gran Grifón*, revealed by the partial erosion of its bore.

just before an adversary was rammed and boarded. In such a situation there was neither the opportunity nor the need for reloading, and in consequence no procedure existed for the disciplined working of artillery as a standard battle drill aboard galleys. Spanish sailing-ship tactics were essentially the same, for they likewise regarded the broadside as a one-off device for crippling and confusing an adversary as an immediate prelude to boarding.

The kind of warfare the English had developed, and applied so successfully at Gravelines, by contrast, involved a continuous close-range bombardment intended to destroy an enemy by the attrition of gunfire alone. Given that their inferior sailing qualities prevented the Spaniards from closing and boarding as they would have liked, the Armada's only counter to such tactics was to attempt to reply in kind. To do this, however, they would have to reload their guns time and again during the course of an engagement. This was more easily said than done. Not only was such a practice outside the training and tactical experience of the Spanish commanders and their crews, it was also one for which their equipment was fundamentally unsuited.

Partly from a close reading of Medina Sidonia's fighting instructions for his own flagship, and partly from evidence provided by the wrecks, the Spanish battle drills can be reconstructed with some confidence. Before action was joined the guns were first loaded and manhandled into position, and then lashed securely to the ship's side with their muzzles protruding through the ports. Each was under the charge of a specialist gunner, and two officers were allocated to each side of the two main gundecks to control and direct the fire. While being prepared, each gun was actually served by a crew of six soldiers, who were withdrawn as required from their battle stations on the ship's decks and in its fighting tops. These men, under the gun captain's direction, carried out the tasks of scouring, sponging and loading; and then heaved on the tackles and handspikes by which the guns were manoeuvred into position and adjusted for traverse and elevation. This done, the men returned to their original positions, for once battle was joined their primary job was to act as marines, whose duty it was to bring down a hail of small-arms fire as the range closed, to wield the pre-boarding weapons of grapnel, shear-hook, missile and incendiary device, and finally to enter and overwhelm the enemy ship. Once the initial artillery discharge had been made, therefore, the guns could not be reloaded until their crews had been called in again from the boarding stations to which they had dispersed.

No doubt, as it became apparent that the English ships could not be grappled and boarded as the Spaniards would have wished, efforts were made to continue working the guns after the first salvo had been discharged. This was probably not too much of a problem with the smaller pieces, a conclusion reinforced by the fact that the *San Martín*, according to Medina Sidonia, did indeed run out of her smaller-calibre shot. Improvising effective reloading drills for the larger-calibre guns would not have been so easy.

Muzzle-loading artillery was worked at sea during the sixteenth century in two ways. The guns could either be brought inboard after firing, and the necessary operations carried out within the ship, or they could be left in the run-out position and reloaded outboard. The much more efficient process of allowing a gun's own recoil to bring it inboard under the restraint of a breeching rope was not developed until well into the seventeenth century. Instead it was customary, after firing, to unhitch the piece and haul it back manually. This process was laborious but reasonably efficient, and during the course of it the crew would be covered from the view, and to some extent from the fire, of the enemy. Outboard loading, although it could be performed with a much smaller crew, was far more awkward and perilous, for it required the loader to straddle the barrel of the gun outside the port and carry out all the clearing and charging operations from this exposed and difficult position.

Which of these procedures the Spaniards used in 1588 is not known for certain, but the inefficient design of their gun carriages, with their wide-diameter wheels and long trails, suggests that it would have been impracticable, mainly because of the lack of working space on the gundecks, for the pieces to have been loaded inboard while a ship was closely engaged. On the other hand, it would have been little short of suicidal to have attempted outboard loading while a ship was within small-arms range of the enemy. The probability is that once close action was joined most Spanish ships only managed to fire off their previously prepared salvo to any serious effect, after which sustained heavy gunfire ceased. This does not of course mean that no further firing was possible.

It seems likely that the galleasses, which carried their heaviest guns at the bow and stern, had room to reload the larger pieces inboard – although no fewer than 2,650 cannonballs were recovered from the wreck of the flag galleass *San Lorenzo*, noted by both sides as being involved in all fleet actions in the Channel, which implies that she had fired relatively few rounds. It would also appear that the galleons of the Portuguese squadron, the only purpose-built sailing warships in the fleet, managed to maintain a high rate of fire. Recalde, in the 46-gun *San Juan*, reported firing 140 rounds on 31 July (although he received 300 incoming rounds), 130 on 3 August and 300 on 8 August (against, he thought, 1,000 incoming); while, according to a gunnery officer aboard Medina Sidonia's 48-gun flagship, the *San Martin* fired 120 rounds on 31 July, 120 again on 2 August ('of which some must have caused much damage to the enemy's ships'), 130 on 3 August and 300 on 8 August.[5]

On most other vessels, however, as we now know from the wrecks and from the records of shot expended, the guns that fired most often were always the smallest. These were either light muzzle-loaders which could with relative ease be hauled back and reloaded, or the numerous breech-loading anti-personnel weapons. Thus of the 314 iron shot fired during the 1588 campaign by the *San Juan Bautista de la Esperanza* (Levant squadron) 'in the fight with the English vice-flagship as well as in others', 41 were 5-pounders, 13 were 3- and 4-pounders, and 260 were 2-pounders or less. Of the 1,640 rounds fired by the nine Armada ships for which detailed records survive, only 175 (11 per cent) exceeded 9 pounds and none exceeded 20 pounds.[6]

Even aboard ships which did not carry particularly heavy guns the same trend is noticeable: the lighter the ammunition, the more likely it was to be used. Gómez de Medina's hulk flagship *El Gran Grifón*, wrecked on Fair Isle, had been issued with four *medias culebrinas* at Lisbon, and these long 10-pounders were the heaviest pieces she carried. Out of the 200 issued to the ship, 97 balls of this calibre have actually been recovered from her wreck indicating that, at the very least, practically half of her most effective firepower was not discharged at the enemy. The true figure is probably much higher, because almost certainly a considerable amount of shot on the wreck site remains undiscovered. The picture for the *Grifón's* 34 lighter guns, 6-pounders and less, is very different. For these we have 273 rounds of ammunition, or only 16 per cent of the total allocation. On the basis of this very substantial sample, therefore, we can confidently say that the *Grifón's* lighter guns were on average fired three times more frequently than her *medias culebrinas*, even though the latter were the only pieces heavy enough to inflict serious damage on an enemy vessel.

The wreck of *El Gran Grifón* has revealed another crucial weakness in the Armada's artillery. The ship had been issued with eight bronze pieces from the crash gunfounding programme at Lisbon just before the fleet sailed: four *medias culebrinas* and four *medios sacres*. An example of each type has been recovered and, in accordance with Juan de Acuña Vela's special instruction, they are plain and undecorated, without the normally mandatory blazon of royal arms. This would not in itself, of course, have affected the performance of the guns, but the intense production pressures evidently caused a dramatic drop in technical standards: the *media culebrina* from *El Gran Grifón* was bored so far off centre that in all probability it could never have been fired. It can certainly not have passed rigorous proofing, for even a much reduced charge would have blown out its dangerously thin-walled breech (FIGURE 23).

Nor was this an isolated case. An Italian *sacre* from the *Juliana*, recovered from her wreck off Streedagh Strand, suffered just such an accident at the muzzle, rendering it useless (FIGURE 24). The early seventeenth-century English gunner Robert Norton may not have been far wide of the mark when he wrote disparagingly of Spanish and Italian techniques that:

> it is apparent that they commit great and absurd faults therein. Some of their pieces (and not a few) are bored awry . . . some are crooked in their chase, other of unequal bores . . . and a great many are come forth of the furnace spongy, or full of honeycombs and flaws . . . [Such guns] will either break, split, or blowingly spring their metals and (besides that mischief they do) they will be utterly unserviceable ever after.[7]

FIGURE 23   One of the four bronze *medias culebrinas* issued to *El Gran Grifón* at Lisbon in 1587 and recovered from the sea off Fair Isle 390 years later. The end of the barrel has broken off to reveal that its bore is badly off-centre.

FIGURE 24   This Italian *sacre* from the wreck of the Levanter *Juliana* off Streedagh Strand has suffered an explosive blow-out close to its muzzle.

A final, insidious difficulty was heaped upon the unfortunate men who had to work the Armada's guns. The fleet was, it must be remembered, not a 'Spanish' Armada at all, but one drawn from across the length and breadth of Europe, and the origins of its 2,431 guns encompassed most of the major foundries from the Baltic to the Adriatic and even beyond. Not a few came from England, by various devious routes. Even within individual foundries there was little enough standardisation of type and bore, while each country (and often each region within the same country) followed highly individual fashions of proportion and design, and employed its own, often widely differing, standards of weights and measures. The confusion this engendered was immense, not least in the apparently simple business of allocating from a central source the calibres of shot appropriate to the guns aboard a particular ship. A further difficulty arose from the habit of expressing all calibres in terms of the weight of shot they represented rather than the actual diameters of the bores, for variations in the specific gravity of different grades of cast iron might easily determine whether or not a shot of a particular weight would actually fit its intended piece.

Artillerymen normally calculated the relationship between bore and shot-weight by means of a simple set of instruments consisting of a gunner's rule and a set of shot gauges. The former was a simple wooden scale, with graduations which determined the weight of shot appropriate to a given bore; the latter a set of matching wooden rings which could be used to gauge a correctly proportioned ball. A gunner's rule and some of its associated gauges have been found on the wreck of La Trinidad Valencera, apparently scaled to one of the many contemporary Italian pounds (FIGURE 25). But the calibration of this scale is so inaccurate, and so full of inconsistencies, as to have rendered it virtually useless. If we multiply this one gunner and his error-laden instruments by the number of guns, gunners and pieces of roundshot in the entire Armada, the scale of resulting muddle at every level begins to emerge.

And muddle certainly existed on the Spanish gundecks at Gravelines. We may obtain a snapshot of what it may have been like, albeit from a source remote from the Armada, in the observations made by the Dutch traveller Jan Huyghen van Linschoten, aboard a large Portuguese carrack when she became involved in an action against some English privateers in 1589. 'Whenever we shot off a piece,' he wrote, 'we had at least an hour's work to lade it in again, whereby we had so great a noise and cry aboard the ship as if we had all been cast away.'[8] This picture of hopeless confusion might well have applied to the Armada a year before. At any event the conclusion is inescapable that, when it came to the test, Iberian sea-gunnery failed almost completely.

What then of the other side? There can be no doubt that the English gunners, particularly at Gravelines, did better, but they were not without their critics. William Thomas, an English master-gunner stationed at Flushing at the time of the campaign, was one of them. On 30 September he wrote to Lord Burghley:

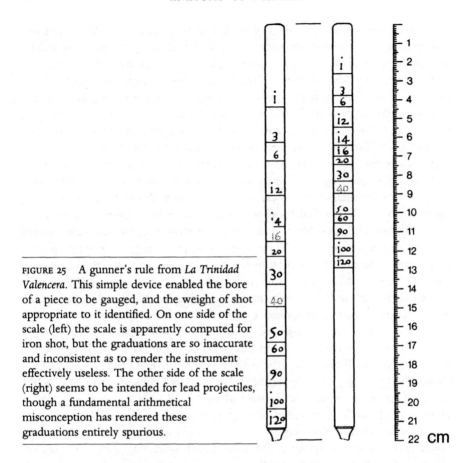

FIGURE 25 A gunner's rule from *La Trinidad Valencera*. This simple device enabled the bore of a piece to be gauged, and the weight of shot appropriate to it identified. On one side of the scale (left) the scale is apparently computed for iron shot, but the graduations are so inaccurate and inconsistent as to render the instrument effectively useless. The other side of the scale (right) seems to be intended for lead projectiles, though a fundamental arithmetical misconception has rendered these graduations entirely spurious.

if it had pleased God that her Majesty's ships had been manned with a full supply of good gunners, according to the forces they carry . . . it would have been the woefullest time or enterprise that ever the Spaniard took in hand . . . What can be said but our sins was the cause that so much powder and shot [were] spent, and so long time in fight, and, in comparison thereof, so little harm.

There was some truth in this. Throughout the campaign Howard and his captains had ceaselessly complained that they did not have enough ammunition. The English shot quota was, initially, probably no more than half the 50 rounds per gun carried by the Spaniards. A trickle of fresh supplies came out of local arsenals as the fleet sailed along the south coast, but without the major haul of powder and shot captured from the *Rosario* and *San Salvador* the situation would have quickly become perilous. Between them the two prizes yielded 229 barrels of powder – perhaps a quarter of the total stock expended by the English in the course of the campaign. Even so, by dusk on 8 August, after only a few hours of combat, the English were almost out of ammunition. According to one source, they 'were fain at last . . . to use plough chains instead of bullets'. Had full replenishment of powder and shot been possible at this point it might indeed have been, as William Thomas speculated, the 'woefullest time' for Spain.

And yet it was woeful enough. The English seem to have surmounted those problems of working ship-killing artillery effectively in a close engagement that had so debilitatingly baffled their adversaries. According to Sir Arthur Gorgas, who had been there, the queen's ships were able to weave in and out among the Spanish fleet 'discharging our broadsides of ordnance double for their single', and this was almost certainly an understatement. Several reasons for this may be adduced. First, the English gunners were all seamen, thoroughly familiar with the guns aboard their own vessels and conversant with the tasks of operating them at sea. Those detailed to work the guns were not expected, as were the Spaniards, to double as soldiers, and so they were not encumbered with military clothing and accoutrements. Drake's men had even undergone training with precious live ammunition (though such prodigality met with official disapproval). The confidence and familiarity thus engendered paid rich dividends. English gunners were, as William Bourne tells us, 'handy and without fear of their ordnance', and 'handsome about their ordnance in ships, on the sea'.

The design of the carriages upon which the guns were mounted greatly increased these considerable advantages of skill and familiarity. Although it had been in service with the navy for at least 70 years – the first known survey of the English Navy, in 1515, already recorded that the large guns aboard Henry VIII's warships rested on 'trotills' or 'on four wheels' – the sturdy four-wheeled truck carriage might well be regarded as England's decisive secret weapon in 1588.[9] Sir Henry Mainwaring's *Seaman's Dictionary*, compiled about 30 years later, entertained no doubt on the subject. 'The fashion of those carriages we use at sea are much better than those of the land', he wrote, 'yet the Venetians and Spaniards (and divers others) use the others in their shipping.' Archival and archaeological evidence confirm his judgement. Some guns aboard the Armada were mounted upon very large two-wheeled carriages, some of them expressly intended for land use. Thus in April 1588 Don Pedro de Valdés, commander of the Andalusian squadron, noted that 'The hulk named *Santa Ana* has a culverin of 31 quintals and 93 pounds of Naples which, because it is very long and is on a land carriage, cannot be used on the said hulk because there is not sufficient space for it.' Valdés therefore ordered the gun to be brought aboard his own, much larger, flagship, *Nuestra Señora del Rosario*, together with 30 rounds and appropriate loading equipment. Excavation of the *Trinidad Valencera*, a Venetian transport embargoed for service with the Armada and wrecked on the coast of Northern Ireland, revealed a massive sea-carriage with a long trail of precisely the type described by Mainwaring, making an assemblage 19 feet long on a deck barely 36 feet wide. Others have been noted among the remains of the *Juliana* off Streedagh Strand. Clearly these inappropriate mountings did not prevail throughout the

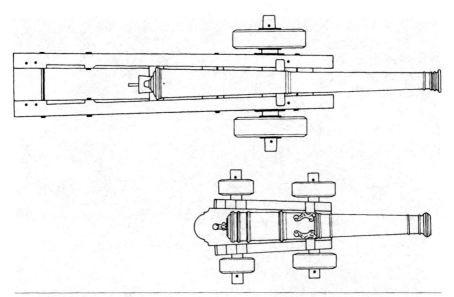

FIGURE 26    Plan view (top) of a Venetian two-wheeled sea-carriage found on the wreck of *La Trinidad Valencera* in 1987. Though no gun was found associated, its dimensions suggest that it would be suitable for a long 18-pounder, as shown. The complete assembly is 19 feet long, most of which would have lain inside the ship. Below it is shown a short 24-pounder from the Swedish royal ship *Vasa* (1628) mounted on a four-wheel truck carriage of the type used by the English in 1588. The lower gun packed a much heavier punch, and occupied far less deck space.

fleet. The new carriages supplied to the Andalusian squadron, for example, had only two wheels. However, since each apparently stood 29 inches high, they were certainly not 'truckles'.[10]

In contrast to the clumsy and inefficient gun mountings on many Spanish ships, which made reloading in action so difficult, the small wheels of the English truck carriages meant that the gun muzzles could protrude further through the gun-ports, while no awkward trail with wide wheels obstructed the sides and rear (FIGURE 26). Adequate working space was therefore available for the crews to serve and fight their guns. Though the pieces were not allowed to recoil inboard for loading, it would not have been necessary to load them outboard, for there was ample room on the decks to haul them in manually after firing. Guns could therefore be brought to bear and fired consecutively while a fight was in progress, at ranges chosen by the English by virtue of the superior sailing qualities of their ships. This surely explains the crippling hull damage they were able to inflict on the Spaniards.

During the making of a documentary series about the Armada in 1988 it was decided to test the relative efficiency of the two types of carriage by building

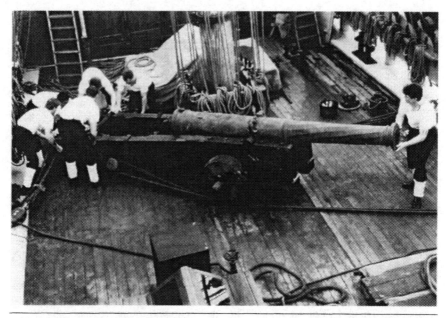

FIGURE 27 A replica Spanish long-trailed two-wheeled sea-carriage, based on finds from the Armada wrecks, undergoing trials in 1988. To reload it was necessary to manhandle the piece inboard and swing it into a diagonal position, as shown in the photograph. The same gun, when mounted on a four-wheeled truck carriage, could be loaded and fired twice as quickly.

replicas and conducting comparative tests. In each case the gun mounted – a replica culverin from the *Mary Rose* – was the same (FIGURE 27). The Portsmouth field-gun team – that year's champions in the Royal Navy's thrilling field-gun race at the Royal Tournament – provided a six-strong crew under a gun captain. It would be invidious to compare these fit, highly motivated, superbly trained and intensely competitive young men with either Spanish or English gunners of 1588: moreover, the Portsmouth team were working under ideal conditions and not in the stress of battle. Even the awkward Spanish gun-rig took them only five minutes to load, fire and haul inboard for reloading. This cannot remotely compare with the likely time the Armada's harassed and under-trained gunners took to reload. What is important, however, is that the modern crew took only half the time to perform the same operation using the same gun mounted on a truck carriage. In comparative terms, then, the latter carriage was 100 per cent more efficient than the trailed version used by the Spaniards. This in itself would explain the much higher rate of fire achieved by the English ships, even had other factors not increased their advantage still further.

The events of 8 August fully confirmed Philip II's worst fears that the dastardly English would indeed fire low, and so inflict damage on the narrow vulnerable belt 'between the wind and the water'. William Bourne, writing in 1587, stressed the importance of co-ordination between gunner and steersman, so that the shots could be timed to hit an enemy's hull below the waterline as it heeled over. The English fleet's commanding position to windward of the Armada throughout almost all of the fighting gave it a considerable advantage in this respect, for it meant that their adversaries were often heeled away from them, presenting the normally submerged parts of their hulls. But the English galleons did not fully exploit this advantage until Gravelines, and by then it was almost too late, for their ammunition stocks were nearly exhausted.

Why had the English delayed so long? Their first encounters with the Armada had been cautious in the extreme: mere 'feather plucking', according to the lord admiral; 'more coldly done than became the value of our nation' thought one of his more outspoken subordinates. The truth was that at the outset no Englishman knew what the strengths, or the weaknesses, of the Armada actually were. It certainly *looked* impregnable, and there seemed no obvious way of attacking it.

So what were they to do? Go in close and risk disablement from those rows of gleaming bronze muzzles? Attempt to board the Spanish ships and be annihilated by their massed companies of troops? Howard's colleagues in the Privy Council had little grasp of his predicament. When, on 31 July, the lord admiral begged desperately for more powder and roundshot, the Council responded by sending a contingent of musketeers to join in the hand-to-hand combat. Howard angrily sent them back. Even on 10 August, when thanks to Howard's efforts the Armada was at last in full retreat, the Council sent a messenger to demand of him 'what causes are there that the Spanish navy hath not been boarded by the queen's ships?' Howard's reply, perhaps fortunately, has not been preserved.

Despite the Privy Council's unhelpful expectations, Howard and his fleet radically improved their tactics as the campaign progressed. In the wake of the dislocation caused by the fireships to the Armada's hitherto tight and steadfastly maintained defensive formation, the queen's ships launched an aggressive close-range gunnery assault on the retreating but fast-re-forming Spanish fleet. But should they not have done this from the beginning? Why did they at first hold back, and what changed that caution to the vigorous and confident close action off Gravelines?

Somehow, it would seem, the bubble of the Armada's apparent invincibility had been pricked, and its shortcomings in gunnery clearly identified. This realisation must have dawned on the English at some point before Gravelines. We do not know how or why it dawned, but it seems certain that Howard and his captains had recognised the fundamental Spanish weaknesses before the Armada reached Calais. After the battles off the Isle of Wight on 3 and 4 August all fighting ceased for three days, while Medina Sidonia progressed towards his uncertain rendezvous with Parma. This suggests that on or before 4 August the English had made a firm decision to conserve their ammunition stocks for an all-out attack on the Armada when it reached its vulnerable station off Flanders. By this point, it would seem, having divined the essential outlines of Philip II's Grand Design they had also discovered that they could come close enough to the Spaniards to deliver really effective broadsides without risking serious retaliation, so long as they used their decisive sailing advantage to avoid being grappled and boarded. They now realised that they had little to fear from the Spanish guns.

Who first made this momentous discovery, and when, may never be known for sure. Perhaps it was a gradual realisation, as events unfolded, in the minds of many men. But a particularly likely candidate for the distinction is Sir Francis Drake, and a number of incidents which may have helped him towards this vital conclusion can be identified.

The first was Sir Francis's capture, on the morning of 1 August, of Don Pedro de Valdés's *Nuestra Señora del Rosario*. Here was the fourth largest and perhaps best-gunned ship in the whole Armada, and yet she had put up only a token resistance. Drake and his officers must have wondered why and, though it is nowhere directly recorded, they must surely have taken the opportunity of inspecting their prize in minute detail. If they examined the ship they could scarcely have failed to notice the cumbersome gun carriages, extending well beyond the centre line of the deck, which made it so difficult to fire frequently or accurately. Perhaps Sir Francis, with his ready wit and infectious charm, extracted a voluble explanation from the disgruntled Don Pedro, with whom he shared his cabin for some days. In any event, he could have seen for himself the contrast between the purpose-built truck carriages of his own guns aboard the *Revenge* and the clumsy two-wheelers of his adversary. And Drake, with his rigorous views on comradely teamwork under a single captain, would certainly have taken careful note of the scratch crews of soldiers who tended the guns, the inefficient and divisive structure of command, and the huge reserves of unspent powder and shot. No one was better qualified than he to appreciate the full significance of all this, and it might be considered that Drake's capture of the *Rosario*, though bitterly criticised by his contemporaries, was in retrospect one of the most significant episodes in the campaign.

It is tempting to link the dawn attack on the straggling flagship of the hulks, *El Gran Grifón*, which took place off the Solent on 3 August, with the discoveries Drake had made aboard the *Rosario* two days before. Here, for the first time, we hear of a really close ship-to-ship action in which the keynotes were mobility and firepower. Is it more than coincidence that the aggressor seems to have been the *Revenge*? Was Drake perhaps testing a developing theory about the Spaniards' inability to fight a mobile artillery action, and wisely choosing one of the less well-armed troubleshooters for his experiment? If so, he must have found the results deeply gratifying, for he struck his target 40 times and killed many soldiers on her decks, while the Grifón's four bronze *medias culebrinas* – the biggest guns she carried – remained virtually silent throughout.

A day later someone (perhaps Drake again) apparently repeated this experiment in full squadron strength, breaking the Armada's right wing off the Isle of Wight. Howard and his officers now had all the information they needed to identify the Armada's fundamental weaknesses, and it was at precisely this point that a decision was apparently made to conserve ammunition, while there was still some left, for the final battle. England, at last, had salvation in her grasp. Even if the Armada could not be defeated or broken at sea, it could be deflected irrecoverably from its junction with Parma, and sent on its perilous homeward voyage. That was the measure of England's success at Calais and Gravelines.

It nevertheless remained a close-run thing. The Armada, even at the last, retained a sting in its tail: some of its ships remained able to fire, reload and fire again with their heavy artillery. Drake, according to his jaundiced critic Sir Martin Frobisher, made a serious tactical error when he 'came bragging up at the first indeed, and gave them his prow and his broadside'. But his Spanish adversary was ready for him, and gave him a full broadside in return: Drake (added Frobisher with relish) was thereafter 'glad he was gone again'. The *Revenge* was 'pierced with shot above forty times', and in the dockyard survey after the battle her mainmast was found to be 'perished with shot'. But this proved the exception. Few Armada ships could administer punishment of this severity, and most of the queen's ships prudently stayed clear of them.

At the last, Lord Admiral Howard resorted to bluff. 'We put on a brag countenance and gave chase', he noted, as the Armada disappeared into the northern seas, 'as if we wanted nothing.' In fact, they wanted everything, for by then the English galleons' shot-lockers were completely bare. Had the Armada at this point been entering the Thames estuary, with Parma's barges shepherded in its midst, the queen's navy could have done absolutely nothing to stop it.

But that terrifying scenario had been averted, and in the process a new form of naval warfare was born. Within a year of the battles Petruccio Ubaldino, the Florentine artist, scholar and historian who had come to England in 1545, wrote a manuscript account of the campaign for Sir Francis Drake. His account clearly reflects, in many ways, the old sea dog's personal views. It also sums up, succinctly and accurately, the tactical doctrines that would, over the coming two centuries, make England the world's most powerful maritime nation. The English fleet, wrote Ubaldino:

> made good use of the most reliable quality of their excellent and speedy ships, not crowded out with useless soldiers, but with decks clear for the use of artillery, so that they could safely play it at any hour to harm the enemy, at any moment which it suited them best to do so . . . It seems to us that next to be praised are the . . . gunners, [because] we must still recognise in that art not only manual practice, which is one of the most important parts of soldiering,

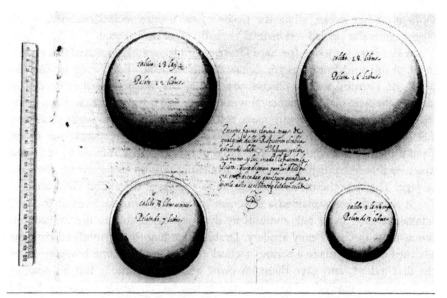

FIGURE 28   After the Armada the Spaniards, recognising what chaos had been caused by the lack of regular shot sizes, attempted to standardise the diameters of their roundshot. This specification, signed by Juan de Acuña Vela at Málaga on 20 January 1590, orders the casting of 9,000 rounds of 3-, 7-, 12- and 16-pound calibres. From now on, he ordains, the diameters are to be *exactly* as indicated in the diagram, irrespective of any variations in the actual weights.

but also the judgement of the eye and mind . . . Among the artillery it had been absolutely decided by the English that all should be of one nationality, one language, and therefore one constant disposition to serve well, and we cannot consider that this was at all so among the enemy.

And yet a thought should be spared for that enemy, now facing the perils of a hazardous return voyage. It had been a gallant effort, and it had certainly not failed because of the cowardice or incompetence of those who took part in it. Among the delivered Protestants, perceptive men recognised in the Armada formidable strengths that, in different circumstances, might easily have prevailed. There was cause for rejoicing, and thanksgiving, but not for complacent triumphalism. The Spanish fleet, to quote Emanuel van Meteren, 'had many great vantages, namely the extraordinary bigness of their ships, and also for that they were so nearly conjoined, and kept together in so good array, that they could by no means be fought withall one to one'.

So, in defiant if somewhat ragged array, the great Armada departed from England's shores. It had fought and failed, but it had not suffered outright defeat. Medina Sidonia and his men had lost much, but they had not lost their honour (FIGURES 28 and 29).

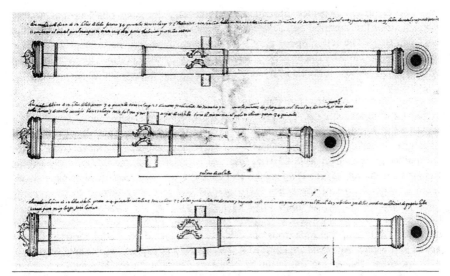

FIGURE 29   Even before the Armada sailed, Spanish naval experts were apparently coming to grips with the operational problems of working heavy guns at sea. This drawing of three different types of *medias culebrinas* was prepared at Lisbon by Don Juan de Acuña Vela, captain-general of artillery, and sent to Philip II on 25 July 1587. The top gun, argues Acuña, is of the old pattern recommended by the marquis of Santa Cruz, but Don Juan considers that it is too slender for safety and too long for shipboard use. The bottom version has been strengthened but it is still too long, and now it is too heavy as well. Acuña's solution is the centre piece, which has been reduced in length and the metal thus saved used to make the barrel thicker and stronger. But these sound ideas evidently took time to work their way down through the system: the *media culebrina* recovered from *El Gran Grifón*, which was cast at Lisbon in late 1587 or early 1588, was still made according to the outdated and discredited 'Santa Cruz' formula.

## Sources

The size of the ships on each side is controversial. Almost all records of the period give the carrying capacity of each ship, not its displacement. Furthermore, the Spaniards and English used quite different formulae for calculating ship tonnages, and neither was intended to give a mathematically exact figure for the burden (let alone the displacement) of the ship. Such calculations were for administrative purposes only – to assess hire charges or port dues: see Martin, 'Spanish Armada tonnages', and Casado Soto, *Los barcos*, 57–94. Jan Glete's magnificent study, *Navies and Nations*, II, 527–30, shows how to calculate displacement from the known length, beam and draught measurements of each ship – usually between 40 and 50 per cent larger than the 'tons burthen' recorded by the documents. We have retained the latter figures because almost all other sources do so, but readers should remember that not all 'tons' are alike.

The campaign provides directly comparable data for only one ship: an English assessment of the captured *San Salvador*, rated by the Spaniards as 958 tons, puts her at only 600 tons. The latter figure may not, however, take into account a 'war rating' increment – one-fifth by the Spanish system, one-third by the English. The question must remain open, though it seems likely that the Spanish method tended to give somewhat higher tonnage figures.

Our account of guns and gunnery rests upon two separate bodies of evidence: archival and archaeological. The archives of Simancas house voluminous accounts for most of the hired ships. At one time at least six 'Libros de quentas fenecidas de las naos que sirvieron en la Armada que fue a Inglaterra' existed. We have come across substantial parts of five: AGS *CMC* 2a/942 and 1012 *Libro segundo*; 2a/772 *Libro tercero*; 2a/460 *Libro quarto*; 2a/963 *Libro quinto*; and 2a/905 *Libro sexto*, with further papers scattered in other *legajos* of the series. *CMC* 1a/1735 and 1736 may belong to the missing *Libro primero*. Most of the ships hired or embargoed by the crown appear in these bundles, and also in the massive volume (3,164 folios) AGS *CS* 2a/280. Neither series includes vessels from the squadrons of Castile or Portugal. Those concerning the former are in AGI *Sección* III, *legajo* 2934 and KML *Medina Sidonia Papers: Casa de la Contratación*, 8/30–41; those concerning the latter have not so far been found (although tantalising fragments may be found in the 'Proveedor's Book': Pepys MS 2269). Material for the English fleet is far more superficial. Detailed accounts of the Ordnance Office's issue and return of munitions to the queen's ships in 1588 clearly once existed, but they have disappeared from the Public Record Office (indeed records only survive for Elizabeth's reign after 1595: WO 55/1626–31: see the tables compiled from them in Parker, 'Dreadnought revolution', 275–7). Accounts for the munitions issued to Drake's western squadron of six royal and 32 merchant ships between October 1587 and April 1588 have survived (West Devon County Record Office, Plymouth, Drake Papers, 1971/4, 'Powder and munitions delivered at Plymouth'); but they do not record quantities expended or returned.

The evidence of the four excavated Armada wrecks – the *Girona*, *Gran Grifón*, *Trinidad Valencera* and *Santa María de la Rosa* – sheds light only on the Spanish side. See the accounts of Sténuit, *Treasures of the Armada*; Martin, *Full Fathom Five*; Martin, 'The equipment and fighting potential of the Spanish Armada'; and various excavation reports published in the *International Journal of Nautical Archaeology*. On a great lost opportunity, the *San Juan de Sicilia*, see McLeay, *The Tobermory Treasure*. Three more wrecks – the *Santa María de Visón*, *Juliana* and *Lavia* – have been located off Sligo, but await full excavation.

The vexed question of the Armada's guns is also discussed by Thompson, 'Spanish Armada guns', which entirely supersedes Lewis, *Armada Guns*, and, in consequence, the conclusions of the same author regarding Spanish and English tactics in his *The Spanish Armada*. For technical data on the external and internal ballistics of smooth-bore artillery we have drawn extensively on Guilmartin, *Gunpowder and Galleys*. On the construction of Master Remigy's siege guns, see the comprehensive account of Roosens, 'Het Arsenal van Mechelen ende de wapenhandel'. For a convincing demonstration that even the English could not have fired a 'broadside' at this time, but only each gun on a side in sequence, see Rodger, 'The development of broadside gunnery'.

## Notes

1   Data on guns from AGS *GA* 347/218, 'Las naves que fueron en esta última Armada'; and Thompson, 'Spanish Armada guns'. Unfortunately, information on the ships of the squadron of Portugal has proved hard to find. Nevertheless the *San Martín*, which in 1588 had carried 48 guns, in January 1591 carried 45, of which the heaviest were two 29-pounder cannon periers; only one other gun fired more than 14-pound balls (AGS *GA* 347/206, 'Relación particular'). RAZ *Rekenkamer* C2983, account of Pieter Willemszoon, recorded the calibre of 38 guns recovered from the wrecked Portuguese galleons *San Mateo* and *San Felipe* (which had originally carried 34 and 40 guns respectively). The heaviest were nine 14-pounders, plus one 11-, seven 9- and five 8-pounders along with sundry small pieces.

2   PRO *SP* 12/220, 'Survey' of the queen's ships carried out on 25 September 1588 OS (see extracts in Laughton, II, 241–9). Although a number of masts and other items are reported as 'decayed', which may be a euphemism for battle damage, they are not numerous; the only specific references to enemy action concerned some sails of the *Elizabeth Bonaventure* 'shot full of holes' (fo. 50). However, a survey carried out three days later reported rather more damage: most notably it described the mainmast of the *Revenge* as 'decayed and perished with shot' (*ibid.*, II, 250–4, at p. 252).

3   Details from the 1588 account of the treasurer of the navy: PRO *E* 351/2225 and (more legibly) PRO *AO*1/1686/23. BL Sloane MS 2450, 'Sea causes extraordinary, A.D. 1588', also includes accounts for numerous repairs carried out in spring 1588, as well as in September (see fo. 54). Our thanks to Nicholas Rodger for helping us to interpret these figures. For some idea of the work required before the queen's ships set forth, see PRO *SP* 12/204/34–5, 'The present state of her majesty's navy', 12 October 1587.

4   Details from AGS *CMC* 2a/772 (*San Francisco* and *Concepción Menor*), 2a/460 (*Santa Bárbara*), 2a/905 (*Santa Catalina*) and 2a/942 (*Trinidad de Scala*), and KML *Medina Sidonia Papers: Casa de la Contratación*, 8/32 and 8/37. See also the tables and further statistics in Parker, '*Dreadnought* revolution', 279–80, and Parker, *Grand Strategy*, 258.

5   AGS *CMC* 3a/1704, no. 45, account of Vicenzo de Bune for salvaging the *San Lorenzo*; AGS *GA* 221/1, 'La felicíssima Armada', fo. A9 (claiming that the galleass carried 2,500 rounds when it left Lisbon); Parker, 'El testamento político', 29–34 (Recalde's *San Juan*); and Duro, II, 377–8, 384–5 and 392 (*San Martín*).

6   AGS *CMC* 2a/905, Papers of *San Juan Bautista de la Esperanza*, pliegos 39–43. See also the table on p. 189 above.

7   Norton, *The Gunner*, 67–8.

8   Burnell, *The Voyage of John Huyghen van Linschoten to the East Indies*, II, 268–9. Almost no explicit contemporary written evidence survives on the question of shipboard gun drills. Some oblique information may be gleaned from William Bourne, *The Art of Shooting in Great Ordnance* and, on the Spanish side, from Diego García de Palacio, *Instrucción nautica*; see also the modern translation by J. Bankston.

9   PRO *E* 36/13, Inventory of the Navy (see pp. 55–62 for the *Mary Rose*, whose excavated remains have yielded truck carriages). 'Truckles', 'extrees' (axle trees) and other items to make sea-carriages feature in, for example, Bodleian Library, Oxford,

MS Rawlinson *A* 204/1, Ordnance Office accounts for 1578 (including carriages made for the *Revenge*) and PRO *WO* 55/1626, Ordnance Office issues for 1596 – every new 'ship carriage' required two 'extrees' and two pairs of 'trucks' (see fos 3, 14, 15, 66–7v etc.). Field carriages, with 'strakes, spikes, nave hoops' and so on, were clearly constructed in an entirely different way (see fo. 36).

10    AGS *CMC* 2a/1210, miscellaneous accounts, order of Valdés dated 22 April 1588; a second copy at *CMC* 1a/1718 fo. 759, noting that the gun (a 9-pound culverin) was exchanged for a much smaller *medio sacre* – one more example of Valdés 'gunning up' his ship. KML *Medina Sidonia Papers: Casa de la Contratación*, 8/30–41 (fos 171–236), accounts of ordnance and munitions supplied to embargoed ships by the duke of Medina Sidonia in July 1587. #32 (for the *Santa Catalina*) called for wheels '3.5 palms high', or 29 inches (the size of the gun it would carry is unstated). Some artistic evidence suggests that there may have been *some* truck-mounted guns on the Armada, particularly aboard the big Portuguese galleons, which may help to explain why that squadron's gunnery performance seems to have been markedly superior to that of the fleet as a whole. See Parker, '*Dreadnought* revolution', 282. Spanish naval gunnery continued to lag, however. Giulio Cesare Firrufino's treatise, *El perfecto artillero*, of 1648, devoted a chapter to the truck carriage, pointedly entitled 'Of the construction of sea-carriages used by the English, Dutch and French' (pp. 96–7, with illustration).

# 12

# 'God breathed'

On the evening of 9 August, with a south-westerly wind blowing the Armada clear of the Flemish shoals and into the North Sea, the duke of Medina Sidonia held a council of war to determine what strategy the fleet should now adopt. Should it, without hope of replenishment or reinforcement, in the face of the prevailing winds, and against an enemy who had already proved his superiority in battle and was operating close to his home bases, attempt the rendezvous with Parma once again? Should it perhaps mount some kind of offensive operation on its own initiative, such as a landing on the Yorkshire coast? Or should it nurse itself back to Spain, now left virtually without naval defences, via the north of Britain?

Tensions ran high. When the duke's felucca came to collect Recalde for the council meeting, he flatly refused to go, 'because he felt disheartened by the lack of courage they had all shown, and by the confusion aboard the flagship, and because his opinion in some other meetings had counted for nothing'. He reluctantly obeyed the second summons, and joined the other surviving general officers, Flores, Oquendo, Bertendona, Bobadilla and Leiva, aboard the *San Martín*. For their benefit the duke gave a brief description of the damage done to the fleet, and summarised its dwindling stock of food and munitions. Then he asked for a vote on what should be done next. According to the duke's journal, the council was unanimous: if at all possible the Armada should turn about and return to the Channel for a second attempt to pick up Parma and invade England. Only if the wind proved contrary should the fleet attempt the long northabout return to Spain. Recalde's journal told a very different story. He claimed that 'although he was of a different opinion, they [the council] resolved to return to Spain'.

Both men wrote their accounts afterwards, with the express intention of sending them to the king, and so we might never have known the truth but for the survival of a subsequent holograph exchange between the two commanders. Two days after the council, in a memorandum to his commander-in-chief, Recalde referred to the 'terrible decision' to return to Spain; the duke returned the note with the tart marginal comment, written in his own hand, 'We could not have done anything else, for the reasons discussed at the council which you yourself attended.'[1] Recalde's version is further confirmed by the public announcement

Ireland and the Armada wrecks, Sept.–Oct. 1588

LA TRINIDAD VALENCERA (Levant)
GIRONA (Naples)
Inish-owen
Bloody Foreland
?
Derry
Dunluce
Burt
Glenarm
Carrickfergus
DUQUESA SANTA ANA (Andalusia)
Loughros Mor Bay
Killibegs
?
ULSTER
JULIANA
all Levant
LAVIA
?
STA MARÍA DE VISON
Streedagh Strand
Sligo
Blacksod Bay
LA RATA ENCORONADA (Levant)
?
Clew Bay
EL GRAN GRIN (Biscay)
FALCON BLANCO MEDIANO (Hulk)
CONNAUGHT
Drogheda
?
Galway
Dublin
Galway Bay
Aran Islands
LEINSTER
?Hulk
Mutton I.
?SAN ESTEBAN (Guipúzcoa)
Doonbeg
Limerick
ANUNCIADA (Levant)
Shannon Est
STA MARÍA DE LA ROSA (Guipúzcoa)
Smerwick
?
Tralee
MUNSTER
Wexford
Dingle
Waterford
Blasket Is.
SAN JUAN BAUTISTA (Merchantman, Castile)
Cork
Kinsale
Cape Clear

0   50 miles
0   50   100 km

to the whole fleet on 10 August, the day after the council, that they were returning to Spain. The duke had clearly decided to cut and run. He accordingly
reduced the daily ration of each man to one pint of water, half-a-pint of wine and
half-a-pound of biscuit a day, 'so that supplies should not run out because of the
long voyage'. Even if all the food aboard was edible, and much clearly was not,
this represented a daily intake of less than 1,000 calories, scarcely enough to
sustain life, let alone health, for any extended period.[2]

The English fleet, sensing the change of plan, altered its own dispositions.
On the 10th, the day Medina Sidonia announced his decision to return to Spain,
Seymour's squadron departed to resume its station in the Channel in case 'anything be attempted by the duke of Parma', and the remaining ships began to
engage in bravado – 'as well they might', Recalde grimly commented, 'because
those who had previously fled from us were now chasing us; and to prove the
point, whenever four or six of our ships turned back towards them, they fled
again'. After two days more of this cautious minuet, the rest of the English fleet
made a final bombastic flaunt in battle array off the Firth of Forth and then
broke off the chase, its commanders protesting that 'if our wants of victuals
and munition were supplied, we would pursue them to the furthest they durst
have gone'.

Although they did not know it, Howard and his commanders now had
nothing to fear. One Armada ship after another – especially the Levanters –
reported difficulties in keeping up with the main fleet. The *Lavia* lacked her
spritsail and foremast topsail; the *San Juan de Sicilia* lacked her foremast mainsail;
the *Trinidad Valencera* had few sails left to set. On 10 August another Levanter
broke her spritsail mast in a collision with one of the smaller galleons of the
Portuguese squadron (which also suffered damage). Recalde favoured slowing
down the Armada's speed, to allow the necessary repairs to be carried out to
these (and other) vessels. He felt this could be done without risk 'because the
enemy does not want our blood' but 'only wants to make us leave'. The duke
refused. Although he chivalrously blamed himself for all the disasters – 'May
Our Lord be praised, because it seems He is punishing us just for my sins, to
which I attribute everything' – he stuck to his decision to head for home as
quickly as he could while supplies lasted.[3]

On 13 August, the fleet's pathetic contingent of already starving draught and
pack animals were dumped overboard to save water and, that same day, the
flagship issued sailing instructions for the homeward voyage. 'The course that is
first to be held', ran the orders, 'is to the north-north-east, until you be found
under 61 degrees; and take great heed lest you fall upon the island of Ireland, for
fear of the harm that may happen to you upon that coast.' After 'doubling the
Cape' (that is, reaching a longitude beyond Ireland's most westerly point), the
fleet was to head west-south-west to a latitude of 58 degrees (somewhere to
the west of Rockall), and thence south-west to 53 degrees, from where a final

south-easterly run might be made to the ports of northern Spain. Two days later the duke gave orders for all ships to make full sail; those that could not keep up would, like Don Pedro de Valdés and the *Rosario*, be left behind. Recalde asked permission to stay and escort the slower vessels, but Medina Sidonia refused 'and sent another order to make sail and follow him, which we did'.[4]

There was nothing remarkable about the Armada's route home. Even in times of peace ships making passage from the North Sea to the Atlantic frequently adopted it, particularly during autumn or winter. The prevailing south-westerlies made the run to the Northern Isles relatively easy, and the islands themselves could usually be rounded without difficulty, often with the assistance of the north-easterly Helm wind which springs from high pressure over Arctic Norway. Once the North Atlantic was reached progress could always be made southwards, even against the prevailing wind, by employing a series of long tacks. This route would have been familiar to many of the Armada's seamen, particularly those aboard the Baltic hulks. What the ships did lack, however, were adequate charts and sufficient pilots. The former were simply not to be had, because no reliable ones existed. The west coast of Ireland remained *terra incognita* for mariners, except for those who had made a personal reconnaissance (as Recalde had done in 1580), until the publication of detailed Dutch charts in 1612. The *Derrotero* and charts issued by Medina Sidonia's cartographic service to every ship in the fleet went no further than the Moray Firth in Scotland and Dursey Head in south-west Ireland. Any officer with the foresight to acquire a copy of the latest guide to navigation – Lucas Waghenaer's *Mariner's Mirror* (Latin edition, 1586) – would have found in it no charts of Ireland.[5]

Medina Sidonia did his best. In the straits between Orkney and Shetland the Armada encountered Dutch and Scottish fishing boats from which the duke 'chose certain pilots, to carry them for the coast of Ireland, and so into Spain'. He also seized as much water and fish as he could, to augment the fleet's rapidly diminishing supplies.[6] On 21 August, as the Armada sailed into the North Atlantic, Don Balthasar de Zúñiga, a staff officer aboard the flagship, was put ashore at Scalloway in Shetland with orders to sail swiftly for Spain, and prepare provisions and reinforcements in Galicia against the moment when the fleet returned. He also carried a copy of the duke's journal, and dispatches for the king which reported moderate casualties (including about 3,000 sick and wounded) but confirmed that 112 vessels remained under Medina Sidonia's command. The Armada had been a costly failure but, as yet, it was by no means a disaster.

But even as Zúñiga departed, disaster began to strike. Four ships, unable to keep up with the more weatherly members of the fleet, lost contact with the main body. They were the supply squadron's flagship, *El Gran Grifón*, two other hulks, the *Barca de Amburg* and the *Castillo Negro*, and the Levanter *La Trinidad Valencera*. Together the four vessels struggled south-westwards for 12 days, making little progress. Then, on 1 September, the *Barca de Amburg* suddenly signalled that she was about to founder. Her company of 250 was transferred to the *Grifón* and the *Valencera* just before she went down.

*La Trinidad Valencera* was a large Venetian grain ship, one of the especially capacious vessels which had been embargoed to carry the Armada's heavy siege train. Under Don Alonso de Luzón, colonel of the Neapolitan *tercio*, she had played a distinguished part in the fighting, but the damage she had sustained had rendered some of her sails useless, and the pumps could no longer cope with her numerous leaks. Luzón therefore decided to run for the nearest land. After sighting the north coast of Donegal the ship ran eastwards, probably with the intention of gaining the shelter of Lough Foyle. Before she got there, however, the *Valencera* grounded on a reef at the western end of Kinnagoe Bay. Stuck firm on the rocks, but with her upper decks still above water, the situation seemed perilous but not hopeless. Don Alonso set off with four companions for the shore in the ship's only remaining boat, evidently quite small. As they approached they saw 20 or so 'savage people' standing on a rock, and when they landed on the adjacent shingle beach 'only with their rapiers in their hands', four or five of the natives came to help them out of the boat and 'courteously used' them. Soon a much bigger crowd of locals had gathered, and the atmosphere became less cordial. The Spanish officers were roughly handled, and relieved of their 'money, gold buttons, rapiers and apparel to the value of 7,300 ducats'.

Such treatment would prove typical of the responses of the indigenous Irish to Armada survivors. They were regarded as fair game for plunder but otherwise, with rare exceptions, were not physically harmed. On some occasions, as on this, they were given active assistance. When the Spaniards' own boat foundered they hired another from the locals, and in due course most of the *Valencera*'s complement came safely ashore. When this boat, too, was lost in the surf, they attempted to hire yet another, but the Irish had now become more intent on salvaging what they could from the ship than on rescuing her occupants. Two days later, when she suddenly split open and sank, several Irishmen and Spaniards still aboard were drowned.[7]

On the beach, Don Alonso rallied the survivors and marched inland. He aimed to reach the west coast, fighting his way through if need be, in order to find other Armada ships on their way back to Spain. Luzón still commanded a formidable, if somewhat dispirited, military force, and sustained by local horsemeat and butter they marched 20 miles to Illagh Castle, seat of Sir John O'Docherty, in whose territory they had landed. Negotiations with the Irish bishop apparently in charge of the castle drew an equivocal response. The Spaniards were asked to make a show of force so that the bishop might surrender to them, and give them assistance, without compromising his own position with the English. Don Alonso viewed this offer with some suspicion. His unease was confirmed when the castle fired its guns, evidently to alert the nearby English garrisons. The Spaniards cautiously withdrew, crossed a wide bog, and took up defensive positions in a ruined castle which stood nearby.

Don Alonso and his men were unaware that an elaborate trap was being sprung. The peninsula of Inishowen, on the northern shore of which they had landed, was bounded at its narrow neck by two parallel strips of boggy ground running between the sea-loughs of Foyle and Swilly. Illagh commanded the crossing of the northern bog, while that to the south was guarded by the much stronger castle at Burt, garrisoned by English and 'affected' Irish troops under Major John Kelly. Through their ignorance of local geography the Spaniards had been lured into a killing ground from which it would be difficult to escape.

With drums beating, the Burt garrison approached the Spanish position, and arranged a parley. What business, asked the queen's officers, had the Spaniards in her majesty's dominions? Don Alonso replied that they had been shipwrecked and wished only to return to Spain. This Kelly refused to accept; they must, he insisted, surrender as prisoners of war. The Spaniards refused, and returned to their trenches. A day later, however, after some skirmishing, Don Alonso resumed negotiations and, seeing his position to be hopeless, agreed to surrender on fair terms. He lived to regret it. After plundering them of all their clothing and possessions, Kelly's men separated the common soldiers and seamen from those of ransomable status. The former were then taken into a field and a cold-blooded massacre began, though a number were able to escape in the confusion and of these a handful eventually reached Flanders via Scotland. The fate of those reserved for ransom was only marginally better. After a nightmare 100-mile march to Drogheda with little food and, for many of them, without adequate clothing or footwear, the survivors were incarcerated while haggling over their maintenance and ransom dragged on interminably. Many died in the process although some, including Don Alonso, were eventually repatriated.

*El Gran Grifón*, the hulks' flagship which had become separated from *La Trinidad Valencera* on 4 September, had meanwhile been enduring her own tribulations. She had been badly shot-up during the battles and, as with the *San Mateo*, the recoil of her own guns had severely strained her hull structure, causing her joints to leak with the working of the sea. Aboard was the squadron commander, Juan Gómez de Medina, together with two companies of soldiers and a small group of priests and expatriate Irish volunteers. Alone, and in almost constantly adverse weather, the ship had beaten south-westwards into the Atlantic, until on 7 September she was hit by a violent storm which caused her weakened seams to gape even further apart. An oncoming sea would certainly have sunk her, and so she ran northwards with the weather until she sighted St Kilda. Then the wind veered into the north-west, allowing her crew to turn once more 'towards our dear Spain'. For three days this favourable wind held, but then it backed into the prevailing south-westerly quarter, driving the ship once more to the north. The exhausted Spaniards toiled ceaselessly at the pumps, and attempted to patch up the worst of the leaks with ox hides and planks. By 25 September they had sighted the Hebrides, at which point they decided to make for the nearest land, even if it meant running the ship ashore. Somehow they negotiated the Orkney archipelago by night, apparently aided by the glow of the Northern Lights. On the morning of the 27th, with the hulk now wallowing with 10 feet of water in the hold, Fair Isle was sighted. At dusk Juan Gómez anchored on its sheltered eastern side, and at dawn *El Gran Grifón* was driven ashore. She fetched up against the overhanging cliff of Stroms Hellier, close to the south-eastern corner of the island, where she wedged fast. Most of those on board escaped by climbing the foremast, which lay against the overhang, but seven perished in the attempt and little could be saved from the ship apart from the squadron pay-chest.

Gómez de Medina's situation, though improved, was still fraught with danger. Fair Isle was small and storm-bound, and there seemed to be no immediate prospect of escape. With winter approaching the 17 crofting families who lived on the island had little to spare for the hungry castaways who, to their credit, made no attempt to take the islanders' provisions by force. Seabirds and fish were plentiful, but could not wholly alleviate the weakness and disease brought on by four months of sustained malnutrition. Fifty of the Spanish soldiers and German seamen, including the hulk's master, Burgat Querquerman, perished on the island.

Six weeks passed before contact could be made with Fair Isle's absentee landlord, Malcolm Sinclair of Quendale, and in due course the survivors were brought to the Shetland mainland. From there they were carried in hired ships to Anstruther in Fife where, on the morning of 6 December, they dropped anchor. Their arrival caused something of a panic in the town, since fears of large-scale Spanish landings were still strong. Tension eased, however, when Gómez de Medina explained their circumstances and friendly intentions to James Melville, the local minister; and, at the cost of enduring a lengthy sermon on the error of their ways, the Spaniards were charitably entertained by the burgh. The soldiers, wrote Melville in his diary, 'were suffered to come a land, and lie all together, for the most part young beardless men, sillie, trauchled, and hungered, to the which kail, porage, and fish was given'. Gómez de Medina was described by Melville as 'a very reverend man of big stature, and grave and stout countenance, grey haired, and very humble like'. After a few days of homely fare for the soldiers and local socialising for the officers (during which they were shown, to their distress, a pamphlet hot from the London presses which gloatingly reported the catastrophes which had befallen the Armada in Ireland) the contingent was shipped across the Forth to Leith, where negotiations for their repatriation began. Technically they were still free men, for Scotland had been neutral throughout the conflict.

It was not so in Ireland, where the scattered English garrisons understandably feared the possibility that Philip II's strategy might still include a direct assault upon them. In August, rumours of the Armada's approach, according to an official in Dublin, 'doth work wonderful uncertain yet calm humours in the people of this country, who stand agape until the game be played, not daring to discover their real intentions'.[8] And then in September numerous Spanish ships *did* appear suddenly and unexpectedly, landing troops on Ireland's shores. A letter from Sir Richard Bingham, governor of Connaught, neatly caught the atmosphere of confusion and fear. There was, he wrote on 20 September:

> further news of strange ships: whether they be of the dispersed fleet which are fled from the supposed overthrow in the Narrow Seas, or new forces come from Spain directly, no man is able to advertise otherwise than by guess, which doth rather show their coming from Spain, both by these falling from the west, and others which coasted along the north parts of Sligo . . . I expect very present news either from the one place or the other, for by all likelihoods they mind to land. I look this night for my horses to be here.

Here was a frightening possibility: were these 'strange ships' indeed 'come from Spain directly' as part of that second Armada of which several prisoners, including Don Diego Pimentel, had spoken? Sir William Fitzwilliam, Elizabeth's lord deputy in Ireland, decided to take no chances in what he described as 'these dangerous and broken times'. His urgent dispatch to the Privy Council on 22 September pointed out that he had in all Ireland fewer than 750 soldiers at his disposal, and no cavalry mounts for want of horseshoes. Any serious Spanish landings, he felt, could not be contained. The chilling instruction therefore went out to his officers in the western provinces 'to apprehend and execute all Spaniards found, of what quality soever. Torture may be used in prosecuting this enquiry.'

His grim order had already been anticipated by some of his scattered agents in the west. On 15 September the *zabra Nuestra Señora de Castro* came into Tralee Bay, because she was leaking so badly. Soldiers rounded up the 24 men aboard and took them to the stronghold of Sir Edward Denny, an English plantation landlord with extensive properties in the district. They were unlucky. Eight years before, Sir Edward had been given the Italian commander of the Castello del Oro at Smerwick for ransom, but the man escaped first. Denny swore that he would kill any Spaniards that he came across, and now he sought his revenge: after a brief interrogation he had all the prisoners summarily executed. Three made unsuccessful efforts to save themselves by claiming that they had friends in Waterford who would ransom them, but when pressed they could not, or would not, name them. They too were hanged.[9]

On 20 September, a large vessel came ashore at Doonbeg on the Clare coast. She was probably the 736-ton *San Esteban* of the Guipúzcoan squadron. Three hundred men were reported drowned, and some 60 captured. On the same day, a few miles to the north, another vessel was wrecked on Mutton Island. Only four survivors reached the shore. The prisoners from both these ships were brought before Boetius Clancy, the sheriff of Clare, and after a brief incarceration they were publicly hanged on a hillock still called *Cnoc na Crocaire* (Gallows Hill). Even Don Felipe de Córdoba, son of Philip II's chamberlain, whose safe return would have commanded a sizeable ransom, was not spared. Clancy's name, tradition asserts, was thereafter cursed in the church of Don Felipe's home town every seventh year, to ensure that his soul would never escape from purgatory.

A little to the south, on the same day that these two wrecks had taken place, another drama unfolded. The 703-ton Ragusan *Anunciada*, another of Bertendona's Levanters, lay at anchor and close to sinking in Scattery Roads, off Kilrush at the mouth of the Shannon. She had arrived there a week before with five attendant pinnaces, leaking badly from damage sustained during the fireship attack off Calais. A day after her arrival she had been joined by the hulk *Barca de Danzig*, which was also in danger of foundering. The *Anunciada*'s carpenters successfully patched up the hulk, but were unable to save their own ship. At length, on the orders of her captain, she was fired and scuttled after the men, guns and stores had been transferred to the other vessels, which then departed.

Up to this point the weather had been unsettled, though not particularly unseasonable. But on 18 September two Atlantic depressions, spawned by tropical storms far to the west, reached the coasts of Europe. By 20 September these had resolved themselves into a single deep depression centred off north-west Scotland, drawing in great frontal masses of cold Arctic air. The resultant gale was described by an English official in Ireland as 'a most extreme wind and cruel storm, the like whereof hath not been seen or heard a long time, which put us in very good hope that many of the [Spanish] ships should be beaten up and cast upon the rocks'.

The gale found Juan Martínez de Recalde and the crew of the *San Juan de Portugal* anchored precariously in Blasket Sound, off the exposed south-western tip of Ireland. A storm on 18 August had carried away the ship's barge carrying 30 sheep and – more critically – 140 pitchers of drinking water. A week later, after a night of thick fog, Recalde found himself with only three other ships and three pinnaces: although he sent out the pinnaces to locate the main fleet, he never saw them again. The admiral, marvelling at the Northern Lights (which he had never seen before), beat against the winds between 59 and 60 degrees north (level with Orkney), and as he tacked other ships joined him until by 7 September the *San Juan* had 22 companions, including the galleass *Zúñiga*. Then another storm struck, dispersing the little fleet. On the 15th, only two remained – Recalde's *San Juan de Portugal* and the *San Juan de Castilla*, commanded by the Basque Marcos de Aramburu – and they found themselves close, too close, to the Irish coast.

With superb seamanship Recalde, who had explored this coast after the landings at Smerwick (only six sea miles away) in 1580, won the shelter of Blasket

Sound by driving through a gap in the outlying reefs barely wider than the beam of his lumbering galleon. Aramburu's ship followed, optimistically 'thinking he must have some knowledge'. There the two ships, together with a small pinnace, made emergency repairs, exchanged anchors and cables, and took on water from the spring on Great Blasket Island. English patrols thwarted attempts to land on the mainland and captured a reconnaissance party of eight men. One of them, a Portuguese seaman called Emanuel Fremoso, told his interrogators of conditions aboard Recalde's *San Juan*:

> He says that out of this ship there died 4 or 5 every day of hunger and thirst, and yet this ship was one of the best furnished for victuals . . . He says that there are 80 soldiers and 20 of the mariners sick, and do lie down and die daily, and the rest, he says, are very weak, and the captain very sad and weak. There is left in this flagship but 25 pipes of wine, very little bread, and no water but what they brought out of Spain, which stinketh marvellously, and the flesh meat they cannot eat, their drouth is so great. He says the Admiral's purpose is with the first wind to pass away for Spain. He says also that it is a common bruit among the soldiers that if they may get home again, they will not meddle with the English any more.

And then, on 20 September, 'the west wind came with some terrible fury, but cloudless and with little rain'. Aramburu, aboard the Castilian *San Juan*, takes up the story:

> The flagship of Juan Martínez drifted down on ours, cast anchor and another cable, and having smashed our lantern and our mizzen tackle and rigging, the flagship secured herself. At midday the *Santa María de la Rosa*, of Martín de Villafranca, came in by another entrance nearer land on the north-west side. She fired a shot on entering, as if seeking help, and another further on. All her sails were in shreds except the foresail. She cast her single anchor, for she was not carrying more, and with the tide coming in from the south-east side and beating against her stern she stayed there until about two o'clock. Then the tide ebbed, and as it turned the ship began dragging on our two cables, and we with her, and in an instant we could see that she was going down, trying to hoist the foresail. Then she sank with all on board, not a person being saved, a most extraordinary and terrifying thing.

The ill-fated *Santa María de la Rosa* was the vice-flagship of Oquendo's Guipúzcoan squadron, a large Basque-built merchantman of 945 tons. There was, in fact, one survivor of the 300 or so men aboard her. Giovanni de Manona, the son of the ship's pilot, managed to cling to a plank and was washed ashore, where he was captured and interrogated by the local English garrison. His story was harrowing and dramatic. The ship's military officers, he said, had tried to save themselves in the ship's boat, but the *Santa María* had gone down so quickly that they had no time to untie it. One of them had accused Giovanni's father of wrecking the ship deliberately and, in a blind rage, had slain him where he stood.

The pilot's 'treason' was probably no more than a seamanlike attempt to get the stricken ship off the isolated reef upon which she had impaled herself, and run for the shore before she sank. To do this he would have had to cut the cable of the fouled anchor and, as Aramburu witnessed, set the ship's only surviving sail. Perhaps the landsmen aboard misconstrued these sensible actions on the part of pilot; at any event, the true sequence of events was revealed in 1968 when the wreck of the *Santa María* was located in deep water at the eye of the tide race which runs through the narrow neck of Blasket Sound. The ship had evidently struck amidships on a pinnacle of rock which rears to within a few feet of the surface, ripping out her bottom so that she sank within a matter of seconds. Her great anchor, which she had dragged across the Sound under the combined influences of tide and wind, still remains hooked foul on the northern edge of the reef.

In the aftermath of the *Santa María*'s sinking, Recalde and Aramburu managed to re-anchor and ride out the storm. While they were doing so the merchantman *San Juan Bautista*, another member of the Castilian squadron, also came into the Sound. She had lost her mainmast, and as she entered a squall blew her foresail to shreds. No assistance could be given that day, but on the following morning, when the storm had abated, some of Recalde's officers went across to assess the damage. They concluded that she would have to be abandoned because her mainmast was sprung and her hold full of water. Recalde and Aramburu now disagreed about the correct course of action: the former wanted to salvage as much as possible, including the guns, the latter wanted to sail for Spain as soon as possible because his provisions were so low. On the 23rd, having agreed to take some of the survivors from the abandoned ship, Aramburu left Blasket Sound, arriving in Santander after a difficult voyage on 14 October. Meanwhile Recalde salvaged what he could and managed to reach the open sea on 28 September. Ironically, his ship reached Spain first, on 7 October.[10]

The gale on 20 September had brought other notable victims to the Irish coast. *El Gran Grin*, the 1,160-ton vice-flagship of Recalde's Biscayans, was driven into Clew Bay, Mayo. Filling fast with water, she ran aground off Clare Island. Don Pedro de Mendoza, the senior officer on board, managed to bring 100 or so of his men ashore, though twice that number were drowned. For a time the Spaniards remained on the island, virtual prisoners of Dowdarra Roe O'Malley. At length, when they made a spirited attempt to escape by stealing their captors' boats, the O'Malleys turned on them, killing 64 including Don Pedro.

About the same time three other ships became trapped in Donegal Bay. They were all large merchantmen of the Levant squadron: the Genoese *Juliana*, the Venetian *Lavia* and the Ragusan *Santa María de Visón*. On board the *Lavia* was Francisco de Cuéllar, a staff officer who had originally shipped aboard the Castilian *San Pedro*, of which he subsequently became captain. He had been relieved of his command after the breach of formation discipline which had occurred after Calais, and for which Don Cristobal de Ávila was hanged. Cuéllar had been lucky to escape with his life. Only the personal intervention of the judge-advocate, Martín de Aranda, saved him from summary execution, and he had been transferred under open arrest to Aranda's ship, the *Lavia*. Of all the accounts given by Armada survivors, that of Cuéllar, contained in a letter written to a friend when he reached Antwerp more than a year later, is the most detailed and dramatic.

In it he tells how the three ships were hit by the great storm of 20 September. They gained some shelter by entering Donegal Bay, but at the fatal cost of surrendering their chance of beating clear when the weather eased. From their anchorage close to the Sligo coast only a wind from the eastern quarter would allow them to weather Erris Head or the western tip of Tirconnell, and of such a wind they had little hope. The next storm, predictably, came from the west, and their anchors failed to grip the loose sand beneath them. Cuéllar now takes up the story in his own words:

> A great gale hit us broadside on, with the waves reaching the sky, so that the cables could not hold and the sails could not be set. We found ourselves driven ashore with all three ships upon a beach of very fine sand, hemmed in at either end by huge rocks. The likes of this had never been seen for, within an hour, all three ships were smashed to pieces, from which less than three hundred men escaped. More than a thousand drowned, among them many important people – captains, gentlemen, and staff officers.

The ships had come ashore on the long beach at Streedagh, a two-mile finger of sandhills fringing the lagoon at Milk Haven, 10 miles north of Sligo. Grounded firm on the unyielding sand, the vessels had been pummelled and smashed by the breaking surf only a couple of hundred yards from the shore. There was time enough for those on board to appreciate the full horror of their predicament, and most of them made desperate attempts to escape through the breakers. On the *Lavia* Don Diego Enríquez had himself battened below the deck of the ship's boat, together with three companions and 16,000 ducats in jewels and coin. The boat was cast adrift, in the hope that it would reach the shore but, as it left, 70 panic-stricken survivors hurled themselves on it, causing it to capsize. It came ashore upside down, and the wreckers eventually hacked it open. By then three of its occupants were already dead. Don Diego, the only survivor, expired as his clothes and valuables were ripped from him.

Captain Cuéllar was more fortunate. Although certain of his fate if he stayed with the breaking ship, because he could not swim, his prospects if he reached land seemed no less dreadful. The beach, he observed, was:

> full of enemies who went about dancing and skipping with glee at our misfortunes. Indeed, when any one of our men reached the shore, two hundred savages and other enemies fell upon him and stripped him of what he had on

until he was left stark naked . . . All of this could be plainly seen from the battered ships.

By now men were drowning on the ships, while others were throwing themselves into the sea or crying out to God in helpless resignation. In an instinctive bid for survival Cuéllar and his erstwhile saviour, Judge-Advocate Aranda, grasped a loose hatch-cover and launched themselves into the surf, but almost immediately a wave swept over their makeshift raft. Cuéllar went under, collided with a piece of timber that gashed his legs, but somehow struggled to the surface and regained his hatch cover. The judge-advocate, however, weighted down with coins sewn into his doublet and hose, lost his grip and, like many another, was never seen again.

At length Cuéllar was thrown up on the beach. Almost naked, and covered in blood, he was spared the attentions of the ghouls who moved casually among the human flotsam which littered the strand, stripping them of whatever they possessed and clubbing them down if they offered the slightest resistance. Inch by inch, and in acute pain, Cuéllar moved slowly towards the comparative shelter of the dunes behind the beach. Soon afterwards:

> a very nice young gentleman, quite naked, came up to me. He was so dazed that he could not speak, not even to tell me who he was; and at that time, which would be about nine o'clock at night, the wind was calm and the sea subsiding. I was then wet through to the skin, dying with pain and hunger, when up came two men – one of them armed and the other with a great iron axe in his hands. We remained silent, as if there was nothing wrong. They grieved to see us, and without speaking a word they cut a quantity of rushes and hay, covered us well, and then went off to the shore to ransack and break open money-chests and whatever they might find, together with more than two thousand savages and Englishmen from garrisons nearby.

Cuéllar fell into a deep sleep, from which he woke during the night to find his companion dead, and English cavalry patrols on their way to pillage and destroy the ships. But he lay undiscovered in his hide until the following morning, when he slipped away inland to start his long and perilous journey home.

Some weeks later Lord Deputy Fitzwilliam himself rode along the strand to view 'the bay where some of those ships wrecked, and where, as I heard, lay not long before 1,200 or 1,300 of the dead'. Scattered the length of the beach, he observed, 'lay as great a store of the timber . . . more than would have built five of the greatest ships I ever saw, besides mighty great boats, cables, and other cordage answerable thereunto, and some such masts, for bigness and length, as in mine judgement I never saw any two could make the like'. Nor was the lord deputy exaggerating. The *Juliana's* great rudder, discovered in 1985 in the shifting sands off Streedagh, was no less than 36 feet long.

Another large Levantine ship lost on the coast of Ireland was the carrack *Rata Santa María Encoronada*. This vessel was the unofficial flagship of Don Alonso de Leiva, the commander of the Armada's vanguard who held a secret commission from the king to take charge of the Armada should Medina Sidonia fall. Leiva's high birth and dashing military career had attracted many young noblemen to the *Rata*, and during the Channel battles she had always been where the fighting was hottest. But like so many of her Levantine sisters, and the unwieldy hulks, she could not keep up with the main body of the fleet during its northabout voyage, and she failed to maintain a safe distance from the Irish coast. Many of these Mediterranean grain ships, moreover, had been severely strained by the recoil of their own artillery, for their iron-fastened hulls were designed to accommodate the evenly spread pressures of a bulk cargo rather than to absorb the localised and violent stresses imposed by the firing of heavy guns.

On 17 September the *Rata* found herself off Blacksod Bay in County Mayo, and Leiva decided to enter this broad and well-sheltered haven to make repairs and, if possible, take on fresh water. After sending a reconnaissance party ashore the ship eventually anchored off Fahy, a creek at the south-eastern end of the bay notorious for its dangerous tide-rips. Before long the *Rata* started to drag towards the sands of Tullaghan Bay where she grounded immovably. Leiva brought his men ashore in good order, and then fired the ship.

The Spaniards dug themselves in at Doona Castle, not far from where they had been wrecked, and took stock of their position. Shortly afterwards they received information that another Spanish ship, the 900-ton hulk *Duquesa Santa Ana*, attached to the Andalusian squadron, had anchored in Elly Bay, on the far side of Blacksod Bay. Leiva gathered his men together and marched 25 miles overland to make contact with the *Duquesa*. With the combined complements of the two vessels crammed on board, the hulk set sail. On 26 September the *Duquesa*, having been driven to the north, ran aground in Loughros Mor Bay, Donegal. Once again Leiva brought his men safely ashore, but was himself injured by a capstan bar as he left the ship. As before, the Spaniards sought out a defensive position in case of English attack, and chose a ruined castle on an island in Kiltoorish Lake, which they strengthened with a light piece of ordnance salvaged from the wreck. Perhaps they intended to hold out there until aid could be sent from Spain, but after a week news reached them that the galleass *Girona* was at Killibegs, some 19 miles to the south. A sedan chair was rigged up for the wounded Leiva, and the Spaniards made their way overland to Killibegs, where they found the damaged galleass under repair.

For the next fortnight Killibegs bustled with activity. Another Spanish ship which had grounded at the harbour entrance was stripped of materials and gear with which to repair the *Girona* and at length, early on 26 October and with some 1,300 souls crammed aboard her, the ramshackle galleass set sail, heading not for Spain but for Scotland. Leiva had decided that the overloaded and crank vessel was unlikely to survive the perils of the open Atlantic, and so the short run to neutral Scotland seemed the safest option. But off the north coast of Antrim the *Girona*'s jury rudder gave way, and she was driven broadside on to the rocky fang of Lacada Point, close to the Giant's Causeway. Leiva and all but a handful of his men perished among the kelp-covered reefs.

The fate of most of those who fell into English hands was little better. The hulk *Falcon Blanco Mediano*, a 300-tonner with a complement of little more than 100 men, had been wrecked on a small island off Galway on about 25 September. Her survivors included Don Luis de Córdoba, another son of Philip II's chamberlain, and his nephew, Gonzalo. For a time they were given shelter by the O'Flaherties of Connemara, but in response to threats from Governor Richard Bingham (the aptly named 'Flail of Connaught'), they were at length delivered under guard to Galway town. Even officers who would have commanded ransoms, and six young Dutchmen forcibly pressed into the fleet, though spared initially by Bingham, were later executed on the personal orders of Lord Deputy Fitzwilliam. In all, Bingham later claimed to have disposed of 1,100 survivors from the Connaught wrecks, though even he regretted the wanton loss of ransom money occasioned by the lord deputy's draconian policy of extermination. But still the hangings continued. On 18 November commissioners were sent out from Dublin 'to make diligent search and enquiry for such of the Spaniards and Italians of the dispersed fleet as came with purpose to invade her majesty's kingdom, and to apprehend and take them, and thereupon to execute them to the death by martial law without respect of person'.[11] Despite all these dreadful measures, Fitzwilliam still complained that 'all the means the Council and I can work will not prevail to take these locusts and grasshoppers'.

The *Girona* was probably the last Armada ship to be wrecked on Ireland. A further drama, however, was soon enacted not far away, in a sheltered harbour on the island of Mull among Scotland's Inner Hebrides. On 23 September a large ship had been sighted close to Isla, and a few days later she dropped anchor in Tobermory Bay. She was the 800-ton Ragusan *San Juan de Sicilia*, yet another member of the ill-fated Levant squadron. Apart from an acute shortage of water and provisions she was not in great distress, and arrangements were made with Lachlan Maclean of Duart, the local chieftain, for replenishment. Maclean agreed to co-operate, for a modest if unconventional price: in return for provisioning he wanted to borrow a company of Spanish troops with which to settle his outstanding feuds. To this the ship's senior officer, Don Diego Tellez Enríquez, readily agreed, though he demanded five Maclean hostages as surety. For more than a month thereafter the ship lay off Tobermory, making repairs and taking on supplies, while a detachment of about 100 Spanish troops ravaged the Macleans' enemies ashore.

But the long arm of Elizabeth's secret service eventually reached this remote part of England's troublesome northern neighbour. Among the merchants engaged in provisioning the *San Juan* was one John Smollett of Dumbarton, who in due course appears to have gained the confidence of the crew and free access to the ship. In reality, it seems, he was an agent of Sir Francis Walsingham. What followed is not entirely clear. On 5 November, while the Spaniards were drying out some of their remaining powder on the forward deck, it appears that Smollett was able to drop a piece of smouldering lint nearby before departing hurriedly ashore. Soon afterwards the ship was rent by a tremendous explosion which sank her and killed almost all still on board, including the Maclean hostages. Of those ashore, Maclean of Duart retained the services of about 50 Spaniards in his local feuds for another year, and then shipped them home.[12]

So far as is known, the coast of England reaped only a single wreck. She was the hospital ship *San Pedro Mayor*, a hulk which, after successfully rounding the British Isles, lost her way and on 6 November ended up on Bolt Tail in Devon, close to where the Armada had begun its advance up the Channel more than three months earlier. Her bedraggled survivors were soon in custody. They included some patients from the *San Salvador*, injured when that ship had exploded early in the fighting. Fortunately the *San Pedro*'s survivors fared much better than their compatriots in Ireland. In sedate Devon they were not perceived as a threat to national security, although an unseemly argument arose between their captors and the state as to who should pay for their meagre rations.[13]

A small number of Spaniards did, however, manage to escape from the horrors of Ireland. Though Fitzwilliam was eager 'in the fury and heat of justice' to slaughter all his prisoners without exception, a few 'ransomable' captives were first imprisoned at Drogheda and then brought to London, where negotiations for their release continued, in some cases for several years. Another group found freedom much more quickly, and in highly dramatic circumstances. Thirty prisoners destined for England had been embarked on the pinnace *Swallow* in Dublin Bay for shipment to Chester. This vessel, which had a crew of eight under a gentleman-captain, belonged to Christopher Carleill, the constable of Carrickfergus. In 1585 Carleill had been Drake's deputy on the great West Indies raid, and was Secretary Walsingham's son-in-law. During the crossing the Spaniards rose and seized the vessel, which they sailed to Corunna. The English crew was subsequently hanged. This was an inequitable twist of fate, for Carleill had been the only Englishman in Ireland whose behaviour had been honourable and humane towards the Armada prisoners, having defied the lord deputy's express orders to execute a batch of 15 which had come into his custody. Instead, he had them shipped to Scotland at his own expense.

It was in Scotland, too, that the humbler survivors – 'the rags that yet remain', as Fitzwilliam contemptuously described them – sought sanctuary. Francisco de Cuéllar, after an incredible catalogue of adventures and tribulations, at last reached Dunluce on the Antrim coast, from where the colourful octogenarian Sorley Boy Macdonnell operated an escape route in collusion with his Scottish kinsmen. Cuéllar made the arduous crossing in an open boat, which almost sank in mid-passage, but lived to write the story of his escape, in Antwerp, almost a year later.

Thirty-two survivors of the Illagh massacre, where the men from *La Trinidad Valencera* had been gunned down, and a handful from the wreck of the *Girona*, had earlier passed through Sorley Boy's hands on their way to Scotland. Their reception there was not unfriendly. The townspeople of Ayr gave them new shoes to help them on their way, and when they arrived in Edinburgh King James VI ordered them to be lodged in the town. Within 30 days they were on their way to France in Scottish ships with letters of safe conduct signed by John Arnot, provost of the city. Twice they had to put into English ports, and on both occasions their credentials were honoured. Finally, on 26 December, they reached Le Havre.

They were lucky. Hard on their heels came the survivors from Fair Isle, to be followed by 300 more from two wrecks off Norway and a pathetic dribble of further refugees from Ireland. King James now adopted a more equivocal stance. Scotland may have been neutral in the conflict, but its young king had well-founded hopes of succeeding to the English throne, and he had no wish to antagonise Queen Elizabeth. His small country, moreover, was far from stable. A strong pro-Spanish faction, mostly Catholic, though it included unprincipled Protestants like the earl of Bothwell, played for high political stakes. The supply squadron's commander, Juan Gómez de Medina of *El Gran Grifón*, the most senior Spanish officer to reach Scotland, became a prime target for intrigue. By the beginning of January 1589 Thomas Fowler, an English agent in Edinburgh, reported to Walsingham that: 'Don John de Medina and divers captains of the Spaniards are going hence with great credit as they say from divers of the nobility here, as Huntley, Bothwell, Seton, and others . . . On Sunday last I dined with Bothwell, where I found four Spanish captains whom he entertains.'

By then 'Don John' was on the point of leaving in a 40-ton barque provided by Bothwell's agent, Colonel Stewart, with an exhortation to 'let the Spanish king know how many well-willers he hath in this country, and to procure but 4,000 Spaniards, good shot, and leaders, with a sum of money to be brought hither by his conduct with speed'.

Gómez de Medina had no intention of getting embroiled in a Scottish revolt, but Colonel Stewart's barque gave him the opportunity he needed to get out of Scotland and so expedite the rescue of his stranded comrades. He departed in secret, taking with him only the small and vulnerable band of priests and Irish expatriates who had come with him from Spain – men whose names, he knew, were high on the English death-list.

The voyage proved eventful, and ended with their wrecking off Cape St Vincent. But Gómez de Medina survived to reach Cadiz, where in a remarkable episode he showed himself to be a man of honour. A trading ship from Anstruther, the town in Fife where he and his men had first landed, had been impounded by the port authorities, and her crew imprisoned. Remembering the succour he and his men had been given by the inhabitants of this small Scottish seaport, he immediately secured their release, and sent them home with kindly messages to his Protestant benefactors. We need not doubt that he acted with similar dispatch to assist his own comrades, still stranded at Leith awaiting their safe conduct and a passage to Flanders. They had not been taken into Gómez's confidence before his escape, and had taken a less than charitable view of his motives in abandoning them. As soon as they heard of his stealthy departure, at the end of January, Captains Patricio Antolinez and Esteban de Legoretta wrote to Philip II accusing their commanding officer of 'an act unworthy of his obligations to your Majesty's flag', and pleading urgently for ships to take them to Spain.[14]

They were not alone. Thirty-two surviving soldiers and their wives from the hulk *Santiago*, 'the ship of the women' wrecked off Norway, were stranded in Hamburg. The galleass *Zúñiga* touched briefly on the Irish coast, where a boatload of her people were captured together with a copy of Medina Sidonia's sailing instructions for the return voyage to Spain. She was then driven by storm to take refuge in Le Havre, where her complement of some 300 waited restlessly for almost a year while the shattered galleass was repaired.[15] At Morbihan in Brittany 168 survivors from the hulk *San Pedro Menor* clamoured for rescue, as did the men of Recalde's first flagship, the *Santa Ana*, abandoned to the English as she tried to return to Spain from her refuge in Le Havre.[16] By the close of 1588, however, almost all of these isolated groups of survivors, including those from the flag galleass *San Lorenzo*, destroyed off Calais during the fighting, had been rescued. This left about 200 prisoners in the Dutch Republic, and some 700 in England itself (most of whom were from the *Nuestra Señora del Rosario* and the *San Pedro Mayor*), as well as the 660 men still in Scotland.

The rank-and-file prisoners were dealt with relatively simply and swiftly. Many had originally been roughly treated in England. As one of their captors put it: 'The peoples' charity to them (coming with so wicked an intent) is very cold.' He added: 'We would have been very glad had they been made water-spaniels when they first were taken.' As the danger abated, however, their treatment improved. In May 1589 the English accepted a ransom of £10 a head from the duke of Parma for 500 of them. Those captured by the Dutch were bought out of prison at the same time, and for the same price.[17] But this did not include persons of rank, who were the subject of separate negotiations. Don Vasco de Mendoza and Don Alonso de Zayas were ransomed for £900; Don Alonso de Luzón of *La Trinidad Valencera* and Don Diego Pimentel of the *San Mateo* for £1,650, and so on. Only the most senior prisoner, Don Pedro de Valdés of *Nuestra Señora del Rosario*, to his mounting fury, remained in custody.

After the Armada had departed, Drake took his distinguished captive to see the queen in St James's Park. Elizabeth refused to speak to Don Pedro, but looked at him meaningfully and said, 'Drake, God give thee joy of this prisoner.'

Valdés went to the house of one of Drake's relatives, and remained there with other well-born prisoners in considerable comfort as a kind of trophy. Sir Francis visited him frequently, and brought along other military and naval commanders to admire his captive. For such occasions music and dancing were provided, during which the Spaniards would emerge to view, and be viewed by, the assembled multitude. Don Pedro spent his time revising the first Spanish-English dictionary, published in 1591, and sending secret reports on English affairs to his master in Spain. Eventually, in 1593, he was repatriated for a ransom of £1,500, plus the exchange of a notable English prisoner in French Catholic hands. As he left England for freedom he discovered that the master of the ship which had fouled the *Rosario*, setting in train the chain of events which led to his surrender, remained in captivity. Observers noted that he laughed, and seemed to sail away a happier man. No doubt he became happier still when two years later he succeeded to the estates of his hated cousin Diego Flores, and he went on to serve for eight years as governor of Havana, Cuba. He died in 1615 at the age of 70, leaving one legitimate and four illegitimate children.

Many of the Armada survivors in Scotland were not so lucky. After the departure of Juan Gómez de Medina they waited in Edinburgh, Leith and Burntisland as arrangements were negotiated for their return journey. The Scots shippers demanded a fare of 10 shillings each to take them to Dunkirk, together with a safe conduct from Queen Elizabeth lest bad weather forced the ships into English ports. Elizabeth herself was anxious to see them go, for she was distinctly worried about what the Spaniards might get up to in the unstable kingdom beyond her northern border.

It was a delicate political situation, resolved in the end by some gentle gunboat diplomacy. In June 1589 two English warships, the *Vanguard* and *Tiger*, dropped anchor at Leith. A third galleon, the *Achates*, kept guard at the entrance to the Forth. Their mission was to pre-empt any Spanish plot in Scotland, and to encourage James VI to send the Armada survivors on their way. Although he might reasonably have objected to this high-handed infringement of his sovereign rights, the Scottish king's reaction was one of profound relief. The English officers were received with all honours at Holyrood Palace, and passes were given to the seamen to come ashore, unarmed, to sample the pleasures of the capital. Their presence created a volatile mix of nations, and a spark soon ignited it. After carousing fraternally with some Scots and Spaniards in a dockside tavern harsh words were evidently exchanged, and in the resulting fracas an English trumpeter was fatally stabbed by a Spanish soldier. For a time the incident – which was condemned by all three nations – threatened to disrupt the delicate process of negotiating the Spaniards' repatriation. Queen Elizabeth, in particular, proved tardy in providing guarantees for the safety of the Spaniards and their Scottish shippers should they be obliged to enter English ports during the journey home.

Early in August, however, Elizabeth confirmed the issue of safe conducts, effective in all English ports. Their safety apparently assured, 600 Spaniards embarked on four Scottish ships bound for Dunkirk. Among them was Francisco de Cuéllar. The small convoy headed southwards, putting in from time to time at English ports, where the safe conduct was scrupulously observed. Then, within sight of its destination, Justin of Nassau's waiting flotilla pounced upon the unarmed Scottish vessels. The safe conduct had said nothing about the Dutch and, too late, the reason for Elizabeth's delaying tactics became clear. In concert with her Protestant allies in Holland, she had used the time to organise an elaborate and deadly ambush.

One ship was captured and everyone on board, Scotsman and Spaniard alike, was peremptorily thrown over the side. The three other vessels ran ashore in an effort to escape, and broke up in the surf under heavy fire from the Sea Beggars. Three hundred men were killed. But Cuéllar's amazing luck held. Wearing nothing but his shirt, and helped by a few other survivors, he managed to stagger to the safety of Dunkirk.

The full extent of the Armada's final casualty list can never be known. Survivors from the various wrecks continued to turn up in Madrid until at least 1597, when Elizabeth released the last prisoners from the *San Pedro Mayor*. A considerable number of veterans from the fleet, perhaps 2,000, entered Parma's army and fought on in the Low Countries throughout the 1590s. A few more may have remained close to the shores on which they had been cast away, to integrate with local families. Some, according to William Asheby in Edinburgh, preferred to remain in Scotland as servants rather than return to King Philip's thankless service, since they were 'better entertained . . . [in] noblemens' houses than they look to be, in following the wars'. Others joined the retinues of Irish chiefs who had sheltered them. Sorley Boy Macdonnell probably retained a few, along with guns and other spoils from the *Girona*, at his castles of Dunluce and Glenarm. Hugh O'Neill, the earl of Tyrone, eagerly welcomed the Spanish troops that came his way, and used them to train his own troops in the arts of modern warfare.

In 1596 eight Armada survivors were still in Tyrone's service, helping him in his great revolt against Elizabeth. One of them, Pedro Blanco, who had escaped from the wreck of the *Juliana* at Streedagh, rose to become the earl's personal bodyguard. In 1607, when after the revolt's collapse his master fled to Flanders and thence to Rome, Blanco went with him. Just before Tyrone died in 1616 he wrote a glowing testimonial for a servant who had become a loyal friend, who had 'fought so valiantly that I never wanted to be parted from him'. Now he was old, and Tyrone begged Philip III to bestow some reward on this faithful adherent of the Habsburg cause.[18]

History does not relate whether this indefatigable veteran of the Armada campaign ever returned to his native land. But in the archives of Spain we have found no indication that he received anything at all for his long and loyal service.

## Sources

As in the preceding chapter, material on the wrecks has been freely taken from the work of Robert Sténuit and Colin Martin. The saga of the *San Juan de Sicilia* is narrated by McLeay in *The Tobermory Treasure*. Cuéllar's story is best followed in the new critical edition, with English translation (which we have followed with some changes), in Gallagher and Cruickshank, *God's Obvious Design*, 193–247. The story of Captain Carleill's prisoners is told by Quinn, 'Spanish Armada prisoners' escape from Ireland'.

The papers of the Spanish government on most of the ships are in AGS *CS* 2a/280 and in the 'libros de quentas fenescidas' of AGS *CMC* 2a *época*. One absentee is the *Santa Ana* of Recalde, but her story can be reconstituted from the correspondence between Parma and the senior officers aboard the ship: see AGS *Estado* 594/130-2 (*relaciones* of events which include transcripts of key letters) and AGRB *SEG* 11/19v, 29v. On the galleys, which dropped out first, see Gracia Rivas, 'El motín de la *Diana*'. On the medical (and religious) services created for the Armada, and on the general health of the fleet, see Gracia Rivas, *La sanidad en la jornada de Inglaterra* (summarised in his 'The medical services of the *Gran Armada*'). Note, however, that to the total who died on the expedition, one must add those who died while the Armada lay idle in Lisbon harbour. Thus of the 500 sailors from Guipúzcoa who died in the Enterprise of England, over 200 died in Lisbon before the fleet set sail: see Gracia Rivas, *La sanidad en la jornada de Inglaterra*, 372.

For attempts to reconstruct the unusual weather conditions which afflicted the Armada, see Douglas, Lamb and Loader, *A Meteorological Study of July to October 1588*, and Daultrey, 'The weather of north-west Europe during the summer and autumn of 1588'. Neither survey seems to take account of the fact that the wind directions recorded in the various Armada 'journals' would reflect the magnetic variation of 11 degrees east that prevailed in 1588. Four centuries later, magnetic variation is 7 degrees west, so all wind directions are one compass point 'off'. This might well affect attempts to reconstruct climatic changes. Moreover, neither survey made use of the meticulous 'journal' kept by Recalde and published in Parker, 'El testamento político', which records wind directions and changes throughout each day of the troubled voyage.

## Notes

1. Duro, II, 245; Parker, 'El testamento político', 27–8 and 35–6.
2. Parker, 'El testamento político', 36. A copy of the order reducing rations, dated 10 August, may be found in AGS *CMC* 2a/772, file concerning the *San Francisco*.
3. Parker, 'El testamento político', 36, from Recalde's exchanges with the duke on 10 and 11/12 August. In the former, the admiral wrote – again with remarkable insight – that 'I think the enemy will leave us in two or three days, unless we see them receive reinforcements of victuals and men, and they send a dozen ships to take us'. Howard turned back on the 12th.
4. *CSPI*, 49–50, prints the only known example of Medina Sidonia's sailing orders, taken from a wrecked Armada vessel, translated (perhaps inaccurately in parts) and sent on to London. Although it is undated, Calderón states that the orders were

issued on 13 August, *CSPSp*, IV, 447; Recalde called the need for sailing orders to the duke's attention the day before (Parker, 'El testamento político', 27). He also noted with obvious disapproval the duke's decision to make sail and abandon those who could not keep up, in *ibid.*, 36.

5    See Voorbeijtel Cannenburg, 'An unknown "pilot" by Hessel Gerritsz, dating from 1612', describing three maps specially prepared for the Dutch fleet sent in 1612 to clear the west coast of Ireland of pirates. The Armada needed nothing less. See also Rodríguez-Salgado, 'Pilots, navigation and strategy in the *Gran Armada*', 171 n. 100, for an example of one 1588 map covering the coast of northern Ireland.

6    BL Cotton Caligula D.1 fos 292 and 305–6, William Asheby to Walsingham, 1 and 18 September 1588 NS (from Edinburgh). Medina also confiscated some of the boats and crews, to replace the *pataches* and sailors he had lost, see AGS *CMC* 2a/1210, unnumbered folio concerning 'Robert Ler, escosés'.

7    PRO *SP* 63/137/16, examination of Balthasar López del Arbol, Drogheda, 23 October 1588 NS.

8    J. S. Brewer and W. Bullen, *Calendar of the Carew Manuscripts*, II, 469, Carew to vice-chamberlain, 4 August 1588.

9    *CSPI*, 26, 28, Thomas Norreys to Walsingham, 18 and 19 September 1588. AGS *CMC* 1a/1736/286, containing the records of eight *zabras*, including the *Nuestra Señora de Castro*, strongly suggest this was the Tralee wreck. Our thanks to Brendan McCarthy for help in identifying the Tralee vessel.

10   Recalde's account from the *Diario* in Parker, 'El testamento político', 37–44; Aramburu's from Tellechea Idígoras, *Otra cara*, 350–7 (also in Duro, II, 315–26: note, however, that the date of the 'great storm' was 20 September, and not 25 as Duro's transcript states).

11   C. McNeill, 'Report on the Rawlinson collection of manuscripts', 95, order to Mr Matthew Smythe, 18 November 1588.

12   See McLeay, *Tobermory Treasure*. The hostages are noted in *CSPI*, 121, lord deputy to Council, 21 February 1589 NS.

13   For a complete list of the 158 survivors from the *San Pedro* see PRO *SP* 12/218/14.I. At first the Privy Council ordered all the 123 Spanish nationals to be executed, though they were reprieved almost immediately. The non-Spaniards were then released (10 French, 10 Dutch and 2 Italians unconditionally; 13 Portuguese on condition that they enlisted with the forces of Dom Antonio, the Pretender). As far as the Spaniards were concerned, it was decreed that since the ship was wrecked on its way home, and not on its way to invade England, the men were shipwrecked mariners rather than prisoners of war, and that responsibility (including payment) for their keep should therefore fall on the local authorities and not on the crown, *Acts of the Privy Council of England*, XVI, 328–9, 357 and 373–4.

14   AGS *GA* 244/257, Patricio Antolinez and Esteban de Legoretta to the king from Edinburgh, 22 January 1589. See also Gómez de Medina to same, 4 March 1589, AGS *GA* 246/159.

15   AGS *Estado* 596/77, Diego de la Barra to Parma, 2 April 1589, on the 'nave de los casados'; and *CSPI*, xxvii; AGS *Estado K* 1568/119, *Relación*; and AGS *CS* 2a/273 on the *Zúñiga*.

16   AGS *GA* 228/117, 236/138 and 236/153 on the *San Pedro*; AGS *Estado* 594/130–2, *Relaciones*, and AGRB *SEG* 11/29v, Parma order of 3 September 1588, on the *Santa Ana*.

17 Elizabeth agreed to accept a ransom for ordinary prisoners of war on 2 October 1588: *CSPF*, XXII, 214. Arrangements for their release can be followed in AGS *Estado* 596 fos 9 and 72, Parma to the king, 13 January and 6 May 1589; and AGRB *SEG* 11/150 and 163v, orders to pay ransoms, 2 and 17 March 1589.

18 Details from M. K. Walsh, *'Destruction by Peace': Hugh O'Neill after Kinsale*, 140, 370; and Walsh, 'The anonymous Spaniard of the flight of the earls'.

# PART IV

# THE ARMADA IN HISTORY
# AND LEGEND

# 13

# Victors and vanquished

By 1616 the story of the Spanish Armada was already ancient history. Most of its leading actors had long since left the stage – many, indeed, in 1588 and 1589: Leicester and Walsingham in England; Santa Cruz, Oquendo and Recalde in Spain; Guise and Henry III in France. Sixtus V followed suddenly in 1590, the 'Pretender' Dom Antonio in 1595, Philip II after a long illness in 1598, Elizabeth in 1603. Parma died in 1592, in the shadow of royal disgrace; Hawkins and Drake perished on an ill-fated expedition to the Spanish Caribbean in 1595–6; Ambassador Mendoza went blind and died in 1604; Bobadilla, Don Pedro de Valdés, Medina Sidonia and Idiáquez all died in their beds between 1610 and 1615, leaving only a handful of important survivors: Don Balthasar de Zúñiga, who, after a distinguished diplomatic career, became chief minister of Spain from 1618 until 1622; Don Diego Pimentel, who became a reforming viceroy of Mexico and provoked a rebellion there in 1624; Lord Howard of Effingham, who remained admiral of England until 1619 and continued to exercise influence at court until his demise in 1624; and Justin of Nassau, who commanded Dutch forces by land and sea almost up to the hour of his death in 1631.

All of these men knew, within a few weeks of the battles in the Channel, almost as much as we do about the outcome of the Armada campaign. But they did not know it at once. When the queen's navy last saw it, the Spanish fleet still numbered over 100 ships, heading north in good formation. That was on 12 August: what would happen next? On the 18th, Howard confessed total ignorance: 'God knoweth whether they go either to the Naze of Norway or into Denmark or to the Isles of Orkney to refresh themselves, and so to return.' Drake agreed. The Armada, he warned, 'I think certainly to be put either with Norway or Denmark' because only there could it find 'great anchors, cables, masts, ropes and victuals; and what the king of Spain's hot crowns will do in cold countries for mariners and men, I leave to your good lordship'. If it could only refit, it would surely return to the Channel and try a second time to join up with Parma. Alternatively, Drake speculated, Parma might attempt an invasion on his own, while the English fleet was out of harm's way in the North Sea: 'I take him to be as a bear robbed of her whelps; and no doubt but, being so great a soldier as he is, that he will presently, if he may, undertake some great matter'. Two weeks later, Drake was still worried: 'We ought much more to have regard to the duke of Parma and his soldiers', he warned the court, 'than the duke of Sidonia and his ships . . . The duke of Parma should be vigilantly looked upon for these twenty days, although the army [Armada] of Spain return not this way.'

These fears were by no means unfounded. We know that some of the Armada's leaders wanted to return to the Channel if they could; and Parma continued apace with embarking his army. In the duke's own words:

> On Monday 7 August, which was the day that Secretary Arceo arrived [with the news that the Armada had reached Calais] and the day I left Bruges, I had 16,000 infantry embarked in Nieuwpoort; and when I arrived at Dunkirk, which was on Tuesday the 8th, the troops who were to embark there had arrived before dawn and were beginning to board, and they finished that same day together with the munitions and all the other things which were ready and prepared. We were embarking at top speed [a furia], and we would certainly have finished had we not called a halt in view of the news we received of the Armada. We could well have begun to sail out that same night, and joined the Nieuwpoort contingent together with that from Dunkirk in order to effect their task [i.e. the invasion] that night and part of the next day, because they lacked nothing that they needed.

He concluded defiantly: 'My statement that we needed no more than three days to embark and be ready to sail forth was not made without justification.' Although his troops had to disembark within a couple of days, Parma did not stand down the forces and the fleet he had assembled until 31 August.[1]

No certainty then existed about the Armada's whereabouts. Parma had dispatched pinnaces in its pursuit, both to Scotland and to Devon, and on 15 August he even wrote a personal letter, urging Medina Sidonia to come back; but to no avail. The last confirmed sighting occurred on 20 August, as the fleet rounded the Orkney islands, where Scottish fishermen saw 'monstrous great ships, being about 100 in number, running westwards before the wind'. But then came silence and, as late as 18 September William Asheby, Elizabeth's agent in Edinburgh, could only speculate that this must mean that the fleet had either sunk, or had left Scottish waters, for otherwise 'we should have heard of them by fishermen'. Just as Asheby's letter reached London, an express courier came in from Dublin with the first firm news of the Armada's doleful progress and of England's miraculous deliverance.[2]

Long before this, the immediate threat of invasion had clearly passed. Queen Elizabeth was hunting in Epping forest when she heard of the Armada's retreat from Gravelines and, according to tradition, in a burst of joyful exultation she galloped her horse up the stairway of a nearby hunting lodge. Still, she kept close to the capital and to her escort, for no one could be sure that some disaffected English Catholic or desperate Spanish hireling might not be waiting to dispatch the last Tudor, as four years earlier an assassin had laid low the prince of Orange.

On 13 August, however, with the Armada reported to be off the Scottish coast, the Privy Council decided it should halt the flow of militia units and new army recruits towards the south-east, although it left intact the 17,000 men mustered around the hastily fortified camp at Tilbury under the earl of Leicester's command. On 18 August it considered the situation safe enough for the queen to sail down the Thames to join them, and soon after her arrival she delivered the short speech which has passed into legend:

> I am come amongst you as you see, at this time, not for my recreation and disport, but being resolved, in the midst and heat of the battle, to live or die amongst you all, and to lay down for my God and for my kingdom and for my people, my honour and my blood even in the dust. I know I have the body of a weak and feeble woman, but I have the heart and stomach of a king, and of a king of England too, and think foul scorn that Parma, or Spain, or any prince of Europe should dare to invade the borders of my realm.

The 'heat of the battle' (such as it was) did not last long, for two days after the speech orders went out to reduce the army in the south-east first to 6,000, and then on 27 August to a mere 1,500 soldiers.

A little later came moves to stand down the fleet. In a macabre sense the 16,000 men crowded about the English ships had already started the process themselves, for death and sickness took a heavy toll. Of the 500 men aboard the *Elizabeth Bonaventure* when she left Plymouth in July some 200 were dead within a month, and Admiral Howard feared that: 'the like infection will grow throughout the most part of our fleet, for they have been so long at sea, and have so little shift of apparel and so [few] places to provide them of such wants, and no money wherewith to buy it, for some have been – yea, the most part – eight months at sea'.

By early September, according to Howard, it 'would grieve any man's heart to see them that have served so valiantly die so miserably', and to see almost all the ships 'foul and unsavoury' with many 'so weakly manned that they have not mariners to weigh their anchors'. But the hearts of the men at court did not grieve. Instead, Burghley callously expressed the hope that 'by death, by discharging of sick men, and such like . . . there may be spared something in the general pay'. He clearly intended that such unfortunates should receive nothing for their part in defeating the Spanish Armada. Howard was appalled. 'It were too pitiful to have men starve after such a service,' he remonstrated; and even if pity did not enter into it, there remained self-interest. At one point he reminded the queen that 'if men should not be cared for better than to let them starve and die miserably, we should hardly get men to serve'.

He was wasting his time. Elizabeth and her ministers were too busy celebrating to pay much attention to the welfare of their destitute seamen. When William Borough went to court to discuss arrangements for discharging the fleet, he found everyone at the windows of the palace, watching a victory parade, and could get no guidance or instruction. When the government later broke down the costs of the defensive effort against Spain, which had involved a total expenditure of nearly £400,000, it transpired that 'rewards to the injured' accounted for a mere £180.[3] And so, in the end, it was left to the commanders to look after their men. Hawkins, Drake and Howard set up a special fund in 1590 for 'poor sailors maimed in the navy'. It was run like an insurance scheme: a small deduction was made from the wages paid to each seaman, and the balance deposited in a large locked chest at Chatham dockyard. As need arose the 'Chatham Chest' then issued pensions to the old, burial money for the dead, and compensation payments for the injured or disabled. But these benefits only became available two years after the Armada's defeat. Those who had fallen ill or suffered wounds in the campaign of 1588 had to rely upon the individual charity of their officers – and here again Lord Admiral Howard set a noble example – or of the towns in which they were discharged. Perhaps only half the men who fought for England in 1588 lived to celebrate the following Christmas. Even at the service of thanksgiving held at St Paul's Cathedral on 4 December, 'a special day wherein all the realm might concur in giving public thanks unto God', at which numerous captured ensigns and other trophies were gleefully displayed, the humble architects of victory were scarcely mentioned. Elizabeth and her ministers presumably felt that to have preserved the Tudor state and the Protestant cause should be sufficient reward in itself.

Of those who sailed on the Armada, too, perhaps only one-half survived the year. As in England, it was many weeks – even months – before the full scale of the disaster became clear. Indeed, the first reports of the Channel battles to reach Spain had been highly encouraging. A report from Dieppe dated 7 August, entitled 'A letter on the encounter of the English and Spanish fleets, and of the Spanish victory', seemed unequivocal enough; and it was forwarded to Spain, together with further confirmatory detail, by Ambassador Mendoza in Paris. It arrived towards the end of the month. As late as 5 September a printer in Seville could still issue a cheerful newsletter on 'What has happened to the most fortunate Armada so far': although it noted the loss of the *Rosario*, the *San Salvador* and Moncada's galleass, the rest of the news concerned great victories won by the Spanish fleet. By then, however, the king (at least) knew it was false.[4]

Writing some 40 years later, Philip II's biographer Balthasar Porreño played down the shock caused by the discovery that the Armada had failed, attributing instead stoic insouciance to his hero. 'I sent my fleet against men', Philip is made to say, when he first heard the news, 'not against the wind and the waves.' Surviving correspondence of the king and his ministers from the autumn of 1588 tells a different – and far more revealing – story. On 7 and again on 14 August Philip signed new missives repeating that the success of the enterprise depended upon his commanders' adherence to the 'agreed plan'. When, on 31 August, a letter arrived from Parma announcing the Armada's failure to 'join hands' with the Army of Flanders, the king at once sought to regain control of the situation with his pen. To Medina Sidonia, wherever he might be, he wrote: 'The news of your great reverse before Calais has caused me more anxiety than you can imagine,' and his officials promptly prepared a long memorandum telling the two dukes what they should do if the Armada had taken refuge in either Scottish or German waters (refit, and discuss ways of effecting the invasion the following year), or if it had started on the journey back to Spain (put some troops ashore near Waterford, in order to create a bridgehead for operations the following year). On 15 September, even as the battered remnants of the fleet anxiously neared the coast of Spain, ministers in Madrid even more unrealistically drafted orders for Medina Sidonia to land in Scotland, ally with the local Catholics, and winter there.

For all that, the king's self-confidence had been dealt a shattering blow. When he read the draft of a letter to Parma, expressing the hope 'that God will have allowed some improvement, and that the reputation of everyone (which is now so compromised) may be recovered', the king hesitated and underlined the passage. 'It might be better', he told his secretary, 'to delete what I have under-lined, because in what God does, and in what we do for God, there is no gain or loss of reputation. It is better not to speak of such things.'[5]

Writing to Parma that same day, 31 August, Don Juan de Idiáquez admitted that:

> I cannot exaggerate the grief caused by seeing something that cost so much time, money and trouble – and is so important to the service of God and His Majesty – placed in jeopardy, just at the point when it was about to bear fruit. His Majesty has felt it more than you would believe possible, and if there were not some remaining hope in God that all this might have achieved something for His cause . . . I do not know how he could bear such a great blow. Certainly this business leaves no time to think about anything else, nor to think of it without excessive grief.

Time brought no relief. Instead, on 3 September, a courier from France brought more detailed news concerning the defeat and northward flight of the Grand Fleet. The cipher clerks and ministers blenched, and debated which of them should break the news to the king. The choice fell upon Mateo Vázquez, Philip's long-serving private secretary and chaplain; but even he did so with great trepidation and indirectly, choosing to forward a tactless letter received from a courtier. 'If we consider', the letter ran, 'the case of King Louis IX of France, who was a saint and was engaged on a saintly enterprise [the Seventh Crusade in 1250], and yet saw his army die of plague, with himself defeated and captured, we certainly cannot fail to fear greatly for the success of our Armada.' Lest there might be some truth in this unfortunate parallel, Vázquez suggested that more prayers should be offered for its safety. This proved too much for the king: 'I hope that God has not permitted so much evil', he scribbled angrily on the letter, 'for everything has been done for His service.'[6]

Then came silence. For two more weeks no further reliable information about the Armada arrived in Spain. Parma's pinnaces sent to Scotland and Devon found no trace of the fleet. Mendoza, in Paris, accumulated an abundance of news, but since most of it came from England he dismissed it. The intelligence concerning Elizabeth's own fleet, however, he treated with greater respect; and this suggested that the queen's ships were regrouping, perhaps in preparation for a counter-attack on Spain. He dispatched an express courier to Madrid, who arrived on 20 September, and the king's ministers promptly sent out orders to all major ports to ensure that, whenever the Armada got home, under no circumstances were the soldiers and sailors to be allowed to disembark. They were to be kept at their posts, come what may, ready to meet any emergency. The folly of all this became apparent a mere four days later, with the arrival at court of a bedraggled Don Balthasar de Zúñiga.[7]

Zúñiga, it will be remembered, had left the fleet off Shetland on 21 August 'at 61 degrees north and 300 leagues from Spain', bearing a full report from Medina Sidonia, Don Francisco de Bobadilla and others on the Armada's proceedings in the Channel and its subsequent plight. He also brought a set of requests for supplies, medicines and provisions to be made ready for the fleet's imminent return. But Zúñiga's pinnace had been buffeted and driven back by the same storms that had so damaged the main fleet – a delay that caused much additional human suffering because, in the event, the remnants of the Armada struggled into various ports of northern Spain before the relief supplies arrived.

On 21 September, two months to the day since their joyful departure from Corunna and after an odyssey in which some ships may have travelled as many as 5,000 miles, Medina Sidonia led eight battered galleons into Santander, Diego Flores took 22 into Laredo and Miguel de Oquendo brought five more to the ports of Guipúzcoa. Two days later, with heavy heart and sick body, the duke dictated his first letter from Spanish soil to his master: 'I am unable to describe to Your Majesty the misfortunes and miseries that have befallen us, because they are the worst that have been known on any voyage; and some of the ships that put into this port have spent the last fourteen days without a single drop of water.'

His flagship was letting in water so fast that she had to be held together with three great hawsers wrapped round her to prevent the seams from opening. And thus, literally tied up with string, she returned. Out of the 500 men who set out with the duke in July, '180 are dead already of sickness, as well as three of the four pilots' (an eventuality which perhaps explained why, having set course for Cape Finisterre, 'when we first espied land, we all believed it was Corunna . . . but in fact we were 100 leagues away from that harbour, without knowing where we were at all'). During the voyage Medina Sidonia had given the two warm cloaks he had taken with him to a frozen priest and a wounded boy; now he had only the thin short cloak he stood up in. Most of the survivors were ill with dysentery, typhus, or both. The duke himself, he reported, had 'arrived very close to death, and so I am in bed and cannot cope with everything, even though I want to . . . Even my own servants, who once numbered 60, have died and sickened so fast that I have only two left. God be praised for all His works.'[8]

The duke did what he could for his wretched men. He sent urgent appeals to the towns and churches of northern Spain, begging for the immediate dispatch of beds, clothes and (rather more surprisingly) of 'sugar, raisins and almond preserves' for the 4,000 sick survivors ashore. That total steadily increased as further ships limped home, some in a terrible state. Purser Calderón's hulk *San Salvador* had no drinking water left at all on the last three days of the voyage, and the crew became too weak to pump fast enough to keep pace with the sea water flooding into the hold. Oquendo's flagship, having made a safe landing, soon afterwards perished by fire when the powder magazine exploded, killing 100 of her crew. Other unfortunate vessels ran straight on to the Cantabrian coast, or else collided with each other, either for lack of anchors abandoned off Calais or for lack of men to work the sails.

At this stage a large number of ships remained unaccounted for but, as September turned to October, news of the losses in Ireland began to arrive. Still the truth proved elusive. Even survivors could not always shed much light on what had happened: one man from the *Trinidad Valencera* was still so traumatised by his experiences that 'it was difficult to understand what he was trying to say'. When asked where his ship sank, he could only 'show on the map that it was on the northernmost promontory of Ireland'. However, on 7 October a witness arrived who confirmed all Spain's worst fears. Recalde, having escaped from Blasket Sound, brought his storm-tossed ship and emaciated crew back to Corunna, and reluctantly stated that he believed there would be no more. He sent to the king his journal, a selection of his correspondence with Medina Sidonia during the campaign, and a trenchant indictment of the overall strategy for the campaign. 'I have read it all', Philip wrote, 'although I would rather not have done, because it hurts so much.' Recalde himself withdrew to a monastery where he died on the 22nd.

It took two weeks for the full enormity of the disaster to sink in. On 10 November the king wrote to his chaplain and secretary, Mateo Vázquez, in total despair:

> I promise you that unless some remedy is found . . . very soon we shall find ourselves in such a state that we shall wish that we had never been born . . . And if God does not send us a miracle (which is what I hope from Him), I hope to

die and go to Him before all this happens – which is what I pray for, so as not to see so much ill fortune and disgrace. All this is for your eyes alone. Please God, let me be mistaken: but I do not think it is so. Rather, we shall have to witness, quicker than anyone thinks, what we so much fear, if God does not return to fight for His cause. We have already seen all this in what has happened, which would not have been permitted except to punish us for our sins.[9]

The final tally of the Armada's losses was truly appalling. Of the 130 ships that had sailed against England, only 60 could now be accounted for: 44 at Santander, 9 at San Sebastián, 6 at Corunna, 1 (the *Zúñiga*) at Le Havre. At the lowest estimate 42 vessels, one-third of the fleet, had been sunk or wrecked. Bertendona's squadron of 10 Levanters, of which only 2 returned, sustained the highest losses. Altogether only 34 major fighting ships survived the campaign, several of them so severely damaged that they were no longer seaworthy. They were, moreover, scattered in sundry ports along 500 miles of coast. Equally serious was the loss of artillery, especially the costly and important siege train cast for Charles V and Philip II by Gregorio Loefer and Remigy de Halut.[10]

Ships and guns could, of course, be replaced in time. It proved harder to replace so many trained and experienced men. Apart from those killed in action, drowned in the surf, or executed in Ireland, exhaustion, dehydration and starvation claimed thousands more. Rations on the fleet had been cut sharply when the decision to return by the northabout route was taken (page 211 above); but even that used up supplies too fast. In the 45 days which elapsed between then and the return to Spain, some of the survivors received only 30 days' rations; and others received even less. Given the remarkably cold weather encountered by the Armada in the North Atlantic – upon which every Spanish account dwells plaintively – it is scarcely surprising that on almost every ship four or five men died every day; or that, even after the longed-for return to Spain, many failed to recover from their privations. Don Agustín Mexía's *tercio*, which had numbered 2,659 men in May, could barely muster 1,000 at the year's end. Altogether, the fleet returned to Spain with fewer than 4,000 of its 7,000 sailors, and only 9,500 of its 19,000 soldiers. In January 1589, according to an eyewitness, the relations and friends of those who had served on the fleet still travelled forlornly from port to port, trying to ascertain what had become of their loved ones.[11]

The exact total of those lost on the campaign will never be known, even though government inspectors soon began work to establish a figure. Thus the chief magistrate of Guipúzcoa received orders to tour the province and record the number of the fallen, their rank and the ship on which they had sailed, their home and the number of dependents they had left. The total stood at 502, including 128 from San Sebastián, almost all of them sailors (only 14 of the total were soldiers). Of these no less than 221 died in Lisbon, before the fleet even set sail, and 102 in Ireland; 49 perished in the explosion of the *San Salvador* and 23 others died in combat. Almost half of the deceased left widows and children (most of them young). Some families were almost wiped out. Three brothers of the Iriarte family of Deva died, 'leaving their parents in great poverty', and not only did Martín de Aranda, Captain Cuéllar's benefactor, perish – so too did every one of his nine cousins aboard the 'Most Happy Armada'.[12]

The Spanish government did its best to care for both survivors and be-reaved. In sharp contrast to the callous indifference of Elizabeth and her minis-ters, Philip II tried to ensure that his faithful soldiers and sailors received proper payment for their service. When, in December 1588, he discovered that some Armada veterans were being discharged without a full settlement of their wages, the king immediately informed his commanders that: 'This is contrary to Chris-tian charity and also very much alien to my will, which has been (and is) that those who have served – and are serving – me should not only be paid what they are owed, but rewarded as far as our resources permit.'[13] So before any veteran was dismissed from the king's army or navy, the council of war had to be notified of his service record, and his arrears, so that proper recompense could be arranged.

Cynically speaking, however, in time even the missing rank and file could be replaced. In the event, by August 1589 30,000 troops once again served on the Spanish fleet or guarded the northern and western coasts of the peninsula. But they now served under different, less experienced commanders. Scarcely any of the Armada's senior officers remained in post by the end of the year. Santa Cruz, Recalde, Oquendo, Leiva and Moncada were dead (the first three probably of typhus); Pedro de Valdés, Luzón and Pimentel had been taken prisoner; Diego Flores was arrested and incarcerated on Philip's orders; Medina Sidonia and Bobadilla, both with shattered health (and eventually writing each other 'sick notes'), left the fleet at the earliest opportunity in order to recover.

As Friar José de Sigüenza, one of the monks at the Escorial, wrote shortly afterwards, the defeat of the Armada was 'the greatest disaster to strike Spain in over six hundred years'. His colleague, Friar Jerónimo de Sepúlveda, agreed: for him, it was a misfortune 'worthy to be wept over for ever . . . because it lost us respect and the good reputation among warlike people which we used to have. The grief it caused in all of Spain was extraordinary . . . Almost the entire coun-try went into mourning. People talked about nothing else.'[14] The same was also true outside Spain, for the 'reputation' of Philip II had received a body blow. In Italy, those who feared or resented Spanish hegemony in the peninsula raised their heads; while in France, those who had supported Spain's grand design lost theirs – in December 1588 Henry III (and his supporters) isolated and murdered the duke of Guise. In the Netherlands, Parma at length abandoned his vigil by the coast of Flanders and, after some diversionary manoeuvres, laid siege to the Dutch town of Bergen-op-Zoom. On 30 October, after six inconclusive weeks in the trenches, Philip II's forces gave up, having received (as Queen Elizabeth gleefully noted) 'no less blemish . . . by land than by sea'.

Needless to say, there was no lack of gloaters among the victorious English and Dutch. In Leiden, the great battle-pennant of the *San Mateo* was hung in the choir of St Peter's church (although it was so long that the end lay rolled up on the ground), and it inspired from the local bard, William Verheyden, a patriotic poem in Latin entitled *Oration on the Fleet of the Spanish Xerxes*. It was declaimed, for the first time, to the Leiden 'Chamber of Rhetoric' on 21 August. Latin verses by Theodore Beza, Philip Marnix and other Calvinist luminaries entertained later meetings. In England, ballads were more favoured than odes, and no fewer than 24 contemporary popular songs about the Armada have survived. Even Elizabeth is supposed to have written one: like most of the rest, it carries little artistic merit. The Protestant creators of the anti-Hispanic 'Black Legend' of course had a field day, which perhaps plumbed the depths of bad taste in the (wisely) anonymous *Skeltonical Salutation or Condign Congratulation and just vexation of the Spanishe Nation*, which assured its readers that the fish which had feasted on Spanish blood could not pass on, through their own flesh, the venereal diseases thereby acquired!

More serious propaganda also appeared. Lord Burghley commissioned (and personally revised) in September a pamphlet known somewhat inelegantly as *The Copie of a Letter Sent out of England to Don Bernardin Mendoza*. It purported to be a report from an English Jesuit to the Spanish ambassador in France, regretting that all his bold promises and boasts had come to nothing, and providing a detailed discussion of Spain's (unjust) reasons for attacking England, Elizabeth's (laudable) countermeasures, the course of the campaign, the names of the Spanish ships and personnel who perished, and the eventual safe return of the English fleet. It concluded with the ringing phrase: 'So ends this account of the misfortunes of the Spanish Armada which they used to call "INVINCIBLE".' The word was capitalised – not unreasonably, since it was not used by the Spaniards themselves – and French, Italian, Dutch and German translations were swiftly issued, all referring with heavy irony to the 'Invincible Armada'. And so Burghley's clever epithet passed into the vocabulary of all Europe.[15]

England's reaction to the Armada's defeat by no means stopped at bluster. Elizabeth had tasted Spanish blood, and she wanted more; but how could it best be obtained? The negotiations for peace, which had reached an advanced stage at Bourbourg early in August, lay shattered beyond repair; and, in any case, the Dutch refused to become involved because Philip offered them no guarantees for continuing religious toleration after hostilities ceased. For the Protestant United Provinces, at least, the Armada changed nothing, and the war continued unabated. In June, indeed, they expanded the theatre of operations by subsidising the French Protestant leader, Henry of Navarre. Although Elizabeth stopped short of following suit for another year, she did ask the Dutch to assist her in a direct attack upon Spain in 1589.

Neither England nor the republic, however, had enough money to spare for such a venture. The cost of fighting Spain had left the United Provinces bankrupt, while the cost of defeating the Armada had absorbed about £400,000 of Elizabeth's resources. So although in September 1588 the queen and her council decided to dispatch a fleet to destroy the Armada's surviving ships as they refitted, they recognised that the expedition could not leave until the next spring. Even then, lack of money forced Elizabeth to take her revenge by proxy: instead of sending a full naval expedition she allowed a consortium of adventurers – including Sir Francis Drake – to take some of her warships along with their own private fleet of some 80 vessels, with support from 60 Dutch transports, on the understanding that they would destroy what remained of the Armada before moving on to take the plunder and prizes that represented their principal objective.

This clear conflict of aims boded no good, but Drake soon made it even worse: he agreed to take with him Dom Antonio, the Portuguese 'Pretender', to make a further bid to regain his ancestors' throne. In the event, by trying to do too much, the expedition achieved virtually nothing. Admittedly it successfully attacked Corunna and destroyed three more Armada vessels, including Recalde's *San Juan* and Bertendona's *Regazona*. But then, instead of sailing east to Santander and San Sebastián where (according to an English spy) Spain's warships 'did ride all unrigged, and their ordnance on the shore', the English sailed to Lisbon.

It proved a disaster. On the one hand it alienated the Dutch by depriving them of their plunder; on the other, since Elizabeth's caution had denied the expedition the royal siege guns it needed for a successful land campaign, Lisbon could not be taken. Instead, the fleet sailed for the Azores in the hope of intercepting the returning treasure fleet and thus injuring Philip II by the 'method of Jason, by fetching away his golden fleece'. Here again the new argonauts failed, for southerly gales drove them back to the coast of England. So £100,000 had been expended for nothing. There were no prizes, and the enemy suffered only minimal losses: on the debit side, the elements inflicted considerable damage on the queen's ships, and some 10,000 of the men aboard either died or became too sick to serve further. Drake, disgraced, received no further naval command until his final voyage in 1595.

Worse still, with the failure of the 'Counter-Armada' died England's only chance of turning the deliverance of 1588 into a lasting victory. For Philip II was not willing to abandon the war. Once he had overcome the spiritual crisis occasioned by the disaster, he convinced himself that Spain's destiny – and God's inscrutable design – could best be served by intensifying, rather than abating, the war against the heretics of northern Europe. Between 12 and 26 November 1588, in a remarkably frank (and hitherto virtually unknown) series of documents, the king invited his council of state to consider the possibility of negotiating rather than fighting. But he left them in no doubt of his own views: 'Right from the start', he began:

I was moved to undertake the Armada campaign for the service of Our Lord, the defence of His Cause, and the advantage of these realms. And I still feel the same now, and greatly desire that our efforts should achieve what has become all the more necessary because of what has happened.

The councillors immediately took the point: unanimously they recommended that the war should go on. The king was ecstatic, praising in extravagant terms their resolution and assuring them that 'I, for my part, shall never fail to strive for the cause of God and the good of these kingdoms, as much as I can.'[16]

A series of orders went out to improve the military and naval state of Spain. Money was sent to refit the ships which had survived the Armada, and 12 new 1,000-ton galleons (predictably known as the 'Twelve Apostles') were laid down in the Cantabrian shipyards. They were to be designed along 'English' lines; shipboard guns were cut down to a more manageable length; and an attempt was made to rationalise calibres. Nor was this regarded simply as an academic exercise: before the year was out, the king had entered into a lively correspondence with Martín de Bertendona, one of the few surviving squadron commanders of 1588, concerning the best way to invade and land troops in England in the near future.[17]

It all came to nothing. Philip II's fleets sailed against England again in 1596 and 1597, but storms drove them back. Instead, during the years 1589–91 alone, English privateers captured some 300 merchantmen, worth perhaps £400,000, belonging to Philip II's subjects, and the spoils flowed until the war ended in 1604. Meanwhile, English forces continued to strengthen Dutch resistance, to assist Henry of Navarre to become king of France after Henry III's assassination in 1589, and to assault and sack Pernambuco in 1595, Cadiz in 1596 and Puerto Rico in 1598. At the same time, the Dutch took the offensive by sea, sending ever larger fleets into the Caribbean, the Indian Ocean and eventually the Pacific in order to usurp Iberian trade and destroy Iberian property. Even after signing a ceasefire in Europe in 1607, Dutch attacks on the Portuguese and Spanish seaborne empires continued unabated.

The Armada had thus clearly failed to attain any of the objectives set out by Santa Cruz, Parma and Medina Sidonia in their proposals of 1586, and by Philip II in his instructions of 1587 and 1588. More seriously still, the spectacular failure of his fleet cleared away many illusions about the power of Spain. Not only did it encourage English and Dutch attacks on Iberian shipping and on Iberian possessions, it helped to silence those voices in the Dutch Republic which had favoured a compromise peace and it confirmed Spain's inability to penetrate the North Sea in order to impose her will. Above all, it sapped Spain's self-confidence. The first work of Spanish literature generally seen to manifest a sense of *desengaño* (disillusion) with empire is a mock-epic poem *Farewell of the Ladies of the Court to the Gallants Sailing on the Armada*, which more or less ridiculed their mission and suggested that all they would gain from the venture was injury, discomfort and disease. After 1588 the genre became prolific.

Looking back, most observers – even Spaniards – saw the Armada's fate as the point at which the decline of Spain as an imperial power began and became obsessed about the reasons for it – the failure to 'adapt the practices of the English and the Dutch' (1620), sending 'an Armada of bulky galleons into the Channel' (1639), and so on.[18] But this was the wisdom of hindsight: at the time, and in the immediate aftermath, there were only two questions on men's lips. First, could the Enterprise of England have succeeded? And, if it could, who then was to blame for its failure?

## Sources

The English response to the Armada campaign may be followed in more detail in the early chapters of Wernham, *After the Armada*; Laughton, II; Whitehead, *Brags and Boasts*; and Lyell, 168–387. The famous Tilbury speech is given in Green, ' "I My Self": Queen Elizabeth's oration at Tilbury camp', who also demonstrates its authenticity. On the Portugal expedition see Kelsey, *Sir Francis Drake*, chapter 12; Wernham, 'Queen Elizabeth and the Portugal expedition of 1589'; and Wernham, *The Expedition of Sir John Norris and Sir Francis Drake to Spain and Portugal, 1589*. The Dutch jubilation is described in Scheltema, *De uitrusting en ondergang van de onoverwinnelijk vloot*, 220ff. The numbing demographic impact upon Spain clearly emerges from Gracia Rivas, *Los tercios*, and *La sanidad*.

The subsequent career of Don Diego Pimentel was bizarre: on his way back to Spain in 1628 after his tempestuous spell as viceroy of Mexico, he again met the Dutch when Piet Heyn defeated and plundered the fleet on which he sailed. See Israel, *Race, Class and Politics in Colonial Mexico*, 176. On the later career of Don Balthasar de Zúñiga, see Elliott, *The Count-Duke of Olivares*, chapter 2; of Howard, see Kenny, *Elizabeth's Admiral*; and of Don Pedro de Valdés, see Martínez, *Cartas de Felipe II*.

## Notes

1   AGS *Estado* 594/163, Parma to Idiáquez, 30 December 1588. This was precisely what Parma had claimed at the time: see *Estado* 594/125, Parma to Philip II, 10 August 1588.

2   BL Cotton Caligula D.I fo. 292, Asheby to Walsingham, 18 September 1588; Laughton, II, 218; and *Calendar of Carew Manuscripts*, II, 470–2, Carew to Walsingham 28 September 1588 NS, with lists of ships lost. Parma interpreted the total silence concerning the Armada to mean it was in Danish waters, preparing to return: see AS, Parma, *Carteggio Farnesiano* 129: *Spagna* 6, Parma to Medina Sidonia, 15 August 1588; and AGS *Estado* 594/130–2, *Relaciones*. AGS *CMC* 2a/1077, accounts of Thorivio Martinez, shows that the Flanders flotilla was only paid off at the end of August. Parma started to issue exeats for individuals who had arrived for the invasion 'attento a haverse, según paresce, alargado la occasión de la Jornada', on 12 September (AGRB *SEG* 11 fos 40, passport for Juan de Anaya Solís, and 46v, to the marquis of Favara).

3   BL Harleian MS 168/180–5, Accounts.

4   [P. le Goux], *Copie d'une lettre envoyé de Dieppe*: see Lyell, nos 95–7; and *Relaciõ de lo que hasta oy a los 5 de septiembre . . . se ha sabido* (Seville, 1588), Lyell, no. 80.

5   See AGS *Estado* 165/144 and 146, Philip II to Medina Sidonia, 7 and 14 August 1588; AGS *Estado* 2219 fos 77, 84 and 87, the king to Parma and Medina Sidonia, 14 and 31 August 1588; fos 85–6, 'Apuntamiento en materia de armada que Su Magestad mandó hazer para que se considere y resuelva entre el duque de Parma, su sobrino, y el duque de Medina Sidonia' (four foolscap sheets); and fo. 91, notes by Idiáquez on 15 September 1588.

6   AGS *Estado* 2219/82, Idiáquez to Parma, 31 August 1588; IVdeDJ 51/190, Vázquez to the king, 4 September 1588, enclosing a note from Pedro Nuñez written the previous day.

7   AGS *Estado* 594/131–2, *relaciones*, on Parma's pinnaces; BL Additional MS 28,376/66–7, Idiáquez to Prada, 20 September 1588, on emergency measures. There can be no doubt about Zúñiga's late arrival, even though historians have always assumed that he reached Spain long before: see *CSPV*, 194, Lippomano to doge, 29 September 1588, and AGS *Estado* 165/149, the king to Medina Sidonia, 27 September 1588.

8   AGS *Estado* 455/5 18ff, Medina to the king, 23 and 27 September 1588; and Oria, 293, same to same, 25 September. The estimate of 5,000 miles is in *CSPV*, 396; the cinching of the *San Martín* comes from the *Relación* of La Torre.

9   AGS *GA* 244/47, Francisco Duarte to the king, 11 January 1589; AGS *Estado* 2851, unfol., undated *billete* from Idiáquez and Moura to the king accompanying Recalde's letter, October 1588. The king's anguished – and hitherto unnoticed – plea for an early death is in HS 145/76, to Mateo Vázquez, 10 November 1588. The king added (understandably) 'This is for your eyes alone.'

10  For a list of ships and their fates, see Casado Soto, *Los barcos*, 379–84 (although it omits the galleys). See also AGS *Estado* 1089/3 39 and 115/223, the king to the viceroys of Naples and Sicily, 23 October 1588, ordering them to send to Spain immediately as much artillery, powder and other munitions as they could spare.

11  *CSPI*, 121, Report of John Brown of Clontarf, recently escaped from Ribadeo, 6 February 1589. Mexía's losses are recorded in AGS *GA* 227/133. Likewise, of 4,638 soldiers in 40 companies mustered at Lisbon in May 1588, only 3,217 were present in November – a loss of almost one-third – and several other companies were lost altogether (calculated from AGS *CS* 2a/276). The rations actually consumed are recorded in AGS *CMC* 2a/29 and 31, accounts with mutineers of La Chapelle (1596), company of Francisco de Frías.

12  The Guipúzcoa survey has been printed and analysed by Tellechea Idígoras, *Otra cara*, 385–516 (who also prints extracts of a survey of 230 Armada dead from Vizcaya), and Gracia Rivas, *La sanidad en la jornada de Ingla terra*, 370–9 and 423–42 (a table based on the survey).

13  The king's autograph order is at HS 122/120, to the captain-general of Guipúzcoa, 26 December 1588.

14  Sigüenza, *La fundación del Monasterio de El Escorial*, 120; and Sepúlveda, 'Historia' in Zarco Cuevas, *Documentos para la historia . . . de El Escorial*, IV, 59.

15  Whitehead, *Brags and Boasts*, chapter 10, gives an excellent account of where the term 'Invincible' originated, and on Burghley's part in *The Copie of a Letter*.

16  AGS *Estado* 2851, unfol., 'Lo que se platicó en el consejo de Estado a 12 de noviembre 1588', and following documents.
17  Lilly Library, Bloomington (Indiana), Bertendona Papers, 14 and 21, on a new invasion strategy. It was Bertendona who eventually took the *Revenge*.
18  Don Diego Brochero and Francisco Feixó de Sotomayor quoted in Goodman, *Spanish Naval Power*, 6–7.

# If the Armada had landed

As soon as the Armada sailed into the North Sea, argument began over where the Enterprise of England had gone wrong. 'There is nobody aboard this fleet', wrote Don Francisco de Bobadilla on 20 August, 'who is not now saying "I told you so" or "I knew this would happen". But it's just like trying to lock the stable door after the horse has bolted.' Bobadilla nevertheless went on to propound his own explanation of the debacle. On the one hand, he asserted, 'we found that many of the enemy's ships held great advantages over us in combat, both in their design and in their guns, gunners and crews . . . so that they could do with us as they wished'. On the other hand, most Spanish ships experienced an acute shortage of ammunition. 'But in spite of all this', he continued, 'the duke [Medina Sidonia] managed to bring his fleet to anchor in Calais roads, just seven leagues from Dunkirk . . . and if, on the day that we arrived there, Parma had come out [with his forces], we should have carried out the invasion'.[1]

This analysis – the earliest one to survive – fully accords with the historical record. In spite of all the defects in supply, design, organisation and leadership, the Armada managed to reach Calais with its order unimpaired. But for the fireships' stratagem, which broke the fleet's disciplined formation before the junction with Parma had been effected, Philip II's Grand Design might have succeeded. So who was responsible for its failure?

Many, like Don Diego Pimentel, blamed the duke of Parma. Why had he not been ready, in spite of repeated messages reporting the fleet's steady progress from Corunna? Why had he not at least attempted a sortie? According to the disillusioned Don Bernardino de Mendoza in Paris, many French observers believed that Parma had deliberately set out to sabotage the Armada. In Italy the duke of Savoy (Philip's son-in-law) offered to take over command of the Army of Flanders because in light of 'the accounts, which seem worse every day, of how badly Parma has carried out his orders (whether through malice or carelessness) to be ready and to aid Medina Sidonia, it seems impossible to the duke . . . that Your Majesty can leave him in the Netherlands'. After the fleet's return a Venetian military expert surmised that 'Parma has reason to be, after King Philip, the most desperate man in the world', while in October the Florentine ambassador in Madrid reported that 'all the Spaniards, and especially those who returned on

the Armada' both 'in public and in private' blamed its failure on 'the delays of
the duke of Parma . . . so the poor gentleman will need a good excuse'.[2]

The duke fully realised his peril. Hardly had the Armada moved into the
North Sea than he wrote to urge his uncle, Cardinal Farnese, who watched over
the family's interests in Rome, to provide immediate refutation 'if it should
happen that, either to exculpate the duke of Medina Sidonia or for some other
reason, the Spaniards wish to blame me for the misfortunes that have befallen
their nation'. In October he sent a special envoy to Italy in order to defend his
conduct. Unfortunately he chose for this mission Count Niccolo Cesi, a somewhat blunt soldier raised in the Farnese household who seems to have blamed
Medina Sidonia instead. The outraged Spanish ambassador in Rome (who
happened to be Medina's cousin) wrote to chide Parma for his disloyalty and
pettiness: 'It was God's will, not your fault – and not Medina's.' And in any case,
the ambassador added tartly, 'explanations of how each commander behaved
are due to his Majesty and to nobody else'.[3]

The duke had already taken care of this, too. On the very day of the battle
off the Flemish coast he penned a preliminary 'explanation' to his master:

> Those who came here off the fleet [Parma explained] and have tried to give the
> impression that we were not ready – because they could not see guns and
> munitions on my ships, nor the troops aboard – are mistaken. Everything was
> prepared as it should have been for the Channel crossing . . . Nothing would
> have been gained by embarking things in advance, because the ships are so small
> that there is not even room to turn round in. Undoubtedly, the men would have
> sickened, the food would have rotted, and everything would have perished.

Others testified that, as soon as Parma learned of the Armada's imminent
approach, he commenced the process of embarkation. According to the Armada's
inspector-general, marooned at Dunkirk:

> The German, Italian, and Walloon troops, to the number of 18,000 were em-
> barked, and the Spanish infantry together with the cavalry were at Dunkirk
> ready for embarkation. As they were boarding, the news arrived that the
> Armada had gone away; but everything remains in the same state, and the duke
> of Parma is present in person and will make no changes until there is certain
> news of our fleet.[4]

It all came down to the crucial delay between the departure of Medina Sidonia's
messengers from the fleet and their arrival in Flanders. As soon as he received
certain news of the Armada's approach – after over a whole year of waiting –
Parma swung into action. Had the messages arrived slightly sooner, therefore,
or had the Armada taken slightly longer, the rendezvous might have become a
reality.

Parma's reputation, after a brief spell under a cloud, was thus vindicated: he
could indeed have done no more. The same was true of Medina Sidonia. The

duke, who had shown unquestioned courage in the face of the enemy, quit his command as soon as possible after leading the Armada back to Spain. After the *San Martín* reached Santander on 21 September Medina Sidonia stayed in port only long enough to ensure the recovery of himself and his personal entourage, and to collect his entire arrears of pay (no less than 7,810 ducats, in gold). He found the leisure to play cards twice (both times he lost), and early in the morning of 5 October, with his baggage loaded on 11 mules and 17 bearers, he set off for home.

Dispersing (according to the accounts of his household treasurer) generous benefactions to clerics and paupers along the way, he reached San Lúcar de Barrameda on the 24th. There was only one ugly moment: as Medina Sidonia tried to snatch a night's rest in Valladolid, his lodgings were surrounded by youths who chanted 'Drake, Drake, Drake is coming' until dawn, and taunted the unfortunate captain-general of the ocean sea with the offensive sobriquet 'duke of Gallina' (chicken duke).[5] To what extent he considered himself responsible for the Armada's disgrace will never be known, but the king never seems to have criticised his personal behaviour or his handling of the fleet. Perhaps Philip recalled the duke's reluctance to accept the command, and how he had begged the king to call off the operation after the return to Corunna; perhaps he also recalled his own foolish insistence that the fleet should press on to Flanders at top speed, regardless of the state of Parma's preparations. He may also have taken into account the praise bestowed by the expedition's survivors on Medina's courageous leadership. According to Don Francisco de Bobadilla, a stern judge, writing after the campaign was over, 'Even our enemies will admit, although it may grieve them, that no commander in the world has done more than this one.'[6]

Instead the duke's naval adviser, Diego Flores de Valdés, was punished for the disaster. He had counselled the duke to abandon his cousin Don Pedro (and the king's 50,000 gold ducats); he had panicked when the fireships came in, ordering all cables to be cut; and he had argued in favour of returning as fast as possible to Spain after the battle off Gravelines, abandoning first the rendezvous with Parma and then all ships unable to keep up. Finally, he was blamed for the fatal collision of two ships in Laredo harbour when the remnants of the fleet limped home to Spain. Many of his brother officers despised the reliance placed by Medina Sidonia on Flores. According to a bitter rumour which went round the fleet, as the duke faced the first furious attack of the English fleet on 8 August and found himself next to the flagship of the Guipúzcoan squadron, he called out to her commander, 'Señor Oquendo, what should we do next?' 'I don't know,' came the sarcastic reply. 'Why don't you ask Diego Flores?' In the months following the fleet's return evidence piled up and, just before Christmas, Philip II had him arrested and sent to prison in Burgos. Diego Flores was not solely responsible for the shortcomings for which he had been charged, but he remained the only scapegoat.[7]

Before long, however, blame for the Armada's failure began to shift from the fleet's principal officers to its supreme commander in the Escorial. The stern Jesuit Pedro de Ribadeneira (who had been one of the most vocal supporters of the Enterprise of England) duly informed the government that:

> The judgements of God are most secret, so that we cannot know for certain the purpose of his Divine Majesty in the extraordinary fate he has decreed for the king's powerful fleet. Nevertheless, seeing that the cause was so much His, and was undertaken with such a holy intent, and was so much desired and assisted by the whole Catholic Church, the fact that He was not moved by the pious prayers and tears of so many and such great devotees makes us fearful that there are serious reasons why Our Lord has sent us this affliction . . . So that it is both necessary and advisable to seek and consider the causes that may have moved God to punish us in this way.

Ribadeneira went on to offer five reasons why God might be offended with Spain in general and with her king in particular. Don Francisco de Bobadilla, by contrast, shivering in the northern seas, took the more pragmatic view of a man on the spot:

> I don't know who had the idea [he began cautiously] that we could join forces [with Parma] in a place with such powerful currents, with a shore so open and liable to cross-winds, and with so many sandbanks . . . But I believe it is imposs- ible to control all the things that must be concerted at the same time, in order to bring together forces that are so separated, unless one has a different sort of ship from those we brought, in the place we were instructed to join.[8]

Once again, hindsight has amply confirmed Bobadilla's judgement. In book V of his *History of the World*, written for the most part in 1613, Sir Walter Raleigh reached a remarkably similar verdict: 'To invade by sea upon a perilous coast, being neither in possession of any port, nor succoured by any party, may better fit a prince presuming on his fortune than enriched with understanding.'

But perhaps this was too glib, too confident? The history of amphibious operations is filled with campaigns that failed in spite of the most confident predictions as well as of enterprises that succeeded in the face of all the odds. To Sir William Winter, even in December 1588, England's deliverance still seemed miraculous. 'When I consider that ships are subject to wind, weather and other haps', he warned, 'it were not good, as I think, for to build our defence only upon them.' And yet that is precisely what Elizabeth had done. England lacked all the vital resources to resist an invasion: if ever the Armada had landed, there were neither fortifications, troops nor money enough to stop the Spaniards.

Parma's orders were clear. It will be recalled that his instructions from the king on 1 April 1588 charged him to lead his troops from Margate through Kent and on to take London by storm (preferably with Elizabeth and her ministers still in it). Perhaps the queen's discontented subjects in the north, in the west and in Ireland would rise in rebellion and aid the invaders, but the success of the plan did not hinge on such a rising. Philip knew that not all English Catholics would support a Spanish invasion, despite the propaganda directed towards them by the exiles at his court, by the pope's pamphleteers and by the doctors of theology at the English College at Douai. All that these polemics achieved, in fact, was to rouse the suspicion of the English government, which first disarmed the recusants and later interned some of their leaders. The English Catholics – like Cardinal Allen and his doctors from Douai – would be important props of the new regime *after* the conquest, but until then they could largely be ignored.[9]

Of much greater concern to the king was the possibility that Parma's invasion might become bogged down before gaining outright victory in the south-east. Here, his instructions were the same as those drafted by Don Juan de Zúñiga in October 1586 (page 96 above). The duke was to use his presence on English soil to force Elizabeth to concede toleration of Roman Catholic worship, and to surrender to Spain all Dutch towns held by English troops (especially Flushing, which commanded the sea-approaches to Antwerp). On top of this, he could attempt to extract a war-indemnity from England, though this might be dropped in return for the main concessions.

Unconditional victory was by no means impossible. Not even Sir Walter Raleigh doubted that the Army of Flanders, once ashore in England, would have proved able to achieve it. Elizabeth's defences, he noted in his *History of the World*, were 'of no such force as to encounter an Army like unto that, wherewith it was intended that the prince of Parma should have landed in England'. Parma's only lack was a siege train; and that, of course, Philip II had thoughtfully provided aboard the Armada itself, ready for disembarkation and immediate use.

This was an advantage of critical importance, since very few towns and castles in south-east England could have withstood heavy bombardment. According to one disgruntled old soldier, the English seemed 'persuaded according to the opinion of the Lacedaemonians, that fortifying of towns does more hurt than good'. Admittedly, Henry VIII had done a good deal to improve the defences of the Kent coast, with five new forts built between the Downs and Rye, and five more along the Thames estuary; but all these defences (as a visit to the still extant castles of Camber and Walmer shows) consisted of thin circular walls and curved, hollow bulwarks. They certainly maximised the potential for offensive firepower – Sandgate Castle boasted 60 artillery and 65 handgun embrasures – but they possessed poor defensive capacity. Parma's siege guns and assault squads would have made short work of them. Recent military experience had clearly demonstrated that only solid angular bastions, protected by wide moats, could withstand heavy artillery; and in south-east England only the small castle of Upnor, built in the 1560s to defend the naval dockyard at Chatham, had those. The larger towns of Kent, Canterbury and Rochester still relied on their antiquated medieval walls, while Rochester Castle, commanding the main crossing over the Medway, was thoroughly decayed. There seem to have been no defence works at all between Margate and the Medway, and Upnor alone could not have stopped Parma. Philip II had deftly selected his adversary's most vulnerable point.

With so few physical obstacles in their path, Parma and his veterans would have been able to move fast. When in 1592 the duke invaded Normandy with 22,000 men, they covered 65 miles in six days, despite tenacious opposition from numerically superior forces. Four years earlier, the invaders might therefore have covered the 80 miles from Margate to London in a week. Such a rapid advance would have brought the advantage of surprise, and also the windfall of copious food supplies, since the Kent harvest would have been in full swing. Even London represented a soft target, for the city still relied on ramshackle medieval walls which had scarcely changed since 1554 when Sir Thomas Wyatt raised an ill-equipped army to protest against Philip's marriage with Mary Tudor. The rebels had marched through Kent, crossed the Thames at Kingston (west of the capital), advanced with impunity through Westminster, and marched down Fleet Street to the city walls at Ludgate before Wyatt, lacking artillery, lost his nerve.

Parma well knew, however, that the state of a town's physical defences did not always prove decisive. Thanks to the determination of their besieged populations, several places in the Netherlands with poor, outdated fortifications had defied capture; conversely, a few strongholds boasting the latest defensive systems had fallen to the Spaniards with ease because their citizens, their garrisons, or their commanders succumbed to bribes. It is by no means certain that the defenders of the major English towns and castles would have resisted the Spaniards to the last man. Elizabeth's own troops in the Netherlands had a distinctly uninspiring record in that respect: in November 1584 the English garrison of Aalst sold their town to Parma for 45,000 ducats, and in February 1587 Sir William Stanley and Captain Roland Yorke, together with over 700 men under their command, betrayed the places entrusted to their care to Parma and (for the most part) began to fight against their former comrades and allies.

One can protest that many of these men were either Irish or Anglo-Irish Catholics, and thus of questionable loyalty to the Tudor state; but it remains true that all had been recruited by, or with the consent of, the English government and had been sent abroad specifically to fight for the Protestant cause in the Low Countries. Elizabeth and her advisers, moreover, set great store by the comrades of these traitors, recalling 4,000 men of the English expeditionary force in Holland to form the nucleus of the army intended to defend London. Its quartermaster-general was the brother of Roland Yorke; its third-in-command, Sir Roger Williams, had fought in the Spanish Army of Flanders for four years in the 1570s. One cannot exclude the possibility that some of these men might have been prepared to sell strongholds to Parma in England, just as their fellows had sold strongholds to him in the Low Countries.

Elizabeth, however, had no choice. She depended on the veterans from Holland because she could call upon very few other experienced troops. A census carried out by her government in July 1588 to ascertain how many 'martial men' (i.e. veterans) resided in England, produced a list of only 100 (some of whom, with service going back to the 1540s, would be too old to use). The 6,000 armed conscripts of the London trained bands, who had been drilling twice weekly since March, were probably capable of putting up a good fight (although some doubted it), but little could be expected from the militias of the inland shires.

To begin with, they were poorly equipped. A survey of the 9,088 men mobilised in Hampshire revealed that many were 'very rawly furnished, some whereof lacketh a headpiece, some a sword, some with one thing or another that is evil, unfit or unbeseeming about him'. In the northern shires, the few men with firearms received only one pound of powder for each fortnight's training so that 'they have been driven hitherto for the most part to train with false fires' (that is to say, they could prime their firearms but lacked charge and bullet for target practice). Most of the shire levies called up to resist the Armada included large contingents of archers – the Kent militia comprised 567 archers and 1,172 'shot' (who were said to lack 'powder, match, lead, nags and carters') – and their quality elsewhere caused despair. The men of Dorset, it seemed to their commander, 'will sooner kill one another than annoy the enemy'.

The queen issued orders only on 27 July for the southern militia units to mobilise, and even then she sent them to the wrong place: Tilbury in Essex, separated by 70 miles and the Thames from the beach-head selected by Philip II. Worse still, the levies brought 'not so much as one meal's provision of victual with them, so that, at their arrival here, there was not a barrel of beer, nor loaf of bread for them'. That was on 5 August. The same day orders therefore went out to the levies coming from London to stop where they stood 'except they had provisions with them'. England could scarcely be defended by starving men.[10]

Other defensive projects also miscarried. A floating boom across the Thames – an improvised affair of masts, chains and cables designed by Giambelli to keep out enemy shipping – broke on the first flood tide; a bridge of boats across the river, intended to link the queen's forces in Kent and Essex, remained incomplete. Even at Tilbury, lynchpin of England's defences, work only began on the fortifications on 3 August, when the Armada lay off the Isle of Wight, and they lacked gun platforms capable of mounting artillery. Three days later, the troops near Dover (most of them raw recruits) began to desert in considerable numbers when the Armada anchored off Calais (perhaps through lack of wages, but more probably through fear). In any case, they numbered only 4,000 men, a ludicrously inadequate force to throw into the path of the seasoned Spaniards.

They also lacked a clear strategy. The local commander in Kent, Sir Thomas Scott, argued that it was better to spread his forces out along the coast in order to 'answer' the enemy 'at the sea side', while the general officer in charge of the south-east, Sir John Norris, more prudently wished to withdraw all but a skeleton force inland in order to make a stand at Canterbury and there 'stay the enemy from speedy passage to London or the heart of the realm'.[11]

Much of this unpreparedness and confusion stemmed from poverty and isolation. Elizabeth could not raise loans at home because hostilities with Spain had caused a trade recession, or abroad because most continental bankers thought Spain would win, forcing her to delay every stage of her counter-invasion plans until the last possible moment to save money. On 29 July her treasurer complained that outstanding bills totalling £40,000 lay on his desk 'with no probability how to get money' to pay them. 'A man might wish', he concluded dourly, that 'if peace cannot be had, the enemy would not longer delay, but prove, as I trust, his evil fortune.' Apart from the Dutch, England stood entirely alone.

By contrast, although on one occasion in 1588 Philip II had to pawn his late wife's jewels to raise money, he laid out huge sums for the Enterprise of England. The duke of Guise, leader of the French Catholic League, received 1,500,000 ducats (£375,000) from Spain between 1587 and 1590, and over the same period the Army of Flanders received some 21,000,000 more. The king later claimed that he had spent 10,000,000 (£2,500,000) on the Armada itself. At the same time Philip's diplomats managed either to win over or to neutralise every other state in Europe. In July 1588, as the Armada entered the Channel, an admiring ambassador at the court of Spain noted that:

> At the moment, the Catholic King [Philip II] is safe: France cannot threaten him, and the Turks can do little; neither can the king of Scots, who is offended at Queen Elizabeth on account of the death of his mother. The one [monarch] who could have made trouble was the king of Denmark, who has just died, and his son is young and so has other things to deal with . . . At the same time, Spain can be assured that the Swiss cantons will not move against him; nor will they allow others to do so, since they are now his allies.

In short, he concluded, no foreign power could prevent the execution of the king's Grand Design.[12]

So it seems reasonable to suppose that had the 27,000 veterans from Flanders, supported by the siege train, munitions and reinforcements brought by the fleet, landed in Kent early in August 1588, their march on London would have been opposed by inferior numbers of badly positioned and largely untrained troops, acting without clear orders, and backed up by only a handful of inadequately fortified towns. The invasion's success would therefore have hinged mainly upon the spirit of the ordinary citizens of south-east England.

How determined would the defence of London and the Home Counties really have been?

Certainly many Englishmen hated the Spaniards, especially in the staunchly Protestant south-eastern shires, their hatred stoked by evocative propaganda and such hair-raising accounts of their cruelty as George Gascoyne's *The Spoyle of Antwerp* (London, 1576) and the English version of Bartolomé de Las Casas's *Destruction of the Indies* (published in 1583). But could hate alone have kept the English fighting on the beaches and in the streets for Elizabeth Tudor, an ageing monarch with no acknowledged successor, and for her compromise Church which (according to a contemporary) 'the common people for the greater part' still called 'the new religion'? The queen's spies reported that some men of Kent during the Armada year openly rejoiced 'when any report was of their [the Spaniards'] good success and sorrowing for the contrary'; while others declared that 'the Spaniards . . . were better than the people of this land'. And, of course, had Elizabeth died – whether by an assassin's hand (as both Henry III and Henry of Navarre would do) or through natural causes – the Tudor dynasty would end with her, leaving a Council of Regency, created without parliamentary authority, to direct the nation's resistance to the invaders.[13]

It would not have been necessary for Parma to conquer the whole of England in order to achieve Philip II's aims, however: the occupation of Kent alone would have offered important advantages. The duke could have exploited his conquests, together with the threat of another Catholic rising in the north or in Ireland, to force England's withdrawal from the Netherlands. After all, alarmed by Spain's preparations for invasion, Elizabeth's commissioners negotiated with Parma throughout the spring of 1588 on this very issue. With Parma on English soil, a deal might have seemed unavoidable.

Without English support, the Dutch could probably not have fought on single-handed for long because there, too, a vociferous peace party already existed. When in December 1587, at Elizabeth's insistence, the States-General of the republic debated at length whether they should send a delegation to the peace talks at Bourbourg, there were a number of voices raised in favour. Although most of the deputies from Holland, Zealand and Utrecht firmly opposed any talks with Spain, some towns dissented, and the inland provinces which had to bear the brunt of the war against Spain (Gelderland, Overijssel, the Ommelanden around Groningen and most of Friesland) argued strongly in favour of a settlement. According to one of Elizabeth's special envoys to the Dutch, 'The Common Wealth of these Provinces consisting of divers Parts and Professions as, namely, Protestants, Puritans, Anabaptists and Spanish Hearts, which are no small number; it is most certain that dividing these in five parts, the Protestants and the Puritans do hardly contain even one part of five.' And, the envoy continued, only the 'Protestants and Puritans' favoured a continuation of the war.[14] Had the Enterprise of England succeeded, leaving the young republic to withstand Philip's power alone, pressure for a compromise would probably have become irresistible. In the context of the Dutch wars also, Medina Sidonia would not have sailed in vain.

Suppressing the Dutch Revolt would have transformed the balance of power in Europe. The pacification of the Netherlands would leave Spain free to intervene decisively in both France and Germany, and to extend its authority (and its language) all around the globe.

Or would it? After 32 years on the throne, Philip II regarded himself as both omniscient and divinely inspired – especially where English affairs were concerned. Having resided in and ruled the kingdom himself in the 1550s, he believed for ever afterwards that 'I can give better information and advice on that kingdom and on its affairs and people than any one else'. Therefore, as we have seen, he attempted to micromanage every aspect of the Armada campaign, starting with the creation of a master plan that rashly involved the junction of a fleet from Spain with an army in Flanders, separated by a thousand miles of sea, as the ineluctable preliminary to invasion, and he refused to allow anyone – whether councillor, general or admiral – to challenge the wisdom of his Grand Design, instead urging them to 'believe me as one who has complete information on the present state of affairs in all areas'. Whenever obstacles threatened the venture, Philip insisted that God would provide a miracle.

Philip's urge to micromanage knew no bounds. Even if Medina Sidonia and his subordinates had somehow managed to avoid the fireships, to wait off Calais until Parma's army had embarked aboard its flotilla of small ships and to escort them to Kent, Philip's desire to meddle would doubtless not have abated. Had his forces occupied only a slice of Kent, the king would probably have insisted that Parma should strive for total victory instead of seeking a compromise, just as he had refused to discuss a compromise settlement after every major success in the struggle against the Dutch (such as the capture of Antwerp in 1585), prolonging instead a stalemate that drained his resources. The results would have been disastrous: with the invasion of England bogged down, Dutch resistance would no doubt have continued and the position of the French Catholics deteriorated, straining Spain's resources and pushing it towards bankruptcy. As it was, Philip's treasury had to suspend all payments in 1596.

At least, however, even partial Spanish success in 1588 would have gone down in the pages of history as a classic 'combined operation'. Historians would have praised the intelligence coups and the selection of an ideal invasion area, the formidable planning and the immense resources, the successful diplomacy that neutralised all opposition, and the operational brilliance which ensured that – against all the odds – an irresistible fleet from Spain 'joined hands' with an invincible army from the Netherlands. Despite all its deficiencies if, in the second week of August 1588, the duke of Parma and his veteran troops had begun their march on London then, whatever the ultimate outcome, everyone today would regard the 'Enterprise of England' as Philip II's masterpiece.

## Sources

Data on England's fortifications from Colvin, *The History of the King's Works*, 415–65 and 602–6; and Bruce, *Report on the Arrangements*. Examples of the equipment of the trained bands are taken from HMC *Fifteenth Report*, Appendix, part V (London, 1897), 40–2; *CSPD 1581–1590*, 485 (order of 30 May 1588); and BL Harleian MS 168/166–74. For a more positive overview of England's chances, see Nolan, 'The muster of 1588', and McGurk, 'Armada preparations in Kent and arrangements made after the defeat'. One must also recall that Elizabeth kept 6,000 men mobilised in the north, in case of a Scottish invasion: see p. 103 above.

On the English Catholics and their possible support for Parma, see Mattingly, 'William Allen and Catholic propaganda in England'; Adams, 'Stanley, York and Elizabeth's Catholics'; Loomie, 'The Armadas and the Catholics of England'; and Wiener, 'The beleaguered isle'.

## Notes

1   Tellechea Idígoras, *Otra cara*, 580–1, Bobadilla to Don Juan de Idiáquez, 20 August 1588.
2   AGS *Estado K* 1568/113, Mendoza to Philip II, 24 September 1588; *Estado* 1261/115, Don Jusepe de Acuña, Spanish ambassador in Turin, to Philip II, 6 September 1588; Malfatti, *Cuatro documentos italianos en materia de la expedicion de la Armada invencible*, 43, Giulio Savorgnano to Filippo Pigafetta, 23 September 1588; and AS, Florence, *Mediceo del Principato* 4919/484v, Alemanni to Florence, 4 October 1588 (a letter full of detail on the criticisms of Parma circulating at the court of Spain).
3   Fea, *Alessandro Farnese*, 308–10: Parma to Cardinal Farnese (undated but presumably 12 August 1588); AGS *Estado* 950/227, the count of Olivares to Philip II, 29 October 1588, and 950/229, to Parma, 15 October 1588, copy.
4   AGS *Estado* 594/125, Parma to the king, 10 August 1588; Oria, 266, Don Jorge Manrique to the king, 12 August 1588.
5   Details from marquis of Saltillo, 'El duque de Medina Sidonia y la jornada a Inglaterra en 1588', 174ff; AGS *CS* 2a/286 fo. 278 (salary paid); and Fray Juan de Vitoria, 'Noticias de la Invencible', in Tellechea Idígoras, *Otra cara*, 188 (see Tellechea's masterful assessment of this much-quoted source: *ibid.*, 133–47).
6   AGS *Estado* 455, unfol., Bobadilla to the king, 27 September 1588. On the other hand, Recalde's whole 'dossier', sent to court on 8 October (the day after he returned to Spain), constituted a sustained critique of Medina Sidonia's leadership, although it seems unlikely that Philip read it all: see Parker, 'El testamento político', 10–14.
7   Oria, 325, Don Orduño de Zamudio to the king, 5 October 1588; AGS *GA* 244/46, Pedro Coco Calderón to the king, 24 January 1589; and Lilly Library, Bloomington (Indiana), Bertendona Papers, 21, Bertendona to the king, 23 June 1589; all blamed Flores for the Armada's failure. So did Recalde, adding that the king should have appointed Oquendo instead (Oria, 334, Andrés de Alba to Don Martín de Idiáquez, 8 October 1588). Diego Flores was imprisoned in Burgos and remained there for three years: see AGS *GA* 228/131, Licenciado Santillán to the king, 23 December 1588; and Tellechea Idígoras, *Otra cara*, 593–6.

8 *Monumenta historica societatis Iesu, LX: Ribadeneira,* 105–11, letter to Don Juan de Idiáquez, December 1588; Tellechea Idígoras, *Otra cara,* 581, Bobadilla to Idiáquez, 20 August 1588.

9 See Parma's instructions, sent with Medina Sidonia (and therefore never seen by Parma himself) in AGS *Estado* 165/174–6, dated 1 April 1588 (precis in *CSPSp,* IV, 250–2).

10 Huntington Library, San Marino, *HA* 30881/76, Huntingdon to Burghley and Walsingham, 15 May 1588 OS and 85v–86, to Walsingham, 20 June 1588 OS; Flower-Smith, 'The able and the willynge'; and HMC *Fifteenth Report* (London, 1897), Appendix, part V, 34–58 (the Foljambe 'Book of musters').

11 PRO *SP* 12/213/45, Sir Thomas Scott to Burghley, 6 August 1588 NS; Scott, 'Pay-list of the Kentish forces raised to resist the Spanish Armada'; and Scott Thomson, *The Twysden Lieutenancy Papers,* 70–1.

12 OÖLA *KB* 4/311–12, Khevenhüller, Imperial ambassador in Spain, to Rudolf II, 13 July 1588.

13 Quotations from Kent in Clark, *English Provincial Society from the Reformation to the Revolution,* 249; on the arrangements for an interregnum, see Collinson, *Elizabethan Essays,* 34–55.

14 *Cabala sive scrinia sacra* (3rd edn, London, 1691), II, 37: Lord Buckhurst to Queen Elizabeth, 27 May 1587 OS.

# APPENDIX I

# Tables of the opposing fleets

## The Spanish fleet[a]

| | Tons | Guns | Sailors at Corunna | Soldiers | Place built | Date built |
|---|---|---|---|---|---|---|
| **SQUADRON OF PORTUGAL: DUKE OF MEDINA SIDONIA** | | | | | | |
| San Martín (flagship: the duke of Medina Sidonia) | 1,000 | 48 | 161 | 317 | Portugal | 1570s |
| San Juan (vice-flagship: Juan Martínez de Recalde) | 1,050 | 50 | 156 | 387 | Cantabria | 1586 |
| San Marcos (marquis of Peñafiel) | 790 | 33 | 108 | 274 | Cantabria | 1585 |
| San Felipe (Don Francisco de Toledo) | 800 | 40 | 108 | 362 | Cantabria | 1583 |
| San Luis (Don Agustín Mexía) | 830 | 38 | 100 | 339 | Cantabria | 1585 |
| San Mateo (Don Diego Pimentel) | 750 | 34 | 110 | 286 | Portugal | 1570s |
| Santiago (Antonio de Pereira) | 520 | 24 | 80 | 293 | Cantabria | 1585 |
| San Francisco de Florencia (Gaspar de Sousa) | 961 | 52 | 89 | 294 | Tuscany | 1570s? |
| San Cristobal | 352 | 20 | 79 | 125 | Portugal | 1570s |
| San Bernardo | 352 | 21 | 65 | 170 | Cantabria | 1586 |
| Augusta (zabra) | 166 | 13 | 43 | 49 | Cantabria | 1585 |
| Julia (zabra) | 166 | 14 | 48 | 39 | Cantabria | 1585 |
| **SQUADRON OF CASTILE: DIEGO FLORES DE VALDÉS** | | | | | | |
| San Cristobal (flagship: Gregorio de las Alas) | 700 | 36 | 116 | 202 | Cantabria | 1583 |
| San Juan Bautista (vice-flagship: Marcos de Aramburu) | 750 | 24 | 90 | 244 | Cantabria | 1585 |
| San Pedro (Francisco de Cuéllar) | 530 | 24 | 90 | 184 | Cantabria | 1584 |
| San Juan (Don Diego Enríquez) | 530 | 24 | 77 | 231 | Cantabria | 1584 |
| Santiago el Mayor | 530 | 24 | 103 | 190 | Cantabria | 1584 |
| San Felipe y Santiago | 530 | 24 | 75 | 204 | Cantabria | 1584 |

| | Tons | Guns | Sailors at Corunna | Soldiers | Place built | Date built |
|---|---|---|---|---|---|---|
| *Asunción* | 530 | 24 | 70 | 170 | Cantabria | 1584 |
| *Nuestra Señora del Barrio* | 530 | 24 | 81 | 202 | Cantabria | 1583 |
| *San Medel y San Celedón* | 530 | 24 | 75 | 200 | Cantabria | 1584 |
| *Santa Ana* | 250 | 24 | 54 | 98 | France | 1581? |
| *Nuestra Señora de Begoña* (Juan Gutiérrez de Garibay) | 750 | 24 | 81 | 202 | Cantabria? | 1585? |
| *La Trinidad* | 872 | 24 | 79 | 173 | Cantabria? | 1586? |
| *Santa Catalina* | 882 | 24 | 134 | 193 | Cantabria | 1586? |
| *San Juan Bautista* (Fernando Horra) | 650 | 24 | 57 | 183 | Cantabria? | 1586? |
| *Nuestra Señora del Rosario* (*patache*) | 75 | 14 | 15 | 20 | Cantabria | 1586? |
| *San Antonio de Padua* (*patache*) | 75 | 12 | 20 | 20 | Cantabria | 1586? |

## SQUADRON OF BISCAY: JUAN MARTÍNEZ DE RECALDE

| | Tons | Guns | Sailors at Corunna | Soldiers | Place built | Date built |
|---|---|---|---|---|---|---|
| *Santa Ana* (flagship: Nicolás de Isla) | 768 | 30 | 101 | 311 | Cantabria | 1586 |
| *Santiago* (vice-flagship) | 666 | 25 | 106 | 204 | Cantabria | 1585 |
| *El Gran Grin* (Don Pedro de Mendoza) | 1,160 | 28 | 75 | 261 | ? | ? |
| *Concepción de Zubelzu* | 468 | 16 | 58 | 161 | Pasaje | 1585 |
| *Concepción de Juan del Cano* | 418 | 18 | 58 | 167 | Cantabria | 1585 |
| *Magdalena* | 530 | 18 | 61 | 183 | Cantabria | 1585 |
| *San Juan* | 350 | 21 | 49 | 141 | Cantabria | 1585 |
| *María Juan* | 665 | 24 | 93 | 207 | Cantabria | 1585 |
| *Manuela* | 520 | 12 | 48 | 124 | England? | ? |
| *Santa María de Montemayor* | 707 | 18 | 47 | 158 | Ragusa | ? |
| *María de Aguirre* (*patache*) | 70 | 6 | 25 | 19 | Cantabria | 1585 |
| *Isabela* (*patache*) | 71 | 10 | 29 | 24 | Cantabria | 1585 |
| *María de Miguel Suso* (*patache*) | 96 | 6 | 25 | 20 | Cantabria | 1585 |
| *San Esteban* (*patache*) | 78 | 6 | 25 | 10 | Cantabria | 1585 |

## SQUADRON OF GUIPÚZCOA: MIGUEL DE OQUENDO

| | Tons | Guns | Sailors at Corunna | Soldiers | Place built | Date built |
|---|---|---|---|---|---|---|
| *Santa Ana* (flagship: Miguel de Oquendo) | 1,200 | 47 | 97 | 341 | San Sebastián | 1586 |
| *Santa María de la Rosa* (vice-flagship: Don Pedro Pacheco) | 945 | 26 | 85 | 238 | San Sebastián | 1587 |

| | Tons | Guns | Sailors<br>at Corunna | Soldiers | Place<br>built | Date<br>built |
|---|---|---|---|---|---|---|
| San Salvador (Don Pedro<br>Priego) | 958 | 25 | 90 | 281 | Cantabria? | 1586? |
| San Esteban (Don Felipe de<br>Córdoba) | 936 | 26 | 73 | 204 | Cantabria? | 1586? |
| Santa Marta | 548 | 20 | 73 | 183 | San Sebastián | 1586? |
| Santa Bárbara | 525 | 12 | 54 | 161 | Cantabria | 1586? |
| San Buenaventura | 379 | 21 | 54 | 154 | Cantabria | 1586? |
| María San Juan | 291 | 12 | 40 | 154 | Cantabria | 1586? |
| Santa Cruz | 680 | 18 | 40 | 127 | Mediterranean | ? |
| Doncella | 500 | 16 | 29 | 112 | Germany | ? |
| Asunción (patache) | 60 | 9 | 16 | 18 | Cantabria | 1586? |
| San Bernabe (patache) | 69 | 9 | 17 | 17 | Cantabria | 1586? |
| Nuestra Señora de Guadalupe<br>(pinnace) | 50? | 1 | 12 | 0 | Cantabria | 1586? |
| Magdalena (pinnace) | 50? | 1 | 14 | 0 | Cantabria | 1586? |

## SQUADRON OF ANDALUSIA: DON PEDRO DE VALDÉS

| | Tons | Guns | Sailors | Soldiers | Place | Date |
|---|---|---|---|---|---|---|
| Nuestra Señora del Rosario<br>(flagship: Don Pedro de<br>Valdés) | 1,150 | 46 | 119 | 345 | Ribadeo | 1587 |
| San Francisco (vice-flagship) | 915 | 21 | 85 | 227 | Cantabria | 1586 |
| San Juan Bautista | 810 | 31 | 84 | 249 | Cantabria? | 1584? |
| San Juan de Gargarin<br>(Tomé Cano) | 569 | 16 | 38 | 175 | Cantabria | 1585? |
| La Concepción | 862 | 20 | 69 | 201 | Cantabria | 1584? |
| Duquesa Santa Ana | 900 | 23 | 65 | 253 | Netherlands | ? |
| Santa Catalina | 730 | 23 | 69 | 238 | Cantabria | 1585? |
| La Trinidad | 650 | 13 | 54 | 198 | Cantabria | 1585? |
| Santa María de Juncal | 730 | 20 | 66 | 219 | Cantabria | 1586? |
| San Bartolomé | 976 | 27 | 56 | 211 | Cantabria | 1585? |
| Espiritu Santo (patache) | 70 | 10 | 15 | 18 | Cantabria | 1585 |

## LEVANT SQUADRON: MARTÍN DE BERTENDONA

| | Tons | Guns | Sailors | Soldiers | Place | Date |
|---|---|---|---|---|---|---|
| Regazona (flagship:<br>Martín de Bertendona) | 1,294 | 30 | 80 | 333 | Venetian | ? |
| Lavia (vice-flagship:<br>Martín de Aranda) | 728 | 25 | 71 | 271 | Venetian | ? |
| Rata Santa María Encoronada<br>(Don Alonso de Leiva) | 820 | 35 | 93 | 355 | Genoa | ? |

|  | Tons | Guns | Sailors at Corunna | Soldiers | Place built | Date built |
|---|---|---|---|---|---|---|
| San Juan de Sicilia (Don Diego Tellez Enríquez) | 800 | 26 | 63 | 279 | Ragusa | ? |
| La Trinidad Valencera (Don Alonso de Luzón) | 1,100 | 42 | 75 | 338 | Venice | ? |
| Anunciada | 703 | 24 | 80 | 200 | Ragusa | ? |
| San Nicolas Prodaneli | 834 | 26 | 68 | 226 | Ragusa | ? |
| Juliana | 860 | 32 | 65 | 290 | Genoa? | ? |
| Santa María de Visón | 666 | 18 | 38 | 183 | Ragusa | ? |
| Trinidad de Scala | 900 | 22 | 66 | 342 | Genoa | ? |
| San Bautista de la Esperanza[b] | 300 | 12? | ? | ? | Castro Urdiales | ? |

## SQUADRON OF HULKS: JUAN GÓMEZ DE MEDINA

|  | Tons | Guns | Sailors at Corunna | Soldiers | Place built | Date built |
|---|---|---|---|---|---|---|
| El Gran Grifón (flagship: Juan Gómez de Medina) | 650 | 38 | 45 | 234 | Rostock | ? |
| San Salvador (vice-flagship: Pedro Coco Calderón) | 650 | 24 | 53 | 218 | Danzig | 1565 |
| Perro Marino | 200 | 7 | 18 | 80 | Netherlands | ? |
| Falcon Blanco Mayor | 500 | 16 | 34 | 182 | Netherlands | 1586 |
| Castillo Negro | 750 | 27 | 46 | 157 | Netherlands | ? |
| Barca de Amburg | 600 | 23 | 30 | 259 | Hamburg | 1577 |
| Casa de Paz Grande | 600 | 26 | 70 | 255 | Netherlands | ? |
| San Pedro Mayor | 581 | 29 | 34 | 110 | Baltic | 1567 |
| Sansón | 500 | 18 | 31 | 184 | Netherlands | ? |
| San Pedro Menor | 500 | 18 | 22 | 176 | Baltic | 1586 |
| Barca de Danzig | 450 | 26 | 28 | 150 | Danzig | 1572 |
| Falcon Blanco Mediano (Don Luis de Córdoba) | 300 | 16 | 23 | 57 | Netherlands | 1564 |
| San Andrés de Málaga | 400 | 14 | 26 | 39 | Netherlands | ? |
| Casa de Paz Chica | 350 | 15 | 21 | 154 | Riga | 1560 |
| Ciervo Volante | 400 | 18 | 39 | 132 | Baltic | ? |
| Paloma Blanca | 250 | 12 | 30 | 67 | Netherlands | ? |
| La Ventura | 160 | 4 | 15 | 49 | Netherlands | ? |
| Santa Bárbara (Don Crístobal de Avila) | 370 | 19 | 24 | 26 | Netherlands | 1559 |
| Santiago ('the ship of the women') | 600 | 19 | 32 | 32 | Baltic | 1551 |
| El Gato | 400 | 9 | 41 | 30 | Netherlands | ? |
| San Gabriel | 280 | 4 | 16 | 31 | Netherlands | 1561 |
| Esayas | 280 | 4 | 24 | 23 | Baltic | 1542 |

| | Tons | Guns | Sailors at Corunna | Soldiers | Place built | Date built |
|---|---|---|---|---|---|---|

### GALLEASSES FROM NAPLES: DON HUGO DE MONCADA

| | Tons | Guns | Sailors | Soldiers | Place built | Date built |
|---|---|---|---|---|---|---|
| *San Lorenzo* (flagship: Don Hugo de Moncada) | 600 | 50 | 124 | 248 | Naples | 1578 |
| *Zúñiga* | 600 | 50 | 100? | 178 | Naples | 1578 |
| *Girona* | 600 | 50 | 140 | 229 | Naples | 1580 |
| *Napolitana* | 600 | 50 | 100 | 221 | Naples | 1581 |

(each galleass also carried 300 oarsmen)

### *PATACHES* AND *ZABRAS*: AGUSTÍN DE OJEDA

| | Tons | Guns | Sailors | Soldiers | Place built | Date built |
|---|---|---|---|---|---|---|
| *Nuestra Señora del Pilar* (Agustín de Ojeda) | 300 | 11 | 59 | 114 | Cantabria | 1584 |
| *Caridad Inglesa* | 180 | 11 | 36 | 43 | England | ? |
| *San Andrés Escocés* | 150 | 12 | 27 | 38 | Dundee | ? |

18 or 19 other *pataches* and *zabras*, 10 caravels and 10 feluccas

GRAND TOTAL: 130–40 ships, carrying perhaps 7,000 sailors and some 19,000 soldiers.

## The English fleet[c]

| | Tons | Guns | Sailors | Gunners | Soldiers | Total men |
|---|---|---|---|---|---|---|

### THE QUEEN'S SHIPS (WITH YEAR BUILT OR REBUILT AND COMMANDER)

| | Tons | Guns | Sailors | Gunners | Soldiers | Total men |
|---|---|---|---|---|---|---|
| *Ark Royal* (1587; Lord Admiral Howard) | 800 | 32 | 270 | 34 | 126 | 425 |
| *Elizabeth Bonaventure* (1581; earl of Cumberland) | 600 | 37 | 150 | 24 | 76 | 250 |
| *Rainbow* (1586; Lord Henry Seymour) | 500 | 26 | 150 | 24 | 76 | 250 |
| *Lion* (1582; Lord Thomas Howard) | 500 | 39 | 150 | 24 | 76 | 250 |
| *White Bear* (1578; Lord Sheffield) | 1,000 | 34 | 300 | 40 | 150 | 500 |
| *Vanguard* (1586; Sir William Winter) | 500 | 37 | 150 | 24 | 76 | 250 |
| *Revenge* (1577; Sir Francis Drake) | 500 | 40 | 150 | 24 | 76 | 350 |
| *Elizabeth Jonas* (1577; Sir Robert Southwell) | 900 | 32 | 300 | 40 | 150 | 500 |
| *Victory* (1586; Sir John Hawkins) | 800 | 39 | 270 | 34 | 126 | 400 |
| *Antelope* (1581; Sir Henry Palmer) | 400 | 24 | 120 | 20 | 30 | 160 |
| *Triumph* (1578; Sir Martin Frobisher) | 1,100 | 36 | 300 | 40 | 160 | 500 |

| | Tons | Guns | Sailors | Gunners | Soldiers | Total men |
|---|---|---|---|---|---|---|
| *Dreadnought* (1573; Sir George Beeston) | 400 | 35 | 130 | 20 | 40 | 200 |
| *Mary Rose* (1580; Edward Fenton) | 600 | 27 | 150 | 24 | 76 | 250 |
| *Nonpareil* (1584; Thomas Fenner) | 500 | 39 | 150 | 24 | 76 | 250 |
| *Hope* (1578; Robert Crosse) | 600 | 36 | 160 | 25 | 85 | 250 |
| *Galley Bonavolia* (1584; William Borough) | 300 | 5? | | | | 250 |
| *Swiftsure* (1573; Edward Fenner) | 400 | 35? | 120 | 20 | 40 | 180 |
| *Swallow* (1580; Richard Hawkins) | 360 | ? | 110 | 20 | 30 | 160 |
| *Foresight* (1581; Christopher Baker) | 300 | 30 | 110 | 20 | 20 | 160 |
| *Aid* (1562; William Fenner) | 250 | 25 | 90 | 16 | 14 | 120 |
| *Bull* (1570; Jeremy Turner) | 200 | ? | 80 | 12 | 8 | 100 |
| *Tiger* (1584; John Bostocke) | 200 | 22 | 80 | 12 | 8 | 100 |
| *Tramontana* (1586; Luke Ward) | 150 | 22 | 55 | 8 | 7 | 70 |
| *Scout* (1577; Henry Ashley) | 120 | ? | 55 | 8 | 7 | 70 |
| *Achates* (1573; Gregory Riggs) | 100 | 7 | 45 | 8 | 7 | 60 |
| *Charles* (1586; John Roberts) | 70 | 12 | 36 | 4 | | 40 |
| *Moon* (1586; Alexander Clifford) | 60 | 9 | 34 | 4 | | 40 |
| *Advice* (1586; John Harris) | 50 | 10 | 31 | 4 | | 40 |
| *Merlin* (1579; Walter Gower) | 50 | 7 | 20 | 4 | | 35 |
| *Spy* (1586; Ambrose Ward) | 50 | 7 | 31 | 4 | | 40 |
| *Sun* (1586; Richard Buckley) | 40 | 3 | 26 | 4 | | 30 |
| *Cygnet* (1585; John Sheriff) | 30 | ? | | | | 20 |
| *Brigandine* (1584; Thomas Scott) | 90 | ? | | | | 35 |
| *George Hoy* (Richard Hodges) | 100 | | 16 | 4 | | 24 |
| *Fancy* | | | | | | 16 |
| *Nightingale* | | | | | | 16 |
| *White Lion* | | | | | | 50 |
| *Disdain* | | | | | | 45 |
| *Marigold* | | | | | | 13 |
| *Edward of Malden* | | | | | | 37 |

34 ships with a total tonnage of 12,620, plus 6 further ships (all small) of unknown tonnage; total men aboard the 40 ships paid by the queen, *c.* 6,500.[d]

## 23 MERCHANT SHIPS WITH SIR FRANCIS DRAKE AT PLYMOUTH INCLUDING

| | Tons | Guns | | | | Total men |
|---|---|---|---|---|---|---|
| *Galleon Leicester* (1578) | 400 | 42 | | | | 160 |
| *Roebuck* | 300 | | | | | 120 |
| *Merchant Royal* (1576) | 400 | | | | | 160 |
| *Edward Bonaventure* (1574) | 300 | 40 | | | | 120 |
| *Golden Noble* (1567?) | 250 | | | | | 110 |
| *Hopewell* | 200 | | | | | 100 |
| *Griffin* | 200 | | | | | 100 |

| | Tons | Guns | Sailors | Gunners | Soldiers | Total men |
|---|---|---|---|---|---|---|
| *Spark* | 200 | | | | | 90 |
| *Minion* (1579?) | 200 | | | | | 80 |
| *Bark Talbot* | 200 | | | | | 90 |
| *Hope Hawkins*ᶜ | 200 | | | | | 80 |
| *Thomas Drake*ᶜ | 200 | | | | | 80 |
| *Bark Bond*ᶜ | 150 | | | | | 70 |
| *Bark Bonner* (1574)ᶜ | 150 | | | | | 70 |
| *Bark Hawkins* (1560) | 150 | | | | | 70 |

Total tonnage: 4,090; total men: 2,294

30 ships and barks paid by the City of London: average tonnage 151; total men 2,130

33 ships and barks (including 15 victuallers), under the lord admiral, paid by the queen: total men 1,561

20 coasters, great and small, under the lord admiral, paid by the queen: average tonnage 97; total men 993

23 coasters under Lord Henry Seymour, 'whereof some were paid by Her Majesty, but the greatest part by the port towns': average tonnage 98; total men 1,093

23 voluntary ships, paid by the queen: average tonnage 95; total men 1,059

GRAND TOTAL: 197 ships; 15,925 menᶠ

## Notes

a   Based on data kindly supplied by José Luis Casado Soto, augmented by our own research. Some data also published in Casado Soto, *Los barcos*, 206–21, and Gracia Rivas, *Los tercios*, 257–62. Figures for the ships' tonnage and armament are taken from the 'Lisbon muster'; the totals of sailors and soldiers come from the last Corunna muster, whenever available, otherwise from the Lisbon muster. Various changes occurred after the musters, and some of the ships were referred to by more than one name. On occasion this creates problems of identification.

b   This vessel was embargoed on 14 June 1588 and served with the Armada throughout, although it has escaped the notice of all 'censuses' of the fleet: see its 'pliego' in AGS CMC 2a/905.

c   Based on the list in Laughton, II, 324–42, augmented from PRO AO1/1686/23 and E 351/2225, the audited accounts of Hawkins as treasurer of the navy for 1588, membranes 10v–19v ('Sea Wages'); Glasgow, 'List of ships in the Royal Navy from 1539 to 1588' (for the date of construction); PRO WO 55/1627, 'The book of the remaynes of Her Majesties shippes returning from the seas' (for the number of guns aboard);

and Dietz, 'The royal bounty and English merchant shipping', 14–15 (for the year of construction of some large private vessels that sailed against the Armada). The totals in the English fleet list come from Laughton, II, 323-7, and all the mathematical errors are original Elizabethan ones.

d    These six additional ships in the 'Navy Royall', all of them small, appear in Hawkins's accounts (see preceding note). They were probably purchased for the campaign.

e    According to Hawkins's accounts, these four ships were only paid until 28 July 1588 OS. They served as fireships and were lost on that day. Sir Francis Drake tried to charge the government £1,000 for the loss of the *Thomas*: see Devon County Record Office, Exeter, Deposit 346/F588, 'Accompte of sondrye charges'.

f    According to Hawkins's account, the hire of the 160-ton *Barque Sanlegier*, 160-ton *Virgin God Save Her*, and 80-ton *Bark Buggins*, also ceased on 28 July OS; these too served as fireships. The total of 197 ships is in Laughton, II.

# Spanish and English guns in 1588

## Spanish guns

Any attempt to classify sixteenth-century artillery carries with it the danger of implying that precise specifications for each type were widely accepted. They were not. In
spite of various attempts to impose standardisation – that by Charles V in 1549 is the
best known – guns of the early modern period are in the main remarkable for their
individuality and profusion of forms.

Even contemporaries were dismayed by the lack of ordered categorisation which
resulted. 'Through an intolerable fault', wrote Cyprian Lucar in 1587, 'all our great
pieces of one name are not of one weight, nor of one height in their mouths.' This
difficulty was echoed in 1592 by the Spaniard Luis Collado, who noted that the guns
in Milan Castle needed more than 200 different sizes of charging implements when 11
would have served had the guns been sensibly standardised. The problems created
by unregulated shot sizes, he added, were just as serious. Gunners who sailed with
the Armada would certainly have agreed with him.

Nevertheless, despite the almost limitless variety of forms sixteenth-century
ordnance might take, gunners usually applied quite specific names to particular types
of gun. These names do not, however, imply any precision in the criteria by which
they were defined, for no such precise definition existed or was agreed upon. The
important factors were the weight and type of metal of which the gun was made,
the charge it could bear, the weight and composition of the projectile it fired, the
proportion of projectile weight to gun weight, and the length of the barrel expressed
as a multiple of its calibre. Beyond these fundamental specifications, as one of the
wisest of the sixteenth-century technical authors put it: 'It does not matter what
their names may be, except to know their sorts and kinds.'

Some attempt must however be made, for descriptive convenience if nothing
else, to group the various 'sorts and kinds' into named families. The Armada documents themselves provide general classification parameters for each named type and
type-group as they were understood by contemporary Spaniards, and this classification is summarised below. The range of shot-weights for each group is taken from
the maximum and minimum figures specified for the guns allocated to that group
within the fleet. This summary is followed by a systematic sampling of actual
weapons, most of which come from Armada shipwrecks. The remainder have been
taken from reliable contemporary sources.

| Family | Type name | Shot-weight (in Castilian *libras*) |
|---|---|---|
| **Cañones** (heavy-shotted guns 25 calibres or less in length) | *Cañón de batir* | 40–50 iron |
| | *Cañón* | 28–35 |
| | *Medio cañón* | 15–27 |
| | *Tercio cañón* | 10–14 |
| | *Quarto cañón* | 9–12 |
| | *Cañoncete* | 10 |
| **Pedreros** (short-barrelled stone throwers with narrowed chambers) | *Cañón pedrero* | 12–20 stone |
| | *Medio cañón pedrero* | 10–12 |
| | *Other pedrero-types* | 4–12 |
| **Culebrinas** (light-shotted guns 30 or more calibres in length) | *Culebrina* | 16–21 iron |
| | *Media culebrina* | 7–14 |
| | *Sacre* | 5–8 |
| | *Medio sacre* | 3–4 |
| | *Falconete* | 2–4* |
| | *Media falconete* | 1–2* |
| | *Falcon* | 1–3* |
| | | *often swivel mounted |
| **Man-killers** | *Falcon pedrero* | 3–6 stone |
| | *Esmeril doble* | 12 oz iron or lead |
| | *Esmeril* | 6–8 oz iron or lead |
| **Obsolescent** | *Verso* | 1–3 iron |
| | *Pasamuro* | 1–2 iron |
| | *Lombarda* | 4–7 stone |

EXAMPLES OF GUNS

The bronze muzzle-loading guns, numbered 1–12, are drawn to a common scale. A larger scale has been used for the smaller swivel pieces and iron guns, numbered 13–21. Wherever possible the guns shown come from one of the Armada wrecks, but where a particular type is not available from this source the gap has been filled with an example drawn from a reliable contemporary source. Each gun is given the name which reflects, as closely as possible, late sixteenth-century Spanish usage. Its origins, decoration and any inscriptions are described, and its technical specifications summarised thus: gun-weight and weight of shot thrown (in Castilian *libras* of 460 grams; where necessary weights specified to other standards have been converted); bore (in inches to facilitate comparison with English examples); length from base-ring to muzzle (also in inches); bore/length ratio; and shot-weight/gun-weight ratio. It should be noted that these calculations depend on a number of factors which may be variable and not always quantifiable, so in some respects the specifications presented here may be arbitrary.

Shot diameter was normally one-twentieth smaller than the gun bore to allow sufficient windage, and this reduction is taken into account in the calculations.

1] *Cañón de batir* by Gregorio Loefer of Augsburg, cast for Charles V in 1538. It carries the emperor's full escutcheon. This drawing is based on a detailed diagram submitted to Philip II in 1587 (AGS *MPyD* V-18). The gun itself, identified by its weight mark, served in the Armada. It was originally shipped aboard the Levanter *Juliana*, but was later transferred to the squadron flagship *Regazona* (AGS *CS* 2a/280 fos 1504–6).
*Weight 5,230 lb; shot-weight 38 lb (iron); bore c. 7"; length 127.5"; bore:length 1:18.2; shot-:gun-weight 1:138.*

2] *Cañón de batir* by Remigy de Halut of Malines, cast for Philip II in 1556. It carries the joint arms of Philip and his wife Mary Tudor, queen of England. On the base-ring is the name (Latinised) of Juan Manrique de Lara, captain-general of artillery. The gun, together with two similar pieces, was recovered from the wreck of *La Trinidad Valencera*. All three bear weight marks which conform to those in the ship's lading documents (AGS *CS* 2a/280 fo. 1461). The same gun is illustrated in AGS *MPyD* V-18 (see above).
*Weight 5,186 lb; shot-weight 41 lb (iron); bore 7.2"; length 106"; bore:length 1:14.7; shot-:gun-weight 1:126.*

3] Full *pedrero*, based on Luis Collado's proportions of 1592. Note the narrow powder-chamber and the thin-walled main barrel. This combination permitted a large diameter projectile of low mass to be fired.
*Weight c. 2,000 lb; shot-weight c. 20 lb (stone); bore 8"; length 67"; bore:length 1:8.4; shot-:gun-weight 1:100.*

4] *Medio cañón*, from a drawing in the 1587 discussion paper (AGS *MPyD* V-19).
*Weight c. 3,500 lb; shot-weight 20 lb (iron); bore c. 5.5"; length 114"; bore:length 1:20.7; shot-:gun-weight 1:175.*

5] Full *culebrina*, from an illustrated casting specification by Don Juan de Acuña Vela, captain-general of artillery, on 25 July 1587 (AGS *MPyD* V-16). The piece was to be decorated as shown. It was to be cast from a mixture of 92 per cent Hungarian copper and 8 per cent English tin.
*Weight 6,000 lb; shot-weight 18 lb (iron); bore c. 5.25"; length 158"; bore:length 1:30; shot-:gun-weight 1:333.*

6] *Media culebrina* from *El Gran Grifón*, one of four 'utility' pieces issued to the ship just before the Armada sailed (see p. 194). It carries no decoration or inscription. The bore of this gun is grossly off centre.
*Weight c. 2,400 lb; shot-weight 9 lb (iron); bore 4.25"; length 139"; bore:length 1:32.8; shot-:gun-weight 1:267.*

7] *Medio sacre* from *El Gran Grifón*, from the same source as above.
*Weight c. 800 lb; shot-weight 2.8 lb (iron); bore 2.9"; length 90"; bore:length 1:31; shot-:gun-weight 1:286.*

8] *Medio cañón* bearing the monogram and attributes of Francis I of France (1515–47), recovered from the wreck of the *San Juan de Sicilia* at Tobermory c. 1740. It is now at Inverary Castle.
*Weight (by mark) 3,253, (by estimation) 3,154 lb; shot-weight 23 lb (iron); bore 5.8"; length 112.5"; bore:length 1:19.4; shot-:gun-weight 1:137.*

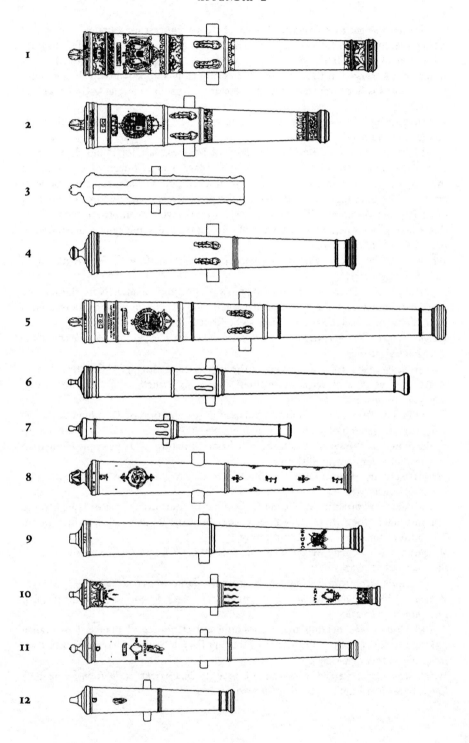

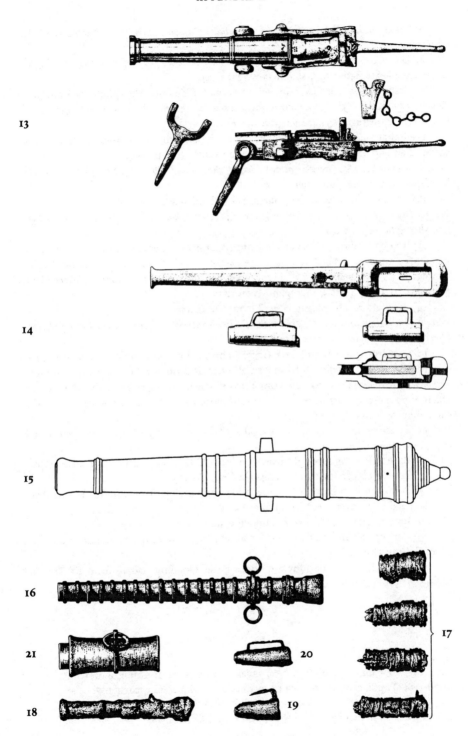

13

14

15

16

21

20

17

18

19

9] Italian *media culebrina* from *La Trinidad Valencera*, perhaps by Nicolo di Conti of Venice.
*Weight (by mark) 2,950, (by estimation) 3,025 lb; shot-weight 13.5 lb (iron); bore 4.9″; length 120″; bore:length 1:24.5; shot-:gun-weight 1:224.*

10] Italian *sacre* from *La Trinidad Valencera* by Zuanne Alberghetti of Venice.
*Weight (by mark) 2,529, (by weighbridge) 2,596 lb; shot-weight 6 lb (iron); bore 3.75″; length 129″; bore:length 1:34.4; shot-:gun-weight 1:433.*

11] Italian *sacre* from the *Juliana*, possibly Sicilian, dated 1570. This gun has suffered an explosive blow-out close to the muzzle (see p. 194).
*Weight (by mark) 2,082, (by estimation) 1,800 lb; shot-weight 5 lb (iron); bore 3.5″; length 118″; bore:length 1:33.7; shot-:gun-weight 1:360.*

12] Italian *pedrero* from the *Juliana*, possibly Sicilian.
*Weight (by estimation) 900 lb; shot-weight c. 7 lb (stone); bore 5.8″; length 64.5″; bore:length 1:11; shot-:gun-weight 1:129.*

13] Breech-loading *falcon pedrero* from *La Trinidad Valencera*. Probably Venetian.
*Weight (by estimation) 300 lb (the 125 mark on the breech refers to the bronze barrel only); shot-weight 1.7 lb (stone); bore 3.4″; overall length 68″; barrel length (excluding breech block) 35″; bore:barrel length 1:10.3; shot-:gun-weight 1:176.*

14] Bronze breech-loading *esmeril* from the *Girona*.
*Weight (by estimation) 200 lb; shot-weight 1 lb (iron); bore 2″; length (excluding missing tiller) 64″; bore:length 1:32; shot-:gun-weight 1:200.*

15] Cast-iron gun from *El Gran Grifón*. This fits into no known Spanish category, but might loosely be referred to as a small *sacre*. It is one of the ship's original guns, and so almost certainly comes from northern Europe – probably Sweden. It has efficient proportions (its bore:length ratio is close to the thoretical optimum), and is extremely well made.
*Weight (by estimation) 1,560 lb; shot-weight 4.5 lb (iron); bore 3.4″; length 87″; bore:length 1:25.5; shot-:gun-weight 1:346.*

16] Breech-loading wrought-iron gun from *El Gran Grifón*. Perhaps a *falconete*.

17] Breech blocks for similar guns (*El Gran Grifón*).

18] Wrought-iron barrel of a breech-loading *falcon pedrero* from *El Gran Grifón*.
Bore 3.4″; 1.7 lb stone shot (*cf.* 13 above).

19] Breech block for a similar gun (*El Gran Grifón*).

20] Wrought-iron breech block for a long iron-throwing swivel gun, perhaps a *verso. El Gran Grifón*.

21] Wrought-iron block for a 6″ bore breech-loading *pedrero* from *La Trinidad Valencera*. The missing barrel was probably of bronze.

*facing*]
Late sixteenth-century Spanish gun carriages, from a series of technical drawings dated 1594. Top, a carriage 'for sea or fortress use', with solid tripartite wheels; bottom, another type of ship carriage. Both have the extended trails which made them awkward to handle aboard ship (AGS MPyD XVIII–47–9).

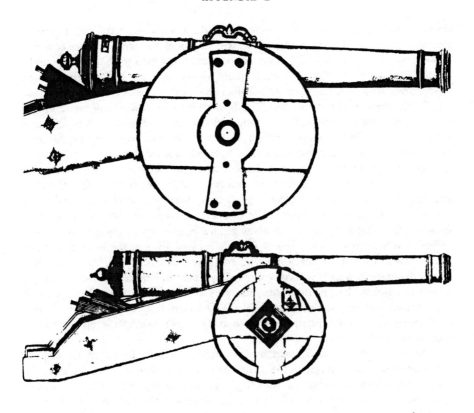

### English guns

Unlike the Spaniards, the English have left no surviving records of the guns aboard their ships, and there are no wrecks to provide us with archaeological evidence. Not a single extant gun can unequivocally be said to have fought against the Armada in 1588. Several dozen Spanish guns were, however, obtained by the English when the *San Salvador* and *Nuestra Señoral del Rosario* were captured during the early stages of the fighting. These were later subjected to careful descriptive inventories, in the course of which each gun was given the type-name the English inventorist considered most appropriate to it. Since these same guns had also been inventoried by the Spaniards before the fleet sailed it is possible to compare the two sets of data and so obtain a 'translation' of Spanish/English gun names.

The result shows some unexpected divergences in the comparative artillery nomenclature of the two sides. When, for example, an Englishmen speaks of a 'cannon' he means the kind of gun a Spaniard would describe as a *cañón de batir* – that is, a battery piece throwing an iron shot of 40 to 50 pounds. But to a Spaniard the term *cañón*, if used without the qualifying *de batir*, meant something altogether different: it was a relatively short-bargelled gun (25 calibres or less in length) firing shot of anything from 28 to 35 pounds. An Englishman would have called guns of this description 'demi-cannons'. But these were not at all the same as Spanish *medios cañónes*, which were pieces of 'cannon' proportions firing balls from 15 to 27 pounds. To an Englishman in 1588 such guns would almost certainly be 'culverins', even though their lengths fell far short of the 30 or more calibres which classification into this family theoretically demanded. The Spaniards were however pedantic in this respect, reserving the term *culebrina* exclusively for the 16–21 pounders of full 'long gun' proportions. In fact there were very few true culverins on either side, for their great length made them too cumbersome to handle aboard ship.

The long-held belief that the English went for 'culverin' types while the Spaniards concentrated on short-range *cañónes* can no longer be sustained. Notwith-standing the misconception about the relationship between barrel length and range (see pp. 185–6 above), the majority of heavier guns on *both* sides were, broadly speaking, short battery pieces of the same general proportions. Only the names were different. What *is* true – though only recently realised – is that the English, and not the Spaniards, carried the heaviest total complement of artillery during the conflict. Their advantage in weight was compounded by a preponderance of shortened tyeps, of all sizes, and by their manifest superiority in working them at sea. The Spaniards were correspondingly disadvantaged by the fact that a large proportion of their medium-category guns – particularly those in the 6- to 16-pounder range – seems to have been of full 'culverin' proportions.

Although the full standardisation of gun types lay far in the future, the English probably came closer to it than the Spaniards and their allies. At the very least, the adoption of a common language and a single standard of weights and measures must have made life on English gundecks a much more straightforward affair than the muddle which, as we have seen, prevailed on the multi-lingual and arithmetically chaotic Spanish ones.

The following table of specifications is taken from a list drawn up by John Sheriffe in 1592 (or perhaps rather earlier). While it appears to be the work of a theorist rather than a practical gunner, and has some evident inconsistencies, it is probably a reasonably accurate guide to English gun classification at the time of the Armada. Probably incorrectly, Sheriffe seems to regard the cannon pedro as an iron-throwing piece. For the distribution of ordnance aboard the queen's ships in 1595–6, see Parker, 'The *Dreadnought* revolution', 272–3 and 287–8.

## English gun specifications, *c.*1592

| Type name | Gun weight | Bore | Shot weight | Shot/gun weight |
|---|---|---|---|---|
| Cannon royal | 7,000 lb | 8″ | 66 lb | 1:117 |
| Cannon | 6,000 lb | 8″ | 60 lb | 1:100 |
| Cannon serpentine | 5,500 lb | 7″ | 53 lb | 1:103 |
| Bastard cannon | 4,500 lb | 7″ | 41 lb | 1:109 |
| Demi-cannon | 4,000 lb | 6″ | 30 lb | 1:132 |
| Cannon pedro | 3,000 lb | 6″ | 24 lb | 1:123 |
| Culverin | 4,500 lb | 5″ | 17 lb | 1:260 |
| Basilico | 4,000 lb | 5″ | 15 lb | 1:262 |
| Demi-culverin | 3,400 lb | 4″ | 9 lb | 1:364 |
| Bastard culverin | 3,000 lb | 4″ | 7 lb | 1:428 |
| Saker | 1,400 lb | 3″ | 5 lb | 1:263 |
| Minion | 1,000 lb | 3″ | 4 lb | 1:250 |
| Falcon | 800 lb | $2^{1}/_{3}$″ | 3 lb | 1:267 |
| Falcon | 660 lb | $2^{1}/_{4}$″ | $2^{1}/_{4}$ lb | 1:293 |
| Falconet | 500 lb | 2″ | $1^{1}/_{4}$ lb | 1:400 |
| Serpentine | 400 lb | $1^{1}/_{2}$″ | $^{2}/_{3}$ lb | 1:601 |
| Robinet | 300 lb | 1″ | $^{1}/_{2}$ lb | 1:600 |

# BIBLIOGRAPHY

*Actas de las Cortes de Castilla*, X (Madrid, 1886).

*Acts of the Privy Council of England*, XVI (London, 1897).

Adams, S., 'Eliza enthroned? The court and its politics', in C. Haigh (ed.), *The Reign of Elizabeth* (London, 1984), 55–77.

Adams, S., 'Stanley, York and Elizabeth's Catholics', *History Today*, XXXVII (July, 1987), 46–50.

Adams, S., 'New light on the "Reformation" of Sir John Hawkins: the Ellesmere naval survey of January 1584', *English Historical Review*, CV (1990), 96–111.

Adams, S., 'The outbreak of the Elizabethan naval war against the Spanish empire: the embargo of May 1585 and Sir Francis Drake's West India voyage', in M. J. Rodríguez-Salgado and S. Adams (eds), *England, Spain and the Gran Armada, 1585–1604* (Edinburgh, 1991), 45–69.

Adams, S., 'The battle that never was: the Downs and the Armada campaign', in M. J. Rodríguez-Salgado and S. Adams (eds), *England, Spain and the Gran Armada, 1585–1604* (Edinburgh, 1991), 173–96.

Alvarez de Toledo, L. I., duchess of Medina Sidonia, *Alonso Pérez de Guzmán, General de la Invencible*, 2 vols (Cadiz, 1995).

Andrews, K. R., *Elizabethan Privateering: English privateering during the Spanish War, 1585–1603* (Cambridge, 1964).

Andrews, K. R., *Drake's Voyages: a reassessment of their place in Elizabethan naval expansion* (London, 1967).

Andrews, K. R., *Trade, Plunder and Settlement: maritime enterprise and the genesis of the British Empire, 1480–1630* (Cambridge, 1984).

Anon, *Relaciõ de lo que hasta oy a los 5 de septiembre . . . se ha sabido* (Seville, 1588).

Bankston, J., translation of Diego García de Palacio, *Instruccion*, privately published (Bisbee, Arizona, 1986).

Bor, P., *Oorspronck, begin ende vervolgh der Nederlantsche Oorloghen*, III, part 2 (Amsterdam, 1625).

Bourne, W., *The Art of Shooting in Great Ordnance* (London, 1587).

Braudel, F., *The Mediterranean and the Mediterranean World in the Age of Philip II*, I (London, 1973).

Brewer, J. S. and Bullen, W., *Calendar of the Carew Manuscripts*, II (London, 1868).

Brown, K., 'The making of a *politique*: the Counter-Reformation and the regional policies of John, eighth lord Maxwell', *Scottish Historical Review*, LXVI (1987), 152–75.

Bruce, J., *Report on the Arrangements Which Were Made for the Internal Defence of These Kingdoms When Spain, by its Armada, Projected the Invasion and Conquest of England* (London, 1798).

Brugmans, H. (ed.), *Correspondentie van Robert Dudley, graaf van Leycester en andere documenten . . . 1585–8*, III (Utrecht, 1931).

Burnell, A. D. (ed.), *The Voyage of John Huyghen van Linschoten to the East Indies*, II (from the English translation of 1598 (London, 1885).

*Cabala sive scrinia sacra* (3rd edn, London, 1691).

*Calendar of State Papers, Domestic Series: Edward VI, Mary, Elizabeth* (1581–90) (London, 1865).

*Calendar of State Papers, Foreign Series, of the Reign of Elizabeth*, XIX, XXI (in 4 parts) and XXII (London, 1916, 1927–31, 1936).

*Calendar of State Papers and Manuscripts Relating to English Affairs Existing in the Archives and Collections of Venice*, VIII (London, 1894).

*Calendar of State Papers Relating to English Affairs Preserved . . . in the Archives of Simancas. Elizabeth*, I–IV (London, 1892–9).

*Calendar of State Papers Relating to Ireland in the Reign of Elizabeth*, IV: 1588–92 (London, 1885).

*Calendar of State Papers Relating to Scotland*, IV: 1571–4 (Edinburgh, 1905).

Calvar Gross, J., González-Aller Hierro, J. I., Dueñas Fontán, M. de and Mérida Valverde, M. del C. *La batalla del Mar Océano*, 3 vols (Madrid, 1988–93).

Casado Soto, J. L., *Los barcos espanoles del siglo XVI y la Gran Armada de 1588* (Madrid, 1988).

Casado Soto, J. L., *Discursos de Bernardino de Escalante al rey y sus ministros, 1585–1605* (Laredo, 1995).

Chaves, Alonso de, *Espejo de navigantes*, a manuscript of *c.* 1540 published by C. Fernández Duro, *Armada Española desde la unión de los reinos de Castilla y Aragón*, I (Madrid, 1895), 379–91.

Chevallier, P., *Henry III: roi shakespearien* (Paris, 1985).

Clark, P., *English Provincial Society from the Reformation to the Revolution: religion, politics and society in Kent, 1500–1640* (Hassocks, 1977).

Clowes, W. L., *The Royal Navy: a history*, I (London, 1898).

Collinson, P., *The English Captivity of Mary Queen of Scots* (Sheffield, 1987).

Collinson, P., *Elizabethan Essays* (London, 1994).

Colvin, H., *The History of the King's Works*, IV (London, 1982).

Constant, J. M., *Les Guise* (Paris, 1984).

Corbett, J. S., *Fighting Instructions, 1530–1816*, Navy Records Society, XXIX (London, 1905).

Corbett, J. S., *Addenda*, Navy Records Society, XXXV (London, 1908).

Corbett, J. S., *Papers Relating to the Navy during the Spanish War, 1585–7* (London, 1898).

Cortesão, A. and Teixeira de Mota, A., *Portugaliae monumenta cartographia*, III (Lisbon, 1960).

Cunha Rivara, J. H. da (ed.), *Arquivo Português Oriental*, III (Nova Goa, 1861).

Daultrey, S., 'The weather of north-west Europe during the summer and autumn of 1588', in P. Gallagher and D. W. Cruickshank (eds), *God's Obvious Design* (London, 1990).

Deleito y Piñuela, J., *El declinar de la monarquía española* (2nd edn, Madrid, 1947).

Dickerman, E. H., 'A neglected aspect of the Spanish Armada: the Catholic League's Picardy offensive of 1587', *Canadian Journal of History*, XI (1976), 19–23.

Dietz, B., 'The royal bounty and English merchant shipping', *Mariner's Mirror*, LXXVII (1991), 5–20.

Donaldson, G., *All the Queen's Men: power and politics in Mary Stewart's Scotland* (London, 1983).

Douglas, K. S., Lamb, H. H. and Loader, C., *A Meteorological Study of July to October 1588: the Spanish Armada storms*, University of East Anglia Climatic Research Unit, publications, VI (Norwich, 1978).

Durand-Lapié, P., 'Un roi détroné réfugié en France: Dom Antoine ler de Portugal (1580–95)', *Revue d'histoire diplomatique*, XVIII (1904), 133–45, 275–307, 612–40, and XIX (1905), 113–28, 243–60.

Earle, P., *The Last Fight of the Revenge* (London, 1992).

Edwards, F., *The Marvellous Chance: Thomas Howard, fourth duke of Norfolk, and the Ridolfi plot, 1570–2* (London, 1968).

Elliott, J. H., *The Count-Duke of Olivares: the statesman in an age of decline* (New Haven, 1986).

Essen, L. van der, *Alexandre Farnèse, prince de Parme, gouverneur-général des Pays-Bas (1545–92)*, 5 vols (Brussels, 1933–7).

Estal, J. M., 'Felipe II y su archivo hagiográfico de El Escorial', *Hispania sacra*, XXIII (1970), 193–333.

Evans, J. X., *The Works of Sir Roger Williams* (Oxford, 1972).

Fea, P., *Alessandro Farnese, duca di Parma* (Rome, 1886).

Feltham, O., *A Brief Character of the Low Countries* (written in the 1620s, first published London, 1652).

Fernández-Armesto, F., *The Spanish Armada: the experience of war in 1588* (Oxford, 1988).

Fernández Duro, C., *La conquista de las Azores en 1583* (Madrid, 1866).

Fernández Duro, C. (ed.), *La Armada Invencible*, 2 vols (Madrid, 1884–5).

Fernández Duro, C., *Armada Española desde la unión de los reinos de Castilla y Aragón*, I (Madrid, 1895).

Firrufino, G. C., *El perfecto artillero: theórica y práctica* (Madrid, 1648).

Flower-Smith, A., '"The able and the willynge": the preparations of the English land forces to meet the Armada', *British Army Review*, XCV (1990), 54–91.

Fruin, R. J., *Verspreide Geschriften*, III (The Hague, 1900).

Gallagher, P. and Cruickshank, D. W. (eds), *God's Obvious Design: papers of the Spanish Armada symposium, Sligo, 1988* (London, 1990).

Gerson, A. J., 'The English recusants and the Spanish Armada', *American Historical Review*, XXII (1917), 589–94.

Glasgow, T., 'Elizabethan ships pictured on Smerwick map, 1580', *Mariner's Mirror*, LII (1966), 157–65.

Glasgow, T., 'The navy in the French wars of Mary and Elizabeth I', *Mariner's Mirror*, LIII (1967), 321–42; LIV (1968), 23–36, 281–96; and LVI (1970), 3–26.

Glasgow, T., 'List of ships in the Royal Navy from 1539 to 1588', *Mariner's Mirror*, LVI (1970), 299–306.

Glete, J., *Navies and Nations: warships, navies and state-building in Europe and America, 1500–1860*, 2 vols (Stockholm, 1993).

Gómez-Centurión, C., *La Invencible y la empresa de Inglaterra* (Madrid, 1988).

Goodman, D., *Spanish Naval Power, 1589–1665: reconstruction and defeat* (Cambridge, 1997).

[Goux, P. le], *Copie d'une lettre envoyé de Dieppe* (Paris, 1588).

Gracia Rivas, M., 'El motin de la *Diana* y otras vicisitudes de las galeras participantes en la jornada de Inglaterra, *Revista de historia naval*, II. 4 (1984), 33–45.

Gracia Rivas, M., *La sanidad en la jornada de Inglaterra, 1587–8* (Madrid, 1988).

Gracia Rivas, M., *Los tercios de la Gran Armada, 1587–8* (Madrid, 1989).

Gracia Rivas, M., 'The medical services of the Gran Armada', in M. J. Rodríguez-Salgado and S. Adams (eds), *England, Spain and the Gran Armada, 1585–1604* (Edinburgh, 1991).

Green, Janet M., '"I My Self": Queen Elizabeth's oration at Tilbury camp', *Sixteenth Century Journal*, XXVIII (1997), 421–45.

Guilmartin, J. F., *Gunpowder and Galleys: changing technology and Mediterranean warfare in the sixteenth century* (Cambridge, 1974).

Heredia Herrera, A. (ed.), *Catálogo de las consultas del consejo de Indias*, I (Madrid, 1972).

Herrera Oria, E., *La Armada Invencible*, Archivo Documental Español, II (Valladolid, 1929).

Hibben, C. C., *Gouda in Revolt: particularism and pacifism in the revolt of the Netherlands, 1572–88* (Utrecht, 1983).

Holt, M. P., *The Duke of Anjou and the Politique Struggle during the Wars of Religion* (Cambridge, 1986).

Hopper, C., *Sir Francis Drake's Memorable Service against the Spaniards in 1587*, Camden Miscellany, V (London, 1863).

Ireland, J. de Courcy, 'Ragusa and the Spanish Armada of 1588', *Mariner's Mirror*, LXIV (1978), 251–62.

Israel, J. I., *Race, Class and Politics in Colonial Mexico, 1610–70* (Oxford, 1975).

Japikse, N., *Resolutien der Staten Generaal van 1576 tot 1609*, V and VI (The Hague, 1921, 1922).

Jensen, J. de Lamar, 'Franco-Spanish diplomacy and the Armada', in C. H. Carter (ed.), *From the Renaissance to the Counter-Reformation: essays in honour of Garrett Mattingly* (London, 1965), 205–29.

Jensen, J. de Lamar, 'The phantom will of Mary queen of Scots', *Scotia*, IV (1980), 1–15.

Keeler, M. F., *Sir Francis Drake's West Indian Voyage, 1585–6*, Hakluyt Society, 2nd series, CXLVIII (London, 1981).

Kelsey, H., *Sir Francis Drake, the Queen's Pirate* (London and New Haven, 1998).

Kenny, R. W., *Elizabeth's Admiral: the political career of Charles Howard earl of Nottingham, 1536–1624* (Baltimore, 1970).

Kostić, V., 'Ragusa and the Spanish Armada', in R. Filipovic and M. Partridge (eds), *Ragusa's Relations with England: a symposium* (Zagreb, 1977), 47–61.

Kouri, E., *England and the Attempts to Form a Protestant Alliance in the Late 1560s: a case study in Elizabethan diplomacy*, Annales Academiae Scientiarum Fennicae, Series B, CXX (Helsinki, 1981).

Lapèyre, H., *Une famille des marchands: les Ruiz* (Paris, 1955).

Laughton, J. K., *State Papers Relating to the Defeat of the Spanish Armada, Anno 1588*, Navy Records Society, I–II (London, 1895).

Lefèvre, J. (ed.), *Correspondance de Philippe II sur les affaires des Pays-Bas*, III (Brussels, 1956).

Leimon, M. and Parker, G., 'Treason and plot in Elizabethan England: the fame of Sir Edward Stafford reconsidered', *English Historical Review*, CVI (1996), 1134–58.

Lewis, M., *The Spanish Armada* (London, 1960).

Lewis, M., *Armada Guns* (London, 1961).

Loades, D., *The Tudor Navy: an administrative, political and military history* (London, 1992).

Loades, D., *Mary Tudor: a life* (rev. edn Oxford, 1995).

Loomie, A. J., 'The Armadas and the Catholics of England', *Catholic Historical Review*, LIX (1973), 385–403.

Lyell, J. P. R., 'A commentary on certain aspects of the Spanish Armada drawn from contemporary sources' (Oxford University B.Litt. thesis, 1932).

Lynch, M. (ed.), *Mary Stewart: queen in three kingdoms* (Oxford, 1988).

Lyon, E., *The Enterprise of Florida: Pedro Menéndez de Avilés and the Spanish conquest of 1565–8* (Gainesville, 1976).

McBride, G. K., 'Elizabethan foreign policy in microcosm: the Portuguese pretender, 1580–9', *Albion*, V (1973), 193–210.

MacCaffrey, W. T., *The Shaping of the Elizabethan Regime: Elizabethan politics, 1558–72* (Princeton, 1968).

MacCaffrey, W. T., *Queen Elizabeth and the Making of Policy, 1572–88* (Princeton, 1981).

McGurk, J. J. N., 'Armada preparations in Kent and arrangements made after the defeat (1587–9)', *Archaeologia Cantiana*, LXXXV (1970), 71–93.

McLeay, A., *The Tobermory Treasure: the true story of a fabulous Armada galleon* (London, 1986).

McNeill, C., 'Report on the Rawlinson collection of manuscripts', *Analecta hibernica*, I (1930).

Malfatti, C. V., *Cuatro documentos italianos en materia de la expedicion de la Armada invencible* (Barcelona, 1972).

Martin, C., *Full Fathom Five: wrecks of the Spanish Armada* (London, 1975).

Martin, C., 'Spanish Armada tonnages', *Mariner's Mirror*, LXIII (1977), 365–7.

Martin, C., '*La Trinidad Valencera*: an Armada invasion transport lost off Donegal', *International Journal of Nautical Archaeology*, 8.1 (1979), 13–38.

Martin, C., 'The equipment and fighting potential of the Spanish Armada' (St Andrews University Ph.D. thesis, 1983).

Martin, C., 'A 16th-century siege train: the battery ordnance of the 1588 Spanish Armada', *International Journal of Nautical Archaeology*, 17.1 (1988), 57–73.

Martin, C., 'The ships of the Spanish Armada', in P. Gallagher and D. W. Cruickshank (eds), *God's Obvious Design* (London, 1990).

Martin, C., 'Incendiary weapons from the Spanish Armada wreck *La Trinidad Valencera*, 1588', *International Journal of Nautical Archaeology*, 23.3 (1994), 207–17.

Martin, P., *Spanish Armada Prisoners* (Exeter, 1988).

Martínez, E. (ed.), *Cartas de Felipe II al General Pedro de Valdés*, Monumenta histórica asturiensia, IX (Gijón, 1980).

Mattingly, G., 'William Allen and Catholic propaganda in England', *Travaux d'humanisme et renaissance*, XXVIII (1957), 325–39.

Mattingly, G., *The Defeat of the Spanish Armada* (London, 1959).

Maura Gamazo, G., duke of Maura, *El designio de Felipe II y el episodio de la armada invencible* (Madrid, 1957).

Meyer, A. O., *England and the Catholic Church under Queen Elizabeth* (London, 1916).

*Monumenta historica societatis Iesu, LX: Ribadeneira*, II (Madrid, 1923).

Motley, J. L., *A History of the United Netherlands*, I and II (London, 1869).

Mousset, A., *Dépêches diplomatiques de M. de Longlée, résident de France en Espagne, 1582–90* (Paris, 1912).

Munby, A. N. L., *Phillipps Studies*, V (Cambridge, 1960).

Nolan, J. S., 'The muster of 1588', *Albion*, XXIII (1991), 387–407.

Nolan, J. S., *Sir John Norreys and the Elizabethan Military World* (Exeter, 1997).

Norton, R., *The Gunner* (London, 1628).

*Notulen van de Staten van Zealand 1588.*

O'Donnell y Duque de Estrada, H., *La fuerza de desembarco de la Gran Armada contra Inglaterra (1588)*, (Madrid, 1989).

O'Donnell y Duque de Estrada, H., 'The requirements of the duke of Parma for the conquest of England', in P. Gallagher and D. W. Cruickshank (eds), *God's Obvious Design* (London, 1990).

Oliveira, F. de, *A arte da guerra do mar* (Lisbon, 1552).

Oosterhoff, F. G., *Leicester and the Netherlands, 1586–7* (Utrecht, 1988).

Oppenheim, M., *A History of the Administration of the Royal Navy and of Merchant Shipping in Relation to the Navy from MDIX to MDCLX* (London, 1896).

Oppenheim, M. (ed.), *The Naval Tracts of Sir William Monson*, IV, Navy Records Society, XLV (London, 1913).

O'Rahilly, A., *The Massacre at Smerwick (1580)*, Cork Historical and Archaeological Papers I (Cork, 1938).

Overeem, J. B. van, 'Justinus van Nassau en de Armada (1588)', *Marineblad*, LIII (1938), 821–31.

Owen, D., *Calendar of the Manuscripts of the . . . Marquess of Bath*, V (London, 1980).

Palacio, Diego García de, *Instruccion nautica* (Mexico City, 1587).

Parente, G., *et al.*, *Los sucesos de Flandes de 1588 en relación con la empresa de Inglaterra* (Madrid, 1988).

Parker, G., *The Dutch Revolt* (London, 1977).

Parker, G., *Spain and the Netherlands, 1559–1659: ten studies* (London, 1979).

Parker, G., *Philip II* (3rd edn, Chicago, 1995).

Parker, G., 'The *Dreadnought* revolution of Tudor England', *Mariner's Mirror*, LXXXII (1996), 269–300.

Parker, G., *The Grand Strategy of Philip II* (London and New Haven, 1998).

Parker, G., 'El testamento político de Juan Martínez de Recalde', *Revista de historia naval*, LX (1998), 7–44.

Pears, E. A., 'The Spanish Armada and the Ottoman Porte', *English Historical Review*, VII (1893), 439–66.

Pierson, P., *Commander of the Armada: the seventh duke of Medina Sidonia* (New Haven and London, 1989).

Pigafetta, F., *Discorso sopra l'ordinaza del'armata catolica* (Rome, 1588).

Pollitt, R., 'Bureaucracy and the Armada: the administrator's battle', *Mariner's Mirror*, LX (1974), 119–32.

Quinn, D. B., 'Spanish Armada prisoners' escape from Ireland', *Mariner's Mirror*, LXX (1984), 117–18.

Rasor, E., *The Spanish Armada of 1588: historiography and annotated bibliography* (Westport, CT, 1993).

Rawlinson, H. G., 'The embassy of William Harborne to Constantinople, 1583–8', *Transactions of the Royal Historical Society*, 4th series, V (1922), 1–27.

Read, C., *Mr Secretary Walsingham and the Policy of Queen Elizabeth*, III (Oxford, 1925).

Read, C., 'Queen Elizabeth's seizure of the duke of Alva's pay-ships', *Journal of Modern History*, V (1933), 443–64.

Read, C., *Lord Burghley and Queen Elizabeth* (New York, 1960).

Riaño Lozano, F., *Los medios navales de Alejandro Farnesio, 1587–8* (Madrid, 1989).

Rodger, N. A. M., 'The development of broadside gunnery, 1450–1650', *Mariner's Mirror*, LXXXII (1996), 301–24.

Rodger, N. A. M., *The Safeguard of the Sea: a naval history of Britain, I: 660–1649* (London, 1997).

Rodríguez-Salgado, M. J., *The Changing Face of Empire: Charles V, Philip II and Habsburg authority, 1551–9* (Cambridge, 1988).

Rodríguez-Salgado, M. J. (ed.), *Armada*, National Maritime Museum (London, 1988).

Rodríguez-Salgado, M. J., 'The Anglo-Spanish war: the final episode in the "Wars of the Roses"?', in M. J. Rodríguez-Salgado and S. Adams (eds), *England, Spain and the Gran Armada, 1585–1604* (Edinburgh, 1991).

Rodríguez-Salgado, M. J., 'Pilots, navigation and strategy in the *Gran Armada*', in M. J. Rodríguez-Salgado and S. Adams (eds), *England, Spain and the Gran Armada, 1585–1604* (Edinburgh, 1991).

Rodríguez-Salgado, M. J. and Adams, S. (eds), *England, Spain and the Gran Armada, 1585–1604* (Edinburgh, 1991).

Roiz Soares, P., *Memorial* (ed. M. Lopes de Almeida, Coimbra, 1953).

Romani, R., *Le corti farnesiane di Parma e Piacenza, 1545–1622*, I (Rome, 1978).

Roosens, B., 'Het Arsenal van Mechelen ende de wapenhandel 1551–1567', *Bijdragen tot de geschiedenis*, LX (1977), 175–247.

Rule, M., *The Mary Rose: the excavation and raising of Henry VIII's flagship* (Greenwich, 1982).

Saltillo, marquis of, 'El duque de Medina Sidonia y la jornada a Inglaterra en 1588', *Boletín de la Biblioteca de Menéndez Pelayo*, XVI (1934), 167–77.

Scheltema, J., *De uitrusting en ondergang van de onoverwinnelijk vloot van Philips II in 1588* (Haarlem, 1825).

Schokkenbroek, J. C. A., ' "Wherefore serveth Justinus with his shipping of Zeeland?" The Dutch and the Spanish Armada', in P. Gallagher and D. W. Cruickshank (eds), *God's Obvious Design* (London, 1990), 101–11.

Scott, J. R., 'Pay-list of the Kentish forces raised to resist the Spanish Armada', *Archaeologia Cantiana*, XI (1877), 388–91.

Scott, W. (ed.), *The Somers Collection of Tracts*, I (London, 1809).

Sigüenza, J. de, *La fundación del Monasterio de El Escorial* (Madrid, 1605; Madrid, 1988).

Skelton, R. A. and Summerson, J. N., *A Description of Maps and Architectural Drawings in the Collection Made by William Cecil, First Baron Burghley, now at Hatfield House* (Oxford, 1971).

Skilliter, S. A., 'The Hispano-Ottoman armistice of 1581', in C. E. Bosworth (ed.), *Iran and Islam* (Edinburgh, 1971), 491–515.

Sténuit, R., *Treasures of the Armada* (Newton Abbot, 1972).

Tassis, J. B. de, *Commentarii de tumultibus belgicis*, in C. P. Hoynck van Papendrecht, *Analecta Belgica*, II, part 2 (The Hague, 1743).

Tellechea Idígoras, J. I., *Otra cara de la Invencible: la participación vasca* (San Sebastián, 1988).

Tenison, E. M., *Elizabethan England*, 14 vols (Leamington Spa, 1933–60).

Thompson, I. A. A., 'Spanish Armada guns', *Mariner's Mirror*, LXI (1975), 355–71.

Thompson, I. A. A., 'Spanish Armada gun policy and procurement', in P. Gallagher and D. W. Cruickshank (eds), *God's Obvious Design* (London, 1990).

Thomson, G. Scott (ed.), *The Twysden Lieutenancy Papers*, Kent Records Society, X (Maidstone, 1926).

Tytler, P. F., *England under the Reigns of Edward VI and Mary*, II (London, 1839).

Vázquez, A., 'Los sucesos de Flandes y Francia del tiempo de Alejandro Farnesio', *Co.Do.In.*, LXXII–LXXIV (Madrid, 1879–80).

Voorbeijtel Cannenburg, W., 'An unknown "pilot" by Hessel Gerritsz, dating from 1612', *Imago mundi*, I (1935), 49–51.

Wagenaer, L., *Speculum nauticum . . .* (Leyden, 1588).

Wagenaer, L., *The Mariner's Mirror* . . . (London, 1590).

Walsh, M. K., 'The anonymous Spaniard of the flight of the earls', *Irish Sword*, III (1957–8), 88ff.

Walsh, M. K., *'Destruction by Peace': Hugh O'Neill after Kinsale* (Monaghan, 1986).

Waters, D. W., *The Elizabethan Navy and the Armada of Spain*, National Maritime Museum Monographs, XVII (Greenwich, 1975).

Watson, R., *The History of the Reign of Philip the Second, King of Spain*, 2 vols (London, 1777).

Wernham, R. B., 'Queen Elizabeth and the Portugal expedition of 1589', *English Historical Review*, LXVI (1951), 1–26, 194–218.

Wernham, R. B., *Before the Armada: the growth of English foreign policy, 1485–1588* (London, 1966).

Wernham, R. B., *The Making of Elizabethan Foreign Policy, 1558–1603* (Berkeley, 1980).

Wernham, R. B., *After the Armada: Elizabethan England and the struggle for western Europe, 1588–95* (Oxford, 1984).

Wernham, R. B., *The Expedition of Sir John Norris and Sir Francis Drake to Spain and Portugal, 1589*, Navy Records Society, CXXVII (London, 1988).

Whitehead, B. T., *Of Brags and Boasts: propaganda in the year of the Armada* (Stroud, 1994).

Wiener, C. Z., 'The beleaguered isle: a study of Elizabethan and early Jacobean anti-Catholicism', *Past and Present*, LI (1971), 27–62.

Williamson, J. A., *Hawkins of Plymouth: a new history of Sir John Hawkins and of other members of his family prominent in Tudor England* (London, 1949).

Wilson, C., *Queen Elizabeth and the Revolt of the Netherlands* (London, 1970).

Woude, A. van der, 'De crisis in de Opstand na de val van Antwerpen', *Bijdragen voor de Geschiedenis der Nederlanden*, XIV (1959–60), 38–57, 81–104.

Zarco Cuevas, J., G. de Andrés, et al., *Documentos para la historia del monasterio de San Lorenzo El Real de El Escorial*, 8 vols (Madrid, 1917–62).

# INDEX

Note: Page numbers in *italics* refer to illustrations on that page.

Lightning Source UK Ltd.
Milton Keynes UK
UKOW030226030912

198383UK00002B/35/A